STUDIES IN HISTORY, ECONOMICS AND PUBLIC LAW

Edited by the

FACULTY OF POLITICAL SCIENCE
OF COLUMBIA UNIVERSITY

NUMBER 351

DEPORTATION OF ALIENS FROM THE UNITED STATES TO EUROPE

BY

JANE PERRY CLARK

DEPORTATION OF ALIENS FROM THE UNITED STATES TO EUROPE

BY

JANE PERRY CLARK, Ph.D.

Instructor in Government, Barnard College
New York City

NEW YORK
COLUMBIA UNIVERSITY PRESS
London: P. S. King & Son, Ltd.
1931

PRINTED IN THE UNITED STATES OF AMERICA

To

MY FATHER AND MOTHER

"Meekly beseecheth your good . . . lordship, (Bishop of Bath and Wells, Chancellor of England), your continual orator. Henry Wakynakght, goldsmith, tenderly to consider that whereas he, by the Mayor's Commandment of London, caused by the subtle suggestion of the Wardens of the Craft of Goldsmiths of London, now late is imprisoned within the Counter in Bread Street, no cause laid against him but only he is a stranger born."

Bland, Brown and Tawney, *English Economic History: Select Documents*, p. 199 (London, 1914), Early Chancery Proceedings, 11, 455, C. 1440.

PREFACE

Periods of war hysteria and economic depression generate a fear of sudden ruin and a desire for panaceas. In the decade from 1920 to 1930 a nostrum often advocated for the ills of the United States was the removal of aliens from the country. The numbers sent forth crept up from 2,762 in 1920[1] to 16,631 ten years later. Nor is the matter finished, for the Commissioner General of Immigration tells us "the task of house-cleaning has practically only just begun. To continue the work and do it thoroughly is the big job ahead."[2]

Considering the importance of the problems involved in sending aliens from the country and the increasing emphasis upon them, it is somewhat surprising that the deportation law and its administration have been so little examined. So far as can be ascertained, no study has been made of the law as it appears on the statute books and in actual administration, nor has the problem been approached in the light of the social and international questions involved.[3] The

[1] The figures for that year are, however, smaller than those for 1913 or 1914, due largely to difficulties of arranging return to Europe in the unsettled conditions there immediately following the war.

Vide infra, ch. i, p. 29, for table of deportation from the United States since 1892.

[2] *Annual Report of the Commissioner General of Immigration for the Fiscal Year Ended June 30, 1930*, p. 7.

[3] The work on the subject to date has been largely concerned with statement of the law. *Vide* J. B. Moore, *Digest of International Law*, vol. lv, sec. 550; C. Bouvé, *A Treatise on the Laws Governing the Exclusion and Expulsion of Aliens in the United States* (Washington, 1912); S. Kansas, *United States Immigration, Exclusion and*

following investigation is therefore an attempt to shed light on some of the problems found in the deportation of aliens from the United States to Europe. As laws pertaining to the deportation of Orientals differ in both inception and administration from other deportation acts, the problems involved in deportation of Orientals are not considered here.[1] Furthermore, as immigration from the western hemisphere to the United States also involves special considerations, deportation to countries of North, Central and South America is not included.

Any such attempt must of necessity be as unbiased as possible, for the snares of propaganda either for or against the alien are legion. The author has no axe to grind and believes neither that all aliens should be deported from the United States nor that all deportations should cease. However, an unbiased attitude toward the problems of deportation does not imply absence of viewpoint, for only an approach which tries to understand the difficulties of the countries of deportation and repatriation can attempt to interpret a procedure which effects more than one country.

It was felt that in addition to the statutes, court decisions

Deportation (Washington, 1927); A. Cook and J. Hagerty, *Immigration Laws of the United States Compiled and Explained* (Chicago, 1929); *Migration Laws and Treaties*, vols. i-iv. While the present book was in progress, Dean William C. Van Vleck of the George Washington School of Law was working on *Administrative Control of Aliens*. This work was done under the auspices of the Commonwealth Fund, legal research committee, and will be published at an early date. Furthermore, Mr. Reuben Oppenheimer was also working simultaneously on *The Enforcement of the Deportation Laws of the United States*, under the auspices of the National Commission on Law Observance and Enforcement. A preliminary draft of Mr. Oppenheimer's report appeared on April 1, 1931, while the present volume was in press. He deals with the subject primarily from the point of view of law enforcement.

[1] Court decisions in such cases are cited only if they touch deportation in general.

and administrative orders, which together constitute the formal organization of the deportation process, there was need for examination of the way in which the procedure appears in the records and personal experiences of various persons deported from the United States. So the author was allowed the privilege of examining records in the files of the bureau of immigration of the United States Department of Labor. It would be impossible, however, within the scope of such a study as the one at hand to attempt to examine more than a very small cross-section of the total number of cases for even one year, so the problem arose of choosing representative cases which would present a fair picture of the situation.

In an effort to delimit the problem and to select cases to illustrate the complete deportation process, it was thought wise to take only cases of actual deportation from the country, not including those in which warrants of arrest or deportation were issued and then cancelled or cases in which deportation could not be carried out. For instance, it is rare that a country will accept deportees not bearing valid passports. In many cases it is impossible to verify nationality because of lack of data or conflicting laws, and so no passport can be obtained. As there are no diplomatic relations between the United States and the Soviet Republic, it is usually impossible to obtain passport for any possible deportee to Soviet Russia. Unless it is possible for the person who cannot secure a passport to be shipped out of the United States as a seaman, in which case only seaman's papers, issued by the master of the vessel, are necessary, he cannot be deported. The problems presented by such individuals are in many respects different from those actually sent out of the country, and so they are omitted from this study.

Cases of seamen are not considered, as the law and regulations for their deportation differ in some respects from the general deportation practice. The author is aware that many persons " sign on " and take the voyage as seamen only for the purpose of entering the United States, but technically they constitute seamen. Nor are persons included in the study who were allowed to "*reship foreign*" or *voluntarily depart* [1] in compliance with warrant of deportation, as a number of such cases include seamen, and as an arbitrary delimitation of cases had to be made.

It was decided to take July 1, 1925 as the date from which to begin to look through the records in the bureau of immigration, for this date had the advantage of securing a normal period of operation within the bureau, with the immigration act of 1924 in full operation; also, on that date the bureau adopted a new system of card records for every case.[2] All the copies of this card record filed between July 1, 1925 and January 1, 1926 were examined; then for comparative purposes and to secure data on the administration of the act of March 4, 1929, the cards of deportation between January 1, 1930 and June 1 of the same year were examined.

In the first group, a total of 518 " cases " was obtained, representing a total of 549 individuals, as each " case " does not of necessity deal with one person alone but often involves a whole family. As each record contains a full hearing for each individual, the individuals were taken as a basis

[1] It must be borne in mind that both "*re-shipment foreign*" and *voluntary departure* constituting deportation. *Vide* chap. xii, pp. 406, 469-470.
For regulations regarding "reshipment foreign" and voluntary departure, *vide* bureau of immigration General Order No. 152: *Transportation and Deportation of Aliens*, March 27, 1930.

[2] These cards give more complete information than under the old system, and from them data can readily be obtained as to nationality, causes of deportation, whether or not deportation was accomplished, etc. This "card record of deportees" (Form 522) is transmitted with the record of the hearing to the bureau.

for study.[1] In the second group, every twenty-fifth case of the categories and period of time specified was selected until fifty were obtained; these fifty consisted of sixty-three individuals.[2] So in the two groups, cases were studied of 612 persons actually deported to Europe.[3]

The statistics of the bureau of immigration from July 1, 1925 to January 1, 1926 give a total of 2,667 cases deported to Europe as contrasted with the 549 studied, but the government report includes seamen, voluntary departures, and "reshipments foreign." As the fifty cases in the later group were selected from the total number of cases between January 1, 1930 and June 1, 1930, no comparison with the total number deported between those dates seems necessary. As the numbers of deportations do not vary greatly from month to month,[4] it is felt a representative group of cases was obtained.

The following tables show the total numbers and causes of deportation for the years in which the cases are found that are included in this study, and the same for the cases included.

[1] On the records of the 549 individuals in the first group there was one instance of voluntary departure to Canada of the wife of a man deported to England and one instance of deportation to Canada of the husband of a woman deported to Poland. These two persons going to Canada were not included in the total, nor is one instance of a mother accompanying her feeble-minded daughter but paying her own passage, as only the daughter was deported.

[2] One record contained the cancellation of the warrant of deportation in the case of a man for whom no passport could be secured. He was not counted in the total, though of course his wife and child were included, as they were deported.

[3] There was considerable inaccuracy in the spelling of place names, etc., and one record was often found to contain several variations in spelling of the same word, particularly in European addresses.

[4] *Vide Annual Report of the Commissioner General of Immigration for,* etc., *1930,* p. 22, for illustration of the numbers deported by months.

Causes and Number of Persons Deported During the Fiscal Years 1926 and 1930.[1]

Causes of Deportation	Number Deported 1926	1930
Insanity, epilepsy	796	509
Other mental conditions	257	221
Loathsome or dangerous contagious diseases	100	251
Other physical conditions	90	61
Likely to become a public charge	887	305
Assisted aliens	42	35
Under 16 years of age (unaccompanied by parent)	54	173
Unable to read (over 16 years of age)	494	2,696
Contract laborers	27	73
Criminals	793	1,712
Under Narcotic Act	...	44
Immoral classes	412	700
Had been debarred or deported	131	653
Entered without inspection	902	131
Under Chinese exclusion act	178	166
Under percentum limit act of 1921 (Excess quota)	536	51
Under Section 17 of Immigration Act of 1924[2]	256	76
Remained longer than permitted as visitor, etc.	...	2,019
Failure to maintain student status	...	12
Without proper visa under Immigration Act of 1924:		
At land border ports	4,582	6,694
At seaports		
All other causes	364	49
Professional beggars and vagrants	2	
Accompnying aliens	1	
Total	10,904	16,631

[1] *Annual Report of the Commissioner General,* etc., for 1926, p. 20, and for 1930, p. 243.

[2] Sec. 17 provides requirements for aliens entering the United States from foreign contiguous territory.

Causes and Numbers Deported in the Two Groups of Cases Studied.[1]

Cause	*1926*	*1930*
Likely to become a public charge	21	4
Public charges (including insanity)	116	20
Criminals	34	7
Prostitutes, other immoral persons and narcotic law violators	16	2
Illegal entries (all categories)	362	30
Total	549	63

As may easily be seen, the same person might come under several of the categories mentioned and so be deportable for more than one cause, or, in bureau of immigration language, more than one " charge " might be placed against the same person.[2]

Thus one person may

(1) enter the United States by water at a time or place other than as designated by immigration officials
(2) enter the United States without inspection
(3) be in the United States in violation of the immigration act of 1924 in that he is not in possession of an unexpired immigration visa
(4) be liable to become a public charge at the time of entry
(5) be unable at the time of entry to read the English language or some other language or dialect, etc., although at that time over 16 years of age and physically capable of reading and not exempted from the illiteracy test.

As some of the charges are " stronger " than others, classi-

[1] The preceding table groups the causes more closely than that of the Commissioner General's Reports, but indicates that the various types of cause for deportation are included.

[2] In all except six criminal and seven liable to become a public charge of the cases studied, several reasons for deportation were listed, and one single "charge" was given only where there was no possible doubt of its validity.

fication is made on the basis of the strongest charges among those listed. For instance, in the case of a woman who entered illegally by land and was liable to become a public charge on entry and was later found practicing prostitution, the prostitution "charge" would be the strongest of the three.

By studying material in statutes, legal decisions and immigration file cases [1] an attempt has been made to explain why and how persons are deported from the United States to Europe. As many aspects of deportation are in a state of flux, before the ink in which this study is written may be dry, changes may have occurred. In any event, it is hoped that it will serve as a flashlight picture of the increasingly prominent deportation scene.

The study would not have been possible had it not been for the very generous cooperation of the Department of Labor. The author desires to express her deep appreciation of the many opportunities and kindnesses extended to her not only by Second Assistant Secretary of Labor Husband and Commissioner General of Immigration Hull but also by the entire personnel of the bureau of immigration with whom she came in contact in the Department of Labor in

[1] Only case records from the files of the bureau of immigration have been used, as it was felt records from social agencies would present a special type of selection. In an attempt to discover how many of the cases studied in the bureau of immigration files were known to social agencies, the cases were registered with social service exchanges where such were available. 16.3% of the total of 612 cases were known to social agencies in the United States, even though many of the cases were located at border points, ill-equipped with social agencies.

The cases used as illustrative examples embody only information in the files from the bureau of immigration. In the few cases where other information obtained from social agencies is used, it is so noted. All cases used in the book have been given fictitious names and addresses to prevent identification. For the same reason the file numbers in the bureau of immigration have been omitted from the cases as summarized.

Washington and in the field. Despite constant pressure of work, officials of the Department and bureau were generous in sharing resources and time, and in explaining points of law and administration.

The author also welcomes this opportunity to express her appreciation and indebtedness to the International Migration Service, a member of whose staff she was when her interest in the subject was aroused and when this study was begun. She also desires to acknowledge her gratitude especially to Professors Samuel McCune Lindsay, Joseph P. Chamberlain and Raymond Moley of Columbia University, Miss Marian Schibsby of the Foreign Language Information Service of New York, Miss Marguerite Schneider of the International Migration Service, and Mr. Max Kohler of the New York Bar, who have all read the study in manuscript form and offered much constructive criticism which the author wishes most thankfully to acknowledge. Above all, she must mention her father, John C. Clark, who has been tireless in interest and encouragement and who has read the manuscript several times. To the many others who have been generous in interest and suggestion this bare word of appreciation must unfortunately suffice.

TABLE OF CONTENTS

PAGE

DEPORTATION LAW AND ITS ADMINISTRATION

CHAPTER VIII

CHAPTER IX

CHAPTER X

CHAPTER XI

CHAPTER XII

CHAPTER XIII

CHAPTER I

Introduction

An Armenian reaching the United States in 1923 and finding the immigration quota in which he belonged filled and himself excluded, provided a modern version of the Flying Dutchman. By American regulation under the quota act of 1921 [1] he could not enter the United States, and by Turkish regulation he could not reenter Turkey once he had left there, so, like the Dutchman, he seemed condemned to wander the Seven Seas. The "quota act" provided that the total number of aliens of any nationality admitted to the United States during any fiscal year should be limited to three per cent of the number of foreign-born persons of such nationality resident in the United States as determined by the census of 1910. By its administrative provisions it created the difficulty of having numbers of people arrive at the gates, only to find that the total number of persons admissible from their respective countries at that time had already entered. In other words, the "quota was full," and those who arrived too late had to turn back. The frantic rush for admission before the quota of a particular country was filled, and the crowd of people sent home as "excess quota" were among the chief reasons why the immigration act of 1924 [2] by its provisions for administration arranged

[1] An act to limit the immigration of aliens into the United States, approved May 19, 1921 (42 Stat. 5) extended to and including June 30, 1924 by act of May 11, 1922 (42 Stat. 540).

[2] Approved May 26, 1924 (43 Stat. 153). This act provides "(a) The

for the allotment of quota numbers at the various American consulates throughout the world, under the direction of "quota control" officers. This alleviated the difficulty of the person who for no other reason than that he arrived a few days, or even hours, too late for admission within the quota of his country was sent back with no more than a glimpse of the skyline of the United States.

"Excess quota" was only one reason for which a person might be sent back. As provided by the basic immigration act of 1917,[1] there are certain excludable categories of aliens. Although "alien" usually means "foreigners,"[2] it is important to note that under some circumstances native-born Americans may be "aliens" in the United States. Thus Frederick Haskins was born in the United States but was naturalized in Canada. He was sentenced to a five-year prison term there but got a "ticket of leave" after serving one year. He then came to the United States and remained five years. While here he apparently used the mails to defraud, and then left for Canada. On entering Canada, he was immediately apprehended at the request of the United

annual quota of any nationality shall be 2 percentum of the number of foreign-born individuals of such nationality resident in continental United States as determined by the United States census of 1890, but the minimum quota of any nationality shall be 100. (b) The annual quota of any nationality for the fiscal year beginning July 1, 1927, and for each fiscal year thereafter, shall be a number which bears the same ratio to 150,000 as the number of inhabitants in continental United States in 1920 having that national origin . . . bears to the number of inhabitants in continental United States in 1920, but the minimum quota of any nationality shall be 100."—Sec. 11. The "national origins" provision did not take effect until July 1, 1929.

[1] Act of February 5, 1917.

[2] "With respect to any country, an alien is a person who is not a citizen, or subject of the country; a citizen or subject of a foreign state; a foreigner; one who does not either by native or voluntary adoption owe allegiance to the government within whose territory he dwells."—*Corpus Juris*, vol. ii, p. 1043.

States post-office authorities and returned to the United States to answer the charge. After serving a prison sentence of a year and a day and paying $1,000 fine, he was taken into custody for deportation to Canada. His case was taken to court, where it was held [1] that according to the provisions in the United States naturalization law [2] an American-born citizen may expatriate himself by becoming naturalized in any foreign state and that mere living in the United States again would not restore American citizenship to such a person. So the American-born Mr. Haskins became deportable to Canada according to the law of the United States.

Persons of course remain aliens even though they have made declarations of intention to become citizens of the United States. In other words, " first papers " do not effect in any way the right of the United States to exclude on reentry or deport after entry to the country.[3] Even if an alien *applies* for naturalization, he is still an alien until citizenship is granted, and so under the disabilities of aliens in regard to reentering or remaining in the country. How far these disabilities may go in regard to liability for being removed from the country is shown by the following:

An alien who was born in another country during a visit of his parents who had previously been admitted to the United States but had not been naturalized, and who was brought to the United States soon after his birth by his parents on their return

[1] Reynolds *v.* Haskins, 8 Fed. (2d) 473.

[2] Act of March 2, 1907 (34 Stat. 1228, § 2).

[3] Frick *v.* Lewis, 195 Fed. 693; Guimond *v.* Howes, 9 Fed. (2d) 412; United States *ex rel.* Bander *v.* Uhl, 211 Fed. 628; United States *ex rel.* Fanutti *v.* Flynn, 17 Fed. (2d) 432.

In the cases studied, a total of approximately 14% had secured their " first papers ". Of these, eight reported service in the American army and one was in the army when apprehended for deportation.

thereto, was subject to deportation on the ground that he had been convicted more than once of crimes involving moral turpitude and had been sentenced therefor to terms of imprisonment of more than one year, although he had lived in the United States all his life, excepting a very short period following his birth, and deportation would therefore in fact be an expatriation.[1]

So a person who is not a citizen of the United States may for various reasons be excluded on entry or reentry to the country or sent away once he has entered. If on any entry to the country, he is found to belong to one or more of the various "excludable classes,"[2] he may be excluded from the country.

Exclusions at ports of entry for a physical, mental, moral or economic reasons are becoming less frequent than formerly, due to a plan of examination abroad begun in Great Britain and the Irish Free State in July, 1925[3] and gradually extended to other points in Europe.[4] It is provided that medical officers of the United States Public

[1] United States *ex rel.* Shladzian *v.* Warden of the Eastern State Penitentiary, D. C. E. D. Pa. no. M-388, Nov. 11, 1930, quoted in *U. S. Daily*, Dec. 10, 1930.

[2] For further discussion, *vide infra*, chs. ii-vii.

[3] Bureau of immigration, General Order No. 51, July 9, 1925.

[4] The countries included by 1930 are England, Scotland, Northern Ireland, Irish Free State, Belgium, Holland, Germany, Poland, Czechoslovakia, Italy, Norway, Sweden, Denmark and (since July 1, 1930) Austria. *Annual Report of the Commissioner General*, etc., *for 1930*, p. 17. *Vide* also *Annual Report of the Surgeon General of the Public Health Service*, etc., *for 1930*, pp. 176 and 187-198.

Such a plan had been suggested some years ago but abandoned as internationally impracticable when other governments were indefinite in their approval or else definitely opposed. *Vide* E. Abbott, *Immigration: Documents and Case Records* (University of Chicago, 1924), p. 201, quoting Report of the United States Immigration Commission, vol. i (1911), pp. 25-49.

Health Service and inspectors of the bureau of immigration of the Department of Labor are attached as "technical advisers" to various American consulates; these advisers[1] give a preliminary examination to those applying for immigration visas, so that obviously ineligible applicants may not start on their way. While the United States of necessity retains right to final rejection, comparatively few who pass the examination abroad are rejected on arrival here. In 1928, of 159,283 persons passing the examination abroad and granted visas, only seventeen were certified with a mandatorily excludable defect on arrival here.

Exclusion on arrival in the United States is therefore becoming a decreasing quantity[2] in American immigration procedure. On the other hand, removal of aliens from the country after they have entered is becoming increasingly important both as to emphasis and numbers. The word *deportation* is sometimes used to refer both to the return home of an alien excluded at entry and to removal after entry, but the tendency of the courts is to hold that "'deportation' as distinguished from 'exclusion,' is depriving a person already in the United States of a privilege which he, at least at the time, is enjoying; whereas 'exclusion' is denial of entry and does not deprive one of any liberties he (*sic*) had theretofore enjoyed."[3] Because of the differences in law, procedure, and social problems involved, it is only in the sense of removal after entry that the word *deportation*[4] is used in this study. In bureau of immigra-

[1] In some cases these consist of immigrant inspectors alone.

[2] For statistics, *vide Annual Reports of the Commission General of Immigration for 1928*, p. 8 and *1930*, pp. 11-12; *Foreign Language Information Service Interpreter Release*, vol. ii, no. 45, p. 2.

[3] *Ex parte* Domenici, 8 Fed. (2d) 336.

[4] It is of note that the term was used in Roman law to denote "a perpetual banishment depriving the banished of his rights as a citizen"

tion language, deportation cases are called "warrant cases," because the procedure of issuing a warrant of arrest, holding a hearing, and issuing a warrant of deportation must be completed before deportation can take place.

There has been a great and definite increase in emphasis on deportation as a matter of legislation and administration, so that in the days of post-war feeling and again in the economic depression of 1930, deportation has become emphasized in the press and in Congress as a cure for the ills of the country. In recent years the Secretary of Labor and the Commissioner General of Immigration have called constant attention to the size and importance of the problem. In 1924 the Commissioner General stated: "The deportation of aliens found to be unlawfully in the United States is rapidly becoming one of the most important functions of the immigration service, and as the laws governing the admission of aliens become more restrictive in character the deportation problem becomes more difficult and exacting." [1] Since then he has annually reiterated its importance, in 1930 saying that the bureau of immigration "has particularly concentrated its efforts to enforce those provisions of the

[*Bouvier's Law Dictionary*, 3rd Revision (8th edition), by F. Rawle] and "a system of punishment for crime, of which the essential factor was the removal of the criminal to a penal settlement outside his own country" (*Encyclopædia Britannica*, 11th Edition, vol. viii, p. 56. *Cf. Webster's New International Dictionary*, 1921, p. 599). The term has almost lost its original connotations of punishment for crime and removal of citizens from their own country and has come to have the meaning of removal of *aliens* simply because their presence is not consistent with the public welfare, and without any punishment being imposed. Deportation is thus also differentiated from *transportation*, which is by way of punishment of one convicted of an offense against the laws of the country (Fong Yue Ting *v.* United States, 149 U. S. 698, 707) and from *extradition* which is surrender to another country of one accused of an offense against its laws, there to be tried, and if found guilty, punished. (*Ibid. Vide* also United States *v.* Hing Quong Chow, 53 Fed. 233.)

[1] *Annual Report for the Fiscal Year Ended June 30, 1924*, p. 12.

1917 act which provide for the deportation from the United States of certain classes of undesirable aliens."[1]

Within the Department of Labor there seems each year to be a race to outstrip the record of the previous year. The increase may be seen by the following table.[2]

ANNUAL DEPORTATIONS FROM THE UNITED STATES, 1892-1930[3]

ear ended une 30th	*Number Deported*	*Year ended June 30th*	*Number Deported*	*Year ended June 30th*	*Number Deported*	*Year ended June 30th*	*Number Deported*
1892	637	1902	465	1912	2,456	1922	4,345
1893	577	1903	547	1913	3,461	1923	3,661
1894	417	1904	779	1914	4,610	1924	6,409
1895	177	1905	845	1915	2,564	1925	9,495
1896	238	1906	676	1916	2,781	1926	10,904
1897	263	1907	995	1917	1,853	1927	12,055
1898	199	1908	2,069	1918	1,569	1928	11,625
1899	263	1909	2,124	1919	3,068	1929	12,908
1900	256	1910	2,695	1920	2,762	1930	16,631
1901	363	1911	2,788	1921	4,517		

Nor is there likely to be a decrease, for according to the Commissioner General of Immigration, "To continue the work and do it thoroughly is the big job ahead."[5]

Congress too has given increased prominence to deportation, for in recent years legislation has repeatedly been con-

[1] *Ibid.* for 1930, p. 70.

[2] The absolute significance of the table depends on its use in conjunction with tables of the total immigration to and emigration from the United States for the same period.

[3] *Annual Report*, etc., *for 1930*, p. 7.

[4] *Annual Reports of the Commissioner General of Immigration for the Fiscal Years Ending June 30, 1925* and *June 30, 1930*. The figures given refer only to numbers of *actual* deportations; if those who left the country by voluntary departure or reshipment foreign were included, the numbers would be greatly increased.

[5] The numbers for the first six months of the fiscal year 1931 show further increase, for they exceeded by approximately 400 the deportations during the same period of the 1930 fiscal year. (Statement of the Commissioner General, Jan. 13, 1931, quoted in *U. S. Daily*, Jan. 14, 1931.)

sidered designed to change and make deportation provisions more drastic than already in force, by adding to the number of deportable categories and lengthening the time limit within which deportation may occur. During the winter of 1925 the committee calendars of the 68th Congress listed not less than twenty-one bills dealing either wholly or chiefly with deportation problems.[1] However, it was not until the passage of the act of March 4, 1929[2] that the trend of Congressional activity made itself felt in actual legislation. That act, forbidding any re-entry to the United States of persons once deported, and making re-entry in violation of the law a felony, punishable by fine or imprisonment or both, was considered so drastic that it was soon thereafter slightly modified[3] so that it no longer applies to persons deported before March 4, 1929 to whom the Secretary of Labor before that date granted permission to reapply for admission.

By 1930 the opposition of organized labor to aliens as a source of undercutting wages, the economic depression in the country, the development of the war against "racketeers" and gangsters, the revived spectre of Communism, the President's message to Congress calling attention to problems of alien deportation, the overcrowding of prisons and jails, and various other factors combined to focus the attention of Congress once more on the alien as a possible source of the difficulties. On December 8, 1930 the Senate adopted a resolution[4] requesting information from the Secretary of Labor in regard to

[1] Among such possibilities for change may be cited H. R. 11796, 68th Congress, which passed the House but remained in the Senate Committee on Immigration. H. R. 11489, 69th Congress, as amended, passed the House but it too was not reported out of the Senate Committee.

[2] 45 Stat. 1551.

[3] By act of June 24, 1929 (public no. 21, 71st Cong.).

[4] S. Res. 355, quoted *U. S. Daily*, Dec. 9, 1930.

First: The estimated number of aliens who have unlawfully entered and are now in the United States.
Second: Approximately what number of such aliens are subject to deportation under existing laws.
Third: What additional appropriations of money are necessary to accomplish the prompt deportation of such aliens.
Fourth: What changes should be made in existing laws to facilitate the deportation of undesirable aliens.[1]

On February 10, 1931, a bill, again adding to the deportable categories and making administrative changes,[2] was introduced in Congress, but it went the way of earlier similar attempts.

What has caused the increasing prominence of deportation? The aftermath of war hysteria was not without its decided influence in reflecting a feeling of the "undesirability" of foreigners merely because of their alienage. Attention directed to one group soon included others of similar category. Then the numerous people who entered the country surreptitiously in evasion of the restrictive provisions of the "quota act" of 1921 or the immigration act of 1924, added greatly to the numbers of possible deportations and served to call attention to the problem of expelling aliens here against the law. Last of all, the serious economic situation in the country beginning during the years 1929, 1930, 1931 brought once more to the fore the need for finding someone to blame for the trouble, and the alien proved a likely possibility.

[1] On January 6, 1931, the Secretary of Labor supplied the information requested, so far as he was able. *Vide infra*, pp. 253, 327.

[2] H. R. 17004, 71st Congress, and S. 6116. The two bills were not exactly the same as first introduced, so the Senate bill was amended to conform to that in the House. The House bill was reported from committee on February 20, 1931 but had not been adopted by either house when Congress adjourned. *Vide infra*, pp. 171, 336, 365, for further discussion.

Let us now turn our attention to just what the problem is which is receiving so much attention. What is the law which governs sending people back to Europe, and how is it administered? It is necessary first of all to make a brief survey of how the legislation governing the matter has grown before we consider the present law and its administration.

CHAPTER II

Growth and Present Status of Deportation Legislation

ENGLISH AND COLONIAL PRACTICE

The theory of sending persons for some reason found undesirable in one locality on to another place is by no means new, for it is found in the poor law and administrative practice in England and in colonial days in this country. Even in the sixteenth century in England " impotent poor " who had become beggars in towns other than their own were conveyed by the town officers " on horseback, cart, chariot or otherwise to the next constable, and so from constable to constable, till they be brought to the place where they were born or most conversant for the space of three years, there to be nourished of alms." [1] However, it was not until the somewhat notorious Law of Settlement and Removal was enacted a century later, 1662, that any person not a property-owner

> who, either to take a situation or merely on a visit to relations or friends, or for any other reason whatever . . . came into a parish in which he had not a settlement, was liable however good his character and conduct, without any application for relief or for other gift or favour, and even after he had secured remunerative employment—unless he could give sufficient security that he would never become chargeable to the parish, to the satisfaction of the Justices to be summarily removed in custody, to-

[1] Report of George Goode . . . on the Law of Settlement and Removal of the Poor, H. C. no. 675 of 1851, p. 11, quoted S. and B. Webb, *English Poor Law History* (London and New York, 1927), pt. i. p. 318.

gether with his wife and children, under ignominious and horribly uncomfortable conditions, to whatever parish, however distant, might be believed to be the place where, according to an extremely complicated and always uncertain code of law, he had his legal settlement." [1]

The same act included a provision for the drastic punishment as a vagabond under the Vagrancy Act of anyone removed to his parish of settlement who then returned to the place from which he had been removed, but this was seldom carried out in practice. The hardships entailed by the act were great and mitigated only to a degree by a system of certificates or testimonials given by parish officers to certain individuals or families, acknowledging them to be settled inhabitants and promising to take them back at the end of a term of years, or in the event of their becoming chargeable to the parish into which they had moved.[2]

The situation of the poor and ill, perpetually wandering from one place to another, became so serious that it aroused criticism,[3] and finally relief was attempted by providing that "with the exception of persons deemed by law to be 'rogues and vagabonds' or 'idle and disorderly persons,' and . . . every unmarried woman with child, no person should be liable to be removed until he had actually become chargeable to the Poor Rate." [4] So those who were liable to become a public charge and those who had actually become such charges early provided vexations and difficulties for the places they inhabited.

[1] *Ibid.*, pp. 322-3.

[2] S. and B. Webb, *loc. cit.*

[3] Adam Smith in his *Wealth of Nations*, bk. i, ch. 10, pt. ii (1776), stated: "to remove a man who has committed no misdemeanor from the parish where he chooses to reside is an evident violation of natural liberty and justice." Smith's chief complaint was directed against the practice of removal as a restriction on the mobility of labor.

[4] S. and B. Webb, *op. cit.*, p. 343.

The English practice was taken over by the colonies and early states in America, until here too commenced the forlorn procession of ill and indigent men, women and children sent wandering from town to town and then from state to state.[1] In some instances the colonies, in a vain attempt to stem the influx of criminals[2] and paupers from other countries, ordered the exclusion or removal of such persons across the seas whence they had come. For instance, as far back as 1639, the settlers at Plymouth, Massachusetts, required the removal of foreign paupers and by that requirement perhaps began the practice of deportation to Europe from this country.[3] In 1740 the province of Delaware had an act "imposing a duty on persons convicted of heinous crimes and to prevent poor and impotent persons being imported," which provided that it might be lawful for any two justices of the peace to compel the master of a vessel, or anyone else who imported

> any infant, lunatick, aged, maimed, impotent or vagrant person or persons to give sufficient security to carry and transport such infant, etc. to the place or places from whence such persons were imported or otherwise to indemnify the inhabitants of this government from any charge that may come or be brought upon them by such infant, etc. coming into or living within this government.[4]

[1] *Vide* G. Abbott, *The Immigrant and the Community* (New York, 1917), pp. 174-6, and R. W. Kelso, *Poor Relief in Massachusetts* (Boston, 1922).

[2] For emigration of foreign convicts to America *vide* House Executive Document, 43rd Congress, 1st Session, no. 253. [Senate Document no. 21, 61st Congress, 3rd Session, p. 22 (1866).]

[3] *Vide* R. Garis, *Immigration Restriction* (MacMillan, 1927), p. 13, quoting Colonial Charters, 1639 and 1692.

[4] E. Abbott, *Historical Aspects of the Immigration Problem* (Chicago, 1926), p. 547.

By 1794 Massachusetts passed a fairly well-developed "act providing for the relief and support, employment and removal of the poor" which set forth that on complaint of the overseers any justice of the peace might

> by warrant directed to, and which may be executed by any constable of their town or district, or any particular person by name, cause such pauper to be sent and conveyed, by land or water, to any other State, or to any place beyond sea, where he belongs, if the justice thinks proper, if he may conveniently be removed, at the expense of the Commonwealth; but if he cannot be so removed, he may be sent to and relieved, and employed in the house of correction, or work-house, at the public expense."[1]

The difficulties of overseas travel were so great that only seldom could a person "conveniently be removed."

In general, efforts consisted in requiring a duty or indemnity to be paid for all such persons brought into the midst of the community rather than in any attempt to send them back. The causes for concern were to a great extent those persons sent from one place to another within the country. Gradually, in this country as in England, sending people from one place to another unless they had actually become public charges became discredited, and as the area of local responsibility widened, the situation was alleviated. Yet to this day the mournful procession of indigent wanderers has not entirely disappeared, for states still in some circumstances return non-resident persons whence they came.[2]

[1] E. Abbott, *Immigration: Select Documents and Case Records*, p. 105.

[2] For instance, *vide 62nd Annual Report of the State Board of Charities for the Year Ending June 30, 1928*, Legislative Document (1929), no. 22, State of New York, pp. 13-14. Repatriation at state expense must not be confused with deportation by the federal government. In the former case, usually consent is necessary on the part of the person removed, while this is not true in the latter case. *Vide* ch. iv, p. 126 *et seq.*

THE ALIEN ACT OF 1798

The possibility of the federal government sending foreigners out of the United States arose not as a method of dealing with the poor, or ill, or even the criminal, but as a political activity resulting from the chaotic relationships between this country and others, especially France, in the period immediately after 1793. English depredations and French spoliations aroused American feeling to such a pitch of resentment that the Federalists determined to take a firm stand and rid the country of foreign agitators of all sorts—English and Irish and particularly French. Accordingly, the year 1798 saw the birth of an Alien Act [1] which empowered the President by executive order to send out of the country those persons of foreign birth whom he deemed inimical to the country's welfare, or those whom he had

some reasonable grounds to suspect were concerned in any treasonable or secret machinations against the government. And in case any alien when thus ordered to depart should be found at large within the United States after the term limited in the order, not having obtained a license from the President to reside therein, or having obtained such license should not have conformed thereto, he should on conviction thereof be imprisoned for a term not exceeding three years, and should never afterwards be admitted to become a citizen of the United States; . . . if the alien thus ordered to depart should prove to the satisfaction of the President . . . that no injury or danger to the United States would arise from suffering him to reside therein, the President might grant a license to him to remain in the United States. . . . The act also provided that it should be lawful for the President, whenever he deemed it necessary for the public safety, to order to be removed out of the territory of the United States any alien in prison in pursuance of the act,

[1] The Sedition Act of the same year, while usually considered at the same time as the Alien Act, does not concern us here. The invectives of the period were usually hurled at both.

and to cause to be arrested and sent out of the United States such aliens as may have been ordered to depart, and had not obtained a license, in all cases where, in the opinion of the President, the public safety required a speedy removal. . . . And that if any alien thus removed or sent out of the United States should voluntarily return, unless by permission of the President, such alien being convicted thereof should be imprisoned so long as in the opinion of the President the public safety might require.[1]

It is of note that the act combined executive order with judicial enforcement.

The Alien Act expired of its own force two years after passage.[2] It had caused a storm of indignation throughout the country and was vehemently denounced by many statesmen, including Madison, Jefferson and Gallatin;[3] its warmest advocates defended it only as a war measure;[4] its opponents denounced it vehemently as dealing with matters over which the federal government had no control. The state of Virginia went so far as to pass condemnatory resolutions,[5] declaring that the Act exercised a power nowhere delegated to the general government and, by uniting legislative and judicial powers to those of the executive, "subverted the general principles of free government, as well as

[1] Fong Yue Ting *v.* United States, 149 U. S. 698, dissenting opinion of Mr. Justice Field, p. 746 *et seq.* *Cf.* A. J. Beveridge, *Law and Order*, Report to a Sub-Committee of the Republican National Committee (1920), p. 86 *et seq.*; A. J. Beveridge, *Life of John Marshall*, vol. ii, p, 381; C. Bouvé, *op. cit.*, pp. 51-2.

[2] Because of the provision for expiration within two years, the constitutionality of the act never came before the Supreme Court.

[3] *Annals of Congress*, vol. ii, pp. 1955, 1958.

[4] *Works of John Adams*, vol. ix, p. 291.

[5] These resolutions and the opposition in general were directed at both the Alien and Sedition Acts.

the particular organization and positive provisions of the Federal Constitution."[1] The resolutions adopted by the Virginia Assembly concerning the Act were sent to the various state legislatures, and their replies in turn were sent to a committee of the Assembly, of which Madison was a member. In his report on the matter he differentiated between alien members of a hostile nation and alien members of friendly nations, and said:

With respect to alien enemies, no doubt has been intimated as to the Federal authority over them; the Constitution having expressly delegated to Congress the power to declare war against any nation, and, of course, to treat it and all its members as enemies. With respect to aliens who are not enemies, but members of nations in peace and amity with the United States, the power assumed by the Act of Congress is denied to be constitutional and it is accordingly against this Act that the protest of the General Assembly is expressly and exclusively directed.[2]

With the expiration of the Alien Act and the disappearance of war-time sentiment in the country, the idea of removing aliens for political reasons during periods of peace became quiescent; only the bitterness and fear engendered by the World War again focused attention sharply on the question. Meanwhile a sufficient number of foreign paupers had entered the United States[3] to shift the emphasis from

[1] Madison's speech before the Virginia Assembly, Dec. 21, 1798. 4 Elliott Deb. 528.

[2] 4 Elliott Deb. 554.

[3] For documents bearing on this subject, *vide* Edith Abbott, *Historical Aspects of the Immigration Problem,* Letters from Pauper Immigrants, p. 75; The Irish Famine Exodus of 1847, pp. 111-17; Immigrants in New York City, pp. 325-8; esp. all of Sec. IV, Pauperism and Crime and Other Domestic Immigration Problems. Also Edith Abbott, *Immigration: Select Documents and Case-Records,* pp. 27-8; Complaints of the Almshouse Commissioner of New York City, 1846, pp. 47-8; American Cholera Epidemics and Emigrant Ships; Part II,

aliens as political liabilities to aliens as economic burdens on the states. With administration of immigration affairs in the hands of the states, those most seriously concerned attempted regulation of exclusion and deportation. For instance, as early as 1837, the Common Council of New York passed a resolution authorizing commissioners of almshouses to send back alien paupers,—provided they gave their consent,—who were in Bellevue or elsewhere.[1]

At this time the right to send back alien paupers once they had been admitted to the country was seriously questioned by foreign powers, whether the sending back be by the individual states or the federal government. It was not long, however, before the idea of expulsion found a secure place in international law. Thus in 1856 Marcy wrote: "Every society possesses the undoubted right to determine who shall compose its members, and it is exercised by all nations, both in peace and in war,"[2] while thirteen years later Fish wrote: "The control of the people within its limits and the right to expel from its territory persons who are dangerous to the peace of the state are too clearly within the essential attributes of sovereignty to be seriously contested."[3] So the publicists and recognized authorities on international law admit the absolute right to exclude or expel in the public interest.[4] However, it is important to

Sec. 1, Admission of Immigrants under State Laws, 1788-1882, nos. 1-6, 9, 10, 14, 18, 20. The two volumes throughout give clear pictures of American attempts at protection against those who were liable to become public charges on her shores.

[1] H. P. Fairchild, *Immigration* (Revised Edition) (New York, 1925), p. 114.

[2] *Wheaton's International Law Digest*, Sec. 206.

[3] *Ibid.*

[4] J. B. Moore, *Digest of International Law*, vol. iv, sec. 550; Clement Bouvé, *Exclusion and Expulsion of Aliens*, quoting 1 Vattel, *Law of Nations*, ch. 19, pars. 230, 231; 2 Ortolan, *Diplomatie de la Mer*

remember that if a nation "exercises either right in an arbitrary or unjust manner it may render itself thereby liable to a demand for satisfaction on the part of the state whose national has been thus expelled or excluded."[1]

FEDERAL LEGISLATION

There was thus sanction in international law for the adoption in federal immigration policy of a law of settlement internationally applied. Economic difficulties caused by Chinese and contract-labor immigration, and the declaration by the Supreme Court that state regulatory laws were unconstitutional, were in large measure responsible for the actual adoption of federal immigration measures. Exclusion by the federal government came with the act of March 3, 1875,[2] which prohibited the importation of alien convicts, of women for purposes of prostitution, and of coolies. But the first general act pertaining to federal immigration was not passed until 1882. The act of August 3 of that year[3] not only imposed a head-tax on all immigrants entering the country but extended the classes excluded by the 1875 act to include "any convict, lunatic, idiot, or any person unable to take care of himself or herself without becoming a public charge,"[4] and "all foreign convicts except those convicted of political offenses";[5] it also provided for the return of

(4th edition), ch. 14, p. 297; 1 Phillimore, *International Law* (3rd edition), ch. 10, sec. 220; Bar, *International Law* (Gillespie's edition), 1883, 708, note 711; Fiore, *Nuov. Di. Int. Publ.* (2nd edition) (Antoine's translation into the French), t. 1, n. 699, t. 3, n. 1297, p. 93; Calvo, *Le droit Publique*, par. 442; Darut, *De l'Expulsion des Étrangers*, p. 14; J. B. Moore, *International Law*, vol. iii, sec. 5; E. Borchard, *Diplomatic Protection of Citizens Abroad* (1916), ch. ii.

[1] Bouvé, p. 14.

[2] 18 Stat. 477.

[3] Sec. 2.

[4] 22 Stat. 214.

[5] Sec. 4.

excluded aliens at the expense of the ship owners and assigned responsibility for the execution of the immigration laws to the Secretary of the Treasury, thus providing a small beginning of a federal deportation policy with federal administration.

As yet the law was concerned with exclusion rather than deportation. But the Chinese Exclusion Act of 1882, and amended two years later,[1] contained provisions for suspending for ten years the admission of Chinese laborers to the United States and for deporting from the country any Chinese person who, on hearing before a "justice, judge or commissioner of a court of the United States," was found not to have a required certificate.[2] Public opinion was rapidly crystallizing, and exclusion was soon firmly entrenched as a fundamental part of United States immigration policy. After the passage of further Chinese exclusion acts [3] the matter came before the Supreme Court, and there

[1] Act of May 6, 1882 (22 Stat. 58) as amended by act of July 5, 1884 (23 Stat. 115). This amended act was continued in force for an additional period of ten years from May 5, 1892 by act of that date (27 Stat. 25); this in turn with all laws on this subject in force on April 29, 1902, was re-enacted and continued unconditionally by the act of April 29, 1902 (32 Stat. 176), as amended by act of April 27, 1904 (33 Stat. 428). *Vide* Cook and Hagerty, *op. cit.*, p. 334.

[2] Sec. 12. Note also secs. 1 and 2. The sections for removal from the country did not apply to any Chinese laborer in the United States on November 17, 1880, or who should have come within ninety days after the passage of the act.

It must be remembered that Chinese deportations are not considered within the scope of this study and the Chinese exclusion acts are only alluded to as relating to the general problem of deportation. *Vide* R. D. McKenzie, *Oriental Exclusion* (Chicago, 1928); E. G. Mears, *Resident Orientals on the American Pacific Coast* (Chicago, 1928); Mary R. Coolidge, *Chinese Immigration* (N. Y., 1908).

[3] Act of July 5, 1884 (23 Stat. 115), and especially those of 1888—Act of September 13, 1888 (25 Stat. 476) and of October 1, 1888 (25 Stat. 504).

the right to exclude from the country was definitely upheld in the cases of Chae Chan Ping *v.* United States [1] and in Nishimura Ekiu *v.* United States.[2] Following the thread they had already begun to spin, legislators now began to expand the list of those generally excludable from the United States by adding contract laborers.[3] From 1885-1888 it was provided that all persons within the contract labor prohibitions should be sent back to the nations to which they belonged at the expense of the vessels in which they came.

The time was ripe for provision for deportation after entry. This question was somewhat more difficult to solve than that of exclusion, for persons already within the country were, both according to the Constitution and the facts, in a different position from those who had never crossed the threshold; but the problem did not prove unanswerable for either Congress or the courts. Aside from the provisions regarding the Chinese, no mention of deportation appeared in the general immigration acts. It was first made in the act of October 19, 1883, an act amendatory to the contract labor law. By it the Secretary of the Treasury, when satisfied that an immigrant had been allowed to land contrary to law, was authorized to cause such immigrant to be taken into custody and returned to the country from whence he came within one year after landing or entry, at the expense of the owner of the importing vessel. Here then are the seeds of the authority later to be vested in the Secretary of Labor in deportation cases.

[1] 130 U. S. 581.

[2] 142 U. S. 651.

[3] The act of February 26, 1885 (23 Stat. 332) prohibited the importation of laborers under contract or agreement, express or implied. The statute was so drawn that it was not difficult to avoid. It was accordingly amended by acts of February 23, 1887 (24 Stat. 414) and October 19, 1888 (25 Stat. 566) to make it inclusive.

Once the entering wedge had been driven, it was easy to widen the opening. By act of 1891 [1] the number of excludable classes had been greatly enlarged by the addition of paupers, persons suffering from loathsome or dangerous contagious diseases, polygamists and persons whose ticket had been paid for by another or who had been assisted by others to come, unless it could be affirmatively shown they were not also in another excludable class.[2] The number of excludable classes had so far been increased to seven [3] and included idiots, insane, paupers or persons liable to become a public charge, persons who had been convicted of a felony or other crime or misdemeanor involving moral turpitude, polygamists, sufferers from a loathsome or dangerous contagious disease, and assisted immigrants (if otherwise excludable.[4] This act of 1891 added a new provision to these excludable classes, for it provided [5] not only for their exclusion but also for the deportation of those who within one year after their arrival, became public charges from causes existing prior to landing. Such persons were to be deemed to have come in violation of law and returned at the expense of the transportation company bringing them, or if that proved impossible, at government expense.[6]

[1] Act of March 3, 1891 (26 Stat. 1084).

[2] Aside from the excludable Chinese and contract laborers.

[3] Sec. 1.

[4] It is to be noted that the act provided (Sec. 1): "That nothing in this act shall be construed to apply to or exclude persons convicted of a political offense, notwithstanding said political offense may be designated as a 'felony, crime, infamous crime, or misdemeanor, involving moral turpitude' by the laws of the land whence he came or by the court convicting." Thus the now notorious "moral turpitude" was inserted in the law as a safeguard for the alien. *Vide infra*, ch. v, pp. 161-171.

[5] Sec. 11.

[6] *Ibid.*

It was, however, the provisions in one of the Chinese exclusion laws that finally caused the Supreme Court to set the seal of its approval on deportation as a matter of general immigration policy. An act of May 5, 1892[1] provided, among other things, that all Chinese laborers within the United States must secure certificates of registration within one year, and anyone found without such certificate was made liable to deportation.[2] Despite the protests of China,[3] the constitutionality of the act was upheld the following year, 1893, by a divided court in the famous case of Fong Yue Ting *v.* United States.[4]

The case formed a landmark in deportation history, for the majority of the court agreed without equivocation on "the right to exclude or expel all aliens, or any class of aliens, absolutely or upon certain conditions, in war or in peace, being an inherent and inalienable right of every sovereign and independent nation, essential to its safety, its independence and its welfare."[5] The majority agreed, furthermore, that

> the order of deportation is not a punishment for crime. It is not a banishment, in the sense in which that word is often applied to the expulsion of a citizen from his country by way of punishment. It is but a method of enforcing the return to his own country of an alien who has not complied with the conditions upon the performance of which the government of the

[1] 27 Stat. 25.

[2] Sec. 6, as amended by Act of Nov. 3, 1893.

[3] *Foreign Relations*, 1892, pp. 106, 118, 119, 123, 126, 134-8, 145, 147-55, 158.

[4] 149 U. S. 698. *Vide* also Lem Moon Sing *v.* United States, 158 U. S. 538; Li Sing *v.* United States, 180 U. S. 486; Fok Yung Yo *v.* United States, 185 U. S. 296.

[5] Fong Yue Ting, p. 711.

nation, acting within the constitutional authority and through proper departments, has determined that his continuing to reside there shall depend. He has not, therefore, been deprived of life, liberty or property, without due process of law; and the provisions of the Constitution, securing the right of trial by jury and prohibiting unreasonable searches and seizures, and cruel and unusual punishments, have no application.[1] . . . The power to exclude or expel aliens, being a power affecting international relations, is vested in the political department of the government, and is to be regulated by treaty or by Act of Congress, and is to be executed by the executive authority according to the regulations so established except so far as the judicial department has been authorized by treaty or by statute, or is required by the paramount law of the Constitution to intervene.[2]

The decision was not reached, however, without vigorous dissent, for Mr. Chief Justice Fuller and Mr. Justices Brewer and Field wrote lengthy and forceful dissenting opinions. All of the dissenting justices agreed in distinguishing the right to deport from the right to exclude, and protested against their assimilation to each other. It may be well to quote from the dissenting views:

Mr. Justice Brewer:

The Constitution has no extraterritorial effect, and those who have not come lawfully within our territory cannot claim any protection from its provisions. And it may be that the national government, having full control of all matters relating to other nations has the power to build, as it were, a Chinese Wall around our borders and absolutely forbid aliens to enter. But the Constitution has potency everywhere within the limits of our territory, and the powers which the national government may exercise within such limits are those, and only those, given to it by that instrument. Now, the power to remove aliens is,

[1] P. 730.

[2] P. 713.

confessedly, not expressed. Even if it be among the powers implied, yet still it can be exercised only in subordination to the limitations and restrictions imposed by the Constitution. . . .

Deportation is punishment. It involves first an arrest, a deprival of liberty; and second, a removal from home, from family, from business, from property . . . it needs no citation of authorities to support the proposition that deportation is punishment. Everyone knows that to be forcibly taken away from home and family, and friends, and business, and property, and sent across the ocean to a distant land, is punishment; and that oftentimes the most severe and cruel. Apt and just are the words of one of the framers of this Constitution, President Madison, when he says (4 Elliott Deb. 555): "If the banishment of an alien from a country into which he has been invited as the asylum most auspicious to his happiness—a country where he may have formed the most tender connections; where he may have invested his entire property, and acquired property of the real and permanent, as well as the movable and temporary kind; where he enjoys, under the laws, a greater share of the blessings of personal security and personal liberty than he can elsewhere hope for; . . . if, moreover, in the execution of the sentence against him is to be exposed . . . possibly to vindictive purposes, which his immigration may have provoked—if a banishment of this sort be not a punishment, and among the severest of punishments it will be difficult to imagine a doom to which the name can be applied."

But punishment implies a trial: "No person shall be deprived of life, liberty, or property, without due process of law." Due process requires that a man be heard before he is condemned, and both heard and condemned in the due and orderly procedure of a trial as recognized by the common law from time immemorial. . . . Its grievous wrong suggests this declaration of wisdom, coming from the dawn of English history: "Verily he who dooms a worse doom to the friendless and the comer from afar than to his fellows injures himself."—Laws of King Cnut, 1 Thorpe, *Ancient Laws and Institutes of England*, 397." [1]

[1] P. 738 *et seq.*

Mr. Justice Field:

The power of the government to exclude foreigners from this country, that is, to prevent them from entering it, whenever the public interests in its judgment require such exclusion, have been repeatedly asserted by the legislative and executive departments of our government and never denied; but its power to deport from the country persons lawfully domiciled therein by its consent, and engaged in the ordinary pursuits of life, has never been asserted by the legislative or executive departments except for crime, or as an act of war in view of existing or anticipated hostilities, unless the Alien Act of 1798 can be considered as recognizing that doctrine. . . .

In no other instance (than the Alien Act) until the law before us was passed, has any public man had the boldness to advocate the deportation of friendly aliens in time of peace. I repeat the statement, that in no other instance has the deportation of friendly aliens been advocated as a lawful measure by any department of our government. And it will surprise most people to learn that any such dangerous and despotic power lies in our government—a power which will authorize us to expel at pleasure, in time of peace, the whole body of friendly foreigners of any country domiciled herein by its permission, a power which can be brought into exercise whenever it may suit the pleasure of Congress, and be enforced without regard to the guarantees of the Constitution intended for the protection of the rights of all persons in their liberty and property. . . .

According to its theory, Congress might have ordered its executive officers to take the Chinese laborers to the ocean and put them into a boat and set them adrift, or to take them to the borders of Mexico and turn them loose there, and in both cases without any means of support; indeed, it might have sanctioned towards these laborers the most shocking brutality conceivable. I utterly repudiate all such notions and reply that brutality, inhumanity and cruelty cannot be made elements in any procedure for the enforcement of the laws of the United States.[1]

The punishment is beyond all reason in its severity. It is

[1] P. 746 *et seq.*

out of all proportion to the alleged offense. It is cruel and unusual. As to its cruelty, nothing can exceed a forcible deportation from a country of one's residence, and the breaking up of all relations of friendship, family and business there contracted.[1]

Mr. Chief Justice Fuller:

Conceding that the exercise of the power to exclude is committed to the political department, and that the denial of entrance is not necessarily the subject of judicial cognizance, the exercise of the power to expel, the manner in which the right to remain may be terminated, rests on different ground, since limitations exist or are imposed upon the deprivation of that which has been lawfully acquired. . . . No euphemism can disguise the character of the Act in this regard. It directs the performance of a judicial function in a particular way, and inflicts punishment without a judicial trial. It is, in effect, a legislative sentence of banishment, and as such, absolutely void. Moreover, it contains within it the germs of the assertion of an unlimited and arbitrary power, in general, incompatible with the immutable principles of justice, inconsistent with the nature of our government, and in conflict with the written Constitution by which that government was created and those principles secured.[2]

It must be remembered that the court in this case dealt with explicit statutory language providing for a judicial hearing [3] previous to deportation of Chinese for non-registration and that deportation by administrative process had not come before the court. In 1903 the Japanese Immigrant Case [4] made deportation by administrative procedure

[1] P. 759.

[2] P. 762.

[3] Deportation of Chinese involves judicial procedure while other deportations are accomplished by administrative fiat.

[4] 189 U. S. 86. Previous to this decision, a United States district court had held in *In re* Yamasaka (95 Fed. 652) that a domiciled alien could not be deported by executive action under the statute as phrased.

an established fact in American immigration policy. Since then, dissenting voices have gradually died away. Now and again they are raised in cases of particular hardship, as in the instance of a boy brought from Poland as a small child and later twice convicted of burglary, serving two terms in prison and then ordered deported to Poland. In regretfully affirming the legality of the order of deportation, Judge Learned Hand of the Circuit Court of Appeals stated that the man was

> as much our product as though his mother had borne him on American soil. He knows no other language, no other people, no other habits, than ours; he will be as much a stranger in Poland as any one born of ancestors who immigrated in the 17th century. However heinous his crimes, deportation is to him exile, a dreadful punishment abandoned by the common consent of all civilized peoples. Such, indeed, it would be to anyone, but to one already proved to be incapable of honest living, a helpless waif in a strange land, it will be utter destruction. That our reasonable efforts to rid ourselves of unassimilable immigrants should in execution be attended by such a cruel and barbarous result would be a national reproach.[1]

Congress now began further to develop the list of reasons for which a person could be excluded or deported from the United States.[2] It was not until 1903, however, that the additions became law. During that year it was provided[3] in a basic act, intended to be a complete codification of the then existing law,[3] that, in addition to the classes already

[1] United States *ex rel.* Klonis *v.* Davis, 13 Fed. (2d) 630.

[2] The acts of February 15, 1893 (27 Stat. 452), March 3, 1893 (27 Stat. 569), August 18, 1894 (28 Stat. 390), March 2, 1895 (28 Stat. 780), June 6, 1900 (31 Stat. 611) dealt largely with administrative provisions and did not add either to excludables or deportables.

[3] By act of March 3, 1903 (32 Stat. 1213), sec. 2.

[4] Contract labor, however, was not mentioned among the excluded

excluded, epileptics, persons having been insane within five years previous, persons having had two or more attacks of insanity at any time previously, professional beggars, anarchists, or persons who believe in or advocate the overthrow by force or violence of the government of the United States or of all government or of all forms of law, or the assassination of public officials, prostitutes and procurers, and "accompanying aliens,"[1] should be excluded. In regard to deportation, the act provided that

> any alien who shall come into the United States in violation of law or who shall be found a public charge therein, from causes existing prior to landing, shall be deported as hereinafter provided to the country whence he came at any time within two years after his arrival, at the expense, including one-half the cost of inland transportation to the port of deportation, of the person bringing such alien into the United States, or if that cannot be done, then at the expense of the immigrant fund.[2]

The following section provided similar deportation within three years after entry for all aliens except public charges found in the country in violation of the act.

The next important immigration act in connection with exclusion and deportation is that of February 20, 1907.[3] It was a second attempt at summarizing and codifying the immigration laws but it, too, added to the ever-growing categories of exclusion and deportation. The excluded

classes. It was held in the absence of such mention that such labor was still excluded by the acts of 1885-1888. This act mentioned such labor, but not among the list of excluded.

[1] Aliens accompanying minor, ill or helpless excluded aliens.

[2] Sec. 20. The immigrant fund was provided by sec. 1 of the same act, by which it was arranged that the money collected from head taxes was to constitute a permanent appropriation to be used for purposes connected with immigration. The provision for the fund was repealed in 1909 (35 Stat. 982).

[3] 34 Stat. 898.

classes were extended to include imbeciles, feeble-minded, persons with tuberculosis, persons found mentally or physically defective, such mental or physical defect being of a nature which may affect the ability of the alien to earn a living, persons who admit having committed a crime or misdemeanor involving moral turpitude, women and girls [1] coming to the United States for prostitution or any other immoral purpose, persons whose ticket had been paid for by any private organization or foreign government in any way,[2] and all children under sixteen, unless accompanied by or going to one or both of their parents (under regulations prescribed by the Secretary of Commerce and Labor).

Most important of all the deportation provisions in the act were those extending the time limit for all deportations to three years after entry.[3] Gradually the time had lengthened from one to two and then to three years, and still further extensions loomed ahead. It is of note that the act arranged for deportable aliens "upon the warrant of the Secretary" (of Commerce and Labor) to be taken into custody and deported to the country whence they came, but pending a final disposition of their cases, they might be released on bail bond, with security "approved by the Secretary." Here too was a foreshadowing of future development.

By 1910 further developments took place. The act of March 26 of that year [4] was devoted especially to strength-

[1] It was not until the 1917 act that "persons" was substituted for "women or girls" in the clause describing the class excluded on grounds of immorality.—Senate Report no. 352, 64th Congress, 1st Session (to accompany H. R. 10384), p. 5.

[2] Sec. 2. This provision did not apply to aliens in transit through the United States to Canada or Mexico.

[3] Secs. 20-21.

[4] 36 Stat. 263.

ening the bar against prostitution and immorality. Its extension of the excludable classes consisted chiefly in the addition of "persons who are supported by or receive in whole or in part the proceeds of prostitution." The time limit for deportation was radically changed by the provision that

> any alien who shall be found an inmate of or connected with the management of a house of prostitution or practicing prostitution after such alien shall have entered the United States, or who shall receive, share in, or derive benefit from any part of the earnings of any prostitute; or who is employed by, in, or in connection with any house of prostitution or music or dance hall or other place of amusement habitually frequented by prostitutes, or where prostitutes gather, or who in any way assists, protects, or promises to protect from arrest any prostitute, shall be deemed to be unlawfully within the United States and shall be deported.

Thus all time limit for such persons was removed. Furthermore, any attempts on their parts to return after deportation became punishable. At the expiration of sentences served for violation of this provision, deportation was to follow.

Without any definite plan of development and by additions made now and then in a hit-or-miss fashion, the immigration law has indeed grown like Topsy, until "there are more than 30 laws on the statute books which relate to immigration control. . . . Congress has necessarily enacted piecemeal laws to meet particular immigration problems as they have arisen. . . . Provisions of law relating to immigration and aliens are . . . widely scattered and interwoven with other statutes."[1] However, the present provisions re-

[1] *Annual Report of the Secretary of Labor for the Fiscal Year Ended June 30, 1930*, pp. 16 and 18.

lating to exclusion and deportation are founded on a basic immigration act of 1917,[1] the first in importance after 1910. Let us therefore turn to that act and to those that follow in an attempt to trace some of the problems of the law as it is administered today.

LEGISLATION SINCE 1917

Since 1882, the whole fabric of the immigration law has been so patched and re-patched, so amended and enlarged, that it has become a veritable crazy-quilt, recognizable only by those who know from use where each individual patch belongs. Even the basic act of 1917, instead of turning out to be a summary and clarification of existing law, became a motley thing, barely intelligible even to the initiate. It has been condemned in no uncertain terms by the Secretary of Labor, quoting from a former Department of Labor official, now on the federal bench, who says:

> the immigration act of 1917 (the general law), as a piece of legislative draftsmanship, is an impossible jumble, unintelligible, confusing and unreadable. Some of the paragraphs are so long, refer to so many subjects, and have so many provisos making exceptions as to what goes before that no human being can possibly know what they mean after reading them.[2]

To no part of the law can the criticism more truly apply than to the provisions regarding deportation, listed as they are in a haphazard, hit-or-miss, unclassified fashion. They are a combination of Sections 20 and 21 of the 1907 act, with additions, corresponding in general to the changes in exclusion provisions. At the time of its passage it was felt

[1] Act of February 5, 1917 (39 Stat. 875).

[2] *Annual Report of the Secretary of Labor for the Fiscal Year Ending June 30, 1929*, p. 19, where consolidation of the immigration laws is urged. A tentative "immigration code" has been drawn up by officials of the Department of Labor but it has not had Congressional action.

that this 1917 act "clarified" the deportation provisions previously existing and "to the fullest extent practicable . . . included all of the classes subject to deportation after having entered the country."[1] Yet Congress did not see fit to provide in this act that aliens falling within certain very definite categories should be deported from the United States. The act and subsequent immigration legislation set up no definite legislative standard but enumerate in somewhat general terms those aliens who are deportable, and divide the general classifications into categories of aliens deportable within three or five years after entry to the United States and those who may be expelled at any time whatsoever after they come to the country. In most cases the terms relating to aliens deportable as members of one or more of these classes are general; as, for example, any "alien who within five years after entry become a public charge from causes not affirmatively shown to have arisen subsequent to entry." There is need for determining whether or not an alien belongs to a certain class. Since the statute here allows the immigration officials power to apply the geenral provisions to particular cases, the question of administrative discretion naturally arises.[2]

The exact statement of the provisions in the 1917 act is as follows:

That at any time within five years after entry, any alien who at the time of entry was a member of one or more of the classes excluded by law; any alien who shall have entered or who shall be found in the United States in violation of this act, or in violation of any other law of the United States; any alien who at any time after entry shall be found advocating or teaching the unlawful destruction of property, or advocating or teaching

[1] Senate Report no. 352, to accompany H. R. 10384, 64th Congress, 1st Session.

[2] *Vide infra*, ch. viii.

anarchy, or the overthrow by force or violence of the Government of the United States or of all forms of law or the assassination of public officials; any alien who within five years after entry becomes a public charge from causes not affirmatively shown to have arisen subsequent to landing: except as hereinafter provided, any alien who is hereafter sentenced to imprisonment for a term of one year or more because of conviction in this country of a crime involving moral turpitude, committed at any time after entry; any alien who shall be found an inmate of or connected with the management of a house of prostitution or practicing prostitution after such alien shall have entered the United States, or who shall receive, share in, or derive benefit from any part of the earnings of any prostitute; any alien who manages or is employed by, in, or in connection with any house of prostitution or music or dance hall, or other place of amusement or resort habitually frequented by prostitutes, or where prostitutes gather, or who in any way assists any prostitutes or protects or promises to protect from arrest any prostitute; any alien who shall import or attempt to import any person for the purpose of prostitution or for any other immoral purpose; any alien who, after being excluded and deported or arrested and deported as a prostitute, or as a procurer, or as having been connected with the business of prostitution or importation for prostitution or other immoral purposes in any of the ways hereinbefore specified, shall return to and enter the United States; any alien convicted and imprisoned for a violation of any of the provisions of section four hereof;[1] any alien who was con-

[1] Sec. 4. That the importation into the United States of any alien for the purpose of prostitution or for any other immoral purpose, is hereby forbidden; and whoever shall, directly or indirectly, import or attempt to import into the United States any alien for the purpose of prostitution or for any other immoral purpose, or shall hold or attempt to hold any alien for any such purpose in pursuance of such illegal importation, or shall keep, maintain, control, support, employ, or harbor in any house or other place, for the purpose of prostitution or for any other immoral purpose, any alien, in pursuance of such illegal importation, shall in every such case be deemed guilty of a felony, and on conviction thereof shall be punished by imprisonment for a term of not more than ten years and by

victed, or who admits the commission, prior to entry, of a felony or other crime or misdemeanor involving moral turpitude; at any time within three years after entry, any alien who shall have entered the United States by water at any time or place other than as designated by immigration officials, or by land at any place other than one designated as a port of entry for aliens by the Commissioner General of Immigration, or at any time not designated by immigration officials, or who enters without inspection, shall, upon the warrant of the Secretary of Labor be taken into custody and deported. . . . *Provided* . . . that the provision of this section respecting the deportation of aliens convicted of a crime involving moral turpitude shall not apply to one who has been pardoned, nor shall such deportation be made or directed if the court, or judge thereof, sentencing such aliens for such crime shall, at the time of imposing judgment or passing sentence or within thirty days thereafter, due notice having first been given to representatives of the State, make a recommendation to the Secretary of Labor that such alien shall not be deported in pursuance of this act; nor shall any alien convicted as aforesaid be deported until after the termination of his imprisonment: *Provided further*, That the provisions of this section, with the exceptions hereinbefore noted, shall be applicable to the classes of aliens therein mentioned irrespective of the time of their entry into the United States: *Provided further*, That the provisions of this section shall also apply to the cases of aliens who come to the mainland of the United States from the insular possessions thereof: *Provided further*, That any person who shall be arrested under the provisions of this section, on the ground that he has entered or been found in the United States in violation of any other law thereof which imposes on such person the burden of proving his right to enter or remain,

a fine of not more than $5000. . . . That any alien who shall, after he has been excluded and deported or arrested and deported in pursuance of the provisions of this act which relate to prostitutes, procurers, or other like immoral persons, attempt thereafter to return to or enter the United States shall be deemed guilty of a misdemeanor, and on conviction thereof shall be punished by imprisonment for a term of not more than two years. . . .

and who shall fail to establish the existence of the right claimed, shall be deported to the place specified in such other law. In every case where any person is ordered deported from the United States under the provisions of this act, or of any law or treaty, the decision of the Secretary of Labor shall be final.[1]

Nor do the various changes and amendments added since those provisions were formulated make the situation any less confusing.[2] Let us then try to untangle the confusing web of provisions concerning deportability, and discover who may be sent out of the country and for what legal causes. So confusing are the provisions of the acts that the courts have fallen heir to the task of construing almost every word of them. Judicial interpretation too has sailed a devious course, often it seems, without chart or compass and in apparent disagreement as to the route. Before attempting detailed discussion, classification of groups of possible deportations according to the length of time after entry within which deportation may take place—within three or within five years after entry, and without time limit—may help to clarify the matter.

Questions have arisen as to the meaning of even apparently simple statements such as " within three years after entry." The courts have held that the three or five year statute of limitations for deportation requires taking the alien in question into custody within three or five years after entry, as the case may be, but that actual removal from the country need not be accomplished within the statutory

[1] Sec. 19, immigration act of February 5, 1917 (39 Stat. 874).

[2] Act approved October 16, 1918 (40 Stat. 1012), as amended by act approved June 5, 1920 (41 Stat. 1008); act approved May 10, 1920 (41 Stat. 593); act approved May 19, 1921, as amended by act of May 11, 1922; act of May 26, 1922 (42 Stat. 596); immigration act of 1924 (43 Stat. 153;) act approved March 2, 1929 (45 Stat. 1512); act approved March 4, 1929 (45 Stat. 1551), as amended by act of June 24, 1929; act approved Feb. 18, 1931.

period.[1] The decision concerning the meaning of the words "after entry" has become a *cause celèbre,* for the courts have held that *last* entry to the country is meant.[2] A foreigner living in the United States for thirty years, but never naturalized, and then crossing the Niagara River to the Canadian side for a few minutes to see the falls would be considered to have *entered* the country on his return from the view of the falls. Should he become ill and a patient in a public institution within five years of that trip, he could be held to have become a public charge within five years after entry, from causes not affirmatively shown to have arisen subsequent to landing, and so deportable to the country from which he came thirty years before. Take another illustration. An alien resident of the United States who entered Canada for the purpose of aiding another alien across the border and reentered the United States two days later, without inspection, was subject to deportation within five years after the reentry from Canada, on the ground that he had entered without inspection, although he had previously entered without inspection from another country, and had lived in the United States for fifteen years. The return from Canada had to be treated as a new entry within the meaning of the immigration act.[3] The interpretation of the word "entry" may lead to consequences socially if not legally anomalous.

Reserving for later discussion all details of various cate-

[1] Bun Chew *v.* Connell, 233 Fed. 220. The third judicial circuit (Philadelphia) held, in the case of Hughes *v.* Tropello, 296 Fed. 306, that deportation must be accomplished within the statutory period. This is contrary to the general trend of decisions.

[2] Lapina *v.* Williams, 232 U. S. 78; Lewis *v.* Frick, 233 U. S. 291; Woo Shing *v.* United States, 282 Fed. 498; *Ex parte* La Matina, 6 Fed. (2d) 468; Guimond *v.* Howes, 9 Fed. (2d) 412.

[3] United States *ex rel.* Natali *v. Day,* Nov. 17, 1930, *United States Daily,* Nov. 17, 1930.

gories of deportation within various periods of time or without time limit, the classes of deportation are very briefly as follows:

Deportation Within Three Years of Entry[1]

I. Aliens found within three years after their entry to have entered illegally by land or water.

For all practical purposes, this provision has been changed, for by the act of 1924 it is provided that any alien entering the United States since July 1, 1924 without an unexpired immigration visa may be deported at any time after entry.[2]

II. Aliens who fall into distress or need public aid, from causes arising after their entry and desirous of returning home may be removed from the United States within the three-year category.

This provision came into prominence during the economic depression of 1930-1931 when persons began to be removed more frequently than formerly on this ground. It is held to constitute repatriation rather than technical deportation and so does not prohibit return to the United States at a later date.[3]

Deportation Within Five Years of Entry[4]

I. Aliens entering or found in the United States in violation of the 1917 immigration law or any other law of the United States.

This provision was commonly used for deportation of aliens violating the 1921 quota act, but for practical purposes has been removed for aliens entering after July 1,

[1] Immigration act of February 5, 1917, secs. 19, 34, and immigration act of 1924, sec. 14.

[2] *Vide infra*, ch. vii.

[3] *Vide infra*, ch. iii, p. 81, and also *Foreign Language Information Service Interpreter Release*, vol. viii, no. 8, March 3, 1931.

[4] Immigration act of 1917, sec. 19.

1924. As indicated above, they may be deported without time limit if they enter without inspection, without an immigration visa, etc., or remain longer than allowed by the act or regulation.[1]

II. Aliens who at the time of entry were members of one or more of the classes excluded by law but not recognized as such on entering the country.

So if an alien is found within five years after any entry to the country to be a member of one of the excludable classes (with certain exceptions) he may be deported from the country. Confusion may arise from the fact that for deportation purposes some of the excludable categories have been removed from the five-year class for deportation, i.e. an alien found on entering the United States to be a prostitute is excludable; but an alien prostitute in the United States may be deported no matter how long she has been here.[2]

Persons excludable at the time of entry who may be deported within the five-year category are, *in brief*:

a. Persons with mental defects, such as idiots, imbeciles, feeble-minded epileptics, persons of constitutional psychopathic inferiority,[3] etc.

b. Paupers, professional beggars, vagrants.

c. Certain diseased, as persons with a loathsome or dangerous contagious disease, or tuberculosis in any form.

d. Aliens not included above, when certified by an examining physician as mentally or physically defective so that their ability to earn a living is interfered with.

[1] *Vide infra*, ch. vii.

[2] For further discussion of exclusion, *vide* Cook and Hagerty, *op. cit.*, ch. iii.

[3] *Vide infra*, ch. iii, p. 117 *et seq.*

Such physical difficulties as the loss of the sight of an eye, the loss of a limb, etc., do not necessarily mean a person is excludable, but depend on circumstances of his financial ability or occupation.

e. Persons who are liable to become a public charge.[1]

f. Contract laborers, etc.,

The provision for the exclusion of contract laborers is very complete and embraces all kinds of skilled and unskilled manual labor, but does not include professional actors, artists, nurses, ministers, professors, etc. Skilled labor if otherwise admissible may be imported if labor of like kind unemployed cannot be found in the United States.

g. Persons previously deported unless deported before March 4, 1929, permission having been granted to reapply for admission before that date.[2]

h. 1. Aliens whose ticket or passage is paid for by another person or persons, unless it is shown that such aliens are not members of another excludable class.

In other words, this category is *in addition to* other reasons for exclusion and the fact alone that a relative pays the passage of an alien is no reason taken by itself for that alien's exclusion.

2. Aliens whose ticket or passage is paid for by an association, corporation, etc.

i. Stowaways

If stowaways are otherwise eligible for admission, they may be admitted in the discretion of the Secretary of Labor.

[1] *Vide infra*, ch. iii.

[2] *Vide infra*, ch. xii, p. 464 *et seq.*

j. Children under sixteen years, coming alone and not coming to one or both of their parents.

If such children are otherwise eligible and are not liable to become a public charge they may be admitted.

k. Natives of certain specified Asiatic districts and islands.

This provision is not applicable to government officers, ministers, lawyers, artists, travelers, etc., nor their legal wives or children.

l. Illiterates.

Aliens over 16, physically capable of reading, who are illiterate, except certain close relatives over fifty-five years of age of admissible aliens or American citizens, or religious refugees.

m. Aliens ineligible to citizenship.

n. Aliens in excess of quota.

o. Aliens entering the United States from foreign contiguous territory applying for admission to the United States must prove they were taken to that territory by a transportation company which had submitted to and complied with the requirements of the 1917 immigration act.

If such compliance is not had, two years' residence is necessary in the foreign contiguous territory before application may be made for entry into the United States.

p. Aliens with defective documents.

q. Polygamists

Deportation Irrespective of Time of Entry[1]

I. Aliens who within five years after entry become a public

[1] Immigration act of 1917, sec. 19, and immigration act of 1924, sec. 14.

charge from causes not affirmatively shown to have arisen subsequent to landing.[1]

II. Alien anarchists.[2]

a. 1. Persons believing in overthrow by force or violence of the government of the United States

2. Persons who advocates the overthrow by force or violence of the government of the United States.

3. Persons who believe in the overthrow by force or violence of all forms of law.

4. Persons who disbelieve in organized government.

5. Persons who advocate the overthrow by force or violence of all forms of law.

6. Persons who are opposed to organized government.

7. Persons who advocate the assassination of public officials.

b. Members of unlawful organizations.

1. Members of or affiliated with organizations entertaining and teaching disbelief in or opposition to organized government, or

2. Advocating or teaching the duty, necessity, or propriety or the unlawful assaulting or killing of any officer, either of specific individuals or officers generally of the government of the United States or other organized government, because of his or their official character, or

3. Advocating or teaching the unlawful destruction of property.

c. Anarchists as defined by act of October 16, 1918, as amended June 5, 1920.

1. Aliens who are anarchists.

2. Aliens who advise, advocate, teach, or who are members of or affiliated with any organization, as-

[1] *Vide infra*, ch. iv, pp. 105-117.

[2] *Vide infra*, ch. vi, pp. 215-231.

sociation, society, or group, that advises, advocates or teaches opposition to all organized government.

3. Aliens who believe in, advise, advocate, or teach, or who are members of or affiliated with any organization, association, society or group, that advises, advocates or teaches: (1) the overthrow by force or violence of the government of the United States or of all forms of law, or (2) the duty, necessity or propriety of the unlawful assault or killing of any officer or officers (either of specific individuals or of officers generally of the government of the United States or of any other organized government because of their official character, or (3) the unlawful damage, injury, or destruction of property, or (4) sabotage.

4. Aliens who write, publish, or cause to be written or published, or who knowingly circulate, distribute, print, or display, or knowingly cause to be circulated, distributed, printed, published or displayed, or who knowingly have in their possession for the purpose of circulation, distribution, publication, or display, any written or printed matter advising, advocating, or teaching opposition to all organized government, or advising, advocating, or teaching opposition to all organized government, or advising, advocating, or teaching: (1) the overthrow by force or violence of the government of the United States or of all forms of law, or (2) the duty, necessity, or propriety of the unlawful assaulting or killing any officer or officers (either specific individuals or of officers generally) of the government of the United States or of any other organized government, or (3) the unlawful damage, injury, or destruction of property (4) sabotage.

5. Aliens who are members of or affiliated with any

organization, association, society or group that writes, circulates, distributes, prints, publishes, or displays or causes to be written, circulated, distributed, printed, published or displayed, or that has in its possession for the purpose of circulation, distribution, publication, issue, or display any written or printed matter of the character described.

d. War-time "undesirables" as defined by the Act approved May 10, 1920. This act includes various categories of aliens undesirable in war-time, such as the interned, those convicted of war-time conspiracies, violation of the espionage acts, trading with the enemy, etc. All persons deported under its provisions are by it denied readmission to the country.

III. Any alien involved in a crime of "moral turpitude", under circumstances that he

a. admits the commission or has been convicted of the commission prior to entry to the United States of a felony or other crime or misdemeanor involving "moral turpitude."

b. has been convicted in this country and sentenced subsequent to May 1, 1917 to a term of one year or more for a crime, etc. involving "moral turpitude," committed within five years after entry.

c. has been convicted in this country more than once and sentenced subsequent to May 1, 1917 more than once to a term of imprisonment for one year or more because of conviction in this country of a crime, etc. involving "moral turpitude," committed at any time after entry.[1]

[1] For discussion of crimes involving "moral turpitude", etc., *vide infra*, ch. v, pp. 161-174.

IV. Any alien

a. found an inmate of or connected with the management of a house of prostitution or practicing prostitution after entering the United States.

b. receiving, sharing in, or deriving benefit from any part of the earnings of any prostitute.

c. managing or employed by, in, or in connection with any house of prostitution or music or dance hall or other place of amusement or resort habitually frequented by prostitutes, or where prostitutes gather or who in any way assist any prostitute or protects or promises to protect from arrest any prostitute.

d. importing or attempting to import any person for the purpose of prostitution or for any other immoral purpose.

Thus bringing an alien into the country for any immoral purpose is sufficient ground for the deportation of the alien importer. However, conviction for violation of the "Mann Act" *within* the United States is not necessarily ground for deportation of the convicted alien.[1]

e. who, after being excluded and deported or arrested and deported as a prostitute, or as a procurer, or as having been connected with the business of prostitution or importation for prostitution or other immoral purpose in any of the ways hereinbefore specified shall return to and enter the United States.

f. convicted and imprisoned for importing into the United States an alien for purposes of prostitution, or for any other immoral purpose or for directly or indirectly importing or attempting to import into the United States any alien for the

[1] *Vide* Cook and Hagerty, *op. cit.*, p. 148, § 296.

purpose of prostitution or any other immoral purpose, or holding or attempting to hold any alien for any such purpose in pursuance of such illegal importation.[1] If after the alien has been excluded and deported or arrested and deported in pursuance of the provisions of this act which relate to prostitutes, procurers, or similar immoral persons, he attempts to return to the United States, he shall be deemed guilty of a misdemeanor, and on conviction thereof, shall be punished by imprisonment for a term of not more than two years.[2]

V. Any alien involved in narcotic traffic under the provisions of the act February 18, 1931. It is now provided that "any alien except an addict, if not a dealer or peddler who shall violate or conspire to violate any statute of the United States taxing, prohibiting, or regulating the manufacture, production, compounding, sale, exchange, dispensing, giving away, importation or exportation of opium, coca leaves, heroin, or any salt, derivative or preparation of opium or coca leaves shall be taken into custody and deported."

VI. Any alien entering the United States illegally since July 1, 1924, or found here after such illegal entry, or who remains here longer than permitted by the 1924 immigration act or regulations made under it.

VII. Alien seamen

Until the case of Philippides *v.* Day, Sup. Ct. No. 92, March 23, 1931, it was held that alien seamen landing

[1] Immigration act of 1917, sec. 4, which provides anyone so convicted shall be punished by imprisonment for a term of not more than ten years and by a fine of not more than $5000.

[2] *Ibid.* However, it must be remembered that the act of March 4, 1929 as amended June 25, 1929 makes it a felony for any alien deported since that date, for any reason whatsoever, to return to the United States. For discussion of deportation of prostitutes and those connected with prostitution, *vide* ch. vi, pp. 231-243.

contrary to the provisions of the 1917 immigration act could be deported only within three years after landing, while those landing contrary to the provisions of the 1924 act were deportable at any time. Since the Philippides case, all time limit is removed for deportation of seamen.

These, then, are in brief the provisions for deportation from the United States. Since the enactment of the law of March 4, 1929 (as amended June 25, 1929) an alien once deported for any of the reasons briefly sketched above may never legally return to the United States. Deportation from the country is now permanent banishment, with no possibility of return except for those few persons to whom permission to return was granted by the Secretary of Labor previous to March 4, 1929. Should any of the others deported from the country even attempt to return, they would be committing felonies.

The numerous provisions for deportation of the various classifications of aliens may be *ex post facto,* for, as the courts constantly remind us, the laws pertaining to the deportation of aliens are not criminal statutes.[1] The inhibition of *ex post facto* laws applies only to criminal statutes. Therefore, unless otherwise stated, the provisions concerning the various categories of deportation apply to the different classes of aliens stated, irrespective of the time of their entry into the United States. So aliens who were in this country at the time of the passage of the act of 1917 may in many instances be deportable by its provisions.

There are many of the various classifications of deportable

[1] Fong Yue Ting *v.* United States, 149 U. S. 698; Mahler *v.* Eby, 264 U. S. 32; Bugajewitz *v.* Adams, 228 U. S. 585.

It is interesting to note in this connection that Governor Roosevelt of New York in his 1929 *Report on Pardons, Commutations and Reprieves* speaks of pardoning aliens after sentence has been served, to prevent the additional *penalty* of deportation. (Italics mine.)

aliens which are not clear from the wording of the law and so need clarification and discussion. Who, for instance, is liable to become a public charge on entering the United States? What does the now notorious "moral turpitude" mean? Who are illegal entries, and how do they succeed in securing admission to the country? Let us turn our attention to these and other problems before discussing the procedure by which aliens are sent out of the United States.

CHAPTER III

Prospective Public Charges

WHAT DOES "LIABLE TO BECOME A PUBLIC CHARGE" MEAN?

THE longest and most checkered career of all phrases in the immigration law doubtless belongs to *Liable to Become a Public Charge,* for it has receded with prosperity and opportunity, and come to the fore with economic stringency, and has varied in meaning according to legislative intent, judicial interpretation, and economic situation. The fear of the newcomer as a possible burden upon the already burdened public is not a new accompaniment of the unemployment difficulties of 1930 but goes back to long before federal immigration problems and policies were thought of. In England and in the early colonies and states, anyone whose financial solvency was in doubt was assiduously "warned out" and told to be on his way. We read that as far back as 1596 the town of St. Albans required officials "to make search for such new comers to the town as being poor may be likely to be chargeable to the same, and if they shall find any such, to give notice thereof to Mr. Mayor, that order may be taken for their sending away,"[1] while two hundred years later the idea had so taken root in the United States that Chelmsford, a town in Massachusetts, warned 211 persons out of the town within the space of fifteen days. We have already noticed that irresponsible and deliberate dumping of paupers, vagrants and criminals

[1] Leonard, *Early History of English Poor Relief* (Cambridge, 1900), p. 25, quoting A. E. Gibbs, *Corporation Records of St. Albans.*

on the towns, colonies and early states well justified the fear of public charges in this country.

It was but natural that so old a fear and phrase should find embodiment in the first comprehensive federal immigration act in 1882 and come down to the present day in its same general form. Since then it has run the gamut of definition and various attempts to clarify its purposely generic expression have served only to raise anew the question, *who* is liable to become a public charge at the time of entry? Only four years after the insertion of the phrase in the law it gave birth to a famous case which has its repercussions today. Seven boys, ranging in age from twelve to fifteen, were sent from a reform school in England to homes in Canada and the United States. Those landing here were ordered excluded by the inspector. The case reached court, where the definition was framed that "the law intends those only that . . . can neither take care of themselves, nor are under the charge or protection of any other person, who, by natural relation, or by assumed responsibility, furnishes reasonable assurance that they will not become a charge upon the public." [1] It was soon found, however, that the process of definition had merely commenced and that a long line of interpretation and extension was to follow. The very next year a group of Irishmen arrived in the United States to find work, but as their passage had been paid by the British government, they were excluded as liable to become a public charge. The men were all healthy and able-bodied, and the court refused to sustain the administrative finding.[2] As a result of the decision, the 1891 statute provided an additional category of exclusion, those whose passage was paid for by the money of another or who had been assisted by others to come. The same year paupers were

[1] *In re* Day, 27 Fed. 678.

[2] *In re* O'Sullivan and 71 other Irish immigrants, 31 Fed. 447.

also added to the list of those forbidden entry to the country. It seemed almost as if a game had begun between the courts and Congress, with the burden of explanation and interpretation tossed continuously back and forth between the two.

A particular dilemma was raised by the question of whether or not scarcity of employment in this country could make a person liable to become a public charge on entering. When the problem arose in 1911, the development it was to undergo during the industrial depression of 1930 was merely foreshadowed. In the former year, a group of Caucasian laborers, all bound for Portland, Oregon, reached the United States but were not admitted. It was said that industrial conditions in Portland were such that they could not obtain employment, and that as they were illiterate and had very little money, they were liable to become a public charge. The matter finally reached the Supreme Court, where it was held that local conditions here were not to determine the public-charge question. The court stated:

> the statute deals with admission to the United States, not Portland. . . . In the act of February 20, 1907 . . . as amended by the act of March 26, 1910 . . . determining who shall be excluded, 'Persons liable to become public charges' are mentioned between paupers and professional beggars and along with idiots, persons dangerously diseased; persons certified by the examining surgeon to have a mental or physical defect of a nature to affect their ability to earn a living, convicted felons, prostitutes and so forth. The persons enumerated . . . (are) to be excluded on the grounds of permanent personal objections accompanying them, irrespective of local conditions unless the one phrase is directed to different considerations than any other of those with which it is associated.[1]

[1] Gegiow *v.* Uhl, 239 U. S. 8. A similar case had previously arisen in the lower courts—*Ex parte* Gregory, 210 Fed. 680.

After this decision, Congress took up the challenge of the court and changed the position of " liable to become a public charge " to its present location [1] immediately following the contract labor provisions. It was suggested that the phrase be changed to read, " persons likely for any reason to become a public charge," but this was not done. It was hoped in Congress [2] that the decision of the court in the Gegiow case might be overcome merely by the change in position of the phrase and that it would be clear that persons might be excluded for economic reasons as well as for personal disqualification. There is some doubt about that interpretation, for the decision in the *Gegiow* case has never been definitely overruled. Despite the change in position, aliens were not excluded from the United States on grounds of economic difficulty within the United States until the 1930 and 1931 unemployment situation.

President Hoover then suggested that the " L.P.C." provision of the immigration act might be used to prevent an influx of aliens, for

> in abnormal times . . . when there is not any reasonable prospect of prompt employment for an alien laborer or artisan who comes hoping to get a job and to live by it, the particular consular officer in the field to whom application for a visa is made, will, before issuing a visa, have to pass judgment with particular care on whether the applicant may become a public charge, and if the applicant cannot convince the officer that it is not probable, the visa will be refused." [3]

Such restriction of the use of the " L. P. C." provision of the law began with regard to Mexico in March 1929, and

[1] From Sec. 2, immigration act of 1907 to Sec. 3, immigration act of 1917.

[2] *Vide* Senate Report no. 352, 64th Congress, 1st Session.

[3] Announcement of President Hoover, in making public a report from the Department of State, Sept. 9, 1930, quoted *U. S. Daily*, Sept. 10, 1930.

then was extended to Canada. The further development of the plan as suggested by the President and the Department of State provided an extension of the restriction to Europe and elsewhere as an unemployment relief measure. In this connection, the words of Mr. Justice Holmes in the Gegiow case may be recalled: "It would be an amazing claim of power if commissioners decided not to admit aliens because the labor market was overstocked." [1]

Whatever its interpretation, the phrase remains as vague as always, and courts and administrative officials vie with one another in the variety and number of their interpretations. Two diametrically opposing lines of thought have become apparent in the decisions of the courts. On the one hand there is a tendency to hold that for a person to be "L.P.C", "some facts or conditions must be shown which make it 'likely' that such person will become an occupant of an almshouse, or otherwise require support at public expense, for want of means to support himself in the future." [2] In other words, "a person liable to become a public charge is one whom it may be necessary to support at public expense by reason of poverty, insanity and poverty, disease and poverty, idiocy and poverty." [3] Furthermore, "whether a person is 'liable to become a public charge' must rest upon a certain condition or necessity, and not on some future speculative contingency and uncertainty as to time." [4] On the other hand may be noted a tendency toward

[1] Gegiow *v.* Uhl, *supra*, p. 10. In that case, the question was whether an alien could be declared "L.P.C." on the ground that the labor market *in the city of his immediate destination* was overstocked, rather than in the country at large.

[2] *Ex parte* Mitchell, 256 Fed. 229.

[3] Wallis *v.* United States *ex rel.* Mannara, 273 Fed. 509; *Ex parte* Hosaye Sakaguchi, 277 Fed. 913.

[4] Cornish *v.* Inhabitants of Parsonsfield, 22 Maine 423.

judicial extension of interpretation which refuses to confine the term to possibility of becoming paupers but includes likelihood of becoming inmates of prisons. "It may be assumed that the words 'likely to become a public charge' do not relate solely to pauperism, and no doubt extend to evil doers generally and particularly to those who commit crime."[1] It is probable that this wide extension of the term is the most generally accepted view, but here as in other interpretations, much depends on the particular judicial district in which the interpretation is made. In any event, the conflict of decisions continues with no tendency to settle the matter. Thus within a short period of time, the courts issued two diametrically opposing statements of the situation: "Congress had in mind those who from infirmity, great age, or small age, want of property, shiftless habits, profligacy, or other things, were apparently such persons as would not maintain themselves in society by the ordinary means, and would thereby become a public charge. I do not think that possible criminal punishments were within the intention";[2] while in another case at about the same time it was stated:

From the evidence it appears that there was no probability of his becoming a pauper, but that he was a persistent and avowed violator of the prohibition laws, from which it is inferred by the department that he was likely, sooner or later, to get into jail, where he would be a public charge. I consider that the statute

[1] United States *ex rel.* Lake *v.* Bullard, 55441/206. *Vide* esp. *Ex parte* Horn, 292 Fed. 455; *Ex parte* Tsunetaro Machida, 277 Fed. 274; *Ex parte* Reeves, 292 Fed. 766; *Ex parte* Britten, 293 Fed. 61; *Ex parte* Fragoso, 11 Fed. (2d) 288; United States *ex rel.* Medich *v.* Burmaster, 24 Fed. (2d) 57. *Contra,* Howe *v.* United States *ex rel.* Savitsky, 247 Fed. 292; Lissotta *v.* United States, 3 Fed. (2d) 108; *Ex parte* Costarelli, 295 Fed. 217.

[2] Skrmetta *v.* Coykendall, 16 Fed. (2d) 783, affirmed Coykendall *v.* Skrmetta, 22 Fed. (2d) 120.

. . . covers, not only those who are entirely lacking means of support, but those who are likely to be boarded at public expense for violation of our laws.[1]

One further case will show how far the courts may go in their interpretation of these vague provisions, for in it a throat ailment and an operation for hernia were held to have rendered a man "L.P.C." on entering. He entered illegally from Canada in 1923. The next year his wife and three children entered illegally. In the spring of 1925 he developed some throat trouble and became a charity patient at the Los Angeles Hospital. Meanwhile his family received aid from a public charitable agency. Deportation proceedings were begun against the family on the ground that they were "L.P.C." and so among the classes excluded by law. The man might have been deported because of illegal entry, but this ground did not figure in his deportation. The court denied him a writ of habeas corpus as he was

a man possessed of no property from which he can derive an income. The fact that he had, before his entry into the United States suffered from an ailment of the throat and that he required hospital treatment in Los Angeles for a similar diseased condition; the fact that he had before coming to the United States been operated on for hernia—all furnish satisfactory evidence to the point that the man at the time of his entry was not physically sound or strong. It is apparent, then, from the record of admitted fact, that said petitioner is, and was at the time of entry, predisposed to physical infirmity and that when suffering from ailments he would likely be incapacitated from performing any work, or earning support for himself and family, and that he would, in such case become a charge upon the public. The fact that he may work at intermittent periods is no assurance that he will earn or save sufficient to provide necessi-

[1] *Ex parte* Riley, 17 Fed. (2d) 646.

ties at all times for himself or his wife and children. It must be said, I think, on the record made before the Immigration Department that the finding upon which the deportation warrant was issued is sustained by substantial evidence. The wife is not shown to have property or any means of earning a livelihood. She is dependent upon the husband for support as are the three children.[1]

The Supreme Court has never set the seal of its approval on any particular definition, but has left the term elastic. This very fact accounts for the administrative development in use of the term during the unemployment difficulties of 1930. As the path of the courts has not been easy to follow, so the road of administrative interpretation has been devious and at times difficult to trace. For a long period immigration officials tended at times to scatter the "L.P.C." charge with a more than generous hand, and in practically every deportation case this charge was entered as a cause for deportation—providing the case arose within five years of the person's last entry to the country. The cases that might be cited are legion, but a few will suffice to show the intensive use of the term by immigration officials. A woman of forty-two, self-supporting and owning property, was held by the immigration service as "L.P.C." on the ground that she was in possible danger of becoming involved in a suit for alienation of a man's affections and so of losing her property in that suit—which incidentally was never brought.[2] A man entering the country with quite a sum of money was excluded as "L.P.C." because he owed the money to another.[3] An able-bodied woman, with a fair education, with

[1] *Ex parte* Turner, 10 Fed. (2d) 816. *Vide Foreign Language Information Service Interpreter Release*, vol. vii, no. 42, Dec. 11, 1930.

[2] *Ex parte* Mitchell, 256 Fed. 229. (Administrative decision reversed.)

[3] United States *ex rel.* Goldberg *v.* Williams, 204 Fed. 828. (Administrative decision reversed.)

no mental or physical disability, with some knowledge of English, skilled as a seamstress and manufacturer of artificial flowers, with a disposition to work and support herself, and having a well-to-do sister and brother-in-law domiciled in this country, ready to assist her, was excluded as "L.P.C." because her husband refused to receive her.[1] A man who could barely read without his glasses unless he looked closely at the print was called "L.P.C."[2] Thus for a considerable period of time the "L.P.C." charge was shaken on deportation cases as though with a large pepper shaker. Only a tiny fraction of the total number ever reach even the lower courts,[3] but in case attempt should be made to secure a writ of *habeas corpus,* it would be important for the immigration officials to know the grounds on which each particular court might grant the writ. Hence the trend of court decisions is followed in the bureau of immigration of the Department of Labor. The number of court decisions against the immigration officials made because of what seemed to some of the courts as almost fantastic rendering of the meaning of "L.P.C." served in some measure to call a halt on the indiscriminate use of the charge. It is of especial note that between the fiscal years 1925 and 1930 there was a drop in deportations for this reason from 887 in 1925 to 305 in 1930, despite the total increase of deportations during that period. This change may be due in large measure to a more careful and discriminating use of the term.

Hardly had care in its use come in when the economic

[1] *Ex parte* Hosaye Sakaguchi, 277 Fed. 913. (Administrative decision reversed.)

[2] *In re* Marcus Stirnberg, not reported. Bureau File 55350/189, Dec. 4, 1923.

[3] *Vide infra*, p. 320.

depression of 1930 offered new possibilities for excluding persons on the ground that because they could not secure work in the United States they were liable to become a public charge should they enter, unless they were possessed of sufficient funds to tide them over the period of difficulty, or else had relatives here who would aid them. Then since aliens have been excluded by consular interpretation of "L.P.C.", in accordance with the possibility of so doing under the immigration act of 1924,[1] the question arises of the possibility of once more clamping down the lid in regard to "L.P.C." deportations and using the provisions rigidly.

A return to the generous use of "L.P.C." in conjunction with other charges seems probable. Many aliens, therefore, are afraid to ask for charitable aid, public or private, during the unemployment crisis, for fear of deportation. Acceptance of aid from a private social or charitable organization does not make a person a public charge; nevertheless, if it is accepted within five years of any entry to the country, it may indicate that he might become a public charge on entering. However, if he accepted such aid from either public or private sources *because of unemployment alone* in a time of economic distress, it would seem that he could not be deported. During 1930, the Department of Labor refused to sanction deportation where unemployment was the sole cause of the alien's dependency, and refused a number of applications for the issuance of warrants of arrest based on that ground alone.[2] As stated by the Commissioner General, "where lack of employment is the only factor which has

[1] *The U. S. Daily*, Dec. 6, 1930, reports that during the month of Oct., 1930 alone there was an under-issuance of 87% of the quota numbers available for issuance to non-preference aliens, because of the consular refusal of visas on "L.P.C." grounds, and that by June 30, 1931 probably 135,000 will have been barred for this reason.

[2] *Foreign Language Information Service Interpreter Release*, vol. viii, no. 2, January 17, 1931.

placed aliens in needy circumstances, they incur no danger of deportation if they accept charitable aid."[1]

VOLUNTARY REPATRIATION

On the other hand, there are a number of aliens who might like to be sent out of the country at such time of economic difficulty, in the hope of finding work elsewhere. So the 1930 unemployment served to bring into renewed force a provision of the law which had been little used of recent years. The 1917 immigration act provides:

That the Commissioner General of Immigration . . . shall have authority to enter into contract for the support and relief of such aliens as may fall into distress or need public aid and to remove to their native country, at any time within three years after entry, at the expenses of the appropriation for the enforcement of this act, such as fall into distress or need public aid from causes arising subsequent to their entry and are desirous of being so removed.[2]

It is the provision for removal within three years after entry to which attention was turned during 1931, when a general order was issued by the bureau of immigration[3] providing for removal of any such alien as falls into distress or needs

[1] *Foreign Language Information Service Interpreter Release*, vol. viii, no. 2, January 17, 1931.

[2] Sec. 23.

[3] General Order no. 168, February 16, 1931. Previous to this order, it had been provided that "any alien not subject to deportation who has fallen into distress or has needed public aid from causes arising subsequent to entry and is desirous of being removed to his native country may, on order of the commissioner general with the approval of the Secretary of Labor at any time within three years after entry, be so removed at government expense." (*Immigration Laws*, etc., *of January 1, 1930*, rule 19, subdivision K, par. 1.) The new order provided that "any alien who has fallen into distress or is in need of public aid from causes arising subsequent to entry," etc. So the *not subject to deportation* was removed from the order.

public aid from causes arising subsequent to entry and is desirous of being removed to his native country may be removed at government expense within three years after entry, whether or not he is subject to deportation. In other words, the alien himself must express a wish to be sent home and may file an application for repatriation.[1] Such repatriation by the government is *not* deportation, and so there is no legal bar to the repatriated alien's return to the United States. However, the possibility exists that he might then be excluded as "L.P.C."[2]

LIABLE TO BECOME A PUBLIC CHARGE CASES INCLUDED IN THIS STUDY

The most noticeable difference between the two groups of cases studied was the greater care used in the second group in the use of the "L.P.C." term and the distinct lessening of its use. At the period covered by the second group of cases the economic depression had not become serious enough to warrant an extension of the use of the term in deportation cases.

Of the 549 individuals in the first group, 542 had the "L.P.C." charge on the warrant of deportation, whatever additional charges there may have been. One of the num-

[1] He must himself obtain a passport, but if he is unable to pay for it the government will do so. It will also maintain him *after* his arrival at the port of embarkation. If he cannot pay his expenses to the port, or no charitable organization will pay them, the government will pay his expenses to the port, provided he has "no objections to occupying the same accommodations as are occupied by regular deports." If it is necessary, the government will also pay transportation from the port of debarkation to his home.

[2] The quota provisions offer other difficulties. If he returns, he must come as non-preference or ordinary quota immigrant. In many countries, such as Poland, Italy, Czechoslovakia, Hungary, etc., the quota is preempted for years to come. *Vide Foreign Language Information Service Interpreter Release*, March 3, 1931, vol. viii, no. 8.

ber had the recommendation made by the District Director after the hearing that this charge be removed, but the board of review and Assistant Secretary sustained it, despite his recommendation, and without stating the reason.

Alfred Stromberg (Case 1).[1]

Alfred Stromberg was born in Sweden in 1899, educated at public schools and a university, followed by study at a school of engineering, from which he graduated with honor as a civil engineer.

He came to the United States in February 1924, first class on a Swedish-American steamer. He was admitted on primary inspection to remain six months for a visit. However, he soon took a position as a draftsman in New York, earning $250 a month, and did not leave the country at the expiration of his six months permit. After he had been here nine months, he filed his declaration of intention to become an American citizen and was immediately reported to the commissioner of immigration on Ellis Island by the district director of naturalization.

A warrant was issued for his arrest four months later, but he was released on his own recognizance because of the excellent appearance he made, and because of his intelligence and education. The hearing was held just a month after the issuance of the warrant of arrest; no lawyer was present, nor did the man attempt to protest his possible deportation. When sending the record to Washington for decision, the commissioner recommended that the charge of "L. P. C." should not be sustained. However, the board of review did not recommend its removal. The warrant of deportation was issued four months after the warrant of arrest, on the grounds that Mr. Stromberg entered the country by means of false and misleading statements, that he entered in violation of the quota act, and that he was liable to become a public charge at the time of entry.

He asked for six months in which to settle his affairs, and this was granted. He was then deported at the expense of the steamship line in September, 1925.

[1] Throughout the case, all names have been changed and identifying information deleted.

The record notes that when he was admitted in February, 1924, he could have been admitted as a member of a learned profession, and so exempt from the quota, but that he had sought admission only as a temporary visitor. As the 1921 "quota act" had expired when deportation proceedings were pending it was felt impossible to make his residence permanent.

A similar case did not have the "L.P.C." charge. Here the man was deported only on the grounds of not living up to his student intentions.

Janos Horthy (Case 2).

Janos Horthy was born in 1901 in a small town in Hungary. After school and university, he secured his degree of Ph.D. and a further degree in chemical engineering in Budapest.

He came to New York in February, 1925, second class, and was admitted as a student going to Columbia University. However, he did not know enough English to fulfill his plans, so he secured a position in the chemical department of a large dye works and studied English at the same time, planning to go to Columbia a year later.

In May, 1925 he filed his declaration of intention to become a citizen. Meanwhile he had decided to go to the College of the City of New York as he thought it would be cheaper than Columbia. He entered in the fall of 1925. However, this college was not on the list approved by the Department of Labor.

A warrant for Dr. Horthy's arrest had been issued in July, 1925, as he had not entered Columbia, according to the plan declared when he arrived here. He was taken into custody the end of August and a hearing was given him the following day on Ellis Island. He was given two weeks to secure legal representation, but when the hearing was held on September 12th, he had not got an attorney, so the hearing was continued without one.

On October 27, 1925 a warrant of deportation was issued, but on the request for a stay of deportation, the board of review recommended on December 1st that deportation be stayed until July, and that Dr. Horthy be allowed to depart voluntarily in the meanwhile.

For some unexplained reason, the notice of the stay of deportation did not reach Ellis Island until December 9th, and Dr. Horthy had meanwhile been deported on December 2nd, at steamship company expense. In response to the vehement protest of a friend over the delay in arrival of the stay of deportation, permission was granted Dr. Horthy to return to the United States as a quota immigrant within a year.

Dr. Horthy wrote the bureau of immigration soon after his deportation to say that $60 had been stolen from him on Ellis Island, while he was awaiting deportation.

Of the total of 549 cases in the first group, three contained the "L.P.C." charge in the warrant of arrest, but had it removed after recommendation by the district director.

Mary Stevens (Case 3).

Mary Stevens was born in 1891 in a town in Cumberlandshire, England. After a grammar school education, she worked as a barmaid until her marriage in 1911 to John Foote. They had a son, born in 1916.

Mr. Foote came to the United States in 1923, leaving his wife and child at home. However, they came to join him in December, 1924, coming third class on a British steamer. The family moved to a mining town in Pennsylvania but had been there only two months when Mr. Foote deserted them and disappeared.

As Mrs. Foote was not well and was strong enough only to do a little work by the day now and then, she applied to the county directors of the poor for aid in August, 1925. They reported the family to the immigration authorities, so a warrant of arrest was issued on September 28, 1925. Mrs. Foote and her child were released on their own recognizance.

The hearing was held on October 5, 1925 and at that time Mrs. Foote said as the whereabouts of her husband was entirely unknown, she wished to return home. The record was sent to the bureau of immigration with the recommendation by the district director that she and her child be deported on the ground that they were liable to become a public charge at the time of entry. However, when the case came before the board of review, it was stated: "at the time of entry the woman was destined to her husband and consequently it does not appear that at that time she was a person liable to become a public charge. The cause which compelled her to seek assistance from the directors of the poor was the subsequent desertion of her husband. There is no relation between the desertion of the husband occurring several months after entry and the status of the woman at the time of entry."

Despite aid of the county directors of the poor, Mrs. Foote was not thought by the bureau of immigration to be a public charge as a person who was liable to become one on entering. The directors of the poor of the county where she lived said they could not afford to send her home. So the nearest British consul offered to pay half the passage of herself and son and secure a reduced rate for her, if she would pay the other half. However, Mrs. Foote could not pay even that much money.

It was finally arranged for Mrs. Foote and her child to be deported under the provision of the act of 1917 which allows "removal to their native country, at any time within three years after entry, at the expense of the appropriations, such as fall into distress or need public aid from causes arising subsequent to entry and are desirous of being so removed." [1] However, the bureau of immigration refused to pay the expenses of conveying the two to Ellis Island, so the directors of the poor agreed to carry that expense, but refused to pay for an attendant. So the bureau of immigration financed an attendant from the Pennsylvania town to Ellis Island.

Mrs. Foote and her son were sent home on November 7, 1925.

[1] Sec. 23, immigration act of 1917, and rule 19, subdivision K, *Rules of January 1, 1930.*

The record contains no warrant of deportation, because of the circumstances of the return.

Michele D'Antona (Case 4).

Michele D'Antona was born near Rome, Italy, in 1899 and worked as a farm laborer until his emigration to Canada in 1913. He came across the border that same year and stayed in the United States until 1916, when he had to return to Italy to serve in the army. He served during the entire war, but was taken prisoner in Austria. There he worked, building roads, and so strained his back badly.

At the end of the war he returned to Italy and was married there in 1919. The following year, Mr. D'Antona and his wife came to the United States. He was admitted on November 9, 1920 as a returning resident, because of his three years residence here before the war.

They went to Rochester to live and there Mr. D'Antona secured work in a bakery. He worked there steadily for three months but then became so weak he was unable to continue. Just at that time a child was born in the family.

When the child was three months old, Mr. D'Antona was admitted to the Rochester General Hospital where he was operated on for displacement of his spine. At first, his wife received aid from some charity, but as soon as she was strong enough after the birth of the child she went to work as a core piler in a foundry. After several years work she averaged $50 a month wages, on which she could support herself and child.

Mr. D'Antona had partially recovered but could not work. His wife felt the burden of supporting her husband as well as the child was too much for her to carry, so she separated from him, and went to live in a place where she could secure room and food for herself and child in return for housework which she did on her return from the factory.

Meanwhile Mr. D'Antona had secured work as a bus-boy in a restaurant, for which he earned $10 a week. He was reported to the immigration authorities by someone, but when the district director requested the issuance of a warrant of arrest for the man and his wife on the grounds that they were liable to become a public charge at the time of entry, the Assistant Commissioner General wrote, on October 24, 1925: "to claim less than three weeks before the expiration of the statutory period that this man and his young wife were persons likely to become public charges when they entered would be a very strained interpretation of the law."

Although Mr. D'Antona had been a public charge in the hospital, no attempt was made to secure the warrant on that ground. However, the inspector brought out the fact that Mr. D'Antona had never been legally admitted and inspected in 1913, and so had not been admissible as an alien returning to any established residence in this country. He was therefore deportable on the ground of having entered by means of "false and misleading statements."

Mr. D'Antona was deported on December 31, 1925, at the expense of the steamship company. His wife remained in this country with her American-born child.

Charles Spelman (Case 5).

Charles Spelman was born in 1893 in London, England. He came to the United States as a valet, arriving in September 1923, first class. He was admitted on primary inspection for two months with the gentleman for whom he was valet.

As soon as he reached New York, he gave up this position, as he had merely used this means of getting to the United States. Soon thereafter he secured a position as a shoe salesman in one of the large department stores of New York, earning $35 a week.

He was reported anonymously to the bureau of immigration, and a warrant was issued for his arrest on September 30, 1925. He was released on his own recognizance, as it was felt he would appear when necessary. The hearing was held at Ellis Island on October 8, 1925, with no attempt at legal representation, for Mr. Spelman was anxious to return to England. After the hearing, the commissioner recommended the removal of the L. P. C. charge which had been placed when the warrant of arrest had been issued. The board of review and Assistant Secretary concurred in this, and the warrant of deportation was issued on other grounds, that is, that Mr. Spelman entered the country by means of false and misleading statements, that the country from which he came had an exhausted quota at the time of his entry, and that his passage had been paid for by the money of the gentleman as whose valet he came.

He was deported December 24, 1925, at the expense of the line which brought him.

Out of the total number in the first group of 549 cases, there were only seven who did not have the "L. P. C." charge.[1] The very comprehensive possible interpretations of the term must be borne in mind, but even so one is tempted to raise the question as to how large a rôle the economic factor plays in deportation cases. The question should be studied in connection with those cases where the deportation process was begun but not carried through to completion. Of the seven cases where deportation was accomplished without the use of the "L.P.C." charge, six[2] have strong reasons for deportation. Two of the six cases involved prostitution and the other four involved crimes of moral turpitude, so in all of them the case for mandatory deportation was strong and would not have been strengthened by the "L.P.C." addition. Furthermore, as the immigration officials have many times been overruled on their interpretation of the term, where cases are at all likely to reach court, as in prostitution and criminal cases, it is safer for them to use only charges that are fairly sure to be sustained, as in the following case.

Nicholas Laskaris (Case 6).

Nicholas Laskaris was born in 1900 near Sparta, Greece, and

[1] Case 2 above is one of these.

[2] The seventh is Case 2 above.

lived there with his parents until he was fourteen, then ran away and secured a promise from his uncle in Pennsylvania that he would receive him. The uncle sent a ticket and so the boy was admitted on primary inspection as going to his uncle.

He went to school intermittently for a year, then began to work as a clerk in a candy store. He held a number of different jobs until 1919 when he was committed to the penitentiary for one year for larceny. He served ten months of the sentence and was released for good behavior. Then in March 1921 he was again committed for larceny to the Western State Penitentiary, for a term of from three years and eight months to five years.

He was in the penitentiary until October 21, 1925. Meanwhile, he had been reported to the district director of immigration by the prison authorities, and a warrant of arrest had been issued on March 5, 1925. The hearing on the warrant of arrest was given him at the penitentiary on July 7th; it had been postponed for him to secure counsel, but he had reconsidered after half an hour: "I have thought it over and I want to go ahead with the hearing. I do not think I should be deported, but if they want to deport me they will. I have not much money. I have only $40 and I won't want to spend the money. I can't go against the government."

On his release from prison, he was immediately sent to the Philadelphia immigration station at Gloucester City, N. J., on October 21, 1925 and was kept there until November 11. While there he wrote a typed letter to the bureau of immigration appealing for a stay of deportation and asking for a copy of the deportation law. The warrant for his deportation was issued on November 10, 1925, with the single charge "that he has been sentenced subsequent to May 1, 1917, to imprisonment more than once for the commission subsequent to entry of a crime involving moral turpitude."

The day after the issuance of the warrant of deportation, he was sent to Ellis Island and deported the next day, at the expense of the United States.

In many of the cases it is clear that the use of " L.P.C." had nothing to do with financial status, as in the following. In still others the use of the term is interestingly defined, as in Cases 8 and 9.

Dimitri Stefen (Case 7).

Dimitri Stefen was born in 1896 in a small town in Bulgaria. In 1913 he came to the United States, but it is not known just when he landed or how long he stayed in New York. However, he went to California and there he worked as a chauffeur.

Mr. Stefen secured his first papers in June, 1923. He kept the same position as chauffeur for a number of years and meanwhile attended night school and learned to speak excellent English. He bought a house and a Ford car and had an account in a savings bank.

In 1924 Mr. Stefen went to Mexico for a trip, stayed about a month, then on August 22nd returned to this country by walking across the border at Nogales. He was immediately apprehended by the immigration border patrol and taken to the Santa Cruz County jail where he was held awaiting trial for implication in the illegal entry of two aliens. On May 13, 1924 he was released on $500 bond, and appeared again at the time of his trial on September 17th. He was acquitted but was sent east to Ellis Island on July 4, 1925, although he did not want to go.

A warrant for Mr. Stefen's deportation was issued July 17, 1925 on the grounds that he was liable to become a public charge at the time of entry, that he entered without inspection in violation of the immigration act of 1924 and that he was not in possession of an unexpired visa at the time of entry.

He was deported on August 4, 1925, at the expense of the United States.

The case above is an illustration of the effects of interpretation of considering entry to the country to be the *last* entry. It also raises the question of whether the " L.P.C." charge is used in cases of illegal entry. The courts have vacillated in their practice, but the latest tendency seems to be to consider that the charge is applicable in such cases.

A particularly noteworthy case is the following.

Henry Thurber (Case 8).

Henry Thurber was born in London 1887 and received a common school education. When he was seventeen he came to the United States and lived in New York. At the age of twenty he was married but deserted his wife just as she was about to have a child.

He went immediately to Montreal with a woman he had come to know in New York and lived with her in Montreal from 1914 until 1921. Meanwhile they had four children. In 1921 they disagreed and Mr. Thurber left her and returned to the United States. He went immediately to Baltimore where he was arrested for defrauding the hotel where he was staying, so he was returned to Canda, where his domicile was. However, he immmediately turned around and came back to the United States where he became an automobile salesman in a New Jersey town.

His " wife " in Montreal had meanwhile made efforts to locate him through various charitable organizations, in a vain effort to make him support her and her four children there. As he would not do it, a warrant was sworn out for his arrest in Montreal, and he was reported to the United States immigration authorities. He was immediately deported to Montreal, where the warrant was served and he was sent to jail for non-support.

Immediately on his release from jail, Mr. Thurber for the third time left Canada for the United States and went to Philadelphia, where he again began to work as an automobile salesman, earning $35 a week and bonus. He was located at the request of the charitable organization and again arrested for deportation to Canada.

Meanwhile his legal wife in New York had also located him and got a warrant for his arrest from the Family Court there; she also had a court order of $5 a week support for herself and child. She did not desire her husband kept in this country but wished the money, as she had had nothing from him since before the birth of her child in 1914.

A warrant of deportation was issued with the charges that he was liable to become a public charge at the time of entry; that he was not in possession of an unexpired immigration visa at the time of his last entry; that he entered the United States within one year from the date of his last deportation without having secured permission to reapply for admission; that he was convicted of or admitted having committed a crime involving moral turpitude prior to his last entry to the United States, to wit, fornication; that he entered by means of false and misleading statements on his last entry to the country.

Canada, however, refused to take him back on the ground that he did not have a domicile there. So the warrant of deportation was amended to read to England, and he was deported to England on December 31, 1925, leaving his wife and child in New York and his other " wife " and four children in Motreal.

The record stated that the board of review and Assistant Secretary maintained the " L. P. C." charge for the following reason: " The record in this case shows him to be quite a worthless fellow, one who recognizes no responsibility. If he were to meet his legal and moral obligations to those for whose existence on earth he is responsible, he would have little or nothing on which to support himself . . .

Enrico Rosso (Case 9).

Enrico Rosso was born in 1887 in Torre del Greco, Italy, where he lived at intervals until 1921. During the intervals he went to sea but always returned home. He was married there in 1910 and had four children.

He came to the United States in 1921, landing on October 15 of that year, and was admitted on primary inspection. He secured work as a fireman, but did not keep it up long. He soon went to Pennsylvania where he worked in a sawmill, then a patent medicine factory. During 1924 he became depressed and on October 28, 1924 he was admitted to a hospital for mental disease.

The doctor in charge stated that Mr. Rosso's disability had not arisen subsequent to landing for the reason (sic) "the disability is more than likely of long standing." After the hearing, the recommendation that accompanied the record to Washington stated: "While neither the medical certificate nor the testimony of the alien shows conclusively that the alien's mental condition arose from 'prior causes', . . . it is reasonably shown that he was a person likely to become a public charge at the time of entry because of his poor financial status, his heavy family responsibility, his small stature, his lack of education, and lack of relatives in the United States legally responsible for his support in case of necessity, and, therefore, that the charges that he was liable to become a public charge at the time of entry and that he has become a public charge within five years after entry from causes not affirmatively shown to have arisen subsequent to entry are to be sustained."

Mr. Rosso was deported to Italy on July 21, 1925 at the expense of the steamship company which had brought him.

Charles De Hogh (Case 10).

Charles de Hogh was born in 1902 in Holland, where he lived throughout his early life, going to lower school and technical school in Amsterdam.

In 1923 he went to Montreal, where he landed on June 21 and remained until October 14th, when he was admitted to the United States as a visitor, entering via the ferry at St. Clair, Michigan. The following day he enlisted in the United States army and was sent to the United States army post at Plattsburg, N. Y.

In May, 1924, he was "A. W. O. L." when he went to Canada for two days. On his return across the border he was held by the board of special inquiry as "L. P. C." and excess quota, but he was then admitted to the custody of the American army.

Nothing further happened until some unknown person reported him to the immigration authorities as being in the country illegally. He was sent to the Clinton County Jail at Plattsburg, N. Y., on the issuance of a warrant of arrest. His hearing was held at the jail on November 30, 1925. Mr. de Hogh felt that he should not be deported because of his two years service in the American army, but he could not afford a lawyer.

The warrant of deportation was issued on December 8, 1925, on the grounds that he was liable to become a public charge at the time of entry, that he entered the United States without inspection, and that he was in the United States in violation of the immigration act of 1924 in that he was not in possession of an unexpired immigration visa.

Mr. de Hogh was sent to Ellis Island on December 25, 1925 and deported the next day at the expense of the steamship company bringing him.

The use of the term " liable to become a public charge " has become so general that it is seldom used alone. When it is the only charge against a person, there is every evidence that that person will prove to be financially unable to care for himself and to need pecuniary assistance. Therefore, when the only cause listed for deportation is " L.P.C.", the meaning of the term is similar to its original meaning of likely to become a pauper. Of course, such use would indicate *strong* likelihood that the person against whom it was used would be likely to have financial difficulties, so that the charge would be sustained should the case come to court.

Of the total number of cases in the first group, fifteen persons were deported for the sole reason that they were found within five years of entry to have been liable to become a public charge at the time of entry. This group of persons is of particular interest because of the social problems involved in the reasons why they were liable to become public charges at the time of entry. The following are summaries of those of particular interest in regard to the " L.P.C."

John Warren (Case 11).

John Warren was born in 1887 in Manchester, England. He had a common school education and then went to work as a shipwright, on a ship canal. He was married in 1910 and had six children. During the war Mr. Warren served in the British army and was discharged in 1918 as medically unfit. He received a pension of $104 annually from the British government.

On April 6, 1923 Mr. Warren came to the United States and was admitted on primary inspection. Soon after his wife and the two youngest children (twins, born in 1919) came to New York on November 1, 1923 and were admitted on primary inspection. The other children had been left with Mrs. Warren's mother in Manchester.

The family went to Buffalo, where Mr. Warren had a brother, but soon moved to Rochester, where Mrs. Warren's sister lived. Mr. Warren began to work for the Rochester Gas and Electric Company, earning $30-35 a week. He was soon troubled with rheumatism and heart trouble, but kept on working.

In July, 1924, the family applied to a loan society for a loan of $90 needed in order to help Mrs. Warren to return to England to get the other children. Because of the good work Mr. Warren had done for the gas and electric company, it was decided that they would lend him the money to be deducted in small amounts from his pay each week, instead of his securing a loan fund.

Mrs. Warren left for England in the fall of 1924 but because she heard her husband was far from well, returned to this country without the four children. Soon after her return, her husband went to a clinic on the advice of the Social Welfare League and it was discovered he needed an operation. He was then referred to the United States Veteran's Bureau because of his army service with the British army and hospitalization was arranged.

While Mr. Warren was in the hospital, the gas and electric company continued to pay half his wages ($15), and the Social Welfare League contributed $6 a week coal, etc. Mrs. Warren was still in receipt of the British war pension of $2 a week for her husband. She was expecting a baby at this time.

The day after Mr. Warren stopped working, at the suggestion of the Social Welfare League, the family reported themselves to the United States immigration authorities and stated they wished to return to England.

Mr. Warren was in the hospital for several months, at the expense of the Veterans' Bureau. A child, Helen, had been born in the Rochester General Hospital, on March 25, 1925. On April 21, 1925, a warrant of arrest was issued and Mrs. Warren and the children were released on their own recognizance. Mr. Warren was still in the hospital.

A hearing was held on April 28, 1925 at the immigration office in Rochester but was postponed until May 8th, as Mr. Warren was to be released from the hospital on May 1st. At this hearing, the family had changed their minds and wished to remain here, as Mr. Warren was not well and able to work. So the district director and board of review recommended waiting for six months to see what would happen.

On November 30, 1925, an immigrant inspector investigated and found Mr. Warren again ill and on December 7th deportation was recommended by the board of review and agreed to by Assistant Secretary of Labor. Two days later a warrant of deportation was issued, on the grounds of the family having been liable to become a public charge at the time of entry. So Mr. and Mrs. Warren and their two children were deported on December 19, 1925 at the expense of the steamship line which had brought them. With them they took their American-born child, paying the expenses of her passage to England.

Bridget O'Donnell (Case 12).

Bridget O'Donnell was born in 1904 in County Cork, Ireland, one of nine children. She had little schooling and tired of working at home, so decided to come to the United States to join an aunt.

She landed in Boston on August 4, 1923, bringing her younger sister with her. They were detained by the board of special inquiry but were released to their aunt, who appeared before the board and stated she had paid their passage here, that she was an American citizen with $5000 property, and intended to send the younger sister to school.

It was not discovered on admission that Miss O'Connell was pregnant. However, four months after her arrival here she was delivered of a child in a hospital in Dorchester. Her aunt paid $350 to a sister of charity for the child's upbringing and care.

As soon as she was well, Miss O'Donnell secured a position at housework, and remained in the same place until April, 1925 when it was found she was again pregnant. She was then admitted to the State Infirmary at Tewksbury, where a second child was born on July 10, 1925. Four days later Miss O'Donnell was reported to the immigration authorities by the Infirmary and a warrant of arrest was issued August 4, 1925. A hearing was given on September 8th at the Infirmary. Miss O'Donnell's aunt had been notified but sent word she did not wish to appear and wanted the girl deported. Miss O'Donnell stated she knew the father of the child but did not wish to bother him; she wanted to stay in this country and board the child out while she worked.

The warrant of deportation was issued October 9, 1925 on the grounds of liable to become a public charge at the time of entry. Miss O'Donnell was deported from Boston on October 31, 1925 at the expense of the steamship company, leaving her child to be placed in this country.

The problem of American-born children accompanying their deported parents is a serious one, whether such children are legitimate or not. It will be discussed later.[1]

Elena Meyer (Case 13).

Elena Meyer was born in 1869 in Switzerland, the daughter of a Swiss father and an Italian mother. She attended school from six to fourteen, then began to work on a farm, then in a restaurant, and finally learned dressmaking.

[1] Pp. 420, 446.

Miss Meyer had two nieces in the United States, both working as domestics in St. Paul, Minnesota. They both planned to be married and wrote their aunt if she came she might have one of their positions. So she came, arriving in New York on August 13, 1922. She was admitted on primary inspection and went immediately to St. Paul.

Before long she was reported to the United Charities by her employer as "acting queerly." Miss Meyer herself felt she was not well enough to work, so she applied to a number of charities in turn. On August 10, 1925 she was reported to the immigration authorities by the United Charities, and a warrant for her arrest was issued the same day, and the hearing was held the following day. The matter was thus rushed as if it were found that Miss Meyer could be deported only in the three-year category after entry, the time limit was about to expire. At the hearing, Miss Meyer said she felt her nieces had brought her here under false pretenses and wished them to return the money it had cost her to come. The nieces testified they were willing for her to be deported.

Subsequent to the hearing, Miss Meyer was adjudged insane and was committed to the state hospital at St. Peter, Minn. on August 21, 1925. The record gives no report from the hospital and no mental diagnosis appears.

The warrant of deportation was issued on September 9, 1925 on the ground of "L. P. C." Miss Meyer was deported on November 10, 1925 at steamship company expense, landing at le Havre, whence she was sent with an attendant to her home in Switzerland and a receipt signed for by a town official there.

Clara Gillespie (Case 14).

Clara Gillespie was born in 1908 in Glasgow, Scotland, and lived there until 1923 when she came to the United States to join her father who had emigrated six months previously.

She reached this country on August 7, 1923 and was detained at Ellis Island five days until her father came to get her and she was released to him. They went to Philadelphia to live and there she began to work in a clothing factory, and remained at work there until May, 1924 when her father heard her mother was very ill in Scotland and returned to her, by working his way back to Scotland as a seaman.

Miss Gillespie went to live with an aunt in a New Jersey town during her father's absence. However, she did not stay long but secured a position doing housework. She disagreed with her employer and soon after was admitted to the hospital with a diagnosis of "gland trouble." Then she was referred to the local family welfare society and by them in turn, referred to the district director of immigration.

A warrant for Miss Gillespie's arrest was issued on October 9, 1925, and she was immediately taken to Ellis Island, where the hearing was held on November 10, 1926. At that time she stated she would like to return to her father.

In recommending deportation, the board of review stated, that the certificate of the United States Public Health Service on Ellis Island said that Miss Gillespie was "unstable mentally and of general psychopathic make-up, which seems to indicate a person of constitutional psychopathic inferiority but does not directly so state." However, the only charge on the warrant of deportation, which was issued on November 23, 1925 was "L. P. C."

Miss Gillespie was deported on December 1, 1925 at the expense of the steamship line.

Johan Lundstrom (Case 15).

Johan Lundstrom was born near Oslo, Norway in 1901. He had some schooling, then worked as a blacksmith for several years before going to sea. He returned home and remained two years before deciding to emigrate to the United States. He arrived in New York on October 15, 1923 and was admitted on primary inspection. He went immediately to Duluth, Minnesota, and soon after his arrival there began to receive free treatments at a city hospital.

It is not known by whom he was reported to the immigration inspectors, but on December 9, 1924, a warrant was issued for his arrest. He was taken to the St. Louis County Jail where a hearing was given him. At the hearing, Mr. Lundstrom was told that he was liable to become a public charge when he entered the country. He said: " What is a public charge? " and was told " one that has to be supported by the Government." Then the conversation continued:

> " I do not understand the public charge.
> Well, you understand if a man is not able to make a living.
> I am able to make a living.
> I want you to get this, if a man is not able to make a living, if he is sick he has to get help from the city or the state he is, a public charge and one that is likely to become a public charge is one that may not be able to make a living.
> I am able to make a living, I have a job in the basement of the Lyceum.
> That is the charge, and you are having a hearing, to have a trial here and to see whether you should be sent back or not.
> Trial, yes. Yes I am able to make a living. I have a job in the basement of the Lyceum. I don't think you need to want me to get a lawyer. I cannot get a lawyer anyway. I am able to make a living. I don't think you can send me back."

The warrant of deportation was issued on February 5, 1925, and Mr. Lundstrom was deported on July 11, 1925 at the expense of the steamship company, on the ground that he had been " L. P. C." at the time of entry.

A decided change is noticeable in the use of the " L.P.C." term in the second group of individuals studied. In 23 the term was not used at all, the other reasons for deportation having been thought sufficient. Thus it was not used in any of the criminal or prostitution cases, and in general not in the illegal entries, though there the practice differed somewhat in various districts of the country, and in some places the term was used and in some not. In six illegal entry cases, the board of review recommended the omission of the charge and this was done when the final warrant of arrest was issued; however in four similar cases, the "L.P.C." was allowed to remain when the final warrant of deportation was issued, nor had there been any recommendation as to its removal. It was used in the cases where the person to be deported had become a public charge within five years after entry from causes not affirmatively shown to have arisen subsequent to entry, in addition to that charge. There were but two exceptions where it was not used, while on one case it was added to the actual "public charge" reason by the board of review and accepted by an Assistant to the Secretary. In only one of this group of cases was "L.P.C." the only cause for deportation. In 24 the "L.P.C." charge was used on the original warrant and on the final warrant of deportation.[1]

Karl Becker (Case 16).

Karl Becker was born in 1898 in a town in Prussia, Germany, and lived there all his early life.

He came to the United States in 1926, landing in New York on April 26th, and going direct to Minneapolis, where he began to work as a sausage-maker, earning $30 a week. After he had got settled there, he sent for Miss Martha Schutt and Grete, their two year old child. They reached the United States on February 17, 1927 and went to join Mr. Becker. He and Miss Schutt were married as soon as she reached Minneapolis.

In 1928 a second child, Heinrich, was born. Meanwhile the family began to have financial difficulties and Mr. Becker could not seem to keep a job for a long period. Various social agencies, especially the Family Welfare Society, helped the family and the city also gave relief.

On August 26, 1929 the Family Welfare Society reported the family to the bureau of immigration but a warrant of arrest

[1] It was not used on 23 cases, was used in 6 additional but deleted after the hearing by the board of review, and in one case was added after that hearing.

was not issued until October 25, 1929. The family was released on its own recognizance, and remained at home until a warrant of deportation was issued on December 13, 1929 on the ground of "L. P. C." About that time Mrs. Becker was arrested for shoplifting but was given a suspended sentence.

Mr. and Mrs. Becker and Grete were deported on March 5, 1930, at the expense of the steamship company. They took with them their American-born child and themselves paid her fare.

Fritz Schlemmer (Case 17).

Fritz Schlemmer was born in 1903 in Bavaria, Germany, and lived in a small Bavarian town until he emigrated to the United States, reaching New York on May 7, 1928.

He worked as a baker until he was taken ill in October 1929 and admitted to Bellevue Hospital. There he was found to have a gastric duodenal ulcer. On his release from the hospital, he was assisted by the German Society, but he could not secure work and so soon went to the Municipal Lodging House. He was reported by them to the immigration officials and a warrant for his arrest was issued on December 5, 1929, as a "public charge."

When the case came before the board of review it was recommended that the additional charge be lodged that he was liable to become a public charge when he entered the country, so the hearing was re-opened and he was told of the change. He did not object and the warrant of deportation was issued on January 15, 1930, on the grounds of his having become a public charge within five years of entry from causes not affirmatively shown to have arisen subsequent to entry, and also the additional charge that he was a "L. P. C."

Mr. Schlemmer was deported on February 1, 1930 at the expense of the steamship company which had brought him to this country.

Despite the apparent increase in care in the use of "L. P.C", it is still a veritable catch-all, vague and uncertain in its meaning, difficult of interpretation for administrative officials and often impossible of comprehension for the alien.

CONCLUSIONS

No exact statutory standard has been set up in regard to definition of liable to become a public charge at the time of entry, so the burden of fitting the vague term to concrete cases and situations has fallen heavily on administrative officials and courts alike. They have often given fantastic renderings to their interpretations of the term and at times have indicated a tendency to hold a person " L.P.C." because of a vague undesirability. Thus " L.P.C." has often come to be a catch-all for cases perhaps not otherwise deportable.

Is a definite and rigid legislative standard the answer to the difficulties caused by the varying interpretations of the term? With such difficult problems as are involved in the determination of who constitute those economically unable to look after themselves, there is need for consideration of many varied factors. Such consideration is not permitted by a hard-and-fast standard embodied in statute such as would be found if " L.P.C." were deleted from the law. This phrase, if properly used, may be a boon to both administrative official and alien alike.

Answer to the difficulties seems to lie in the direction of common-sense interpretation of the term rather than in statutory change. There should be no tacit and predetermined assumption on the part of the administrative official that a person is a liability to the community merely because he is a foreigner. There is need for careful investigation of whether or not a particular alien was *really* an economic liability at the time of his entry here. After such investigation, interpretations by administrative officials and courts alike need always be tempered by common sense, and the use of the term should be confined to its original meaning. Undiscriminating use of terms adds neither to efficiency of administration nor to understanding of the law.

CHAPTER IV

Actual Public Charges

From the day when whole almshouses were vacated to send their inhabitants to America, when convicts, ill, and insane, reached this country in unending procession,[1] the cry has gone up from town, city and state that the burden of public charges of foreign birth is too great to be borne. Indeed, it was the failure of state attempt at head tax[2] to be used for the support of foreign paupers and public charges that sounded the death-knell of state regulation of immigration and led to the beginning of federal legislation on the subject, for the states protested that without a source of financial income from arriving immigrants they could not afford to maintain the foreign public charges already within their borders.

Yet the assumption by the federal government of immigration regulation did not settle the question and states have continued to complain of the unjust burden they perforce must bear. They have indicated their strong feeling that if foreign countries cannot be made to assume responsibility for their dependent citizens in this country, the federal gov-

[1] *Vide supra*, p. 35 *et seq.*, and esp. E. Abbott, *Historical Aspects*, etc., *op. cit.*, pp. 682-6.

[2] Declared unconstitutional by the Supreme Court. *Vide* the "Passenger Cases", 7 How. 283; Henderson *v.* the Mayor of New York, 92 U. S. 259; People *v.* Compagnie Générale Transatlantique, 107 U. S. 59. The opinion in this last case was not delivered until 1883 when federal immigration legislation had already begun.

ernment should do so.[1] New York state, for instance, has attempted for some time to recover $17,447,616 from Congress for the care of insane aliens in New York state hospitals from 1882 to 1921. No headway has been made in such recovery, however,[2] despite the fact that a high federal official indicated his sympathy with the state attitude. Former Secretary of Labor James J. Davis stated:

> If the Federal Government had to maintain all of these inadequates at its own expense, there would be more poetic justice in the whole situation. As the matter stands, the Federal Government has the authority in relation to immigration, whereas the several State Governments have the responsibility and expense of caring for dependent immigrants and their children. . . .[3]

The protest and outcry became so strong that it was determined to ascertain the number of alien public charges in this country. Dr. H. H. Laughlin of the Eugenics Record Office of the Carnegie Institution at Cold Spring Harbor, N. Y., was asked to investigate the matter. He reported to the House Committee of Immigration and Naturalization on April 26, 1926 that in 689 state and federal institutions for the "socially inadequate" in the United States, there were 77,859 foreign-born, or a total of 19.45% of the inmates.[4] The following year, the bureau of immigration of

[1] *Vide Proposed Deportation Legislation,* Hearings before the Committee on Immigration and Naturalization, House of Representatives, 68th Congress, 2d Ses., Dec. 10, 12, 16, 1924 (Serial 1-B), p. 23.

[2] On February 25, 1924 a special subcommittee on alien insane of the New York State Hospital Commission was appointed to help secure such reimbursement and to study questions relating to the refusal of admission and removal of alien insane. *Vide Annual Report of the State Hospital Commission, New York State, for the Year July 1, 1923–June 30, 1924* (Albany, 1925), pp. 96-7.

[3] *Selective Immigration* (New York, 1925), pp. 91-2.

[4] Of these, 2480 were not deportable under the law, for many of them had been in the United States over five years after entry when they became public charges, or their nationality could not be verified, or it could be affirmatively shown that their condition arose subsequent to entry, etc.

the Department of Labor made an independent investigation in continental United States, Alaska, Honolulu, and Porto Rico covering a somewhat larger group of institutions—of penal institutions, insane asylums, hospitals and poorhouses. It was found that prisons, penitentiaries and jails contained 45,193, insane asyulms and other institutions for the care of such cases 37,470, hospitals and sanitaria 14,383, and poorhouses 16,059—a total of 113,105.[1]

"WITHIN FIVE YEARS AFTER ENTRY"

Who are these alien public charges and what is the law pertaining to their deportability? The law says, "any alien who within five years after entry becomes a public charge from causes not affirmatively shown to have arisen subsequent to landing . . . shall, upon the warrant of the Secretary of Labor, be taken into custody and deported."[2] On its face, the provision is clear and simple. But let us examine somewhat more closely into the matter. As already indicated,[3] "within five years after entry" has been held by the courts to mean within five years after *any* entry to the country from a foreign country, whether such entry be legal or illegal, or after a visit of only a few hours. This definition seems to touch the public-charge category with particularly tragic consequences.

Further question has arisen in regard to the "five years." Does it mean that a person must be deported within five years after his entry, or that deportation proceedings must be begun within five years, with actual deportation occurring

[1] *Annual Report of the Commissioner General of Immigration*, etc., *1927*, p. 11. The type of institution covered in its relation to the *public charge* question is not defined. The Commissioner General calls attention on p. 25 to the lack of officers to investigate the individuals to determine how many of these were subject to deportation.

[2] Immigration act of February 5, 1917, sec. 19.

[3] *Supra*, pp. 58-59.

afterward, or that the person must have become a public charge within five years, with the proceedings begun during that time and deportation accomplished any time thereafter? Here too there has been some difference of opinion. The more general trend of opinion in the courts seems to be that the five-year limit refers to the time after entry during which the public dependency must occur, not to the initiation of deportation proceedings.[1]

In cases where an alien became a public charge within five years after entry from causes not shown to have arisen since landing, the general, though not universal, practice, is to add the further charge that the person had been liable to become a public charge at the time of entry. However, if this additional charge is used, deportation proceedings must be begun *within* five years of entry, as " L.P.C." belongs to the excludable category where there is a five-year limit to the institution of deportation proceedings. In other words, in cases where " L.P.C." is used, the warrant of arrest must be applied for by the local immigration office within the statutory period, even if only a day before its expiration.[2] If the proceedings are instituted within five years, there is no legal hurry as to their termination. For instance, a woman who became an insane patient within five years after an entry into the country, if it could not be shown by her friends or relatives that the cause of her insanity arose after her last arrival here, might have deportation proceedings instituted at any time within the five years, if the immigration officials declared her to have been " L.P.C." on entry.

[1] *Ex parte* Reeves, 292 Fed. 766; *Ex parte* Horne, 292 Fed. 455; *Ex parte* Britten, 293 Fed. 61; Greenwood *v.* Frick, 233 Fed. 629; *Ex parte* Mitchell, 256 Fed. 229. *Contra*, Hughes *v.* Tropello, 206 Fed. 306.

[2] United States *ex rel.* Davis *v.* Tod, United States *ex rel.* Schnirmacher *v.* Same, 289 Fed. 60; Nocchi *v.* Johnson, 6 Fed. (2d) 1; United States *ex rel.* Patton *v.* Tod, 297 Fed. 385. *Contra,* Hughes *v.* Tropello, 296 Fed. 306, *supra.*

If the "L.P.C." charge were not lodged, deportation proceedings need not have been begun within five years after entry, for she needed merely to become a public charge within that time to make her deportable. The immigration service in practice usually institutes proceedings before the expiration of five years, whether or not "L.P.C." is used. It is probable that there are enough cases within the time limit to keep the immigration officials busy deporting them. Furthermore, a number of countries may grant a passport more readily to a person who has not been in this country very long than to one who has been here many years and has possibly expatriated himself from his country of nativity.

An alien may become an inmate of a public institution or receive public aid in other ways after he has been here more than five years following his last entry. He would not then be liable for deportation from the country.[1]

WHAT IS A PUBLIC CHARGE?

The question that doubtless provokes the most difficulties in this connection is, what constitutes a *public* charge? Does it mean paupers, those without any financial resources, held in city, county, state or semi-public institutions? Is a person a public charge if he pays part of his expenses in a public institution, or can he be a public charge even if he pays all of his expenses? Would he be liable to deportation if he subsequently paid the money which his illness or detention had cost the state or place where he was kept? Would he be considered a public charge if he were confined, as so many aliens are, in a jail or prison of any description whatsoever? Would relief or aid given by a voluntary social agency, such as a charity organization or family welfare society, bring him into the class of public charges?

[1] Unless he entered illegally after July 1, 1924, or was an extreme radical or criminal of a certain category, or connected with prostitution. Then he could be deported on those grounds instead of having become a public charge.

The words " public charge " mean a financial liability on, or expense to, the public for support and care; such support, however, must be received from funds raised by taxation and not by private or voluntary subscription. If *any* public funds are so used, even though part of the money is raised by private subscription, the charge is a public one. Receiving aid from a private social agency alone does not constitute receiving public support.[1] " By public money is meant money raised by taxation not only in the state at large but in any city, county or town." [2]

Where a hospital is paid the full amount of its charge, even though such hospital is a public one receiving any or all of its support from public funds, the patient who pays such charges is not a public charge.[3] An interesting case of this kind is that of Antoinette Martinis, born in 1902 in Jugoslavia, who came to the United States to join her father when she was about seventeen years old. At the age of twenty-one she married, and very shortly after became insane. She was cared for in a private sanitarium for six weeks and then was committed to a Washington state hospital. Within six months she had recovered and her release had been recommended by the hospital superintendent, who said he had found nothing in her history to indicate any cause existing before the attack. The girl's husband paid all of her hospital bills and had $1500 left from his year's earnings. Yet the immigration authorities started deportation proceedings. A writ of *habeas corpus* was secured

[1] However, such aid is often indication that the person receiving it is *liable* to become a public charge.

[2] People of the State of New York *ex rel.* State Board of Charities *v.* N. Y. S. P. C. C., 162 N. Y. 430; also 42 N. Y. App. Div. 83.

[3] *Ex parte* Kichmiriantz, 283 Fed. 697; United States *ex rel.* Brugnoli *v.* Tod, 300 Fed. 913; United States *ex rel.* Donatello *v.* Commissioner of Immigration at the Port of New York, 4 Fed. (2d) 808.

and the girl was released, for the court held she had not become a public charge and might not be deported on that ground. Another case worthy of note is that of a boy who within five years after entry was sent to a state school for defective children and kept there at public expense. His parents were able and willing to pay for his support but did not understand the commitment arrangements and so did not make the payment required of them by state law. When deportation proceedings were instituted, the parents took the matter to court and indicated their willingness to pay any necessary charges. So the boy was held to be not deportable under the circumstances.

In some states it is a policy not to render statements of account to persons maintained in hospitals supported by public funds, even though request is made by the persons or their relatives for a hospital bill.[1] Despite the wish of the states where this practice is carried on, the Department of Labor will not institute deportation proceedings in such instances, as in the case of Terese Mandel, who became insane and was sent to the observation ward of Bellevue Hospital in New York. From there she was transferred to Central Islip Hospital for the Insane. From the beginning of her stay at Central Islip, her father and family paid all the charges. However, when her father requested a bill from Bellevue Hospital he did not receive it. Later the bill came, and he paid it immediately and the court refused to hold the girl a public charge.[2] If an alien is forced to accept public aid without his knowledge or agreement, he is held not to be a public charge.[3] But if he pays *after* deportation proceedings have been begun, or attempts to pay then, he is held to *have become* a public charge and so liable to deportation, if

[1] Cook and Hagerty, *op. cit.*, p. 143, § 286.

[2] United States *ex rel.* Mandel *v.* Day, 19 Fed. (2d) 520.

[3] Nocchi *v.* Johnson, 6 Fed. (2d) 1.

it cannot be shown that the causes for his entering the public institution as a charge did not arise subsequent to his last entry to the United States. If a person pays only part of the bill rendered him by the hospital, he is still a public charge, even though he intends to complete payment at a later date. Thus if a woman were ill in a hospital and her husband paid 60% of her expenses at the time, she would have been a public charge then, even though the remainder were paid later.

Even though the person in the institution or his relatives or friends pay the hospital bill and as far as their knowledge and ability go he is not a public charge, some states contend that he is still such a charge if the nominal fee charged for hospital care does not completely cover the cost of his maintenance. Federal authorities and the courts have usually refused to agree to this interpretation,[1] despite the vehemence with which some states have urged it. Thus Dr. Spencer Dawes, medical examiner of the former New York State Hospital Commission, stated in testimony given before a Congressional committee in 1924:

Some years ago I made the contention and it was upheld in the federal courts that the fact that an alien paid to the state of New York the sum of $1 a day for care and maintenance in a State Institution—I made the contention that they were still public charges, because they were only paying a part of their keep, and that it cost considerably more than a dollar a day for care and maintenance. That contention was upheld by the federal courts and they are deporting aliens right along from the State of New York [2] who are only partly paying their way. I am very particular about that phase of the work. In no case do I permit the acceptance of money from the family of any

[1] *Ex parte* Kichmiriantz, 283 Fed. 697.

[2] By this is meant repatriation at state expense rather than deportation by the federal government. For further discussion, *vide infra*, pp. 126-133.

deportable alien without first warning them that under the rules of the State of New York we cannot accept more than a dollar a day. I do not want to take advantage of them and I advise them that their paying this money will not stop deportation of the alien.[1]

The per-capita daily cost in New York state public hospitals was $3.08 in 1925, $3.17 in 1926 and $3.29 in 1927.[2] Thus the state of New York is in the peculiar situation of *not allowing* an alien to pay more than the partial cost of his maintenance and at the same time considering him a public charge. An *impasse* had been reached between the federal and the state authorities over the question; for however frequently New York state may at its own expense send home those aliens who are willing to go, whether or not they have paid the charges demanded of them, yet ordinarily the bureau of immigration of the Department of Labor will not deport such cases.

At the same hearing, Dr. Dawes further testified that the public-charge provisions of the law prevent deportations by allowing those who have paid their expenses in institutions to remain here while those who cannot pay are deported. He said he felt that the present interpretation of the law means that those unable to pay are deported, while others in institutions, possibly with the same illness, who can pay the small charge required of them, are kept here. Dr. Dawes also seemed to feel that patients are sometimes maintained in private institutions until they have been in the United States five years and then, when the statutory period has elapsed

1 Here again repatriation by the state is probably meant. *Hearings on Proposed Deportation Legislation before the House Committee on Immigration and Naturalization, op. cit.*, p. 23.

2 *Annual Report of the State Board of Charities of the State of New York for the Year Ending June 30, 1927*, p. 20, and *for the Year Ending June 30, 1928*, p. 32.

within which they must become public charges to be deportable, they are turned over to public institutions for care. No figures are available showing the number of such cases. In any event, from the social point of view an ethical question is raised which is not easy to answer, for consideration of conditions in one country may result in a lack of consideration of the individuals involved and of the country to which they were returned, and *vice versa*.

There are still further complications. In a few states, such as Washington, Maine, Michigan and California, the state authorities can by law sequester or assume jurisdiction over funds or property held by an insane patient at the time of his commitment, or in the possession of those legally responsible for his support.[1] Thus if the person has money in the bank at the time he is admitted to a public institution, that money must be used to pay his expenses to the state. As long as their care is being paid for by their own money or the proceeds of their property, such persons are not public charges.

Technically a person who receives care and treatment at a municipal lodging house, free public dispensary, etc., would be a public charge but practically this very strict interpretation has not been used. However, "L.P.C." has been used in this connection, particularly where the alien involved wishes deportation.

A somewhat different interpretation of the term "public charge" has arisen on a number of occasions. Is a person committed, for whatever cause, to a prison or jail within five years after entry, also a "public charge"? It has been held that "as used in Section 19 of the Immigration Act of February 5, 1917, providing for the deportation of any alien who within five years after entry becomes a public

[1] *Ex parte* Kichmiriantz, 283 Fed. 697; *Ex parte* Antoinette Marinis, 55223/332, 283 Fed. 697.

charge from causes not affirmatively shown to have arisen subsequent to entry, 'public' means the people or government of the United States, and a person becomes a public charge *when committed to a department of the government* by due course of law." [1] This very broad interpretation of the term has never reached a higher court but a similar understanding has been reached by the federal courts in other cases. It would seem that the difficulty in the way of interpretation lies in the explanation of "causes not affirmatively shown to have arisen subsequent to landing."

"CAUSES NOT AFFIRMATIVELY SHOWN TO HAVE ARISEN SUBSEQUENT TO LANDING"

That particular wording of the law was arranged with a definite purpose in mind, for the 1907 act had authorized the deportation of any alien who becomes a public charge within the specified time limit, from causes existing prior to entry. As many cases arose where it was very difficult for the government to accomplish deportation under the wording of the act, the Commissioner General of Immigration and the Secretary of Labor recommended [2] that a change be made. So, after being passed by the Senate and then dropped in conference and added again by the House Committee, the provision was finally embodied in the 1917 act to read "from causes not affirmatively shown to have arisen subsequent to landing." [3] So under the present provision, if the alien cannot definitely show that the causes of his becoming a public charge arose after his coming to the country, it is assumed those causes were existent at the time

[1] *Ex parte* Tsunetaro Machida, 277 Fed. 239.

[2] *Senate Report No. 355*, 63rd Congress, 2nd Session, and *Senate Document* 451.

[3] *Senate Report No. 352, to accompany H. R. 10384*, 64th Congress, 1st Session.

of entry. The burden of proof is upon the alien to show that they came into existence in the United States, as in any event the burden of proof is upon him to show that he should not be deported, and this is a further emphasis upon that point. It is often difficult to show that a certain disability arose after reaching the United States, but if a doubt exists as to when the onset occurred, the wording of the phrase "causes not affirmatively shown to have arisen subsequent to landing," makes deportation possible. Thus a man who entered a public tuberculosis hospital within five years after entry would have to give definite proof, which might be difficult to secure, as to the date of the beginning of the disease here, should he wish to avoid deportation. The statutory increase in time from one to two to three and then to five [1] years after entry, within which deportation may occur, has made the possibility of onset of illness here greater; yet the difficulty of proving that a disease " begins " at a definite date may be so great that despite the length of time the alien has been here he cannot show affirmatively that the illness began after his entry.

Then the interpretation of " entry " to mean last entry to the country gives a peculiar twist to the effect of " causes not affirmatively shown to have arisen subsequent to landing." In numerous instances, disabilities which do not arise after a person's last landing in the United States nevertheless arise *in* this country. However, the act uses the word " landing " rather than entry, so in this instance it would seem that entry can only be by water.

In some cases, the only charge on the warrant of deportation is that the person became a public charge within five years after entry from causes not affirmatively shown to have arisen subsequent to landing, but more often than not other charges are listed as well. In any instance where a

[1] *Vide supra*, pp. 58-59, 107.

disability was present but undetected at the time of entry, the person suffering under it could be deported for the additional reason that he belonged to one of the classes excludable by law, but, as already indicated in the case of "L.P.C.", proceedings in such instances must be begun within five years from the date of the last entry of the alien. Thus persons found to be feeble-minded within five years of their last entry and placed in public institutions for the feeble-minded, or those who within five years are found to have had attacks of insanity prior to their last entry, no matter where such attacks occurred, and who then become public charges within the five-year period, would be deportable not only as "public charges" but for the additional reason that they were excludable at entry. A common additional ground within the five-year period is that the alien is one whose ticket or passage money was paid for with the money of another, or who was assisted by others to come. Such reason can be used, however, only if the alien already belongs to a deportable category; it is an *additional* and not a primary cause for deportation. The number of aliens whose passage is paid for by relatives or friends is legion, and they would not because of that alone become deportable. Only should they fall into another deportable class could this be an added charge against them.

"CONSTITUTIONAL PSYCHOPATHIC INFERIORITY"

A further charge is often used in conjunction with the ground of being a public charge, namely that the person who becomes a public charge within five years after entry was of constitutional psychopathic inferiority at the time of entry. This ground has an especially favored place in New York state practice. The theory behind this coupling of terms is that a person who becomes insane from any cause whatsoever must be of constitutional psychopathic inferiority or the immediate cause would not have resulted in insanity. If, in an insane case, a certificate declared that the person was a constitutional psychopathic inferior at the time of entry, it would be exceedingly difficult to show that subsequent cause could bring on the insanity. The feeling of New York state officials in regard to this question is shown in the following excerpt from a hearing on a warrant of arrest.

Counsel to Dr. Barton:

Q. Have you any statement here to make with reference to your certificate?
A. I want to testify that I still am of the opinion that the patient was of a constitutional psychopathic inferior make-up when she entered the United States and also that the experience of birth of a child acted simply as a secondary cause in a constitutional psychopathic make-up.

Inspector to Counsel:

Q. Is it not true that in practically all cases or most cases of insanity, there was previous to the insanity a condition, at least in some degree, of constitutional psychopathic inferiority?
A. Yes, all except organic cases.
Q. Is this an organic case?
A. No.
Q. This is not?
A. No.
Q. Your conclusions then are based more on the general run or line of cases and not particularly with reference to this patient?
A. That is correct.
Q. In other words, in most cases you have here on the Island, when you find a case of insanity, your conclusions are that the person is of a constitutional psychopathic make-up, except organic cases?
A. Yes, that is correct.

Q. There is nothing that you know of, Doctor, in detail or in particular, about this patient which leads you to come to that conclusion?
A. No, there is nothing in the patient herself, it is based on general experience of myself and others.
Q. Have you examined the patient?
A. Not since June of this year.
Q. At that time did you come to any conclusion of the matter, or had you not reached any conclusion?
A. Yes, I concluded at that time she belonged to another manic depression from which they recover to get another attack. I was evidently wrong, it has been changed in the hospital to Dementia Praecox. Sometimes a diagnosis is changed after long residence in the hospital. When I saw her she was so excitable and restless I thought at that time she was a case of manic depressive insanity.
Q. From your previous observations and examinations of the patient, would you say that the patient shows some improvement as you look at her to-day from the last time you saw her?
A. Superficially, I should say yes. I have not spoken to her. I don't know what her mental content is.[1]

The courts have not lent a favorable ear to the unsupported interpretation of New York State. The District Court of the Eastern District of New York says:

the rule of this circuit is if an alien is ordered deported on the ground that at the time of entry he was a person of constitutional psychopathic inferiority, the record must contain evidence as to the previous mental or medical history of the alien. Accordingly, where no reasons whatever are assigned through or by virtue of which the decision was arrived at, the conclusion is that the cause of the alien's psychosis could not have arisen subsequent to landing, and the court will refuse to uphold the action of the immigration authorities. . . . In answer to the

[1] Record in files of bureau of immigration.

question, " state whether or not the disabilities described constitute the sole cause why the alien is a public charge," the certificate states " constitutional psychopathic inferiority and general mental instability at the time of entry." There are no reasons assigned by which the physician shows the cause of the alien's psychosis could not have arisen subsequent to landing and there is no statement of the previous mental or medical history of the alien. . . . Since no facts are given and no process of reasoning advanced by which the doctor arrived at his conclusions, . . . the order of deportation must be vacated and the alien discharged from custody.[1]

However, New York continues to use the charge, on the ground that such types of mental disease as *dementia praecox* or *manic depressive insanity* show a defect in the " germ cell " which must have existed from birth. Therefore it would be difficult if not impossible to show that a person thus afflicted had become so from causes arising subsequent to landing. But independent of that reason, no matter when the latent germs of insanity were formed, deportation could occur for anyone who had become a public charge in an institution for the insane within five years of his entry.[2]

How in general are medical decisions reached in deportation cases? If a person is ill and it is found he was excludable at the time of entry, but he is not a public charge, the doctors of the United States Public Health Service make an examination and certify mental or physical defects or diseases for the information of immigration officers. In an institutional case of a public charge, the institution may,

[1] United States *ex rel.* Mandel *v.* Day, 19 Fed. (2d) 520. *Vide* also United States *ex rel.* Brugnoli *v.* Tod, 300 Fed. 918. The Brugnoli case had previously stated there must be some previous history upon which to predicate the conclusion that the alien at the time of entry was a member of one or more classes excluded by law.

[2] United States *ex rel.* Donatello *v.* Commissioner of the Port of N. Y., 4 Fed. (2d) 808.

through its chief resident, certify as to causes of the deportability of the alien; or even a reputable private physician may so certify. The inspectors of the immigration service consider themselves in practice bound by the certificate of such a doctor, for they maintain they should not interfere with medical decisions which they are not technically qualified to judge. The final decision is, of course, in the hands of the Secretary of Labor. It has been decided in court that

> an alien, arrested on the warrant of the Secretary for deportation, was denied a fair hearing where the immigration officers did not exercise their own judgment as to whether he should be deported, but considered themselves bound by the decision of a medical examiner and the report of a medical board that he was feeble-minded.[1]

State institutions where aliens are patients, are supposed to report all cases of possible deportability to the immigration service, but the procedure and frequency with which the states do this varies widely from state to state, and even sometimes within the same state. Some states, such as Maine,[2] require report to be made by law while others seldom report a case. In many instances the immigration inspectors

[1] Billings *v.* Sitner, 228 Fed. 315. *Vide* also United States *ex rel.* Haft *v.* Tod; United States *ex rel.* Brugnoli *v.* Tod, 300 Fed. 918.

[2] "Whenever any person shall be admitted or committed to the State Penitentiary, State Reformatory, county jail or any other state, county, city or private institution which is supported wholly or in part by public funds, it shall be the duty of the warden, superintendent, sheriff or other officer in charge of such institution to inquire at once into the nationality of such person, and if it shall appear that such person is an alien, to notify immediately the United States Immigration officer in charge of the district in which such penitentiary, reformatory, jail or other institution is located of the date and the reason for such alien's admission or commitment, length and time for which admitted or committed, county of which a citizen and the date on which and port at which he last entered the United States."—Maine Stat. 1927, ch. i, § 1.

must call on institutions to determine the number of deportable aliens there. Much depends on the initiative of the individual inspectors, although in states with a small foreign-born population the cases are few and far between, no matter how active the inspector. Usually one inspector in a local district is assigned to institutional work, but if pressure of other cases, especially illegal entries, is great, action on institutional cases is postponed, for it is felt that they cannot escape and are safely detained where they are, at the expense of the state rather than of the federal government.

FEDERAL VS. STATE GOVERNMENT IN PUBLIC CHARGE CASES

This very point has caused unending friction between state and federal authorities. Several states, especially New York, are loud in their complaints about the slowness and inefficiency which they claim characterizes the immigration service in its removals of public charges. Dr. Spencer Dawes, medical examiner of the Bureau of Special Examination in the Department of Mental Hygiene of New York state, said that in 1927, " while the bureau certified as deportable 337 aliens, the Federal government removed but 250, a greater disproportion than usual. . . . Permit me again to emphasize that had the Federal government been alive to its responsibilities a major part of the expenditure of more than $19,000 need not have been incurred." [1] Indeed, the situation had become so serious between state and federal officials that under the impetus given by the then existing State Hospital Commission of New York, an Interstate Conference on Immigration was held in the New York office of the State Hospital Commission on October 24, 1923, in " order to secure the cooperation of other states in

[1] *Annual Report of the Department of Mental Hygiene, New York*, June 1, 1926 to June 30, 1927, pp. 79-80.

obtaining legislation from Congress to relieve New York and other states from the burden of the alien insane." It was recommended by the conference

That each State take the earliest opportunity to present to their United States Senators and representatives in Congress a copy of the minutes of the Conference outlining the laxity in enforcement by the Federal government, the misuse of funds by Congress, and urge upon them their cooperation with the State of New York: (1) in an endeavor to obtain the changes in the immigration law approved by the Conference and the appropriation by Congress of sufficient money from the immigrant fund, not only to enable a proper enforcement of the law but to reimburse the several states for the care and maintenance of alien public charges as provided in the immigration law, Act of May, 1917; (2) To cooperate in obtaining permission from Congress for New York State to submit claims against the United States for $17,247,616.71 now due such State for the care and maintenance of insane aliens in State hospitals; (3) To aid in bringing about the following changes in the immigration law:

(a) Regarding warrants of arrest, providing that they shall be issued upon the order of the Commissioner of Immigration of the district in which the alien is a public charge.

(b) Providing that the Secretary of Labor shall give due notice with an opportunity to be heard either in person or by letter to the department or officer issuing the certificate before a warrant either of arrest or of deportation, is cancelled.

(c) Regarding the examination of aliens, that there shall be provided as a prerequisite to the granting by an American Consul of a visa to the immigrant, that he shall present a medical certificate on a blank provided by the Commissioner General of Immigration, embodying personal and family history, and certifying that the emigrant is not of the excluded classes, and made by a physician in the employ of the transportation company which would bring him to the United States; providing a fine, based upon the cost of transportation, of not less than three times such cost and leaving in the law the provisions of sections 9 and 19.

(d) Regarding alien seamen, providing that they shall be admitted and deported under the same conditions as other aliens not only as to time in the United States but as to hearings.

(e) Regarding stowaways, providing that there shall be no time limit as to deportation when they are public charges.

(f) Regarding geographically excluded aliens providing that they, excepting these specifically exempted, may be deported at any time and without verification of landing when they are public charges.

(g) Regarding admission under bond, providing that no aliens belonging to the class of mandatorily excludable aliens suffering from " idiocy, insanity, imbecility, feeble-mindedness, epilepsy, constitutional psychopathic inferiority, or chronic alcoholism " shall be admitted under bond and in any other case admitted under bond the amount shall be not less than $5,000 and a surety company bond.

(h) Regarding time of deportation, providing that an alien proved to be a public charge may be deported at any time when deportation proceedings have been commenced within five years after entry and that for the purposes of the law the " commencement of proceedings " shall be the request for a verification of landing by a responsible officer of any state.

It is the opinion of the Committee that the States should be reimbursed by the Federal Government in the case of alien public charges from the day of their admission to a State institution where it is proven that the alien is in the United States contrary to law and at a rate of not less than $1 per day.

The Committee further advises that where failure to deport is due to laxity or negligence on the part of the Federal Government, the latter should remove the alien to a Federal institution.

> That the failure on the part of Federal officials to obey the law should be ground for prosecution for malfeasance in office.[1]

The recommendations at least serve to show the pitch of feeling to which some of the states have been aroused.

It has also been suggested that the present law be amended to provide for the deportation not only of aliens who have become public charges, but of all aliens who become inmates or patients of any city, county, municipal or state hospital within five years after entry, from causes not affirmatively shown to have arisen subsequent to entry.[2]

Whether the accusation by the states of negligence in deporting public-charge cases is true or not is an open question. It *is* true, however, that there is a tendency on the part of immigration officials to regard public-charge cases maintained at state expense as less urgent than illegal entries, detained at federal expense in county jails or other detention quarters. The lack of general detention facilities, the overcrowding of jails, especially at border points,[3] and the possibility of escape of the well and able-bodied make it practical for immigration officials to turn their attention where it seems most needed.

It is of note that there has been a decrease in public charge deportations in the last few years, together with a corresponding increase in deportations for illegal entry. The number of public charges deported in recent years are as follows:

[1] *Report of the State Hospital Commission, New York State*, etc., *for 1925.*

[2] *Proposed Deportation Legislation, op. cit.*

[3] *Vide infra*, ch. xi, p. 389 *et seq.*

Statistics of Public Charge
Deportations 1925-1930[1]

1924	*1925*	*1926*	*1927*	*1928*	*1929*	*1930*
716	803	1087	817	938	647	961

There may be a number of reasons for this variation. It would seem that increased emphasis on deportation of those illegally crossing the border or deserting the ship may be one contributing factor and it is barely possible that the present restrictive immigration law and the increased care in Europe in issuing immigration visas may already have become effective.[2]

In pursuance of the traditional policy of transferring paupers from one locality to another to avoid their support, the states themselves may make removals to other places within the United States or even outside the country. Yet care must be taken to distinguish between such removals and deportation, for the states have no power to deport under either the commerce clause of the Constitution or federal control over foreign affairs. However, a state may send a person home *if he consents to the removal.* With the development of Poor Law practice, it has become customary to remove no one without his consent,[3] and this is

[1] *Annual Report of the Commissioner General of Immigration for the Fiscal Year Ended June 30, 1930.*

[2] In a letter to the author in July, 1930 the Second Assistant Secretary of Labor writes concerning this point: "While there was a considerable falling off in public-charge deportation in 1929, I do not believe that the decrease has any particular significance. The unpublished figures for the past fiscal year show 961 public-charge deportations. It seems to me inevitable that this class of cases will decrease materially as time goes on because of reduced immigration and also because great care is exercised in the examination of applicants for immigration visas." To the author it would seem too soon for marked results to show in regard to deportation after entry, particularly with the wording of the phrase in the present law "from causes not affirmatively shown to have arisen subsequent to landing" and the difficulty of proving onset of disease here.

[3] *Annual Report of the State Board of Charities of the State of New York*, 1880, p. 229.

particularly necessary where removals are made to a foreign country.

THE NEW YORK STATE PRACTICE OF REMOVAL OF ALIEN PUBLIC CHARGES

The practice of New York State is of especial note. The law of that state provides that

> when any person who is an inmate of any public home or is otherwise cared for at the expense of the state or of any public welfare district belongs to or has friends willing to support him or to aid in supporting him in any other state or country, the superintendent of state and alien poor may cause his removal to such state or country, provided, in the judgment of the superintendent, the interest of the state and the welfare of such person will be thereby promoted. The expense of such removal shall be paid from the state treasury on the warrant of the comptroller pursuant to a verified account submitted by the superintendent of state and alien poor or other person legally incurring the expenditure.[1]

The State Board of Charities maintains a superintendent of state and alien poor, charged with the duties of carrying out the provisions of the state law. The state feels that,

> with a few exceptions, dependent aliens are not deportable by the immigration authorities unless it can be established definitely that the cause of dependency existed prior to arrival in this country [2] and dependency occurred within a period of five years after arrival. Aliens who have lived in this country more than five years, or those here under five years who are not deportable by the Immigration Service, but who are under public care and likely to remain dependent, may be proper sub-

[1] Chap. 965, Laws of 1930, "An Act in relation to the public welfare, constituting chapter forty-two of the consolidated laws," sec. 73.

[2] Author's note. — This is not an exact statement of the law, for, as already noted, the burden of proof is the other way around.

jects for repatriation to their native country. They cannot, however, be removed unless they express a willingness to return. This is due to the present passport rules and regulations which do not permit an alien to depart from this country without a passport, for which application must be made by the individual.[1] The cooperation of the United States Immigration Service in cases of aliens becoming dependent from causes existing prior to landing, and who are thus properly deportable under the federal laws, has been of great assistance to the Department, not only from the financial standpoint but in cases where there was unwillingness on the part of the poor person involved to return to the country from which he came.[2]

Of the alien poor who had been more than sixty days in some county in New York state and therefore were not state poor, during the fiscal year 1928, 319 were repatriated to other countries, 111 sent at state expense, the same number at the expense of relatives or friends, and 97 by the United States immigration service to whom the cases had been referred.[3] These persons were sent to 29 different foreign countries, at a cost for those sent at state expense of $5,571.29.[4] "All those removed were poor persons incapacitated by disease or disability, infancy, old age or for other reasons which were likely to make them dependent indefinitely or permanently." [5]

[1] Author's note.—That is, the individual must sign the application. A further reason for inability of state to repatriate without the consent of the individual or the country to which he is returned is that the exclusive power over foreign affairs as well as commerce rests of course with the federal government.

[2] *Annual Report of the State Board of Charities for the Year Ending June 30, 1928* (Legislative Document, 1929, no. 22), pp. 14-15.

[3] It is not known whether these were voluntary deportations under the three-year statutory limitation or regular deportations.

[4] *Ibid.*, p. 15.

[5] *Ibid.* State removals of public charges to other countries decreased during the last few years, as shown by the following table:

Repatriation of insane aliens presents a somewhat different situation, for their care and removal is arranged for by the Bureau of Special Examinations of the New York State Department of Mental Hygiene.[1] This department is entirely separate from the New York State Department of Social Welfare. Each department covers its own work, so that whereas the number of repatriations claimed by the former department for the fiscal year 1928 was 490 insane,[2]

STATE REMOVALS OF PUBLIC CHARGES TO OTHER COUNTRIES, 1923-8

1923-4	*1924-5*	*1925-6*	*1926-7*	*1927-8*
500	473	380	353	319

[1] The former State Hospital Commission became merged with the newly organized Department of Mental Hygiene by act of 1927 (New York Stat. 1927, art. 2 of chap. 426) and the work of the Bureau of Deportation of that Commission has been transferred to the Bureau of Special Examinations.

[2] The Bureau of Special Examinations investigated and arranged for the return of these 490, but of that number 313 were actually deported by the immigration service, 120 were sent back at the expense of relatives or friends, and 57 were removed at state expense.—*Annual Report of the Department of Mental Hygiene, State of New York, July 1, 1927–June 30, 1928*, p. 63.

It is evident that insane aliens removed at state expense must have had the consent of relatives, for it would be impossible in many cases to obtain the consent of the aliens.

The following table of removal of insane aliens from New York State shows the total of such removals since 1894. It does not distinguish between deportation and state removal, but includes both.

REMOVALS FROM NEW YORK STATE FOR INSANITY, 1894-1928

1894	13	1904	176	1914	825	1924	425
1895	16	1905	299	1915	6490	1925	453
1896	40	1906	307	1916	208	1926	458
1897	638	1907	352	1917	52	1927	436
1898	48	1908	424	1918	53	1928	490
1899	692	1909	489	1919	142		
1900	48	1910	613	1920	337		
1901	103	1911	784	1921	496		
1902	94	1912	1171	1922	367		
1903	147	1913	865	1923	442		

Ibid., p. 64.

the latter claimed 309. For the year 1929, of the 403 removed, 206 were deported and 197 repatriated by the State Department.

The state has had the same trouble as the federal government [1] in procuring passports for those persons of foreign birth whom it desires to remove. The Medical Examiner of the Bureau of Special Examination says: "The number (repatriated) might have been considerably greater except for the obstacles in the way of obtaining passports imposed by a number of foreign governments, notably Poland, Italy and Germany." [2]

Other states, especially those with large foreign-born population, have arrangements for repatriation to other countries. For instance, Massachusetts in 1926 removed a total of 72 persons to other countries, 79 the following year and 57 in 1928; [3] Illinois in 1929 removed 77 alien patients; [4] Pennsylvania in 1928 returned 11 persons to other countries. [5]

[1] *Vide infra*, p. 400 *et seq.*

[2] *Ibid*,, for the year 1927, p. 79.

[3] Removals are made through its Department of Public Welfare, Division of Aid and Relief, Subdivision of Settlements. *Vide Annual Report of the Department of Public Welfare for the Year Ending November 30, 1928*, Massachusetts Public Document no. 17, p. 6.

[4] *Twelfth Annual Report of the Department of Public Welfare, July 1, 1928 to June 30, 1929*, p. 49, "Report of the State Deportation Agent."

[5] *Fourth Biennial Report of the Secretary of Welfare, June 1, 1927–May 31, 1928*, p. 41. It cannot be ascertained how many of these were returned at the expense of relatives rather than of the state. The same report gives figures of an investigation in state institutions, where it was ascertained that out of a total of 26,640 patients, 6,494 were foreign born. Of these, 1,886 were known to be aliens, but of these only a few appeared to be deportable.—*Ibid.*, p. 41.

THE PRACTICE OF OTHER STATES

It is beyond the scope of this book to study the bewildering assortment of laws and arrangements of different states for removals to other countries. Suffice to say that the situation in regard to the possibility of removal depends on variations on the theme of gaining and losing settlement. And that situation is indeed a chaotic one.[1] In eleven states, removal may be made from one district to another *within* the state, while

in eight others the law is not explicit, saying only that the pauper may be removed to their (sic) place of residence or such a vague phrase as " elsewhere " or " from the state ". In thirteen states, including California, Massachusetts, Minnesota, New York, and others, the enforcing agency is authorized to return the pauper to " the country or state " where his residence may be. In Arizona, Oregon, and Wisconsin explicit authority is given for the removal only of non-resident paupers who have been committed to state institutions. Fourteen states have no express provision for removal.

Besides these three states (Arizona, Oregon and Wisconsin) which arrange for the deportation of inmates of institutions only, California, Connecticut, Illinois, Indiana, Kansas, Minnesota, Vermont and Wisconsin have such a provision in addition to the general authority to deport non-residents making eleven states in all. . . . There is a tendency . . . toward a state authority assuming responsibility in such cases as involve transportation from one state to another. In some cases, as in Arizona and Kansas, the board of trustees of the state institution where the non-resident is an inmate is responsible for making the necessary arrangements for his return; but more often this responsibility is given to some general state agency or official. There is such a state authority in California, Connecticut, Illinois, Indiana, Massachusetts, Minnesota, New Jersey, New

[1] *Vide* Charlotte C. Donnell, " Settlement Law and Interstate Relationship," *Social Service Review*, vol. iv, no. 3, September, 1930.

York, Oregon, Vermont and Wisconsin. . . . In Connecticut, Indiana, Massachusetts, New Jersey and New York the law applies to all dependents; in the other states to those committed to state institutions. In Vermont and Wisconsin it applies only to the insane.[1]

As there are variations and difficulties not only between states, so there are difficulties within states, shown by the following case in Minnesota.[2] There a village

operating under the town system of caring for the poor, under statutes defining the settlement of a pauper as the city, town, or village " in which he has longest resided within " the year during which he has continuously resided in the county in which such city, town, or village is located, could not recover from the county the cost of deporting aliens who had lived in the village in the year preceding deportation, since the statutes defining settlement are applicable to aliens, and since the statute authorizing the transportation of a pauper to the place of his settlement and providing for reimbursement from the county does not apply to the deportation of aliens to another country.

Not only is there a miasma of difficulty concerning the varying state laws, but in many cases the connection between state repatriation policy and federal deportation law and activity is not clear.

PUBLIC-CHARGE CASES INCLUDED IN THIS STUDY

Of the total number of cases in the group from 1925-6, 116 were deported as public charges. In no case in that group was the only cause for deportation the fact that the person deported had become a public charge within five years after entry from causes not affirmatively shown to have

[1] *Ibid.*, p. 443 *et seq. Vide ibid.* for amplification of the above, with citation to statutes of different states. The author of the article considers the interstate rather than the international aspects of the question.

[2] Village of Litchfield *v.* County of Meeker, Minn. Sup. Ct., no. 28310, Dec. 19, 1930, quoted in *U. S. Daily*, December 30, 1930.

arisen subsequent to entry. It was doubtless thought that a person in a public institution would reveal other disability, ranging from illness to crime, which would make him a public charge, and that disability would doubtless put him in an additional category for deportation.

In all this group, the individuals were listed as "L.P.C." as well as public charges, and so deportation proceedings had to be begun within the five-year statutory period. Several cases brought up the question as to whether or not the alien had actually become a public charge, or was merely "L.P.C."

Sigurd Nielson (Case 18).

Sigurd Nielson was born in 1898 in Sweden, where his father and mother and two brothers were still living at the time of his emigration in 1923. The men were all smelters by trade and Mr. Nielson had worked at that until he sailed to the United States.

He was admitted on primary inspection from the III class of a Swedish-American steamship and went directly to a friend in the state of Washington. He secured work immediately in a stove and stamping works and worked steadily until he was admitted to the Northern State Hospital in January, 1925, with a diagnosis of maniac depressive insanity, manic type.

On January 22 of that year, he was reported by the hospital to the immigration authorities, but on the report (Form 534) it was stated: "there will be a complete cure, probably within a few weeks." It was also said that the man's history could not be determined at that time.

Two months and a week elapsed before a warrant of arrest was issued, by mail, with the charge that Mr. Nielson was likely to become a public charge at the time of entry, although the inspector in charge had recommended the further charge "that he had become a public charge," etc. On issuing the warrant, the bureau notified the inspector in charge that the latter ground was not used as the doctor had not stated whether or not the man's illness arose subsequent to entry or not.

A month (all but six days) later, a hearing was held at the hospital, where Mr. Nielson waived his right to a lawyer. No interpreter was considered necessary. Mr. Nielson stated that his mother had always been nervous but never seriously so, or in a hospital. He had never been ill himself except with influenza in 1918. He also said: "I had my bed in the Pacific Stove and Stamping Works and it was noisy and it was so hard work and I could not sleep at night. I think it was that that caused my trouble. . . . I went to the night school that the church ran."

On May 7, 1925 the commissioner of immigration at Seattle consulted the superintendent of the hospital who refused to certify that Mr. Nielson had become a public charge within five years of entry from causes not affirmatively shown to have arisen subsequent to entry; also, that Mr. Nielson was almost normal again.

A month and four days later, the commissioner recommended to the bureau in Washington that action be deferred for six months, and a further report then submitted. Ten days after that the state deportation agent of Washington wrote direct to the bureau asking the reason for deferring action, but before the bureau had replied, on July 17, 1925 the hospital superintendent sent a second copy of Form 534, secured by the state deportation agent, to the bureau. The paragraph concerning the "alien's history" now read: "It is generally conceded that in this class of cases there is a hereditary predisposition to this particular form of insanity". The form was accompanied by a letter from the state deportation agent saying that Mr. Nielson *was* a public charge within five years of his entry from causes not affirmatively shown to have arisen subsequent to entry, and protesting the deferring action for six months. The agent stated: "If he should not be a public charge in six months, it is entirely probable that he will become a public charge later with the probability that he could not then be deported under the law."

On August 1, 1925, a hearing was held by the board of review in Washington, rescinding the order deferring the case, and reopening the case with the additional charge that Mr.

Nielson had become a public charge, etc. It was there stated: "Notwithstanding the fact that the original medical certificate did not definitely indicate a prior cause, the facts shown in the record are in harmony with the presumption that the cause of the alien's condition was constitutional and this is now indicated in the later medical certificate."

A month and eight days later, a reopened hearing was given Mr. Nielson at the hospital, but no statement was made on either side concerning the new charge.

On September 30, 1925 a warrant of deportation was issued with the two charges, "L. P. C.", and that Mr. Nielson had become a public charge, etc. On November 5, the Swedish consul was notified of the deportation, which took place on November 17, at the expense of the steamship company which had brought him. On November 29 of that year he was delivered to and signed for by his father at his home town.

Margaret Phillips (Case 19).

Margaret Phillips was born in 1883 in London, England, the child of an Irish father and an English mother. She lived in Devonshire with her parents and four sisters until her marriage in 1905 to James Winter. They had two daughters, one born in 1907 and one in 1909.

After the birth of the last child, the family emigrated to Canada and were immediately admitted and went to reside in Winnepeg, where they stayed until 1921. Then they returned to England for a visit of four months, but went back to Winnipeg to live. In 1923 a third daughter was born.

The family decided to visit the United States and were admitted as temporary visitors at Noyes, Minn. on April 27, 1923. They went right to Los Angeles where Mr. Winter engaged in the grocery business and decided to remain.

At the beginning of June, 1924 Mrs. Winter was admitted to the Los Angeles General Hospital, but was transfered to the Norwalk State Hospital on June 25th. Almost eight months later,—on February 11, 1925, the hospital reported the case to the immigration office. The certificate stated in regard to the "alien's disabilities": "patient is insane; affidavit of insanity states that patient has been failing mentally for about five weeks; has ideas of grandeur, thinks she has plenty of money and wants to buy property. The fact is she has no money to buy anything. . . . Disease requires a manic depressive make-up which existed from birth".

A warrant of arrest was issued and sent by mail on February 27. The hearing was opened at the hospital on May 12, but was postponed until June 15, so the hospital superintendent could testify. He was asked "Is the woman a public charge?" and answered "Partially. Her husband has paid about 40% of her care and maintenance and the state has had to pay the other 60%. She is therefore a public charge".

On account of Mrs. Winter's long residence in Canada, the district director and the board of review both recommended that she be deported to Canada. When the case was referred to the Canadian Commissioner of Immigration on June 23, he stated that Mrs. Winter by her residence in the United States had lost her Canadian domicile and had been "regularly admitted to the United States" and so was no longer a citizen of Canada, so would not be readmitted.

The warrant of deportation had been issued on June 18, with the same charges as the warrant of arrest.

On September 12, Mrs. Winter left Los Angeles for New York, where she was detained in the psychopathic ward at Ellis Island Hospital until January 2, 1926 when she was deported at the expense of the steamship company which had brought her and her family to Canada in 1923 after their four months visit abroad. She landed at Southampton on January 9 and was sent by car to an institution there and signed for by the senior master of the institution.

Her husband and children remained in Los Angeles, as far as the record states and there is no mention of the possibility of deporting them for having entered as temporary visitors and remained longer than allowed.

Out of the group of 116, a number had other charges beside having become a public charge, etc., and "L.P.C." The 39 cases from New York state who had become public charges in institutions for the insane all had the additional reason that they were of "constitutional psychopathic inferiority at the time of entry." The following case shows the New York use of the term:

Joachim Herz (Case 20).

Joachim Herz was born in Nürnberg, Germany, in 1903. After attending a gymnasium there for nine years he went to the University of Freiburg, and worked to help pay his way through.

He decided to come to the United States to study and reached New York, October 12, 1924 and was admitted on primary inspection as a student coming to Rochester University. He went there immediately, and cared for furnaces to help pay expenses.

Probably from work, Mr. Herz became nervous and depressed and finally was admitted to the Rochester State Hospital, on January 23, 1925. A diagnosis was made of "manic depressive insanity, manic phase." On February 2, the Dean of the University of Rochester reported to the immigration authorities that Mr. Herz had been forced to leave college and be sent to a hospital, because of his mental condition.

On April 23 a warrant of arrest was issued, and a hearing was held on May 6th at the hospital, with no one testifying but Mr. Herz. A warrant of deportation was issued on June 22, on the grounds (1) "L. P. C.", (2) public charge, etc., (3) that he was a person of constitutional psychopathic inferiority at the time of entry.

A sister of Mr. Herz, living in the west, wrote she would be willing to repatriate him to Germany to avoid deportation, and a friend would accompany him, but the record contains nothing further than the offer itself. On November 14, 1925, Mr. Herz was sent to Ellis Island and was deported December 12, at the expense of the line bringing him him to this country. The record does not state by whom he was received.

Two cases from Massachusetts had the same charge, but one from that state did not. One from California also contained it, and is of particular interest in its relationship to the time limit for deportation.

Manuel Velasquez (Case 21).

Manuel Velasquez was born in 1903 in Aibor, Spain. The names of his parents are unknown, as is their present whereabouts. He came to the U. S. on December 30, 1919, destined to a friend, in Hollywood, California.

What he did and where he lived in the U. S. are not known, but he was admitted to the Stockton State Hospital on August 20, 1924. It was stated he was noisy, restless, incendiary and that he had a mental inferiority with a psychosis of dementia praecox, hebephenic type.

He was reported to the immigration authorities by the Stockton State Hospital on December 16, 1924.

On January 3, 1925, the local immigration office applied for a warrant of arrest. On January 8 the bureau wrote that the statutory period had expired when application was received. On March 3 the district director wrote the bureau of immigration stating no reply had been received to the application for the warrant.

The warrant was issued, without comment, on June 16, 1925. The hearing was held at the hospital, July 28, 1925. There was no lawyer, but an interpreter was present. Although the hospital had stated the man was of constitutional psychopathic inferiority, and although this was mentioned in the hearing before the board of review, the only technical charge for the warrant of arrest or of deportation (later issued September 29, 1925) was that the man had become a public charge within 5 years after entry from causes not affirmatively shown to have arisen subsequent to entry. He was sent to Ellis Island, October 16, 1925. He was deported on October 29, 1925. The original warrant of deportation had stated that he was to be deported at the expense of the government, but was amended to read " at the expense of the S. S. line ". The line protested that the deportation proceedings had not been instituted within 5 years, so the amendment was cancelled and the man was deported at the expense of the government. He landed November 7, 1925, at Vigo, Spain, and on November 12, 1925 was delivered by the attendant sent from the steamship to the Mayor at Aibor, Novaro, who turned him over the same day to his mother. The receipt was signed for by his mother with a cross, as she could not write.

The other causes of deportation on this total group of cases were as follows:

4 epileptic at the time of entry.
5 entered without inspection.
4 whose ticket or passage to the United States was paid for with the money of another, or who were assisted by others to come to the United States. From the records, it is indicated that this reason could have been used on a number of other cases.[1]
3 who were unable at the time of entry into the United States to read the English language, or some other language or dialect, although at that time over 16 and physically capable of reading and not exempted from the illiteracy test. However, two of the three were insane at the time the test was given. The record of one of these states: " His school knowledge could not be tested because the patient is Finnish. He does not know any American history or geography or current events " (Report of the hospital).
3 who were feeble-minded at the time of entry.
2 who were afflicted with chronic alcoholism at the time of entry.
3 who were afflicted at the time of entry with a loathsome or dangerous contagious disease.
1 who had had one or more attacks of insanity previous to entry.
4 who were in the United States in violation of the 1924 immi-

[1] This charge must always be in *addition to* other causes.

gration act in that they had no unexpired visas at the time of entry.

2 who entered the United States by water at a time or place other than as designated by immigration officials.

5 who were afflicted at the time of entry with tuberculosis in any form.

4 who entered without inspection.

2 who had been sentenced subsequent to May 1, 1917 to imprisonment for a term of one year or more because of conviction in this country of a crime involving moral turpitude committed within five years after entry.

The second group of twenty public-charge cases showed no marked difference in charges, except that there were four where the *only* charge was that the person had become a public charge within five years of entry from causes not affirmatively shown to have arisen subsequent to entry. Another case contained only that charge in the warrant of arrest but "L.P.C." was added in the warrant of deportation:

Hans Lagemann (Case 22).

Hans Lagemann was born in 1903 in Germany and lived there until he emigrated to the United States in 1929. He worked as a laborer after he was admitted, and remained in New York where he had landed.

After about seven months here, he became ill and could work only intermittently, so received aid from a German society. Then he was admitted to Bellevue Hospital, where a diagnosis of gastric ulcers was made. After he was a little better, he was released but because of his ill health and the unemployment situation could not get work, so he was admitted to the Municipal Lodging House in March, 1930. He was reported by them to the immigration authorities.

A warrant for his arrest was issued March 22, 1930, and he was sent to Ellis Island on April 1, 1930. A hearing was given him there that day, and a warrant of deportation was requested from Washington on the grounds that he had become a public charge within five years after entry from causes not affirmatively shown to have arisen subsequent to entry. When the case came before the board of review in the bureau, they recommended that the charge that he was liable to become a public charge at the time of entry be added. On April 17, 1930, the hearing was re-opened to ask if Mr. Lagemann had any objection to the additional charge, but he did not. So the warrant of deportation was issued on May 7, 1930, on the two grounds, and deportation took place on May 20, at the expense of the steamship company by which he had entered the country.

Other charges beside the public charge ground in the second group of cases were:

2 who were mentally deficient at the time of entry.
2 who were of constitutional psychopathic inferiority at the time of entry.
1 who overstayed a temporary visit.
1 who had had one or more attacks of insanity previous to entry.

Other charges might have been added in other cases, but apparently only the strongest were used.

The great problem in many of the cases seems to have been caused by the becoming a public charge within five years of entry, *from causes not affirmatively shown to have arisen subsequent to entry*. The fact that the person held for possible deportation must prove the onset of his disability to have arisen in the United States, doubtless explains the vague wording of many of the medical certificates as to the "alien history." A few of these will serve to illustrate:

A complete restoration is likely to be greatly delayed, if at all possible, due to the patient's youth at the time of the present attack. He is predisposed to recurrent attack for which this type of mental disease is significant. Also owing to youth, the likelihood of complete or partial recovery is diminished. It is unlikely that this patient or his descendants, if any, become efficient citizens. . . . This type of mental disease is usually based on some hereditary deficiency in the individual makeup. That the patient is young in years and in his mental organization, has early given way to an incompatibility in his social conduct before the struggle for existence became a great factor and at the period when his responsibility was not greatly taxed, thus supporting the view that there was a deficiency in his ability to bear even a minor strain of youth in the social plan.

Patient has never made a success in life. Has always been a drifter, having previously left his home in England. Visited South Africa and other parts of the Empire previous to coming to Canada, and was a ne'er-do-well with a deficient mental stability which was instilled into his makeup by heredity, handicapping him.

The underlying cause of her condition must have been of long duration beyond the time of her arrival.

The disability is more than likely of long standing.

Dementia praeox is generally conceded as based on some constitutional defect. No family history is obtainable here.

The reason for the fact that the illness did not arise subsequent to entry: The daily observation of the alien since admission; the physical and mental examination.

She has been somewhat peculiar all her life.

A definite record of the patient's condition prior to coming to this country cannot be obtained; however, his mental condition shows marked impairment. Most likely, a form of dementia praecox which has been present since early youth.

The character of his mental disease and the present state of his condition is such that it is reasonable to believe that the disease is of long standing and probably existent previous to landing in the United States.

He has been unable to hold a job since landing, being constantly discharged because of his slowness. It would appear that he is naturally unable to take care of himself because of intellectual dullness.

My opinion is that a predisposition existed through heredity.

Dementia praecox usually develops in an individual constitutionally inferior in type of personality.

All the above are *reasons* why the disability did not arise subsequent to entry. There is obviously great difficulty of determining the date of onset of mental disease, or of tuberculosis, for instance.

All but four of the cases were reported by the hospitals, or such centralizing organizations as the New York State Hospital Commission. One of the four cases was reported by a man's landlady, one by a minister, and two by relatives who were anxious for deportation to occur as quickly as possible. Deportation often offers a way for relatives to relieve themselves of burdens they are unwilling to bear.

There was no uniformity in the methods of reporting used by hospitals either in the same or different states, with the exception of New York. All the medical certificates sent from hospitals in that state were made out on a form basis, almost completely identical for all cases studied, with variations only in the name of the diseases, relatives, etc.

The dates of original report from the hospital as to possible deportability were not always given, and the only way of judging the report from the records was from the *Proof of Alien's Having Become a Public Charge* (Form 534). The length of time from that original report to the issuance of the warrant of arrest varied from one day to four months. The warrant of arrest was issued by letter in all the cases studied, with one exception, as there was no immediate hurry; that one exception was of a case where "L.P.C."

was an additional ground, and so the period for that case was within the five-year limit. The time that elapsed between the issuance of the warrant of arrest and the warrant of deportation varied from one day to a year and two months, with the modal length of time at two and a half months.

One case of particular interest is that of a man who, although he contracted an occupational disease in this country, was anxious to be deported to his home country:

Anton Krakes (Case 23).

Anton Krakes was born in 1891 in Czechoslovakia, near Prague, but moved to Prague while still small. He continued to live and work there, marrying in 1916 and working at the trade of file maker. He had one child, a boy, born in 1917.

In 1923 Mr. Krakes emigrated to the United States, arriving May 15, of that year, leaving his wife and child in Prague, with the intention of having them follow him when he became established in this country. He went immediately to his brother-in-law at Monaca, Pa., and soon secured work with a plumbing and bathroom fixture factory. He continued to work there until November 15, 1924, when he appealed to the Beaver County Welfare Department for aid in getting back to Europe, as he was in poor health and had spent his money on treatments instead of saving it as he had hoped. A doctor testified that Mr. Krakes had chronic mitral myocarditis and chronic metallic poisoning, the latter received from his work.

As Mr. Krakes was unable to work, he wanted to return home but could not afford it, particularly as the state of Pennsylvania has no system of occupational disease compensation and did not pay him anything for his illness. The Beaver County Welfare Commissioners felt the satisfactory way to secure deportation would be to have Mr. Krakes admitted to the Beaver County Home as a public charge, and an application made for deportation. So he was admitted there four days after his application to the Welfare Department, but he was not reported to the immigration authorities until three months after, February 18, 1925. A warrant of arrest was issued June 20th.

The report from the institution as to Mr. Krakes having become a public charge from causes not affirmatively shown to have arisen subsequent to entry states: " The metallic poisoning was caused by the work in the United States . . . ; the heart disability probably existed many years before. A complete cure is impossible.

A hearing was held at the Beaver County Home on September 18, 1925, when the following statements were made (through an interpreter):

Q. From the medical certificate, form 534, rendered in your case it appears that the cause of your becoming a public charge in this institution existed prior to your entry into the United States. What have you to say to that?

A. No, that is not true, I got this ailment in the Standard Sanitary Works where I worked since I came to this country.

Q. Have you any documentary evidence such as medical certificate or other document to show the immigration authorities that the cause of your becoming a public charge has arisen since your entry into the United States?

A. No, I have no documents with me but in the old country before coming to the United States I was examined by doctors and pronounced as being in good health.

Q. Where were you working that made you sick?

A. United States Sanitary Manufacturing Company, Pa.

Q. Where were you working?

A. I was working at a furnace where the iron was powdered and then placed in the form.

Q. How long did you work in the furnace?

A. Since I came to the United States last year.

Q. Were you ever in the hospital in the home country?

A. No. never.

Q. Were you never treated in your home by a doctor in the old country?

A. No. never.
Q. Did you ever suffer in your native country with the same trouble?
A. No. never.
Q. Have you suffered with stomach trouble in your native country?
A. I've never been sick.
Q. It appears from the medical certificate, form 534, that you suffered with heart trouble in the old country, what have you to say to that?
A. No, I've never suffered with any heart trouble or the ailment from which I suffer now.

Mr. Krakes said he wished to return home to his wife and child in Prague. The warrant for his deportation was issued October 12, 1925, with the charges (1) "L. P. C.", (2) that he has become a public charge, etc., (3) that his ticket or passage money was paid for by the money of another (His brother-in-law in Monaca had advanced the money to Mr. Krakes to come).

On October 31, 1925, he was sent to Buffalo where he was kept several days (exact number unknown) in the county jail, then sent to Ellis Island whence he was deported on November 11th, at the expense of the steamship line which had brought him here.

This case further illustrates the long periods of delay which may arise in carrying a case through to a conclusion.

The general run of public-charge cases may be seen from the following, selected from among the cases studied. It is in this type of case that the social problems involved in deportation become particularly apparent, with the consequent need for international social care. Furthermore, they all demonstrate the length of time for procedure in this type of case.

Henry Hewitt (Case 24).

Henry Hewitt was born in 1898 in London, and lived there until 1920, when he emigrated to Canada and secured work with an insurance company in Montreal. After two years in that city, he married Helen Thompson, who had been born in Lynmouth, England in 1902 but had gone to Canada at the age of three with her parents.

Two days after their marriage, Mr. Hewitt lost his position, and was unable to get another, so his wife supported him for six months. Then she found a position for him as salesman with a large Montreal store where she too was working, but he remained only a few days and soon thereafter, Mr. and Mrs. Hewitt went to the United States and were admitted on November 1, 1923 as temporary visitors.

They went to New York immediately and both secured work at a 5 and 10 cent store. After about a month, Mr. Hewitt lost his position, and they moved to New Jersey, where he tried work as a carpet salesman, then longshoreman, without success at either. While they were there, a baby was born in the Jersey City Hospital, Mrs. Hewitt, being a free patient at the time. After several changes of work and one forced change of residence because of non-payment of rent, the family managed to finance a move to Jacksonville, Fla.

They arrived there with the baby on December 22, 1924, and soon thereafter Mr. Hewitt began the same story of irregular work. So a year and a half later, Mrs. Hewitt left him, taking the baby with her, and going to live with an American who deserted his own wife and two children for her. Almost immediately he was arrested and Mrs. Hewitt was taken by the Duval County Welfare Board, who also cared for the little girl and placed it with the Children's Home Society. One day Mr. Hewitt went and took the child away, and placed her with someone to board, telling Mrs. Hewitt he would not let her see the child unless she returned to him. She refused and said he had never taken care of either her or the child and said she wanted to divorce him, but that the only reason she had gone off with another man was because she "was tired of going hungry."

Mr. Hewitt was meanwhile out of work again and receiving emergency relief from the County Welfare Board. He received this relief intermittently from January to April, 1925, and at times did some work for a grocery store. He had reported his wife's desertion to the police, who reported her to the immigration authorities.

Warrants of arrest were issued on October 11, 1925 for both Mr. and Mrs. Hewitt, but of course it was impossible to issue them for their American-born child, Margaret. They were both detained in the Duval County Jail, but Margaret was cared for by the Children's Home Society, to whom she had been returned. On October 12, a hearing was given Mrs. Hewitt at the jail, and two days later her husband was given one. On October 24th, Mrs. Hewitt's mother came from Canada to Jacksonville and requested the immigration authorities to allow her daughter and grandchild to return to Canada. In view of the history of non-support of her husband, Mrs. Hewitt was allowed to return to Montreal with her mother, and Canada accepted Margaret too.

Meanwhile, Mr. Hewitt remained in jail. A warrant for his deportation was issued on December 19, on the grounds that he was liable to become a public charge at the time of entry and that he had become a public charge, etc. An attempt had been made to deport him to Canada, but he had lost domicile there, so deportation was directed to England at government expense. The British Consulate was notified January 8, 1926 that he was being deported, as he had been deported December 31, 1925.

Ole Hanson (Case 25).

Ole Hanson was born in Norway in 1903 and lived in the small town where he was born until 1923 when he emigrated to the United States and was admitted on primary inspection as a quota immigrant. He went immediately west to Washington and secured work in a logging camp, where he stayed until June, 1924, when he developed a cough. He continued to work, however, and by August had a pain in his right side. He saw a physician, but no diagnosis was made and he remained in the logging camp until December, 1924.

He then went to Seattle, where a doctor told him he had moderately advanced tuberculosis, and so he was admitted to a state sanitorium on March 12, 1925. On June 11 of that year he was reported to the immigration authorities, with the statement: " He has moderately advanced tuberculosis, now involving the upper and lower left lobe of his lung. He has been here three months and is greatly improved, but for some years he cannot work. He has no means." As to whether or not the disease occurred subsequent to entry, the report continued: " Pulmonary tuberculosis is an infection acquired in childhood, developing as pulmonary tuberculosis in adult life. I am of the opinion that he had tuberculosis when he came although the symptoms did not appear until June, 1924. . . . We know that tuberculosis trouble develops slowly, is extensive, and involvement is the chronic type widely distributed, and must be of some years standing."

A warrant of arrest was issued on grounds of " L. P. C." and that he was a public charge, etc. just two months after the case was reported to the immigration officials, and the hearing held on August 24th. Mr. Hanson stated " I should like to go back. I have no folks here. I cannot work."

The warrant of deportation was issued October 31, 1925, with the charges the same as on that of arrest. Mr. Hanson was then sent to New York on November 7th, remaining at Ellis Island until his deportation on November 15 at the expense of the steamship company bringing him.

Miguel Joaquin (Case 26).

Miguel Joaquin was born in 1903 in Lisbon, Portugal. He lived there with his father and paternal aunt, as his mother did not live with his father. In 1913 his father came to the United States, leaving him with his aunt.

In April, 1921, the boy came to this country to join his father, but had been here only eight months, when he was committed to a reform school near Providence where his father was living. He was released, but three times after that was returned for being a " thief and a vagrant ", and each time it was recommended that he be transferred to the Exeter School for the Feeble-Minded.

On July 15, 1925, his admission to that school took place, and he was certified as a " moron, with criminal tendencies ". He was reported by the school to the immigration authorities on August 6, and a warrant of arrest for him was issued on August 18th. A hearing was held at the school on October 14, and there a social worker for the school testified that she had talked with Mr. Joaquin, who was willing to have the boy returned to Portugal and for that reason the inspector did not interview the father.

A warrant of deportation was issued October 26, 1925, the charges being the same as those on the warrant of arrest,—that the boy was " L. P. C.", that he had become a public charge, etc., and that he was feeble-minded at the time of entry. He was deported on November 12, 1925, at the expense of the line bringing him to the country. He landed at Lisbon, November 23, was signed for by a police officer and sent to the police station there.

Maria Prezzo (Case 27).

Maria Prezzo was born in 1881 near Naples, Italy. She was married in 1898 to Giuseppe Rocco, who emigrated to the United States in 1902, leaving her at home. Soon after his departure, a son, Giovanni, was born.

In 1921 Mrs. Rocco and her son came to the United States to join Mr. Rocco. They arrived in New York, were admitted on primary inspection, and went immediately to join Mr. Rocco in Erie, Pa.

On July 23, 1923, a child, Catarina, was born in Erie. On February 23, 1925, Mr. Rocco died, and soon afterward Mrs. Rocco applied to the Erie Associated Charities for aid. Her son Giovanni had heart trouble and could not work steadily enough to support his mother and sister.

On August 14, the Erie Associated Charities reported the case to the bureau of immigration and warrants of arrest were issued on September 22nd, on the grounds that Mrs. Rocco was liable to become a public charge at the time of entry, and that Giovanni, who had received free hospital care, had become a public charge, etc. Both Mrs. Rocco and her son were released on their own recognizance, as both wanted to return to Italy. The hearing was held at their home on October 29, through an interpreter. Warrants of deportation were issued on December 3, with the same charges contained in the warrants of arrest.

Mrs. Rocco and Giovanni were deported January 1, 1926 at the expense of the steamship line. They took with them Catarina, the American-born child, whose expenses were paid by the Directors of the Poor in Erie.

Margaret O'Connell (Case 28).

Margaret O'Connell was born in 1902 in southern Ireland, where her parents, three sisters and three brothers lived until one sister emigrated to the United States to be with an aunt in Michigan.

Miss O'Connell went to Dublin at the age of 17 and began to work in a department store, but left because she became despondent and annoyed at meeting people. She went to England. There she worked as a barmaid four months. Then she returned home, where she stayed a year. In 1922 she decided to join her sister in the United States, coming with an aunt who was returning here after a visit to Ireland.

On reaching the United States, Miss O'Connell was admitted on primary inspection and secured work in a hospital. She soon gave it up as she felt it was too hard, and decided to go to Michigan, where she had another aunt. Miss O'Connell began to work as a domestic servant near her aunt's home in Detroit, but before long met a man by whom she became pregnant. The child was born in the Herman Kiefer Hospital in Detroit, on February 26, 1925, but was taken by the sisters of St. Vincent de Paul and immediately put in their orphanage.

Apparently the fact of having given birth to an illegitimate child worried her so greatly that it was a contributing cause in her admission to the Pontiac State Hospital, with a diagnosis of dementia praecox, on May 25, 1925. On June 16, the case was reported by the hospital to the immigration officials, and a warrant of arrest was issued July 24, 1925, on the grounds that Miss O'Connell was liable to become a public charge at the time of entry and that she had become one within five years, etc.

She was given a hearing on August 10, at the hospital, with her aunt and sister testifying as follows: (Sister) "The greater part of our family are over here now. My mother will be coming soon, my father has just arrived, and it would be a hardship to send her back. I am willing to help out; pay her expenses." (Aunt) "She should not have been sent to the hospital. If I had known it she would not have become a public charge. I am willing to take her out and provide for her. If she is sent back to Ireland the baby will become a public charge."

The warrant of deportation was issued October 3, 1925, with the same charges as in the warrant of arrest. Miss O'Connell was deported November 10, at the expense of the steamship company bringing her. Her American-born child was left here.

Arturo Cucetti (Case 29).

Arturo Cucetti was born in 1893 near Milan, Italy, where he lived, working as a weaver until he decided to emigrate. On December 23, 1920 he landed in New York and was admitted on primary inspection, and then went immediately to St. Louis, where a cousin lived.

Mr. Cucetti worked as a laborer until February 16, 1925, when he was admitted to the St. Louis City Hospital. Five days later the case was reported to the immigration authorities and a warrant of arrest was issued on the 23rd of the month. On the report from the hospital it was stated that Mr. Cucetti was suffering from "evident dementia praecox and alcoholic hallucinations", but that it was not known whether or not the disability arose subsequent to entry. The report continued: "Since entering the hospital, the patient has cleared somewhat; however, his manner is irritable; his replies give one the impression of anger due to the fact that he does not speak English well. Satisfactory mental examination is difficult to obtain."

A hearing was given Mr. Cucetti at the hospital on February 27th, with an interpreter. On March 16th a warrant of deportation was issued on the same grounds as the warrant of arrest, that he was (1) "L. P. C.", (2) afflicted with chronic alcholism at the time of entry (3) a public charge within five years after entry, etc.

Two days after the issuance of the warrant of deportation, the St. Louis district director of immigration wrote the bureau that the Italian consul in St. Louis had filed a certificate, signed by two doctors, stating that a physical examination disclosed no "organic disease of the central nervous system or otherwise" and that Mr. Cucetti was at that time free of any definite disease. So the Italian consul was reluctant to grant an extension on Mr. Cucetti's Italian passport and to receive him.

Furthermore, the congressman from the district wired the bureau concerning Mr. Cucetti's desirability and requested a stay of deportation pending investigation. But the case was brought before the board of review on March 27th and there it was recommended that all the charges be sustained. Three days later, the district director in St. Louis wrote the bureau that the hospital had changed its original diagnosis and the Italian consul had refused to extend Mr. Cucetti's passport. On April 9th, a lawyer engaged by Mr. Cucetti wrote the bureau requesting a new examination by physicians of the U. S. public health service.

On April 13th, the board of review re-opened their hearing and again recommended that the charges be sustained and Mr. Cucetti be deported. On April 15th a letter was received from the congressman interested, asking for reexamination, and on April 30 the board of review again recommended deportation, stating that the latest certificate from the hospital did not conflict with any of the three charges calling for Mr. Cucetti's deportation. However, the request for reexamination was granted "in view of the interest of the congressman, the request of the lawyer."

The bureau received a wire on May 14 saying that Mr. Cucetti had been placed in a government hospital for observation and that the public health service officials stated there was no sign of dementia praecox. The public health service appointed a board of physicians to pass on the case. They stated that Mr. Cucetti was " not now suffering from any psychosis, either alcoholic or otherwise. History admitted by Cucetti . . . shows that he has used alcohol excessively at times. We found no evidence, however, of dementia praecox. It was the opinion of the admitting physician at the St. Louis City Hospital that he was suffering from acute alcoholism at the time of his admission February 16, 1925. From his history we may infer that Cucetti will be a useful citizen provided that he abstains from the use of alcohol."

The case came before the board of review once more on June 22nd but there the evidence was brought out by the recommendation of the district director that Mr. Cucetti had been a public charge in the St. Louis City Hospital for ten weeks. Furthermore, there was " nothing in the medical or other evidence that the conclusions that the alien is afflicted with chronic alcoholism was liable to become a public charge at the time of entry is not wholly justified. Neither is there any showing that the cause of becoming a public charge for a few months arose subsequent to entry."

Meanwhile, the City Hospital would not keep Mr. Cucetti, and he was released from the custody of the immigration officials on a bond of $1000. On July 14, the same congressman wired the bureau stating Mr. Cucetti was employed and that he appealed for the order of deportation to be rescinded. However, three days before the telegram was received, Mr. Cucetti had been sent to Chicago from St. Louis, and on to New York the next day. He was deported July 15, 1925, at the expense of the steamship line which had brought him. To the end, he protested his deportation and felt it was all caused by a cousin who wanted to make trouble for him.

On only one other of the cases was a private practitioner called in to testify concerning the condition of a public charge:

Catherine Aron (Case 30).

Catherine Aron was born in 1898 (or 1899) in what is now Czechoslovakia. After finishing common school, she worked in a restaurant for a while but decided to come to the United States to join her sister. She arrived in New York II class on July 12, 1921.

Almost immediately, Miss Aron began to work as a domestic, and remained until January, 1925 when she began to "act queerly", so her sister took her to Bellevue Hospital on February 12, 1925 and two weeks later she was admitted to Central Islip Hospital, where a diagnosis was made of *manic depressive insanity, manic type.*

On April 24, 1925, the hospital reported her for deportation and on May 23, the immigration service issued a warrant for her arrest. Just two months later, Miss Aron was given a hearing, but as she stated she wished a lawyer, the hearing was postponed until August 3rd, to give time to secure legal advice. At that time, Miss Aron's sister and the lawyer testified.

Ten days later the lawyer submitted a brief, stating there was no history of insanity in the family, and requesting an examination by a reputable private physician. On September 10 this examination was given, with the report that Miss Aron had suffered from a "mild attack of manic depressive psychosis, induced by great worry over the ill health of her mother and brother to whose support she could not contribute. She could be paroled to her sister and with suitable care would never have a recurrence."

The board of review took up the case on September 25, and there it was stated: "In view of the conflict between the state certificate and the certificate of the private practitioner, the official certificate of the institution in which the alien is confined, should be accepted." A warrant of deportation was issued five days later, on the grounds (1) L. P. C., (2) public charge, etc., (3) that Miss Aron was a person of constitutionally psychopathic inferiority at the time of entry.

Miss Aron had her "first papers," dated June 26, 1924. She also had $500 saved in a savings bank, but of this $200 was paid to the doctor for examination and $200 was used for a dentist bill she had owed. What happened to the other $100 is not shown on the record.

On December 29, 1925, the Czechoslovak consulate in New York was notified of deportation, and Miss Aron was deported on January 1, 1926 at the expense of the line which had brought her. No report was on the record of her condition or delivery at her destination.

Two of the cases in New York state contained testimony that the relatives were each paying $7.00 a week maintenance at a state hospital, and would have paid more if more had been requested of them. Nevertheless deportation took place on the grounds of having become a public charge, etc.

Adelaide Davis (Case 31).

Adelaide Davis was born in 1907 in Manchester, England, and lived with an aunt during her childhood. At the age of 17, she decided to emigrate to the United States, to be with an uncle in Chicago.

She landed in Boston on November 3, 1924, and was admitted on primary inspection as a quota immigrant. She went immediately to her uncle in Chicago, but as he died within a few months of her arrival, she left and took a room in a boarding-house and worked in a factory. After about a month, she began to work as a maid in a large hotel, and there became intimate with a waiter, from whom she probably contracted venereal disease. So she was admitted to the Cook County Hospital for three weeks treatment; from there she was sent to the House of the Good Shepherd, where she was kept and treated for two months.

It is unknown by whom she was reported to the immigration service, but a warrant for her arrest was issued August 13, 1925, by wire, followed the next day by a formal warrant. She was kept at the House of the Good Shepherd, to prevent being sent to the county jail, but the immigration service paid her expenses (55 cents a day) there. On August 20, Miss Davis was given a hearing, and there she stated it would be better for her to go back to her aunt in England. The record contains the report of a psychologist of the Juvenile Protective Association that Miss Davis had an age of 18, but a mental age of 9 years and 7 months and an I. Q. of 60 on the Stanford-Binet tests, so that her mental status was that of a medium moron.

On August 29, a warrant for Miss Davis' deportation was issued on the grounds (1) "L. P. C.", (2) Public charge, etc., (3) that she was feeble-minded at the time of entry. She was sent to Ellis Island on August 29, and on September 3rd the British Consulate in New York was informed that her deportation would take place two days later. She was then deported at the expense of the steamship company who brought her. She was destined to her aunt, but there is no record of her arrival there.

Adele Müller (Case 32).

Adele Müller was born in 1902 in Baden, Germany. After leaving school, she began to work in a factory. While she was working there, she began to have epileptic seizures, and had them periodically after 1924. She felt her health might be better in the United States, so arrived in New York on January 3, 1925, and was admitted on primary inspection as a quota immigrant, destined to her aunt in Buffalo.

Miss Müller secured work as a domestic, and remained six months in one position, then took another. On September 10, 1925, she was arrested for shoplifting stockings in a Buffalo department store. She denied the charge to the policeman who arrested her, but the judge committed her to the county jail to await deportation proceedings.

After 5 days in the county jail, the county superintendent ordered her sent to the Buffalo State Hospital as an epileptic whom it was unwise to keep in jail. She was admitted to the hospital on September 15, and an immediate diagnosis of epilepsy was made. That day she was reported to the immigration officials by the superintendent of the poor, and a warrant was issued for her arrest on October 8, 1925.

Miss Müller was given a hearing on October 10, with the inspector acting as interpreter. A warrant of deportation was issued October 27, on the grounds of (1) "L. P. C.", (2) public charge, etc., (3) that she was an epileptic at the time of entry. She was detained at the hospital until November 1st, when she was sent to Ellis Island, and deported on the 7th, at the expense of the steamship line which had brought her. The captain of the boat reported that she had an attendant all day and all night and that she had had three epileptic seizures on the way home. She landed in Bremen on November 20, 1925, and was signed for by the local authorities who were to take her to Ludwigshaven, where her parents are living.

CONCLUSIONS

There are many and varied methods of reporting cases of alien public charges in state institutions to the United States immigration service. There is need for careful and exact study of the different methods of reporting and of the length of time before the immigration service acts on the reports of public-charge cases from different states, to the end that there may be some correlation in methods of procedure and more understanding between the state and federal governments as to what both are doing. In this connection, the varying use of the same terms by different states should be noted, as for instance "constitutional psychopathic inferiority." Some states are inclined to use this term as a catch-all for insane public charges, in the same way that immigration officers use "L.P.C." to denote a kind of vague undesirability. There is need for care in its use and adherence to definite psychiatric standards of definition.

There is no doubt but that in several ways an *impasse* has been reached between the state and federal governments in regard to alien public charges. Chief among the problems is that of cost of maintenance. If a person completely pays all the charges asked of him by the state, he can do no more.

In some localities, the only hospital available for care is a public one, and it seems that a person in such an institution paying all that he is asked should not be considered a public charge by any state.

Further attention should be given the matter of federal payment for aliens in state institutions. As immigration regulation is in the hands of the federal government, and as deportation is a part of that problem of regulation, it would not seem unreasonable to demand that the federal government assume the burden of expense of at least such aliens as have not been here over five years before becoming public charges from causes not shown to have arisen since landing and who are therefore deportable. There will then be unified responsibility without divided authority for such cases. There is a further possibility that some day international cooperation will so far have developed that nations will pay the expenses of their citizens who have become public charges in other countries, when the reason for becoming such has not arisen subsequent to leaving the home country. But that day is so far distant that more immediate practical problems are to be faced in connection with international cooperation regarding deportation.

There is particular ground for international misunderstanding in the removal of ill or insane from the United States to other countries. There is pressing need for study in Europe of what has happened in a number of cases of repatriation of such deportees from the United States,[1] so that the way may be opened to further international cooperation in their care. It is certain that the government of the country to which the deportee is to be returned should be notified at the earliest possible moment not only of the

[1] The files of the International Migration Service contain information on this subject, but there is need for a definite study of the repatriation procedure and facilities of various countries.

need for passport but of particulars of the person's condition so that plans may be made in advance of his arrival for adequate care. It is of course necessary that the forms providing special care in transportation of ill and insane be followed in the most careful and painstaking way but it is not enough that such people be merely signed for and dumped. Plans for their adequate care on arrival must be made and carried out, for the international problem is a greater one than alone ridding the United States of ill and insane, important as that may be from the national point of view.

In this connection, the practice of states within the United States should be remembered. Little is known about the varying practices of state removals to other countries and there is need for study of what is done by different states and how they do it, for here state practice touches international relations in a little-understood way. Yet states remove only those willing to go. Perhaps that idea will pave the way for the future of federal practice.

CHAPTER V

Criminals Involved in "Moral Turpitude"

WHAT IS MORAL TURPITUDE?

A NOTORIETY such as has befallen few sections of the immigration law was acquired by the words "moral turpitude" when during the winter of 1926 an attempt was made to order Countess Vera Cathcart excluded from the United States because she admitted the commission of a crime involving moral turpitude previous to her entry here, whereas the Earl of Craven, the other party to the crime, had omitted to mention the facts which the Countess Cathcart saw fit to disclose and so had already quietly entered the country. Whatever the merits of that particular case, it added geographical definition of moral turpitude to the already bewildering list of interpretations of that vaguest of phrases, and served to focus attention on this particular part of the law.[1]

The early history of the United States shows the country to have been a refuge for those driven from their own countries by political oppression. With political refugees came a crowd of convicts of less desirable qualifications for the

[1] The court did not uphold the immigration officials in their attempt to exclude the Countess on the ground that her previous adultery in South Africa involved moral turpitude. It was held that she was not within the prohibition of the statute as adultery was not a crime in South Africa. Matter of Cathcart, 10 Misc. Dockets, S. D. N. Y. 335 (1926). *Vide* also *New York Times*, Feb. 10, 1926, at 1, and *idem.*, March 6, 1926, at 1. The court did not decide the question whether adultery was a crime involving moral turpitude but turned its attention to the position of adultery under South African law.

upbuilding of the country.[1] The framers of the immigration law were faced with the problem of excluding the really undesirable and yet letting into the "asylum for all oppressed" those who were mere political convicts in the countries from which they came. The early immigration act of March 3, 1875 prohibited the importation of alien convicts, while the general immigration law of August 3, 1882 provided that "all foreign convicts except those convicted of political offenses, upon arrival, shall be sent back to the nations to which they belong and from whence they came." [2] By 1891, humanitarian friends of the politically oppressed in other countries had hit upon the happy thought of preventing exclusion for commission of mere political crimes by inserting the "moral turpitude" phrase in the law of that year. Thus, among those excluded were "persons who had been convicted of a felony or other infamous crime or misdemeanor involving moral turpitude." But it was explicitly stated that "nothing in this act shall be construed to apply to or exclude persons convicted of a political offense, notwithstanding said political offense may be designated as a 'felony, crime, infamous crime, or misdemeanor involving moral inturpitude' by the laws of the land whence he came or by the court convicting." [3] In that day our national fears had not been actively aroused and we had not yet been led to put up the bars against political radicals. Even anarchists convicted of conspiracy in Russia and ordered to long and desolate exile in Siberia might instead find refuge here.

The chaos engendered by the World War and the subsequent emphasis on the "crime wave" led to an increased development of methods of attack on the criminal, and the

[1] *Vide supra*, p. 35 *et seq.*, 105.

[2] Sec. 4.

[3] Sec. 1.

alien criminal in particular, culminating perhaps during the economic depression of 1930. President Hoover in his message to Congress on December 2, 1930 called attention to the need for " strengthening our deportation laws so as to more fully rid ourselves of criminal aliens." He was followed by the Secretary of Labor, who on December 12 of the same year announced that the Department of Labor was undertaking a " thorough investigation into the history of leading underworld figures with a view to their eventual deportation " [1] and was planning to ask Congress for an increased appropriation for an enlarged staff of investigators. Furthermore, cities such as New York and Chicago also began to check up their " public enemies," with a view to deporting those whom it was possible to remove from the country. New York City, for instance, on December 19, 1930 established a new bureau as a part of the detective division in the police department " to round up and investigate all aliens with criminal records to establish possible grounds for deportation." [2] Eight men are assigned to the new bureau, to learn the name, address, date of arrival and port of entry and the circumstances of any crime charged or proved against every one of the 1200-odd aliens arrested yearly by the New York police. Before the establishment of the bureau, there was no special police detail to look into the records of these men so far as immigration laws are concerned. Now, when investigation shows that an alien charged with or proved to have committed a crime is deportable, the information is turned over by the Police Commissioner to the immigration commissioner for action.

[1] *New York Times*, December 12, 1930. It is noteworthy that in this entire statement as quoted in the *Times* the word *alien* does not appear, bu that assumption is made throughout that gangsters and gunmen are *all* aliens.

[2] *New York Times*, Dec. 20, 1930.

The increased emphasis on alien criminals and their possible deportation gives pause for thought as to just what the law is at present and wherein its difficulties lie. First and foremost, there are the problems involved in defining "moral turpitude." This classification inserted in the law from purely humanitarian motives, has become a bugbear to administrative officials and aliens alike. A legion of definitions has been evolved, from Will Rogers' explanation as "telling the truth when you ought not to"[1] to the more legalistic but perhaps no clearer distinction between *malum in se* as against *malum prohibitum*.[2] The plethora of definition but leads one back to the starting point, for if "moral turpitude is anything done contrary to justice, honesty, principle, or good morals; an act of baseness, vileness, depravity in the private and social duties which a man owes to his fellow man, or to society in general, contrary to the accepted and customary rule of right and duty between man and man,"[3] solution is no easier than before because these questions immediately arise: what is contrary to justice, honesty, principle, or good morals, and what constitutes an act of the baseness, vileness or depravity alluded to in the definition? Nor does the solicitor of the Department of Labor clarify the situation very much by excepting from crimes involving moral turpitude "offenses the outcome merely of natural passions, of animal spirits, of infirmity of temper, of weakness of character, or of unstable principles, unaccompanied by vicious motive or corrupt mind."[4]

The slow process of judicial inclusion and exclusion has

[1] *Washington Post*, February 28, 1926.

[2] Distinction is here drawn on the basis of whether or not origin is statutory. 4 Bl. Comm. 8; *vide* State *v.* Trent, 122 Ore. 444, 450; 259 Pac. 893, 898.

[3] *Cyclopædia of Law and Procedure*, vol. xxvii, p. 912.

[4] Quoted, United States *ex rel.* Mongiovi *v.* Karnuth, 30 Fed. (2d) 826.

attempted to prick out a line of definition, but the dots in the line often trace a zig-zag and devious course. It would be impossible to attempt to trace the complete course of explanation reached in the decisions of the various courts, for the number is legion; however, citation of a few of the varying grounds will call attention to the many difficult problems involved in "moral turpitude." An alien convicted of stealing $15 in Massachusetts was held subject to deportation because of conviction of a crime involving moral turpitude, notwithstanding the fact that the crime was one defined as petit larceny and misdemeanor, under the Massachusetts laws, since "theft or larceny was a crime at common law, involving an act intrinsically and morally wrong and not acquiring additional turpitude from being declared unlawful by municipal law."[1] Violation of the Volstead Act also involves moral turpitude[2] whereas violation of a state liquor law does not.[3] A man and woman living together fifteen years, though each was married to another person, had not been convicted of nor did they admit the commission of a crime involving moral turpitude and so were not deportable. The warrant for their deportation which the court refused to uphold "does not find that either has been convicted of, or that he admits, but finds that he did one *or* the other, which is in effect no finding."[4] A similar case arose of a man and woman who had admitted sexual intercourse with each other some eight or ten times, although

[1] Tillinghast *v.* Edmead, 31 Fed. (2d) 81. Circuit Judge Anderson dissented on the ground that the logical result of the majority opinion would be that "a foolish college student stealing a sign would be guilty of moral turpitude."

[2] Riley *v.* Howes, 17 Fed. (2d) 647, reversed on other grounds, 24 Fed. (2d) 686.

[3] United States *ex rel.* Iorio *v.* Day, *U. S. Daily*, Sept. 4, 1929, at 1558 (C. C. A., 2d, 1929).

[4] *Ex parte* Rodriguez, 15 Fed. (2d) 878.

each was married to someone else, but did *not* admit adultery *as such* nor even habitual intercourse, and in the state of Texas, where the man lived, it was held that "mere sexual commerce does not constitute adultery. The act of intimacy must be either while living together or habitual." [1] Therefore, the couple had not committed adultery and so were not guilty of a crime involving moral turpitude.

This case indicates the prime difficulty that moral turpitude may depend on geographical location. This geographical determination of morality became notorious in the Cathcart case. Previously the immigration officials had extended definition to include what would be considered moral turpitude in the United States, regardless of the status of the crime where it was committed. Since the Cathcart case, an alien desirous of entering the country who has committed a crime possibly involving moral turpitude will have his right to enter determined by the status of the crime where committed. It is, however, the status of the crime *when* committed that determines the answer, for even though the crime has been wiped out by pardon, the alien cannot enter.[2] But if the crime committed did not involve moral turpitude where committed, the alien may enter, regardless of the status of the crime in this country. Thus the validity of a marriage ceremony is to be determined by the law of the place where it was performed and the right of a woman to enter the United States depends on the legality of her marriage where it was performed. Such right to enter is a federal question, not dependent on the law of the particular state where her husband may be domiciled.[3]

Once the alien enters and commits a crime in this country, the status of the crime must be determined by the statutes

[1] *Ex parte* Rocha, 30 Fed. (2d) 823.

[2] *Vide infra*, p. 176.

[3] *Ex parte* Suzanna, 295 Fed. 713; Kane *v.* Johnson, 13 Fed. (2d) 433.

of the state where the crime is committed.[1] The record of conviction for a crime involving moral turpitude in a state court is conclusive evidence of the crime.[2] This geographical factor in morality is of interest in connection with assault and battery, for apparently in Pennsylvania moral turpitude is not implied in a charge of aggravated assault and battery [3] while in New York it is so implied.

How has this much used and much abused term come into being? The following note from the *Harvard Law Review* [4] interestingly suggests the history and development of the term:

At common law this term was rarely used [5] to distinguish

[1] United States *ex rel.* Mongiovi *v.* Karnuth, 30 Fed. (2d) 825. In this case the court held that in New York State manslaughter in the second degree does not involve moral turpitude, as it does "not include evil intent or commission of an act wilfully or designedly, and includes an act resulting in death without design to injure or affect death."

[2] United States *ex rel.* Castro *v.* Williams, 203 Fed. 155; Hawes *v.* Tozer, 3 Fed. (2d) 849; Tillinghast *v.* Edmead, 31 Fed. (2d) 81.

[3] United States *ex rel.* Griffo *v.* McCandless, 28 Fed. (2d) 287; Ciambelli *ex rel.* Maranci *v.* Johnston, 12 Fed. (2d) 465; United States *ex rel.* Mazillo *v.* Day, 15 Fed. (2d) 391; United States *ex rel.* Morlacci *v.* Smith, 8 Fed. (2d) 663; Weedin *v.* Tayokichi Yamada, 4 Fed. (2d) 455, reversing *Ex parte* Tayokichi Yamada, 300 Fed. 248.

[4] Vol. 43, p. 117, November, 1929.

[5] No English case using the phrase has been found. But *cf.* "Partialitie in a Judge is a Turpitude which doth soyle and stayne all the actions done by him." Coke, Speech and Charge (at the Assises in Norwich, 1606), (1607)5. In the United States, the term was first used in defining slander. Brooker *v.* Coffin, 5 Johns, 188 (N. Y. 1809) (to call the plaintiff a prostitute does not charge her with a crime involving moral turpitude). But this use has apparently not reached England. *Cf.* Odgers, *Libel and Slander* (5th ed., 1911), pp. 38-51. The phrase has had a limited popularity in quasi-contractual law. Courts which ordinarily rejected the rule of Britton *v.* Turner, 6 N. H. 461, allowing an employee discharged for cause to recover the reasonable value of services already performed, did permit recovery if the discharge was not for a cause involving moral turpitude. Lindner *v.* Cape Brewery Ice Co., 131 Mo. App.

between more and less heinous crimes. The classifications in vogue included felony [1] and misdemeanor, crimes mala in se and mala prohibita,[2] crimen falsi,[3] and infamous crimes.[4] Uncertain connotation, conflicting precedent, and unsuccessful redefinition made these categories objectionable. Legislators called upon to draft civil statutes that referred to criminal offenses needed a classification less tenuous. Instead of cataloguing the separate crimes at which their enactments were directed, they employed the general term, "crimes involving moral turpitude." It is not clear whether this established a new criterion, or was merely a synthesis of previously recognized distinctions; [5] at any rate, the phrase has been widely employed, in legislation dealing with immigration . . . [6]

Almost all courts have construed the words as embracing every form of stealing. Larceny,[7] embezzlement,[8] burglary,[9]

680, 11 S. W. 600. Another line of decisions allowed a person who had transferred property under an unlawful contract to recover it if the contract did not involve moral turpitude. Pullman Palace-Car Co. *v.* Central Trans. Co., 65 Fed. 158. Cases are collected in note, L. R. A. 1917 A, 1026.

[1] (Note in *Harvard Law Review* article omitted.)

[2] (Note in *Harvard Law Review* article omitted.)

[3] (Note in *Harvard Law Review* article omitted.)

[4] (Note in *Harvard Law Review* article omitted.)

[5] See United States *ex rel.* Griffo *v.* McCandless, 28 Fed. (2d), 287, 288. But see Bartos *v.* United States Dist. Ct., 19 Fed. (2d) 722, 724.

[6] 39 Stat. 875 (1917), 8 U. S. C., § 136 (1926) (exclusion of aliens). 39 Stat. 879 (1917), 8 U. S. C., § 155 (1926) (deportation of aliens).

[7] United States *ex rel.* Ulrich *v.* Kellogg, 30 Fed. (2d) 984 (1929) (alien excluded); Tillinghast *v.* Edmead, *supra,* note (alien deported); *In re* Henry, 15 Idaho, 755, 99 Pac. 1054 (attorney disbarred); Jones *v.* Brinkley, 174 N. C. 23, 24, 93 S. E. 372, 373 (slander); Pendergraft *v.* State, 296 S. W. 885 (Tex. Cr. App 1927) (witness impeached).

[8] *In re* Turner, 104 Wash. 276, 176 Pac. 332 (attorney disbarred); *In re* Cruickshank, 47 Cal. App. 496, 190 Pac. 1038 (same); *cf.* State *v.* Anderson, 117 Kan. 117, 230 Pac. 315 (official ousted for using public funds for private benefit).

[9] Drazen *v.* New Haven Taxicab Co., 95 Conn. 500, 111 Atl. 861, 862.

receiving stolen property,[1] obtaining money under false pretenses,[2] conspiring to defraud,[3] and issuing a check without funds,[4] are all crimes involving moral turpitude. Only an occasional dissent has philosophically suggested that in an acquisitive society the immorality of those who commit petit larceny may be debatable.[5] There is also unanimity in condemning various forms of false swearing; it involves moral turpitude not only to commit perjury,[6] but to file consciously false information with the income tax department,[7] the pension office,[8] the comptroller of the currency,[9] officials in charge of military exemptions,[10] and trustees in bankruptcy. This line of decisions simply duplicates the list of wrongs denominated *crimen falsi* at common law.

Numerous cases defining moral turpitude are concerned with those crimes to which the older terminologies were badly adjusted. Whether or not it involves moral turpitude to assault with a deadly weapon depends on the jurisdiction.[11] And al-

[1] *In re* Thompson, 37 Cal. 344, 174 Pac 86 (attorney disbarred); *In re* Kirby, 10 S. D. 322, 73 N. W. 92 (same).

[2] State *v.* Guyer, 91 Vt. 290, 100 Atl. 113 (witness impeached).

[3] *In re* Williams, 64 Okla 316, 167 Pac. 1149 (attorney disbarred).

[4] United States *ex rel.* Portada *v.* Day, 16 Fed. (2d) 328 (alien deported).

[5] See Anderson, J., dissenting, in Tillinghast *v.* Edmead, *supra*, note.

[6] Kaneda *v.* United States, 278 Fed. 692 (alien excluded); *In re* O'Keefe, 55 Mont. 200, 175 Pac. 593 (attorney disbarred).

[7] *In re* Diesen, 173 Minn. 297, 217 N. W. 356 (attorney disbarred).

[8] *In re* Hopkins, 54 Wash. 569, 103 Pac. 805 (attorney disbarred).

[9] *In re* Peters, 73 Mont. 284, 235 Pac. 772 (attorney disbarred).

[10] *In re* Wiltse, 109 Wash. 261, 186 Pac. 848 (attorney disbarred).

[11] In the following cases aliens were deported for assaults: United States *ex rel.* Mazzillo *v.* Day, 15 Fed. (2d) 391; United States *ex rel.* Morlacci *v.* Smith, 8 Fed. (2d) 663; Weedin *v.* Tayokichi Yamada, 4 Fed. (2d) 455, reversing *Ex parte* Tayokichi Yamada, 300 Fed. 248. *Contra:* Ciambelli *ex rel.* Maranci *v.* Johnson, 12 Fed. (2d) 465; United States *ex rel.* Griffo *v.* McCandless, *supra*, note. *Cf.* United States *ex rel.* Mongiovi *v.* Karnuth, 30 Fed. (2d) 825.

though in most communities commercial vice[1] and rape[2] are regarded as obloquious, it is uncertain whether fornication, adultery[3] and bigamy[4] are. Decisions dealing with violations of liquor statutes but demonstrate the geographical variability of morals.[5] A few war-time cases held that interference with the military branches of government involved moral turpitude . . .[6]

But it is in the Immigration Act that the phraseology seems most unfortunate. . . . Though proceedings under the act are not criminal,[7] they are in their nature penal. Men who are

[1] Dossett *v.* State, 94 Tex. Cr. Rep. 145, 249 S. W. 1048 (bawdy-house keeper impeached as witness). This aspect of the problem is not raised by the Immigration Act, since prostitutes, procurers and pimps are not specifically dealt with. 39 Stat. 875, 889, 8 U. S. C., § 136g, § 155.

[2] Bendel *v.* Nagle, 17 Fed. (2d) 719 (alien excluded for rape); Siniscalchi *v.* Thomas, 195 Fed. 701 (alien excluded for rape).

[3] *Ex parte* Rocha, *supra,* note (alien not deported for fornication not shown to be contrary to statute); *Ex parte* Isojoki, 222 Fed. 151 (alien not deported for fornication, not amounting to prostitution); United States *ex rel.* Huber *v.* Sibray, 178 Fed. 150, reversed on other grounds, 185 Fed. 401 (alien not deported for fornication); *cf.* Matter of Cathcart, *supra,* note. *Contra:* Morrison *v.* State, 85 Tex. Cr. Rep. 20, 209 S. W. 742 (witness impeached for adultery); *Ex parte* Rodriquez, 15 Fed. (2d) 878, 879 (alien deported for adultery).

[4] United States *ex rel.* Rennie *v.* Brooks, 284 Fed. 908 (alien deported); United States *ex rel.* Rosen *v.* Williams, 200 Fed. 538, certiorari denied sub. nom. Rosen *v.* Williams, 232 U. S. 722 (same). But see Wong Yow *v.* Weedin, 33 Fed. (2d) 377, 378.

[5] In the following cases violation of a liquor statute was held to involve turpitude: Roussean *v.* Weedin, 284 Fed. 565 (alien deported); Riley *v.* Howes, *supra,* note (same); Rudolph *v.* United States *ex rel.* Rock, 55 App. D. C. 362, 6 Fed. (2d) 487 (pension discontinued); State *v.* Bieber, 121 Kan. 536, 247 Pac. 875 (attorney disbarred); State *ex rel.* Young *v.* Edmunsen, 103 Ore. 243, 204 Pac. 619 (same). *Contra:* United States *ex rel.* Iorio *v.* Day, *supra,* note (alien not deported); Coykendall *v.* Skrmetta, 22 Fed. (2d) 120, affirming 16 Fed. (2d) 783 (same); Bartos *v.* United States Dist. Ct., *supra,* note; Bough *v.* State, 215 Ala. 619, 112 So. 157 (witness held not impeachable).

[6] Matter of O'Connell, 184 Cal. 584, 194 Pac. 1010; *In re* Hofstede, 31 Idaho 448, 173 Pac. 1087; *In re* Kerl, 32 Idaho 737, 188 Pac. 40.

[7] E. g. Mahler *v.* Eby, 264 U. S. 32; Bilokumsky *v.* Tod, 263 U. S. 149; Zakonaite *v.* Wolf, 226 U. S. 272.

menaced with the loss of civil rights should know with certainty the possible grounds of forfeiture.[1] And the terminology of moral turpitude hampers uniformity; it is anomalous that for the same offense a person should be deported or excluded in one circuit and not in another. . . .

The conclusion seems inevitable that in the classification of crimes it is perilous and idle to expect an indefinite statutory term to acquire precision by the judicial process of exclusion and inclusion. The legislature can ordinarily better accomplish its purpose by enumerating the proscribed offenses, or by dividing them on the basis of penalty imposed. Either method would replace with a uniform standard the apocalyptic criteria of individual judges.

It would be a well-nigh impossible task to steer an unruffled course amid such shoals of opinion as that conviction for carrying concealed weapons is not for a crime involving moral turpitude,[2] and that in one district, at least, mere assault and battery does not involve commission of such a crime, but assault with a dangerous weapon does.[3]

Interpretation of "moral turpitude" has become enshrouded by an impenetrable mist, so that various attempts have been made to change it. In recent Congressional sessions, bills have been introduced and considered which in a general way eliminate the requirement that a crime involve "moral turpitude" and base the liability to deportation upon a sentence or sentences of imprisonment amounting to the minimum time specified in the bill. For instance, the latest of these proposals was for the deportation of:

An alien who is convicted of any offense (committed after

[1] On the inadvisability of using flexible standards in such a case, see E. Freund, "The Use of Indefinite Terms in Statutes" (1921), 30 *Yale L. J.* 437, 444.

[2] *Ex parte* Saraceno, 182 Fed. 955. Bureau File 53895/121 B.

[3] United States *ex rel.* Morlacci *v.* Smith, 8 Fed. (2d) 663.

the enactment of this Act and at any time after entry) for which he is sentenced to imprisonment for a term of one year or more, and who is thereafter convicted of any offense (committed after the enactment of this act and at any time after entry) for which he is sentenced to imprisonment for a term of one year or more.

An alien who is convicted of any offense (committed after the enactment of this Act and within ten years after entry) for which he is sentenced to imprisonment for a term which, when added to the terms to which sentenced under two or more previous convictions of any offense or offenses (committed after the enactment of this Act), amounts to two years or more.[1]

By 1930 the situation was still unimproved. The Commissioner General of Immigration in 1926 had stated that "the moral turpitude problem is one that has vexed the law officers of the bureau and department for almost 20 years,"[2] while the Secretary of Labor in his 1930 Annual Report again called attention to the fact that

[1] *H. R. 17152*, 71st Congress, 3rd Session, reported to the House on Feb. 10, 1931. Similar legislation had previously been recommended and attempted. *Vide S. 5094*, Union Calendar no. 752, 70th Congress, 2nd Session, and report no. 2418, Committee on Immigration, House of Representatives. *Vide* also report of the Secretary of Labor made on Jan. 6, 1931, on *Sen. Res. no. 355* (Dec. 8, 1930), quoted in *U. S. Daily*, Jan. 7, 1931.

On the other hand, the immigration act of July 3, 1930 (S. 3691) uses the term "moral turpitude" in providing that an American citizen by birth and if he served in the World War, may bring his wife to this country even though she is inadmissible, if their marriage occurred prior to July 3, 1930, and if the offense involving "moral turpitude" which rendered her inadmissible was committed while she was a minor and more than five years before the adoption of the act, and if the sentence of imprisonment imposed for the offense or offenses was for less than three months. Women guilty of serious crimes, prostitutes, polygamists, etc. are excluded from the benefits of the act.

It is probable that the act, which had its inception in a particular case, will not be of wide application.

[2] *Hearings, Deportation Bill of 1926, op. cit.*

[3] Pp. 18-19.

we now have a law for the deportation of criminals if their crimes involve moral turpitude, but it does not reach the great number of aliens who persistently violate other laws, both Federal and State, but who cannot be expelled from the country because it has been held that their offenses are not within the scope of the present law.

An illustration of the type of criminal not covered by the "moral turpitude" provisions of the law is found in the case of a man convicted in 1918 and given three years' maximum sentence for carrying concealed weapons,[1] and again sentenced two years later to two years in the United States penitentiary on conviction for violation of the Harrison Anti-Narcotic Act of December 17, 1914.[2] He was not deportable because neither crime for which he was convicted involved moral turpitude, even though each sentence was for more than a year. Yet under the present law a man in Massachusetts convicted of stealing $15 was held to have committed a crime involving moral turpitude[3] and so was deportable.

If a criminal receives one or more sentences for crimes not involving moral turpitude, committed within five years after entry, the only possibility of his deportation would be on the ground that he was "L.P.C." on entry.. The recent tendency of the courts, however, is to hold that "L.P.C." is not applicable in such cases in general.[4] In no event, of course, would the "L.P.C." provision apply to such crimes if they were committed after the expiration of five years from entry.

[1] *Ex parte* Saraceno, 182 Fed. 955, held that a sentence for carrying concealed weapons did not involve moral turpitude.

[2] United States *ex rel.* Andreacchi *v.* Curran, 38 Fed. (2d) 498, held that violation of this act did not involve moral turpitude, as the act is for revenue only.

[3] Tillinghast *v.* Edmead, 31 Fed. (2d) 81. *Vide supra*, p. 165, note.

[4] Iorio *v.* Day, 34 Fed. (2d) 920; Browne *v.* Zurbrick, 45 Fed. (2d) 931.

However, "moral turpitude" is not the only element of the law pertaining to the deportation of criminals which has provided ample food for controversy. Let us turn to some of those other elements.

THE STATUTE OF LIMITATIONS REGARDING DEPORTATION OF CRIMINALS

There are three important categories of those committing crimes involving "moral turpitude." In the first place, those "who have been convicted of or admit having committed a felony or other crime or misdemeanor involving moral turpitude" are found among the excludable classes. In order that their deportation may take place even after five years, the statute provides the deportation, without time limit after entry, of "any alien who was convicted, or who admits the commission prior to entry, of a felony or other crime or misdemeanor involving moral turpitude."[1] In the second place, any alien sentenced subsequent to May 1, 1917 "to imprisonment for a term of one year or more because of conviction in this country of a crime involving moral turpitude, committed within five years after the entry of the alien to the United States";[2] third, any alien sentenced subsequent to May 1, 1917 "more than once to such a term of imprisonment because of conviction in this country of any crime involving moral turpitude, committed at any time after entry."[3]

Let us consider each category separately. In the first class, those excludable at the time of entry, but from whom the five-year statute of limitations has been removed for deportation, are aliens convicted of a crime involving moral turpitude before their last emigration.[4] Here, too, the defi-

[1] Immigration act of 1917, sec. 19.

[2] *Ibid.* *Ibid.*

[4] United States *ex rel.* Castro *v.* Williams, 203 Fed. 155; Preatue *v.* Stathakos, 192 Fed. 469, and 278 Fed. 694.

nition of " entry " takes its place of importance, as in the case of an alien who came to the United States in 1913, lived here eleven years, was convicted in Minnesota of having concealed assets from a trustee in bankruptcy and sentenced to a prison term of 18 months. As this conviction, eleven years after entry, was the man's only conviction, he was not deportable. However, after serving his sentence, he moved to Buffalo, New York, where he engaged in the taxicab business. One day he transported a company of teachers across the border to a place in Canada and returned the same day, thus becoming liable to deportation for conviction of a crime involving moral turpitude before entering the country, although the commission of the crime and the conviction for it took place *in* the United States, and had he not journeyed across the border in his taxi he would not have been deportable under the present deportation laws.[1]

Whether a crime committed before entry is a felony or misdemeanor is immaterial; that it involves " moral turpitude " is enough, for the statute mentions only that. If the alien was *convicted* before entry, whether or not he admits the commission of the crime, he is excludable from the

[1] United States *ex rel.* Medich *v.* Burmaster, 24 Fed. (2d) 57.

A recent case runs counter to the established definition of entry. " Where an alien who had lawfully entered the United States in the first instance was convicted, after residing in the country for eight years, of taking indecent liberties with a girl 15 years of age, and was not imprisoned but was placed on probation for two years, and where he was regularly employed at a salary of $2,400 both before and after his conviction, he was not subject to deportation, on his subsequent re-entry from Canada after spending ten days of his vacation therein, either on the ground that he was likely to become a public charge, by reason of his prior conviction, or on the ground that he had been convicted of a crime involving moral turpitude, since the commission of the crime was not in itself sufficient to establish his status as a person likely to become a public charge, and conviction, prior to entry, to constitute ground for exclusion, must have been abroad and not in the United States." Browne *v.* Zurbrick, C. C. A. 6, no. 5682, quoted in *U. S. Daily*, Dec. 27, 1930.

United States. Nor is it material whether or not he could be convicted for the same offense in this country.

Even if he were pardoned in the foreign country where the crime was committed, he would still be excludable and deportable after entry, should he succeed in entering. For instance, Nicolo Palermo came to the United States in 1919 at the age of sixty-six and remained until 1924, when he was arrested for deportation to Italy because he had been convicted and sentenced to death there in 1883. The following year the sentence had been commuted to life imprisonment. He had served in Italy from 1884 until 1919, when he was pardoned. When the case of his possible deportation to Italy came to court, it was held that the provisions of the 1917 immigration act referring to pardon were intended to apply only to aliens convicted after entry to the United States, and that Mr. Palermo, at the age of seventy-one, was deportable to Italy.[1]

If a person had not been actually convicted but merely admitted the commission of a crime or misdemeanor of "moral turpitude" before his entry here, he would likewise be inadmissible, and if admitted, deportable within five years.[2] But the admission must be an "unequivocal acknowledgment of guilt, an acknowledgment which shall leave no fair ground for doubt or debate. . . . The . . . evidence that warrants deportation is an unqualified admission, by the alien."[3] Yet if such actual admission is made, the alien

[1] United States *ex rel.* Palermo *v.* Smith, 17 Fed. (2d) 534. *Vide* also Weedin *v.* Tayokichi Yamada, 4 Fed. (2d) 455; Hawes *v.* Tozer, 3 Fed. (2d) 849; United States *v.* Brooks, 284 Fed. 908.

The effect of pardons granted in other countries must not be confused with the provisions in the immigration act of 1917 concerning the effect of pardon in this country. *Vide infra*, p. 185 *et seq.*

[2] United States *ex rel.* Castro *v.* Williams, 203 Fed. 155.

[3] Hawes *v.* Tozer, 3 Fed. (2d) 849. The immigration authorities are

who makes it is liable to deportation. Whether or not he was sentenced has, however, no bearing on the matter. The admission is what counts. Should he refuse to admit the crime of "moral turpitude," there might still be evidence which would tend to show that he was a person liable to become a public charge within five years of entry. As already indicated,[1] the courts have on some occasions held that a person in a prison, jail, or other penal institution is a public charge. Such courts might hold that a person who has served sentence, or committed such a crime in a foreign country, might be apt to become a public charge in the United States by reason of his previous conviction. Other courts have given an opposite interpretation [2] and would not be apt to designate as "L.P.C." a person who refused to admit the commission of such a crime.

It was to this question of *admission* of a crime that the Cathcart case drew attention, and it is here that confusion has become worse confounded. If there is no conviction, it is possible that the "crime" admitted might be such in this country and not in the country where it was committed, or vice versa. To what, then, does the admission refer,—to the commission of an offense which would be regarded as involving "moral turpitude" where it took place, or to an offense which *would* be a crime involving moral turpitude if committed *here*? It has recently been held that the question revolves around how the crime was considered *in the country* where it was committed.

Once a person has been admitted to the country, he may fall in either of the other two classes of those who commit

without jurisdiction to try the question of the alien's guilt or innocence, or to infer his admission against his denial from testimony given by him in another case.

[1] *Ex parte* Fragosa, 11 Fed. (2d) 988. *Vide supra*, pp. 114-115.

[2] Coykendall *v.* Skrmetta, 22 Fed. (2d) 120. *Vide supra*, p. 76.

crimes involving "moral turpitude." If he is sentenced to imprisonment for a term of a year or more[1] because of conviction in this country of such a crime, committed within five years after entry, he may be deported at any time. If he is sentenced more than once to imprisonment for a term of a year or more[2] because convicted in this country of such a crime, committed at any time after entry, he comes under the provisions allowing deportation for more than one such crime committed at any time after entry, no matter how long the offender may have been in this country. This section of the law is not retroactive, and sentences under it can be given only for convictions subsequent to May 1, 1917.

THE SENTENCE

A question further arises over the meaning of one or more sentences for "one year or more." Could a man, sentenced to six months and a fine, who could not afford to pay the fine, but worked it out, so that he would as a matter of fact be in prison a year, be said to be sentenced for "one year"? Here again the alien's deportability may depend on the district in which he lives. In some districts, if a man during his first five years here, received a sentence of six months plus a fine sufficient to constitute a year's sentence for an offense involving moral turpitude, if he worked the sentence out, he would have the equivalent of a year in prison and so be deportable. If the man could pay his fine, he would not be liable to deportation, as the actual sentence would be only for six months. However, the practice varies, and it is common to have an actual sentence of a year imposed as the least which will furnish ground for deportation.

What is the relationship of an indeterminate sentence to

[1] Subsequent to May 1, 1917, § 19, Immigration act, 1917.

[2] *Ibid.*

the requirement of a sentence for "one year or more"? An indeterminate sentence under which the prisoner cannot be released within one year is a sentence for one year or more as regards deportability.[1] In other words, the minimum term to be served must be at least a year. But in general,

> an indeterminate sentence . . . is a sentence for the maximum term prescribed for the offense committed, coupled with a provision which permits but does not require an earlier release . . .[2]

So a prisoner may not as of right demand earlier release than the maximum. Because of the questions involved in time served in indeterminate sentences, it has been proposed to enact a statutory provision that:

> In the case of a sentence for an indeterminate term in which the minimum term under the sentence is less than one year, the term actually served shall be considered the term for which sentenced.[3]

If a judge gives a sentence for a year or more and then suspends sentence for another year, the alien so sentenced may be deported at the expiration of his sentence, if that sentence was imposed within his first five years here or if he had had a previous similar sentence. He cannot be deported if the sentence is indefinitely suspended, unless the sentence is suspended to require deportation.

Furthermore, a designation of separate periods of time under different counts of the same indictment, the second sentence to commence with the expiration of the first, would

[1] United States *ex rel.* Morlacci *v.* Smith, 8 Fed. (2d) 663; United States *ex rel.* Sirtie *v.* Commissioner of Immigration, 6 Fed. (2d) 465; Ciambelli *ex rel.* Maranci *v.* Johnson, 12 Fed. (2d) 465.

[2] State *v.* Page, 57 Pac. 514; Oliver *v.* Oliver, 169 Mass, 592; Murphy *v.* Com., 172 Mass. 264; People *v.* State Reformatory, 148 Ill. 413; State *v.* Wolfer, 119 Minn. 368; State *ex rel.* Petkoff *v.* Reed, 138 Minn. 465.

[3] *H. R. 17152,* sec. 2 (2), 71st Congress, 3rd Session.

constitute not separate sentences but a single aggregate one and would represent but one punishment.[1] Hence, for example, an alien convicted and sentenced under one information charging him in eleven counts with eleven different offenses in statutory arson, would not be subject to deportation, as there would be only *one* act of sentencing, though several sentences might be imposed.

This matter has been discussed in detail in relation to sentences where the terms of confinement for several crimes ran concurrently. A man named Nishimoto entered the United States in 1919, and after more than five years here was charged with issuing five separate fraudulent checks, the issuance of each check constituting a separate felony. He was sentenced to a term in the California state prison on each of the five counts, but the sentences and terms of imprisonment for all five were to run concurrently. Mr. Nishimoto claimed that this constituted but a single sentence, that he therefore had not been sentenced, " more than once " and that since he had lived here more than five years, he was not subject to deportation. The court stated, however, that the fact that the sentences ran concurrently merely meant that the convict was given the privilege of serving a portion of each sentence each day and that, in effect, if he served the sentence, he was discharged at the expiration of the maximum term imposed on any one of the five counts. If, however, the sentence upon each count were of a different length of time, he could not be discharged until he had served the longest sentence of all. Even if the sentences were all of the same length, a pardon upon all but one of the counts would not relieve him from serving the full term imposed upon the count for which no pardon was granted. Last but not least, the statute requiring deportation does not limit the power

[1] United States *v.* Thompson, 202 Fed. 346; United States *ex rel.* Pepe *v.* Johnson, 26 Fed. (2d) 288.

of deportation to a second conviction after five years in the United States but is based on the commission of a number of offenses for which an alien has been sentenced.[1]

Further questions arise concerning the important matter of parole, and here there has been considerable confusion between the state and federal authorities. By 1927 an *impasse* had been reached in this situation as in that of public charges, and the Secretary of Labor called attention to it in his Annual Report:

It was at one time the practice of immigration officers to take into custody and deport aliens sentenced to imprisonment, when such aliens were released on parole, or otherwise than at the termination of imprisonment in a legal sense. In some instances deportations were affected of aliens released on parole where parole was granted for the express purpose of giving the alien into the custody of the local immigration officer. The department is anxious that its machinery be used to its utmost capacity in effecting deportation of these classes, but it must of necessity keep within the wording of the statute. To effect a deportation which is not in accordance with the law is not due process as required by the Constitution of the United States.

The practice has been, and still is, upon being advised of the conviction of an alien under conditions which require deportation at " termination of imprisonment " to serve a warrant of arrest and grant a hearing to the prisoner while in the custody of the penitentiary. After the hearing has been completed and the case reviewed in the department, a warrant of deportation is issued, and nothing further may be heard of the case by the administrative officers until the deportation has been accom-

[1] Nishimoto *v.* Nagle, C. C. A. 9th, no. 6154, Nov. 3, 1930, cited in *U. S. Daily*, Nov. 18, 1930, pp. 7-8. The court stated: "The purpose of Congress undoubtedly was to provide for the deportation of a man who committed more than one offense involving moral turpitude for which he had been convicted and upon which conviction and sentence has been imposed; whether the sentences run concurrently or consecutively is entirely immaterial from the standpoint of the purpose of the law."

plished and the warrant returned satisfied, or a protest against deportation is filed at the time of the alien's release by the prison authorities. Protests have in a few cases been received against the deportation of criminal aliens who had been paroled, on the grounds that a parole did not constitute "termination of imprisonment," as the law requires. The solicitor and courts have held that this interpretation of the law is correct and that a paroled alien may not be deported until the legal termination of imprisonment.

In general the States have been anxious to be rid of alien criminals and have cooperated with the department in bringing this about as speedily as possible. While a parole does not terminate imprisonment, a commutation of sentence does, and the executive authority of most of the States are willing, if deportation is to be effected, to commute the sentence for that purpose when the imprisonment is to be for many years' time. In that way communities are relieved of the burden of caring for these criminals at State expense, and frequently, also, the aliens themselves request that such procedure be followed.

At least one State, however, has officially stated that it expects to defeat deportation of an alien by the granting of pardons for the offenses committed. The counsel for the governor of that State reported to the department that it was the practice to parole prisoners, and in case the prisoner were an alien to consider his case with a view to granting a pardon for the purpose of preventing deportation at the time the sentence was legally completed. It was further stated that, if immigration officers were to take aliens into custody for deportation upon their parole, the governor would be compelled to resort to pardons rather than paroles, but that he disliked to discriminate in favor of the alien as against the citizen. It was intimated, however, that if the department, when these cases were brought to its attention, should fail to stay deportation until the expiration of the period of parole, pardons would be issued to defeat the Federal statute requiring deportation.

Here again it was New York state which proved the

thorn in the flesh of the immigration service. As deportation is not a punishment for crime, the state thought that a paroled alien would still be in the custody of the state, and if the federal government were to take over such an alien, it would not only be taking the person from the power of the state but would also allow deportation to take the place of continuing custody to the state,[1] such as obtains when the person is accountable to state parole officials.

In an attempt to clarify the situation between state and federal authorities, the act of March 4, 1929 provides that

> an alien sentenced to imprisonment shall not be deported under any provision of law until after the termination of the imprisonment . . . the imprisonment shall be considered as terminated upon the release of the alien from confinement, whether or not he is subject to rearrest or further confinement in respect of the same offense.[2]

If imprisonment is terminated upon the release of the alien from confinement, he may be deported as soon as eligible for parole and paroled, for though still under state custody on parole, he is not confined. Here, as often happens, administrative interpretation was written into the statute.

The new act is thus supposed to include answer to the further difficulties involved in the indeterminate sentence. Before its passage, a person sentenced to a term of from one to three years, supposedly was to serve the full length of sentence which he would have to serve if there were no deportation possibility. Thus deportation would not serve to shorten his sentence or make the lot of the alien easier than that of the native-born. However, there was a differ-

[1] United States *v.* Marrin, 227 Fed. 314; Commonwealth *v.* Ramsey, 1 Brewster 422. *Vide* J. Duncan, unpublished memorandum on deportation of aliens within the jurisdiction of the state.

[2] Sec. 3.

ence of opinion between various state and the federal authorities:

Many states have legislation covering indeterminate sentences; that is, defendants are sentenced, for example in New York, to serve from six months to three years for a specified offense. The District Court for the Southern District of New York has held such a sentence to be one of three years within the meaning of the immigration law and that the alien could be deported upon the expiration of his imprisonment.

There are several States, however, where, were the question tried in the courts, we could not with confidence look forward to similar favorable decisions.[1]

Prisoners in federal institutions have until recently been in a somewhat different situation, for an alien in such prison had to remain within the jurisdiction of the court while under parole, and so could not be deported. By act of March 2, 1931,[2] it was provided:

that where a Federal prisoner is an alien and subject to deportation the board of parole may authorize the release of such prisoner after he shall have become eligible for parole on condition that he be deported and remain outside of the United States and all places subject to its jurisdiction, and upon such parole becoming effective said prisoner shall be delivered to the duly authorized immigration official for deportation.

So where an alien federal prisoner becomes eligible for parole, where application for Departmental warrant of arrest is made, formal advice of such action is furnished to the appropriate prison authority, followed subsequently by formal advice as to the decision in the case, and, if deportation is ordered, the date when surrender for deportation under parole may be accepted.[3]

[1] *Hearings, Deportation Bill of 1926, op. cit.*, p. 68.

[2] Public No. 777, 71st Congress, H. R. 9674.

[3] Bureau of immigration, General Order No. 172, March 17, 1931.

THE EFFECT OF PARDON ON DEPORTABILITY

If a foreigner is pardoned for an offense in the United States, his record is completely cleared, for the 1917 immigration act states that the provisions for criminal deportation

> shall not apply to one who has been pardoned, nor shall such deportation be made or directed if the court, or judge thereof, sentencing such alien for such crime shall, at the beginning of imposing judgment or passing sentence or within thirty days thereafter, due notice having first been given to representatives of the State, make recommendation to the Secretary of Labor that the alien shall not be deported in pursuance of this act . . . [1]

A judge may therefore recommend that a man convicted of a crime involving "moral turpitude" be not deported,[2] but the judge's recommendation must be not later than thirty days after sentence, "shall be given a mandatory effect when a right to a person is lost by failure to do an act within a limited time." [3]

Of course, pardons are granted by both federal and state authorities to prevent deportation. During the fiscal year 1930, the President pardoned seven persons convicted for federal crimes, to prevent their deportation. It may be well to examine some of these cases to see in what type of situation the President pardons criminals to save them from being sent out of the country.

A similar power is exercised by the Governor of New York state, for example. In his annual statements he gives a list of pardons issued "after completion of sentence to save from deportation," on the ground "that in the opinion

[1] Sec. 19.

[2] Such recommendation may be made only for crimes involving "moral turpitude". Rodriguez *v.* Campbell, 8 Fed. (2d) 983; United States *ex rel.* Arcara *v.* Flynn, 11 Fed. (2d) 899.

[3] United States *ex rel.* Arcara *v.* Flynn, *supra.*

of the Governor special circumstances existed which were sufficient to induce the removal of this additional punishment." [1] There were seven such pardons in 1929 and nineteen the previous year. The following shows the type:

Joseph Gerani. Convicted in New York county of confessed attempted grand larceny, second degree, and sentenced in June, 1927, to Sing Sing prison for a term of 2 years, 6 months; released in June, 1929 (upon expiration of term).

A pardon was granted in this case by Lieutenant Governor and Acting Governor Herbert H. Lehman, so as to permit Gerani to remain in this country, where he has resided since he was 14 months of age. He married an American citizen and has 2 children. He has no relatives in Italy, and his deportation to that country would not only mean the breaking up of his home, but sending him to a strange country.[2]

If a pardoned alien leaves the United States, he is not liable to exclusion on his return, for it is as if the crime had never been committed.[3]

The pardon, however, must be a definite one, and commutation of sentence will not serve, as it is not pardon.[4]

[1] Message of the Governor, transmitting *Statement of the Pardons, Commutations and Reprieves Granted During the Year 1929*, State of New York Legislative Document (1930), No. 79.

For discussion of the use of the word punishment to refer to deportation, *vide supra*, pp. 45, 69.

[2] *Ibid.*, p. 27.

[3] If he leaves the country under circumstances where his crime has *not* been pardoned, he is excludable on return, as having been convicted of a crime involving moral turpitude prior to entry. This would be the case even if the penalty imposed were less than a year, or if he had resided in this country more than five years before he committed a crime, and his conviction was for only one crime after the expiration of the five-year period.

[4] United States *ex rel.* Brazier *et al.* *v.* Commissioner of Immigration, 5 Fed. (2d) 162. Nor would a *nunc pro tunc* order serve as a bar to deportation.—United States *ex rel.* Klanis *v.* Davis, 13 Fed. (2d) 630. *Vide* Cook and Hagerty, *op. cit.*, p. 140, § 278.

PARDONS TO PREVENT DEPORTATION, 1929–30 [1]

Name	Offense	Sentence and Date	Recommendation of Attorney General
N. Medich	Violation sec. 29 (b), national bankruptcy act.	Jan. 13, 1925. 18 months U. S. penitentiary.	Had completed sentence, wanted for deportation. Resided in U. S. since boyhood and had lost all connection with the country of nativity. Wife and family dependent on him for support and it appeared deportation would cause undue hardship. U. S. attorney recommended favorably. Attorney General advised that pardon be granted to prevent deportation. Granted July 31, 1929.
C. Gib	Possession and concealment of narcotics (2 cases) in violation Harrison Anti-narcotic Act and narcotic drug import and export act.	Jan. 29, 1923. (1) 1 year U. S. penitentiary. (2) Feb. 1, 1923, 11 months. Sentence to run concurrently.	Completed sentence Dec., 1923, and deportation order issued against him. He was 67 years old, had been in U. S. many years, and, except this offense, had, as far as is known, been law-abiding and industrious. U. S. attorney recommended clemency; Dep't of Labor did not oppose it. Attorney General advised full and unconditional pardon. Granted Aug. 2, 1929.
E. Bracho	Stealing from U. S. mails in violation of sec. 194 U. S. C. C.	Jan. 31, 1927. 3½ years in U. S. penitentiary.	Completed sentence and wanted for deportation. His mother, who assisted in his apprehension, pleaded that her son be given another chance. Solicitor of P. O. Department did not object. Attorney General advised full and unconditional pardon to prevent deportation. Granted Nov. 7, 1929.
H. Shibata	Selling and possessing narcotics.	July 16, 1926. 3 years house of correction, Worcester, Mass.	Served term and wanted for deportation. Resident of U. S. for 25 years. Had wife and 3 children who were U. S. citizens and from whom he would be separated if deported. Trial judge and U. S. attorney recommended pardon. Attorney General advised full and unconditional pardon to prevent deportation. Granted Mar. 10, 1930.

[1] *Annual Report of the Attorney General of the United States for,* etc., *1930.* The last case, however, is taken from the 1929 report, p. 334.

S. Bill[1]	Transportation of a stolen motor-cycle interstate.	Sept. 20, 1927. 18 months U. S. penitentiary.	By reason of conviction was subject to deportation. Was about 19 years old, with previous good reputation. His family lived in this country, with no connections elsewhere. Trial judge and the Attorney recommended full and unconditiona. pardon to prevent deportationl Concurred in by Attorney General. Granted Jan. 22, 1929.

The court has stated that no commutation of sentence or liberation on parole could prevent the operation of a general law, and, speaking of an attempt made by the President to commute sentence to prevent deportation, stated:

If these men had served their sentences in full, they would plainly, "if undesirables," be subject to deportation . . . if the Executive by the device of shortening their sentences, subject to executive pleasure at all times, wished by this "cat and mouse" procedure to keep undesirable aliens in this country, it would be beyond Executive power; because such substantial regulation of the status of aliens bears no relation whatever to the constitutional pardoning power as described in the United States Constitution.[2]

While the President may not commute sentences to prevent deportation, he may commute them to *hasten* it, as he often does, and as is shown by the table on the next page.

One case is of particular interest, as it involved both commutation and pardon:

Romeo Forlini was sentenced on September 3, 1925 to 7 years in the United States penitentiary in Atlanta and fined $100 for possessing false obligations of the Italian government, and altering obligations of the United States. When he had nearly

[1] From the 1929 report, p. 334. The other cases are all from the 1930 report.

[2] United States *ex rel.* Brazier, *supra*.

COMMUTATION TO SECURE DEPORTATION [1]

Name	Offense	Sentence and Date	Recommendation of Attorney General
G. Dahlin	Stealing and transporting a stolen automobile interstate.	Feb. 2, 1929. 1 year county jail, Lincoln, Neb.	Offense made him subject to deportation. Sentence to expire Dec. 4, 1929. A group was being gathered for deportation the latter part of Nov., 1929. Assistant Secretary of Labor and assistant U. S. attorney recommended commutation. Attorney General advised sentence be commuted to expire Nov. 26, 1929. On Nov. 11, 1929, the President commuted sentence to expire Nov. 26, effective upon prisoner's delivery to immigration officer for deportation.
P. Uljee	Bringing stolen property into District of Columbia.	Mar. 2, 1929. 360 days Washington Asylum and Jail.	Served all but 2 weeks of sentence. Wanted for deportation. Father in Holland seriously ill, and deportation could be conveniently arranged. U. S. attorney and trial judge recommended favorably. Attorney General advised commutation of sentence to expire Dec. 13, 1929, on condition that the prisoner be deported and remain outside U. S., etc.
A. Stevens [2]	Entering U. S. illegally.	Nov. 18, 1929. 8 months county jail, Moscow, Idaho.	Served major portion of sentence and was wanted for deportation. Was 21 years old. Had entered U. S. wrongfully to secure employment as a farm hand, but without any malicious purpose, and bore a good reputation. The U. S. attorney recommended commutation. Attorney General advised sentence be commuted to expire at once upon condition that man be deported. Commutation granted Mar. 31, 1930, on condition he be deported.

[1] *Annual Report of the Attorney General of the United States for the Fiscal Year Ended June 30, 1930* (also 1929 report). There were 12 cases of commutation in the 1930 report.

[2] Nothing is said in this case about the necessity for remaining outside the United States, etc., although the act of March 4, 1929 would preclude return.

COMMUTATION TO SECURE DEPORTATION.—*Continued*

Name	Offense	Sentence and Date	Recommendation of Attorney General
A. Amelas [1]	Entering U. S. on a passport issued to another in violation of act of May 26, 1924, Sec. 22.	May 11, 1928. 3 months in county jail at Tucson, Ariz.	In a serious physical condition and had but little more than a month to serve. District attorney recommended his immediate release and judge was favorable. Attorney General advised sentence be commuted to expire at once on condition that prisoner be deported. Sentence commuted July 3, 1928, to expire at once on condition that applicant be immediately deported.
F. Stanley [1]	Stealing property of another on high seas.	Oct. 10, 1927. 15 months in U. S. penitentiary.	British subject, kept in jail over 4 months awaiting sentence. Had served actual imprisonment more than 13 months. In very serious condition physically. Attorney General advised the sentence be commuted to expire at once to allow prisoner to be immediately deported. Commutation granted July 30, 1928, but warrant of commutation was not delivered; term expired before immigration authorities could arrange for deportation.
F. Henry [1]	U. S. consular court at Alexandria, Egypt. Murder in the second degree.	Sept. 15, 1920. 20 years in the Alexandria Central (Hadra) Prison. Later transferred to U. S. penitentiary, Atlanta, Ga.	Had served actual imprisonment of about 8 years and 5 months and was subject to deportation. The British government was willing to receive him, and his release and deportation would not jeopardize the interests of society in this country. The Attorney General advised that the sentence be commuted to expire at once upon condition that the applicant be deported and remain outside the U. S. and all places subject to its jurisdiction, to become effective upon his delivery to the immigration official authorized to receive him for deportation.

[1] From the 1929 report. All other cases from the 1930 report.

completed his sentence he was wanted for deportation. He has assisted the United States government in the prosecution of other cases and both the United States attorney and the judge recommended clemency. The Attorney General advised that the sentence be commuted to expire at once upon condition that the prisoner be deported and never return to the United States or any territory or place subject to its jurisdiction. On June 25, 1930 the President commuted the sentence to expire at once, on condition that the man be deported and not return. The prisoner declined to accept the commutation, although the reason was not given, and was later, on July 10, 1930 granted a full and unconditional pardon, so that he was not deported.[1]

CRIMES INVOLVING "MORAL TURPITUDE" IN THE CASES STUDIED

Of the first group of cases studied there were thirty-four criminals who had committed crimes involving moral turpitude, while in the second group there were seven. The charges involved many types of offense, such as murder in the first and second degrees, grand and petit larceny, forgery, highway robbery, defrauding the government, and perjury. None of the thirty-four in the first group, however, had only the charge connected with moral turpitude, and all were charged with being "L.P.C." A change was noted in the later group, for of the seven cases studied, five had the warrant of deportation issued on the ground connected with moral turpitude alone, with no other reason for deportation. One of these five had the "L.P. C." charge on the warrant of arrest, but this was not recommended as sustainable by the board of review and so was not contained on the warrant of deportation. Two of the cases in the first group were also charged with having become a public charge within five years of entry, etc. Various other charges occurred as additional reasons for deportation:

[1] *Ibid.*, p. 352.

Additional Charges

	Group 1	Group 2
Entered without inspection	6	1
Unable at entry to read, etc.	2	
Entered by false statements, etc.	3	
Entered by water at time or place other than designated, etc.	2	
Entered within one year from date of exclusion or deportation, without permission to reapply	2	
Violation of "passport law"	2	
Not in possession of unexpired immigration visa	4	2

The word "entry" is of particular importance in both groups, for out of the forty-one, seventeen lived in the country from periods varying from two to twenty-nine years and had then left for short visits of from three months to four years, and were convicted after their return from the visit. In six cases where the crime occurred before "entry," it occurred *in* the United States before the visit out of the country.

From the first group there were 11, and 1 from the second who were convicted or admitted having committed a felony or other crime or misdemeanor involving moral turpitude, such as adultery, prior to entry into the United States.

Henrietta Phillips (Case 33).

Henrietta Phillips was born in 1890 in Leeds, England, where she lived during her early life. There she married Paul Dunham in 1910, but was deserted soon after her marriage, and has not seen or heard of her husband since. She worked at housework until she decided to emigrate to the United States.

Mrs. Dunham arrived in New York on December 24, 1924, and was admitted on primary inspection as a quota immigrant, destined to an uncle in Ohio. She went immediately to Canton, near where the uncle lived, and began to work as a waitress in a restaurant, earing $12 a week. There she met one of the patrons and went to live with him for a while. She soon found she had contracted venereal disease, and so went to a physician for treatment.

It is not known by whom Mrs. Dunham was reported to the immigration service, but a warrant was issued for her arrest on August 19, 1925, and she was taken to the Stark County Jail in Canton for detention. There she was given a hearing on August 20th. At that time the Union Gospel Mission, to whom Mrs. Dunham had appealed, sent a representative, and also to the board of review in Washington when the case came before them on September 1. The Salvation Army of Canton was also interested and hoped that Mrs. Dunham would not be deported.

The request of the Union Gospel Mission for a stay of deportation was denied and a warrant of deportation was issued on September 17, with the charges (1) "L. P. C.", (2) that Mrs. Dunham had committed a crime or misdemeanor involving moral turpitude prior to her entry: adultery. At the hearing she had admitted immoral relations with one man in England before coming to the United States.

She was deported on November 7, 1925, at the expense of the steamship line which had brought her to this country.

Albert Holden (Case 34).

Albert Holden was born in 1871 in London, England. He lived there throughout his school and college days. In 1886 he graduated from College and began work.

In 1903 under an assumed name he was sentenced to serve six months in Wandsworth prison for stealing money from his employer. The following year he served six weeks in St. Albans prison for vagrancy, under a different name, then under still another name, he was in Cardiff Prison for two months for stealing money from the man in whose house he lived. His next sentence was in 1916 when he served three months in Swansea Prison, North Wales, for stealing money from his employer. The following year he spent six months in the same prison for obtaining money under false pretences. In 1918 he served three years in Dartmoor Prison for sodomy.

In 1924, Mr. Holden secured work as a fireman on a steamer going to Cuba. There he left the ship and took passage for the United States, landing in Florida, and being admitted on primary inspection. He went to New York, then to Waukegan, Ill., where he was married on September 21, 1925 to an American-born girl.

A month after their marriage, Mrs. Holden reported her husband to the immigration authorities, stating he cruelly abused her, and she wanted him to leave the country, as he had entered illegally.

A warrant was issued for his arrest on October 5, 1925, and he was taken to the Cook County Jail in Chicago. He was given a hearing on October 10, at the jail. On November 4, a warrant of deportation was issued, with the same charges as in the warrant of arrest, namely (1) "L. P. C.", (2) that he had been convicted of a crime involving moral turpitude prior to entry into the United States, and (3) that he was not in possession of an unexpired immigration visa at the time of entry.

Mr. Holden was sent to the Philadelphia Immigration Station at Gloucester City for detention because of the crowded conditions in the Cook County Jail. He arrived at Gloucester City on November 2, 1925. On January 13, 1926 he was sent to Ellis Island, and was deported the following day at government expense.

There is no mention in the record of notice being sent to the British consulate in New York or elsewhere previous to his deportation.

Adelaide Grant (Case 35).

Adelaide Grant was born in Preston, England in 1890. She left school at 16 and began to work as a cotton weaver, which she continued until her marriage in 1913 to John Carr. She left her husband the same year she married him, as he drank and abused her.

About two years after this she met Edward Perry, and in 1916 went to live with him. She took his name, and, as her legal husband had disappeared, she thought she was Mr. Perry's common-law wife. She even received a bonus from the British government for his services in the war.

In 1923 Mr. Perry came to the United States, and on September 26 of that year, Mrs. Perry came to join him. She was homesick, and went back to England for a short time, but came over to the United States again, landing in New York on April 14, 1925, as a non-immigrant, here for 60 days for pleasure. She went directly to join Mr. Young, who was working on a talking moving picture patent in Boston.

The Perrys were anonymously reported to the immigration service. They were taken into custody on September 1, 1925, and the warrants for their arrest were issued the same day. They were taken to the East Boston immigration station for detention. A hearing was given them there on October 10. Warrants of deportation were issued on October 24, 1925 for Mrs. Perry, (1) "L. P. C.", (2) that she remained longer than the time allowed her for visit, and (3) that she admitted having committed a crime or misdemeanor involving moral turpitude before entering the United States: adultery. On the warrant of arrest, the additional charge had been made that she entered the United States for an immoral purpose, but this was not sustained and recommended by the board of review and so did not appear on the warrant of deportation. The warrant of deportation for Mr. Perry, issued the same day, contained the same charges as those of Mrs. Perry, except that the additional charges were sustained in his case, that he imported a person for an immoral purpose, and also that the quota or the country from which he came was exhausted at the time of his entry, and also, that he entered by means of false and misleading statements.

They were deported to England on October 31, 1925 at the expense of the steamship company which had brought them.

The following cases of people who admitted the commission of or conviction for crimes involving moral turpitude *before entry* shows that the commission of such crimes may be *in* the United States and yet be *before* entry to it. One case is of a man examined at the border, committing perjury there; technically he was not in the country though he was actually on American territory.

Pietro Kotor (Case 36).

Pietro Kotor was born in 1901 in Istria, now belonging to Italy. He worked as a blacksmith until 1923, when he went to Mexico, landing there in September and going to work in Tiajuana.

Mr. Kotor remained there until May 24, 1924, when he entered the United States by walking across the border. He was examined by a board of special inquiry of the immigration service, but was admitted on his statement that he was a returning resident of the United States.

It is not known by whom Mr. Kotor was reported to the immigration service, but a warrant for his arrest was issued on March 19, 1925, the day of his apprehension. He was immediately released on bond of $1000. A hearing was given him on April 28, at the Los Angeles immigration service office. An interpreter was present, but Mr. Kotor said he wished the hearing postponed a day so he could get a lawyer. This was done, but in the meanwhile, a lawyer had stated to Mr. Kotor his services would be of no use.

Two days later, Mr. Kotor was sentenced to serve three months in the county jail for perjury. A warrant for his deportation was issued June 13th, previous to the expiration of his sentence, on the grounds (1) "L. P. C.", (2) that he was convicted of a crime or misdemeanor involving moral turpitude before he entered the United States: perjury, and (3) that he was not in possession of an unexpired immigration visa. The charges were the same as on the warrant of arrest.

Mr. Kotor was sent to Galveston on July 29, and deported the next day, at government expense. He was to land in France, but he was given a ticket to Italy.

Henvar Simkowicz (Case 37).

Henvar Simkowicz was born in 1875 in the countryside of

Galicia, Poland, and was married in his home town in 1897. He had three children by this marriage.

In 1913 Mr. Simkowicz came to the United States and lived here until 1919, working with the Standard Steel Car Company in Pennsylvania. His wife and children never came to this country, but during his stay here, Mr. Simkowicz lived with a woman by whom he had two children.

In 1919 he returned home to his legal wife and children for a visit, and stayed four years. He came back to the United States on October 9, 1923, and was admitted that day on primary inspection, destined to his brother in Butler, Pa.

It is not known by whom Mr. Simkowicz was reported to the immigration authorities. A warrant for his arrest was issued November 16, 1925; the same day he was taken to the Allegheny County Jail for detention. The hearing was held there two weeks later, with a lawyer, and an interpreter. The lawyer presented a brief in which he charged unfairness and no attempt to follow the rules of evidence on the part of the inspector conducting the hearing. The attorney's objections were entered in his brief, which he presented after the hearing, to be forwarded to Washington.

At the hearing it was stated of Mr. Simkowicz, "having no relative in the United States, in the event of becoming ill and incapacitated for work he would, beyond doubt, become a public charge."

A warrant of deportation was issued on December 1, 1925, with the charges the same as those in the warrant of arrest, namely (1) "L. P. C.", (2) that he admitted the commission of a crime or misdemeanor involving moral turpitude prior to his entry: adultery, and (3) that he was admitted by means of false and misleading statements. The commission of the act involving moral turpitude had, of course, occurred *in* the United States, previous to the visit home which Mr. Simkowicz paid in 1919.

He was deported January 11, 1926, at the expense of the steamship company which had brought him to the United States in 1923.

The record states it was said the woman with whom he had lived in this country had returned to Poland, with her two children, and was in the same town with his wife.

Carlo Pacelli (Case 38).

Carlo Pacelli was born in 1894 in the province of Teramo, Italy. Nothing is known of his early life. He came to the United States in May, 1913, and soon after joined the American army. He went overseas with the American Expeditionary Force and served four years and seven months, with an honorable discharge from the army on November 12, 1919. He had secured his "first papers" on entering the army, and said he thought his second papers were automatically granted for honorable discharge from the army.

After his return to the United States in 1919, Mr. Pacelli lived in Washington, D. C. and worked as a truck driver, store manager, and real estate salesman until February, 1925, when he went to Canada for two days visit from Detroit. Just before he left the United States, he had been indicted, on February 16, for defrauding the government (Sec. 35, District of Columbia Criminal Code). So he was apprehended on his return to Detroit from Canada and sent back to Washington, where he was taken to the local jail.

A warrant was issued for Mr. Pacelli's arrest on August 20, 1925. He was given a hearing at the jail on September 3rd, but it was postponed until September 17 for him to secure a lawyer. The same lawyer appeared in Mr. Pacelli's behalf before the board of review when the case came before it on October 9th. The lawyer stated that the criminal prosecution was for defrauding the United States Veteran's Bureau of $300 for payment to a woman supposedly his wife, but in reality not.

On October 13, a warrant of deportation was issued, on the same grounds as those in the warrant of arrest, namely (1) "L. P. C.", (2) that he was convicted of or admitted the commission of a crime involving moral turpitude previous to entry, and (3) that he entered without inspection. The crime involving moral turpitude was of course the one committed *in* the

United States before Mr. Pacelli went to Canada for the two days visit, but it was before his entry after that visit.

The lawyer applied for an extension of time, on October 26, 1925, so that Mr. Pacelli could attend proceedings for annulment of his marriage, and trial for bigamy, as it was found he had been married in 1915, and again in 1924. The bureau of immigration refused to grant the extension of time, so Mr. Pacelli applied to a Representative in Congress, who wrote the bureau to ascertain the facts rather than request action. However, Mr. Pacelli was not deported until January 1, 1926, at government expense. There is nothing in the record mentioning the bigamy trial after the lawyer's letter of October 26.

The following case originally contained the charge that the woman had been convicted or admitted having committed a crime involving moral turpitude prior to her entrance into the United States, but this charge was not sustained, and she was deported on other grounds:

Jeanne Maylan (Case 39).

Jeanne Maylan was born in 1896 near Lyons, France, where she lived until her marriage on May 15, 1916 to Charles Auban. They moved to Paris and remained there until December, 1921, when Mrs. Auban secured a decree of divorce from her husband.

She then began to work in a dressmaking firm, then as mail clerk in a bank. There she met an American to whom she became engaged, so she came to the United States to join him, arriving in New York, October 3, 1924, II class, and being discharged to the care of the Travelers' Aid Society. They in turn sent her to the care of Mrs. Hunter, the sister-in-law of the man to whom Mrs. Auban was engaged.

Mrs. Auban soon discovered that Mr. Hunter had a wife and two children, but as he reported he could not find the whereabouts of his wife to get a divorce, Mrs. Auban took an apartment with him. The Travelers' Aid meanwhile had found that Mr. Hunter had been married in 1907 in Malone, N. Y., and that his wife and four (not two as Mr. Hunter had stated) children were living in Philadelphia, having been deserted in 1918 by Mr. Hunter.

At that time he went to Europe and had not been heard of since. So. Mrs. Hunter had placed the children through the Catholic Children's Bureau, as she could not look after them alone, and had also tried to locate her husband, through the American Red Cross. They had been unsuccessful, as he was in Europe three years. Mrs. Auban later said she had lived with him part of that time.

So the Travelers' Aid reported the case to the immigration authorities on May 22, 1925, but a warrant of arrest was not issued until July 1. Mrs. Auban was taken to Ellis Island, but was released on bond of $1000, which Mr. Hunter provided. A hearing was held on Ellis Island on July 18th. There Mr. Hunter testified he earned $12 a day, that he wanted a divorce, and would support his wife and children, and his second wife, if he could marry Mrs. Auban.

A warrant of deportation was issued on September 15, with the following charges (1) "L. P. C.", (2) that Mrs. Auban's ticket or passage to the United States was paid for by the money of another, (3) that she entered by means of false and misleading statements, thereby entering without inspection, (4) that she entered the United States for an immoral purpose. The warrant of arrest had contained the additional charge that Mrs. Auban had been convicted or admitted the commission of a crime involving moral turpitude prior to entry into the United States, but this was not sustained or recommended when the case came before the board of review, as there was doubt about the status of Mrs. Auban's act in France.

Mrs. Auban was deported on October 28, 1925, at the expense of the line which had brought her to the United States, destined to her mother who lived at St. Ouen sur Seine, France.

There were 19 out of the 34, and 4 out of the 7 who who were sentenced subsequent to May 1, 1917 to imprisonment for a term of one year or more because of conviction in this country of a crime or other misdemeanor involving moral turpitude, committed within five years of entry. As this five-year term refers to *any* entry, an alien who left the United States for no matter how short a time would, as already indicated, have the period for deportation date from his last entry.

The following cases from among those studied illustrate the type where a conviction was involved for a crime involving moral turpitude, with a sentence for a year or more in each instance:

Enrico Castrucci (Case 40).

Enrico Castrucci was born on June 17, 1902 in Naples, Italy. His father emigrated to the United States in 1907, and married again there, leaving his mother in Italy without support. So the boy left school at an early age and learned the trade of a plasterer, to help support his mother.

On April 9, 1920, the boy emigrated to join his father, who meanwhile had become an American citizen and was living in Mount Vernon with his second wife, and his 15-year old stepdaughter. The son went to live with them, and secured work as a plasterer, earning $30 a week, with $15 for overtime.

It appears that Mr. Castrucci, Sr., had assaulted an uncle in Italy, and been sentenced to prison, but had been allowed to come to the United States when he still had eight months to serve. In 1912 he had been sentenced to 8 years in prison for implication in the killing of a policeman, but had been paroled at the end of five years. According to his son's story, his father made improper advances to the fifteen-year old daughter of his wife, so Mrs. Castrucci had asked Enrico to take the girl away and marry her.

So Enrico Castrucci and the girl, Elena, went to Boston together and applied for a marriage license, but were told they had to have their parents' permission, as Elena was under age. So they took an apartment together in Boston, but were reported to the police by one of their neighbors. The police got in touch with Mr. Castrucci, Sr., and on his request, his son and step-daughter were arrested. So the boy was sentenced on April 2, 1925, by the Municipal Court in South Boston to a term of one year in the House of Correction. At the trial, the boy repeated his desire to marry the girl but his inability to on account of his father's refusal of permission. While he was sent to the House of Correction, Elena was sent to the House of the Good Shepherd.

The House of Correction reported the case for deportation (date unknown) and a warrant of arrest was issued on February 24, 1925. The hearing was called the next day at the House of Correction but was adjourned so that the boy's uncle, who lived in Boston, could get a lawyer for him. The hearing was continued on March 12, when the uncle and a lawyer were both present. The uncle said he had $3,000 in savings and was earning $60 a week and would be glad to take his nephew to live with him. He furthermore corroborated the history of Mr. Castrucci, and the fact that he had never supported his first wife in Italy. A friend of the family also testified as to the excellent record and reputable life the boy had led in Italy previous to emigration, while the brief submitted by the lawyer to the board of review contained the same statement. The boy was released on $1000 bond on March 17.

On June 9, the Secretary of Labor wrote a letter asking for a reinvestigation of the facts leading up to the trial and conviction, to ascertain whether Enrico or his father had been responsible for what happened, and whether or not his father's wife had definitely requested him to go off with her daughter. Investigation showed that the day of the arrest, Mrs. Castrucci had gone from Mount Vernon to Boston and had refused to allow her daughter to marry. It was said that Elena had written a letter saying the boy's statements about his father were untrue, but the investigation failed to reveal the letter.

In view of the complicated social factors in the case, the lawyer retained by the uncle and a congressman from Massachusetts wrote and then wired requesting a three weeks stay of deportation while an attempt was made to secure the boy's pardon, which was not secured, however, though the reasons are not given in the record.

A warrant of deportation was issued on October 8, 1925 for Enrico on the grounds which had been used in the warrant of arrest, that he was (1) " L. P. C.", (2) sentenced subsequent to May 1, 1917 to imprisonment for a term of one year or more because of conviction of a crime involving moral turpitude committed within five years of entry, to wit: lewd and lascivious cohabitation.

Enrico was deported on December 2, 1925, at the expense of the steamship company which had brought him to the United States, destined to his mother in Italy.

Catherine Heppe (Case 41).

Catherine Heppe was born in 1903 in Donetz, a town in Austria, but moved to Vienna, when she was still a small child. She went to school and then business college there.

Her aunt, Mrs. Margaret Heppe, came to visit the family in 1922, and Catherine went to the United States with her aunt on her return, landing in New York on August 22, 1922, as a first class passenger, and admitted on primary inspection in the quota from Austria.

Miss Heppe then went to New Britain, Conn., where she went to live with her second cousin, but soon secured a position as maid, earning $8 a week and board. She soon became involved in an affair with a man she met one evening, but when she found he was married, she became angry and went to live with another man she had met the same time. She was arrested on November 21, 1924, charged with lascivious carriage, and soon thereafter, Miss Heppe was committed to the Connecticut State Farm for Women at Niantic, she was examined and found to have venereal disease, which she had contracted from the man with whom she had lived.

On January 4, 1925, Miss Heppe was reported to the immigration authorities by a probation officer in New Britain, and a warrant of arrest was issued on January 24. A hearing was given her at the State Farm on February 14. There Miss Heppe stated, " because I am sick, and I was not sick in my country, I do not want to be sent back. I was all right until I came over here. I want to live in this country; my father is mad at me, and my mother is very sick." Her aunt was called on for testimony and said the girl's mother was ill with tuberculosis and wanted to have her daughter at home, but if she knew of her daughter's physical condition, it might kill her.

A warrant of deportation was issued on October 8, 1925, with the charges (1) "L. P. C.", (2) that Miss Heppe had become a public charge within five years of entry, etc., (3) that she was sentenced to imprisonment for a year or more because of conviction of a crime involving moral turpitude commited within 5 years after entry. The charges on the warrant of arrest had been the same.

Miss Heppe was deported on December 18, at the expense of the steamship line which had brought her to the country, destined to her parents in Vienna.

There were 4 out of the 34, and 1 of the 7 who were sentenced subsequent to May 1, 1917 to imprisonment more than once for a term of one year or more because of conviction in this country of a crime involving moral turpitude committed within five years after entry.

Joseph Andirjic (Case 42).

Joseph Andirjic was born in 1883 in Jugoslavia. He never went to school but went to work at an early age in a flour mill. He was married in 1903, and had one child, but it died soon after birth.

In 1907 Mr. Andirjic left his wife at home, and emigrated to the United States, going to join his brother in Akron, Ohio. He worked there in various rubber factories until 1916, when he was given an indeterminate sentence in the Ohio State Penitentiary for robbery. The sentence was suspended, and he was put on probation. In March of the next year, he was arrested in Pittsburg, under a different name, for violation of his probation. On November 1, 1919, he was sentenced in Buffalo under a third name for a term of from 2½ to 5 years for grand larceny committed in August of that year. He served 21 months at Auburn Prison. He was sentenced again on November 17, for from 1-7 years for grand larceny, committed June 6, 1924 in Akron. For this last sentence he was committed to the Ohio State Penintentiary in Akron.

On July 30, 1925, a warrant was issued for his arrest. A hearing was given him at the penitentiary on August 20. There Mr. Andirjic stated he wished deportation as soon as possible to get out of prison. On October 14, a warrant of deportation was issued on the same ground as that in the warrant of arrest, namely, that he was sentenced subsequent to May 1, 1917 to imprisonment more than once for a term of one year or more for the commission of a crime involving moral turpitude (grand larceny).

On December 3, 1925, the legation of Jugoslavia wrote the Department of Labor, saying they had issued a passport for the man, but wanted to be informed regarding the date and boat on which he was to be deported. The record, however, does not contain a copy of such notification. Mr. Andirjic was deported on January 2, 1926, at government expense.

Karl Nordsen (Case 43).

Karl Nordsen was born on May 31, 1891 in Aalborg, Denmark. He came to the United States with his parents in July, 1909, having landed in Montreal, and being legally admitted at Rouses Point. His life in this country is unknown, save that his father died here, and his mother is still living here, but has never been naturalized.

On January 3, 1921, Mr. Nordsen was sentenced to 1-10 years, to be served in the State Prison of Utah for grand larceny, but he was paroled in October, 1922. On June 18, 1925 he was sentenced at Phoenix, Ariz. to the United States Penitentiary at Leavenworth, Kan., for 2 years each on each of 3 indictments, for violation of the so-called Dyer Act (transportation of stolen motor vehicles in interstate commerce.) He was reported to the immigration authorities by the penitentiary in September, 1929.

A warrant was issued for Mr. Nordsen's arrest on October

31, 1929, and a hearing was given him at the penitentiary on November 11. The case came before the board of review a week later, and it was said there that one of the Utah senators was interested and wished information. A warrant of deportation was issued on November 21, on the ground that Mr. Nordsen had been sentenced subsequent to May 1, 1917 to imprisonment more than once for a term of one year or more for the commission subsequent to entry of a crime involving moral turpitude. This was the same ground as in the warrant of arrest.

The Danish legation requested a certified copy of the 2 sentences for larceny and also wished information as to when deportation would take place. On March 5th, 1930, they were informed by the bureau of immigration that deportation would take place on March 8th, which it did, at government expense.

It is of note that in a number of these cases where persons were convicted and serving sentences for offenses involving moral turpitude that there was desire for deportation, and attempt made to hasten it rather than prevent it. Three men out of the total number of cases in both groups objected strongly to deportation, as they had lived in the United States since early childhood and did not wish to go to their country, which would be entirely foreign to them. Twenty-one out of the total stated they definitely desired deportation, to secure release from prison, while eleven said they did not object; the other six made no statement.

That deportation was desired not only by the prisoners but also by the state, to save expenditure and overcrowding and to rid the state of undesirable residents, is shown by the following. Here aliens in the country less than five years and committing crimes, etc. of moral turpitude and sentenced to a term of imprisonment for a year or more had their prison terms shortened, as a matter of actual fact, in order to hasten deportation.[1]

[1] The same might be done on their last sentence with those sentenced *more* than once after five years.

1. Sentence December 31, 1917, for 8-12 years murder in the 2nd degree which had been committed on December 24, 1916. This crime was committed within 5 years after the man's entry, though the commission was prior to the passage of the immigration act of 1917. However, the man was sentenced after the passage of the act.
2. Indictment April 1, 1924 for robbery, 1st degree; grand larceny, 2nd degree; and assault, 2nd degree. Conviction for robbery 3rd degree on confession and plea of guilty. Sentence for 10 years and commitment to the New York State Reformatory at Elmira, N. Y. Paroled June 7, 1925 for deportation, which took place October 6, 1925.
3. Indictment for forgery. Application for probation denied on July 9, 1925 and an indeterminate sentence (meaning in Illinois, where the crime was committed, a sentence from 1-11 years) given, to be served in the Southern Illinois Penitentiary. Sentence suspended to permit deportation, which took place on September 5, 1925.
4. Sentence February 9, 1929 to 9 months—5 years for larceny, to be served in the Michigan State Reformatory. Parole to the immigration service on January 9, 1930 for deportation, which took place January 25, 1930.

Since pardon in the United States for a crime committed here wipes out the offense, it is natural that in studying cases of actual deportations none of those where pardon was granted to prevent deportation would be found. However, two cases were among the total where pardon was granted; in one case so that deportation, which otherwise would have been impossible, might take place, and in the other, that it might take place more speedily than otherwise:

Nicola Baratovic (Case 44).

Nicola Baratovic was born in 1886 in Dalmatia, Jugoslavia. Nothing is known of his early life. He entered the United States in 1914, but it is impossible to verify his entry. He worked as a barber in various places after his entry. In 1917 he secured his " first papers " in Detroit.

On January 19, 1919, Mr. Baratovic was sentenced at St. Clairsville, O. for a life term in the Ohio Penitentiary at Columbus, for 1st degree murder, committed on May 29, 1918. Under the Ohio laws, an alien cannot *ask* for parole, but the board of pardons can parole him if it wants. The warden, deputy warden and chaplain of the penitentiary recommended that Mr. Baratovic be released from prison for deportation, and the recommendation was concurred in by the prosecuting attorney, trial judge, sheriff and 5 jury members, as well as the board of pardons. So on January 2, 1929, the Governor of Ohio granted a conditional pardon to be effective that day, on condition that Mr. Baratovic be turned over to the immigration service for deportation to his country. This was done on January 8, when he was transferred from the penitentiary to the county jail in Cincinnati, but ten days later he was released on bond of $1000. In other words, he was pardoned to be deported.

The warrant of arrest and deportation had been outstanding since July 10 and October 17 respectively, in 1923. Mr. Baratovic was deported on January 2, 1930, destined to Jugoslavia, and at government expense.

Mario Fedele (Case 45).

Mario Fedele was born in 1896 in Gioia Santica, Caserta, Italy. He came to the United States when he was a small child, though at what age is not known, nor is anything known about his family. When he was about 15 or 16 years old, he was sentenced to the state reform school at Meriden, Conn., though for what offense is not known.

On April 1, 1913, he was sentenced to 4-10 years in the Weathersfield Prison for highway robbery, and served until May 26, 1921. Then he went to Europe, and returned to the United States in 1913, bearing a Spanish passport, for which he had paid $20 in Barcelona. His entry could not be verified.

In January, 1924, he received his third prison sentence in this country, at Lansing, Mich., for one year, for transportation of liquor. He received a suspended sentence, and then one year later was convicted at South Bend, Indiana, for 10-20 years for first degree burglary. He was reported to the immigration service by the Indiana Reformatory at Pendleton, Ind., where he began to serve his sentence. A warrant was issued for his arrest in deportation proceedings on May 25, 1925. On October 30, he was given a hearing at the reformatory, but did not secure a lawyer as he wished deportation.

A warrant of deportation was issued for him on November 25, on the grounds (1) "L. P. C.", (2) that he was sentenced subsequent to May 1, 1917 to imprisonment more than once because of conviction in this country of a crime involving moral turpitude committed within five years after entry: burglary, first degree, (3) violation of the passport law, (4) that he had been convicted or admitted having committed a crime or misdemeanor involving moral turpitude prior to entry into the United States. The fourth charge was added after the hearing and was not contained in the original warrant of arrest.

Mr. Fedele was deported on January 5, 1926 at the expense of the government, destined to Italy.

The reason that deportation could take place before the expiration of ten years in the Indiana Reformatory was that the Governor of Indiana pardoned him on condition that he be deported to Italy.[1]

There is one case of particular interest among the group studied, for every effort was made by those interested to prevent deportation, except to seek a pardon. Why that was not tried is not stated in the record. The case also shows how much easier it is to start proceedings for deportation than to stop them once they are begun:

[1] Information sent the author by the Secretary of the Board of County Charities, Pendleton, Ind., as the statement concerning pardon was not in the record of the bureau of immigration.

Arturo Costarelli (Case 46).

Arturo Costarelli was born in 1904 in Isola delle Femine, Italy. As his father died, and his three older sisters and mother emigrated to the United States and were living in Pittsburg, California, he decided to join them, but it took some time for him to be able to secure a quota number. However, he landed on June 2, 1926, and went right to join his family in California. The whole family were fisher people in Italy, and now were employed in the fish canneries in Monterey.

Mr. Costarelli had not been in the United States a year when he became engaged to Francesca Orsini, who lived near him. They were engaged from December 1927 for almost a year, but in October, 1928 she broke the engagement, without giving a reason. Then several months later, she heard that he was interested in another girl, so she told her mother that she had had intercourse with him. As she was 17 years and 9 months old when it had occurred, she accused Mr. Costarelli of statutory rape, and reported him to the immigration service for deportation.

On March 6, 1929 he was sentenced to one year in the Contra Costa County Jail in Martinez for statutory rape, but received a 60 days' reduction of sentence because of good behavior. Meanwhile, a warrant was issued for his arrest on April 22, 1929, and a hearing was given him at the jail on May 15, with a lawyer and witnesses present in his behalf. The witnesses testified as to his excellent character, and the lawyer presented a brief requesting his stay in this country. Furthermore, Miss Orsini said she regretted her action against him, as he had at all times been willing to marry her, and she had changed her mind and was now willing to marry him. She presented an affidavit to that effect, which was sent with the lawyer's brief to the board of review in Washington. The affidavit and brief stated that if the girl had been three months older there would have been no offense, and that in any case, there was no moral turpitude involved, as the man had wanted to marry the girl and still did.

Two Congressman became interested and wrote the bureau, while one of them sent a telegram to President Hoover. The

Commissioner of Immigration replied to all of the communications that in a case where there was *conviction* for a crime or misdemeanor involving moral turpitude committed within 5 years of entry to the United States, deportation was *mandatory*, with no discretion vested in any of the officials of the Department of Labor. So a warrant of deportation was issued on December 10, 1929, on the one ground indicated.

Mr. Costarelli was deported January 2, 1930, from Galveston, Tex., to Italy, via Vera Cruz, Havana, Coruna, Santander and Le Havre, where debarkation took place. Mr. Costarelli had a ticket to his home in Italy.

He can never return to the United States.

The following cases are illustrative of the fact that the convictions for moral turpitude must involve sentences of at least a year, for the men involved in these cases received sentences of less than a year each time. Furthermore, there is the question of whether or not the offenses for which they were convicted involved " moral turpitude." As they both entered illegally, they were deportable on that ground, whereas if they had not so entered, they would not have been deportable.

James Rice (Case 47).

James Rice was born in 1902 in London, where his parents still reside. He was trained as a bookeeper and accountant and worked as an assistant bookkeeper previous to his emigration to Canada in 1922.

In some way which is not known, he entered the United States, going immediately to Baltimore. There he was arrested the latter part of the year for stealing a suitcase full of clothes from a club in a Baltimore hotel. The case was " nolle prossed " as the attorney for Mr. Rice promised that his client would leave the country immediately.

He went to England, but decided to return to the United States and took ship for Canada, landing at Halifax in May, 1922. He went immediately to the border, crossing on foot at one of the bridges at Niagara Falls. He was not seen or inspected, and the exact date of his entry is not known.

Then Mr. Rice went to Chicago where he passed worthless checks in a scheme known as a " con game." On February 27, 1925, he received a sentence in the Municipal Court in Chicago of a term in the House of Correction or a fine. In lieu of paying the fine and costs, he went to serve time of 113 days.

Two days after entering the House of Correction, a warrant was issued for his arrest, and a hearing was given him at the House of Correction on March 24. Mr. Rice stated he had no money to pay a lawyer to represent him, and that he preferred deportation to Canada, but that if that were impossible he would like deportation to England as quickly as possible so that he might secure employment before the following winter set in.

A warrant was issued for Mr. Rice's deportation, on July 28, 1925, with the same charges as on the warrant of arrest, namely, that he was (1) "L. P. C.", (2) entered without inspection, (3) was not in possession of an unexpired visa at the time of entry. He was sent to Ellis Island on November 10, and deported at government expense, destined to England.

Albert Kamin (Case 48).

Albert Kamin was born in Finland, near Helsingfors, in 1896. He early began the trade of painter.

In 1923 he landed in Quebec, and on November 27, just eleven days after landing in Quebec, came to the United States in the box-car of a train, crossing the border at Sault St. Marie, Mich. He went immediately to Chicago, where he began to work as a painter.

Mr. Kamin was sentenced in May, 1925, to a term of six months in the House of Correction in Chicago, for assault with a deadly weapon. A warrant for his arrest was issued on September 11, on the grounds (1) "L. P. C.", (2) entering without inspection, (3) violating the " passport law." He was given a hearing at the House of Correction on September 26, and a warrant of deportation was issued on October 29, on the same grounds as those in the warrant of arrest.

On December 14, 1925, Mr. Kamin was sent to Ellis Island from Chicago, and then was sent to St. Johns, New Brunswick, for deportation on December 16, 1925 at the expense of the steamship company which had brought him to Canada.

CONCLUSIONS

It seems that the " moral turpitude " provision of the deportation law has outlived its usefulness and become a trap for the unfortunate administrator as well as the luckless alien who runs afoul of this section of the law. Attempts to remove it have been opposed by those friends of the alien who feel it to be a safeguard against heaping of sentences followed by deportation. They argue that an alien violating traffic regulations and serving enough sentences therefor would be liable to deportation, even though otherwise an entirely acceptable member of the American community. The question arises as to whether even such an extreme case would be any worse than a provision by which a man in Pennsylvania charged with aggravated assault and battery is not involved in a crime involving moral turpitude while a man in Massachusetts who stole $15 is. Vague provisions which are impossible to interpret are no solution for the alien.

The Secretary of Labor has said that " the time has come for taking vigorous measures to rid the country of alien criminals of every class." [1] Mere international dumping alone will not effectually accomplish the desired end of ridding the country of alien criminals. The law violator who has been in prison is probably the person least apt to fear those provisions of the law which deny him reentry after deportation. So mere sending him out of the United States is not a solution of the problem either for the United States or for the criminal, to say nothing of the other country in-

[1] *Annual Report*, etc., *for 1930*, pp. 18-19.

volved. At international conferences on criminology it has been resolved that the problem of international criminals could be facilitated in handling if different states could agree to allow direct intercommunication between the judicial and police authorities of different countries with a view to the exchange of information with respect to dangerous criminals.[1] In that way the habitual alien criminal would not be passed from the United States to another country there to commit further crime, serve sentence and perhaps return to this country surreptitiously. On the other hand, the exchange of such information should be made only with respect to dangerous criminals, for the non-habitual alien criminal in the United States, who may have served sentence on a technical charge alone, should not be branded as a criminal to be kept under police surveillance on his return to Europe. The case of Arturo Costarelli (Case 46) above is an illustration of such situation. Here, as always, care must be taken to distinguish between the habitual alien criminal and the incidental one.

Obviously international "passing on" offers no real solution for the problem of the criminal as such, and for the social causes of crime. The roots lie deeper than the alien. The assumption often current in the United States that aliens are malefactors because of the mere fact of their alliance has not been borne out in investigations of criminologists, who have shown that aliens have not contributed more than their proportionate share of crime in the population. The task infinitely more difficult than lumping together persons who are not citizens in the United States and assuming that because of that accident of birth they are lawbreakers is to study the social causes of crime, and the cures for them.

[1] *Journal of Criminal Law and Criminology*, 1926, p. 608.

CHAPTER VI

Anarchists, Prostitutes, and Other "Undesirables"

ANARCHISTS AND OTHER RADICALS

In time of war or other stress, human beings seem to seek surcease from their fears and troubles by trying to find a scapegoat who will bear the onerous weight of their difficulties, whether he will or not. Then we forget the wise words of Mr. Justice Holmes, that "we should be eternally vigilant against attempts to check the expression of opinions that we loathe and believe to be fraught with death, unless they so imminently threaten immediate interference with the lawful and pressing purposes of the law that an immediate check is required to save the country."[1] The problem resolves itself into discussion of when the immediate check is necessary and *when* there is need for saving the country. Lack of agreement as to how great shocks the country can stand has caused continued vacillation in legislative, administrative and judicial policy with regard to radical activity in the United States. In times of peace and prosperity we sometimes forget how "undesirable" political dissenters may be, and in times of war and depression we suddenly call them to mind.

As already indicated, the United States was long hospitable to those convicted of political offenses in other countries. So it inserted the now too famous "moral turpitude" phrase into the immigration law to allow admission to those who might have served prison terms previous to emigration

[1] Abrams *v.* United States, 250 U. S. 616, 624, dissenting opinion.

for none other than political offenses and who came to the United States as a refuge.[1] Thus a philosophical anarchist who had served imprisonment in Siberia for unwise expression of opinion might have been allowed to enter this country as a land of freedom of thought and opinion. However, the assassination of President McKinley by a self-styled anarchist, and the Haymarket riots in Chicago, probably kindled the flame of fear of "foreign anarchists." They were an inciting cause to the inclusion in the immigration act of March 3, 1903, among those excludable from the country or deportable within three years of their arrival here, of anarchists and persons who believe in or advocate the overthrow by force or violence of the government of the United States or of all government or of all forms of law, or in the assassination of public officials.

The act of February 20, 1907 reenacted and affirmed the clause. A question immediately arose as to what constituted an anarchist,[2] but the cases were few and far between until the hysteria of the World War brought in its train a pronounced fear of anything alien.[3] The immigration act of

[1] Under the 1917 and subsequent immigration acts, if the only ground of exclusion from the country is the admission of a crime involving moral turpitude, and that crime is of a political nature, the person so excluded may be admitted on appeal to the Secretary of Labor, if he is otherwise admissible. As the statute now definitely excludes anarchists, an anarchist would not be admissible to the country as a political refugee from any other country. *Vide* United States *ex rel.* Castro *v.* Williams, 203 Fed. 155, and *Ex parte* Chun Wang, 18 Fed. (2d) 119.

[2] United States *ex rel.* Turner *v.* Williams, 194 U. S. 279 (1903).

[3] By act of May 10, 1920, aliens found "undesirable" by reason of their war activities were made deportable from the country. The list of persons included in the act comprises, among others, interned aliens, those who possess explosives in war-time, those who make threats against the President, those who trade with the enemy, or interfere with the neutrality or foreign relations of the United States, etc. Deportation of such aliens can take place at any time after entry. The act is, of course, a dead letter in times of peace, but it is on the statute books.

1917 attempted to define just who constitute anarchists, by providing for the exclusion from the United States, or deportation at any time after entry, of those who believe in the overthrow of the government of the United States by force or violence,[1] advocate the overthrow by such methods, believe in or advocate the overthrow by force or violence of all forms of law,[2] do not believe in or are opposed to organized government,[3] advocate the assassination of public officials, advocate or teach the unlawful destruction of property; and all members of or persons affiliated with

> any organization entertaining or teaching disbelief in or opposition to organized government, or who advocate or teach the duty, necessity or propriety of the unlawful assaulting or killing of any officer or officers, either of specific individuals or of officers generally, of the Government of the United States or of any other organized government because of his or their official character.[4]

Anarchists of whatever sort, whether advocating violence or not, alike fall under the ban. Thus a Spanish anarchist, who believed in and taught anarchy as a philosophical theory but did not advocate violence, was found deportable, despite the fact of his fifteen years' residence in the United States.[5]

[1] Colyer *v.* Skeffington, 265 Fed. 17; *Ex parte* Caminita, 291 Fed. 913.

[2] United States *v.* Stupiello, 260 Fed. 913.

[3] *Ex parte* Caminita, 291 Fed. 913.

[4] Immigration act of 1917, sec. 3. *In re* Olson, 4 Fed. (2d) 417.

[5] Lopez *v.* Howe, 259 Fed. 401. *Vide* also *Ex parte* Peltine, 259 Fed. 733; United States *ex rel.* Georgian *v.* Uhl, 271 Fed. 676; United States *ex rel.* Diamond *v.* Uhl, 266 Fed. 34; United States *ex rel.* Rakics *v.* Uhl, 266 Fed. 646. In 1921, after the law was made more inclusive than before, a Russian opposed to the government of the country and who published propaganda intended eventually to result in or facilitate its overthrow, was held deportable, though he did not advocate its immediate overthrow by violence.

It was not long before fear of anarchists was destined to be supplanted by a new menace to those who feared for the safety and stability of the United States. The downfall of the Russian Empire and the upbuilding of the Union of Soviet Socialist Republics led to a wave of dread of " Bolsheviks " and Reds and to an identification of communists with anarchists as the most undesirable of many undesirable foreigners. To make assurance doubly sure in regard to the exclusion and deportation of all such radicals, Congress passed an act " to exclude and expel from the United States aliens who are members of the anarchistic and similar classes," approved October 16, 1918 and amended by the act approved June 5, 1920. An attempt was thus made to extend the existing provisions and render them more inclusive and more definite in their application to excludable and deportable aliens. The aliens included in the act are:

(A) Aliens who are anarchists.

(B) Aliens who advise, advocate, or teach, or who are members of or affiliated with any organization, association, society or group, that advises, advocates, or teaches, opposition to all organized government.

(C) Aliens who believe in, advise, advocate, or teach, or who are members of or affiliated with any organization, association, society, or group that believes in, advises, advocates or teaches: (1) the overthrow by force or violence of the Government of the United States or of all forms of law, or (2) the duty, necessity, or propriety of the unlawful assaulting or killing of any officer or officers (either of specific individuals or of officers generally) of the Government of the United States or of any other organized government because of his or their official character, or (3) the unlawful damage, injury, or destruction of property, or (4) sabotage.

(D) Aliens who write, publish, or cause to be written or published or who knowingly circulate, distribute, print or display, or knowingly cause to be circulated, distributed, printed, published, or displayed, or who knowingly have in their possession for the purpose of circulation, distribution, publication, or display any written or printed matter advising, advocating or teaching: (1) the overthrow by force or violence of the Government of the United States or of all forms of law, or (2) the duty, necessity, or propriety of the unlawful assaulting or killing of any officer or officers (either of specific individuals or of officers generally) of the Government of the United States or of any other organized government, or (3) the unlawful damage, injury or destruction of property, or (4) sabotage.

(E) Aliens who are members of or affiliated with any organization, association, society, or group that writes, circulates, distributes, prints, publishes or displays or causes to be written, circulated, distributed, printed, published, or displayed or that has in its possession for the purpose of circulation, distribution, publication, issue, or display any written or printed matter of the character described in subdivision D.[1]

For the purpose of this section: (1) The giving, loaning, or promising of money or anything of value to be used for the advising, advocacy, or teaching of any doctrine above enumerated shall constitute the advising, advocacy, or teaching of such doctrine; and (2) the giving, loaning, or promising of money or anything of value to any organization, association, society, or group of the character above described shall constitute affiliation therewith, but nothing in this paragraph shall be taken as an exclusive definition of advising, advocacy, teaching, or affiliation.[2]

Such aliens are excludable under the act and may be de-

[1] United States *ex rel.* Kasparian *v.* Hughes, 278 Fed. 262.

[2] Act approved October 16, 1918, as amended by the act approved June 5, 1920, sec. 1.

ported at any time after any entry into the country, regardless of how long they may have been here and whether or not those beliefs which render them deportable have been acquired in this country or some other. The act is retroactive, for its provisions "shall be applicable to the classes of aliens mentioned . . . irrespective of the time of their entry into the United States."[1] Last but not least, here is found a harbinger of the future provisions in regard to all deported aliens,[2] for an alien excluded or deported under its provisions against radical activity can never attempt to return, or return without being deemed guilty of a felony and on conviction thereof being sentenced to imprisonment for not more than five years and thereafter deported.[3]

It seemed that now various categories of radicals were defined with sufficient clarity and definiteness to let the matter rest. Not only legislators but others felt that "the law goes about as far as it is possible to go in providing for the exclusion of radical aliens. Under it our country could be purged of every such alien if the law were properly enforced."[4] It was not long before the purging process was to begin, and with it difficulties for citizen and alien alike crowded thick and fast one upon the other. The long story of the arrests and raids during the troubled days of 1919 and 1920, when the Departments of Labor and Justice, in the wave of "Red" fear sweeping the country, tried "strong-arm" methods of ridding the United States of all types of radicals, has been told elsewhere and need not be rehearsed here.[5] Between November 1, 1919 and April 26,

[1] Sec. 2.

[2] Act of March 4, 1929, as amended. *Vide infra*, p. 464 *et seq.*

[3] Act approved October 16, 1918, as amended by act approved June 5, 1920, sec. 3.

[4] R. Garis, *Immigration Restriction, op. cit.*, p. 140.

[5] *Vide* Louis F. Post, *The Deportations Delirium of 1920* (Chicago,

1920 warrants were issued by the Department of Labor for the arrest of 6,350 aliens alleged to be radicals. Approximately 3,000 arrests were made. About 2,500 of those arrested were members of the Communist Party and the remainder were probably members of the Union of Russian Workers. After hearings were held, only 762 were ordered deported. Between the dates mentioned, 271 were actually deported, and of these 249 were carried by the steamship *Buford,* leaving the United States on December 21, 1919 and depositing its load of deported radicals in Finland, there to be sent across the Russian border. The twenty-two remaining behind the *Buford* when it left were subsequently deported to various places.

During those sad days the courts too had their troubles, for the questions of free speech and especially of "due process of law" in proceedings against radical aliens came

1923); C. M. Panunzio, *The Deportation Cases of 1919-1920* (Federal Council of Churches, 1921); Zechariah Chafee, *Freedom of Speech* (N. Y., 1920), ch. v; Kate H. Claghorn, *The Immigrants' Day in Court* (N. Y., 1923), chs. ix, x; G. M. Stevenson, *History of American Immigration* (N. Y., 1926), ch. xiv.

H. Bevis, "Deportation of Aliens," *University of Pennsylvania Law Review,* vol. xlviii, no. 2, and "Deportation of Seditious Aliens," 23 *Law Notes* (N. Y.) 64; J. L. O'Brian, "The Menace of Administrative Law," *Proceedings of the 25th Annual Meeting of the Maryland State Bar Association,* June 24-6, 1920, p. 153 *et seq.*; A. J. Beveridge, "Law and Order and the Administration of Justice," Report of Sub-Committee on Platform and Program, Republican National Committee, 1920; *To the American People: Report upon the Illegal Practices of the United States Department of Justice,* National Popular Government League, May, 1920.

Investigation of L. F. Post on Deportation Cases, House Committee on Rules, 66th Congress, 2d Session, on *H. R. 522; Investigation of the Activities of the Department of Justice,* Sen. Doc. no. 53, 66th Congress, 1st Session, "Exclusion and Deportation of Radical Aliens," *Cong. Record,* Jan. 5, 1920, p. 1114 *et seq.*; "Deportation of Anarchist Aliens," *ibid.*, p. 1116 *et seq.*

Various articles in popular periodicals, i. e. Winthrop Lane, "The Buford Widows," 43 *Survey* 391, Jan. 10, 1920.

up again and again. The courts laid down definite criteria as to what constitutes a fair hearing,[1] so that aliens, however radical and subversive their views might be, nevertheless might be afforded at least some degree of Constitutional guarantee as to their rights.

The courts had other difficulties aside from those presented by administrative procedure; for, despite the verboseness of the acts pertaining to radical deportability, there were still questions of definition to be decided. Thus what constituted *membership in* or *affiliation with* an organization advocating the radical principles outlined, and what *organizations* fell under the ban? After a somewhat devious process of reasoning the courts decided that membership in the Communist Party warranted deportation, while membership in the Communist Labor Party did not.[2] Likewise, membership in the " I. W. W." came within the prohibited pale.[3] The important factor was not the particular beliefs of the individual foreign member but his exact relationship to or membership in such organizations.[4] In fact, so constantly have the courts dwelt on this aspect of the matter [5] that the all-important question has become that of proving membership. This, however, is not always easy to do, for the general membership of many organizations, and particularly of those engaged in radical activity, is secret, and as indi-

[1] *Vide infra*, ch. x, p. 369 *et seq.*

[2] Skeffington *v.* Katzeff, 277 Fed. 129; Ungar *v.* Seaman, 4 Fed. (2d) 80; United States *ex rel.* Lisafeld *v.* Smith, 2 Fed. (2d) 90; Antolish *v.* Paul, 283 Fed. 957; United States *ex rel.* Alberu *v.* Wallis, 268 Fed. 413; Petition of Brooks, 5 Fed. (2d) 238.

[3] *Ex parte* Bernat, 255 Fed. 429.

[4] Colyer *v.* Skeffington, 265 Fed. 17.

[5] The immigration act of 1917 refers to membership in prohibited organizations. If a person is actually a member, his individual beliefs may differ widely from those of the organization to which he belongs, but the question turns on his membership.

viduals are often inclined to deny their affiliation, there is often no means of securing evidence of such membership. The tendency of the courts in many such cases since the 1919-20 deportations is shown in the opinion of Federal Judge Thatcher, delivered in 1929:

The relator is held for deportation under an Executive Order in the usual form, upon the sole ground that he is a member of or affiliated with an organization, association, society or group that believes in, advises or teaches the overthrow by force or violence of the Government of the United States or of all forms of law.

There is a finding that the relator was a member of the *Communist Party* but there is no evidence of this. It may be that the finding intended was that the relator was a member of the *Workers (Communist) Party*, a political organization which has participated in our national elections, but the only basis for this is the hearsay statement of a woman affiliated in some way with this party that she thinks the relator is a member.

In the face of the relator's positive denial, this could not rationally be accepted as proof of membership. But even if it could there is no proof that this organization believes in, advises, or teaches the overthrow by force or violence of the Government of the United States or of all forms of law, or any evidence in this record as to what its aims and purposes are.

The relator consorted with radical agitators, and no doubt sympathized with their views; but this is not enough to warrant his deportation, unless prejudice is to take the place of proof. The Statute is specific. There is no evidence to bring the relator within its terms.[1]

[1] United States *ex rel.* John Voich alias Vujevich, Relator, *v.* Commissioner of Immigration, Ellis Island. No. M. 12-265, District Court for the Southern District of New York. Unreported. In *U. S. Daily*, July 19, 1929. The Annual Report of the American Civil Liberties Union, *The Story of Civil Liberty*, 1929-1930, erroneously states that Judge Thatcher's decision holds that "mere membership in the Communist Party does not make an alien deportable" (p. 6). What Judge Thatcher did

Another difficult thread for the courts to unravel was found in the receiving and distributing of seditious literature. If a foreigner living in Detroit received a package mailed from New York and did not know the contents of what he had received, would he fall under the ban if it proved to be incendiary propaganda against the government? The statute [1] provides the connection with the seditious literature must be knowing,[2] but the courts have held that a man may be deported even if he does not know the contents of *all* the literature he is circulating.[3] Exact states of knowledge concerning the contents of literature is, however, difficult to prove, but if the alien made the distribution of inflammatory literature knowingly, he must needs have knowledge of its character.[4]

The gradual subsidence of war-time psychology, the talk of "prosperity" and "return to normalcy," the insistence of the courts that alien radicals, though anathema in our eyes, be given their measure of "due process" before being expelled from the country, and the impossibility of deporting aliens to Russia because of lack of diplomatic relations with the Soviet government, all proved factors in lessening the activity in regard to radical deportations during the

hold was that there was no evidence in the record that Voich was a member of the Communist Party, and the fact that he consorted with radical agitators and no doubt sympathized with their views did not make him deportable. *Vide* letter of Carol Weiss King, *The Nation*, July 23, 1930.

[1] Act of October 16, 1918, as amended, sec. 1 (1).

[2] United States *ex rel.* Tisi *v.* Tod, 264 U. S. 131; United States *ex rel.* Gasparian *v.* Hughes, 278 Fed. 262; United States *ex rel.* Georgian *v.* Uhl, 271 Fed. 676; Gebartus *v.* Paul, 3 Fed. (2d) 145; Hush *v.* Davis, 3 Fed. (2d) 273.

[3] United States *ex rel.* Tisi *v.* Tod, *supra*; United States *ex rel.* Vojewvic *v.* Curran, 11 Fed. (2d) 683.

[4] United States *ex rel.* Gasparian *v.* Hughes, *supra.*

decade from 1920-1930. Yet the statutes formulated during the heat of war were left on the books, and hold within them the potentiality of repetition of the activities of 1919 and 1920.

That the matter is not yet ended is shown by the fact that the disturbance in the textile industry in the fall and winter of 1929 and 1930, with its accompaniment of Communist agitation, the serious economic depression of 1930 and 1931, and the renewed development of fear of Soviet Russia, served to arouse anew the question of radical activity in the United States. The way to Congressional investigation was paved by the Department of Labor, for in response to much urging, it delegated an officer to make a two months' survey, concluding March 15, 1930. He reported on the difficulties facing the Department in securing deportations of radicals, such as the problem of proving membership in a particular organization and that of the impossibility of deporting Russian Communists to Russia. He further called attention to the fact that during the ten immediately preceding years not only had the Department of Labor laid less emphasis on radical deportations than during the chaotic post-war days, but the bureau of investigation of the Department of Justice had made no investigations and taken no action concerning radical activity for about the same length of time, due doubtless to the same causes. From 1926 to 1929 only fifteen persons were deported under the various laws against radicals and each of the fiscal years 1928 and 1929 saw only one individual sent for such radical activity.[1] The investi-

[1] *Annual Report of the Commissioner General of Immigration for the Fiscal Year Ended June 30, 1929*, p. 224. Deportations as anarchists or violators of the act of October 16, 1918 as amended June 5, 1920 are as follows:

Deportation of Radicals

1918	*1919*	*1920*	*1921*	*1922*	*1923*	*1924*	*1925*	*1926*	*1927*	*1928*	*1929*
2	37	314	446	64	13	81	22	4	9	1	1

gator of the Department of Labor reported that the difficulties of deportation had been so great under existing acts that during the latter part of the decade from 1920-1930 hearings in deportation procedure were arranged to provide requests for deportation only in case of actual distribution of Communist literature. He stated there had been difficulty in proving, especially to some courts, that the Communist Party of the United States teaches and advocates the overthrow by force and violence of the government of the United States. He recommended a division in the bureau (temporarily at least) to handle communist matters, and an inspector in each field district where communists are active to study the problem and help prepare deportation cases. The report hopes for a "happy medium or middle course by which the Government may proceed, careful at all times to distinguish the unfortunate man unable to find employment and naturally disgruntled, from the real communist."

Congressional investigation was soon to follow, for nation-wide discussion of the subject was begun by a Committee of the House on July 15, 1930. It reported at length six months later.[1] Among its numerous recommendations are several which have special bearing on the deportation of radicals. These are:

1. Enlarging the authority of the Bureau of Investigation of the Department of Justice, for the purpose of investigating and keeping in constant touch with the revolutionary propaganda and activities of the Communists in the United States; and to provide for additional appropriations for skilled agents to devote their entire time to investigating and preparing reports on the personnel of all entities,

[1] *Vide Report of Special Committee to Investigate Communist Activities and Propaganda in the United States, in Accordance with House Resolution No. 220*, House of Representatives, 71st Congress, 2d Session, Supplement to *U. S. Daily*, vol. v, no. 270, sec. ii, January 19, 1931.

groups, individuals, who teach or advocate the overthrow of the Government of the United States by force and violence.

2. Strengthening immigration laws to prevent the admission of Communists into the United States, and providing for immediate deportation of all alien communists.
3. Providing for additional appropriations to the Bureau of Immigration for vigorous handling of deportation cases.
4. Amend (*sic*) the naturalization laws so as to forbid the naturalization of a Communist.
5. Amend (*sic*) the naturalization laws so as to cancel the United States citizenship of a Communist.

It seems that among the train of evils brought in the wake of the depression, one of the greatest is the renewal of a fear psychology. Should the recommendations of the committee be carried into legislation[1] before the return of a normal economic situation, the group of those who may be deported for radical activity will be enlarged by the inclusion of communists as such. The Secretary of Labor has recommended the change, saying:

I am firmly convinced that the law relating to the expulsion of extremists ought to be amended to provide that any alien who at any time after entry to the United States becomes affiliated with any organization the purpose of which is to supplant our form of government with a totally different system, or who engages independently in advocating such change, through force or violence, and not by the exercise of the peaceful methods provided by the Constitution, should be deported from the United States.[2]

REVOCATION OF AMERICAN CITIZENSHIF

The proposal of the Congressional investigating committee, that citizenship of Communists be revoked, was not

[1] H. R. 16296, introduced January 17, 1931, proposed this change.

[2] *Annual Report*, etc., *for 1930*, p. 19.

entirely new, for citizenship had already been revoked in the cases of some radicals, on the ground of not believing in the government of the United States at the time of naturalization and so fraudulently securing citizenship.[1] It was not until 1929, however, that a beginning was made in revocation of Communist citizenship. In that year a Pennsylvania district court revoked the citizenship of one John Tapolcsanyni on grounds of being a Communist, and the following year the revocation was upheld by a higher court.[2]

Revocation of citizenship may have implications for deportation. If the country of which the person whose American citizenship is revoked had not recognized his expatriation, would it receive him if he were deported for radical activity in the United States? In most cases, the "denaturalized" person would be a man without a country, but not always.[3] The possibility of deporting those who have once been American citizens is worthy of note.

Radicals in the Cases Studied

Since the periods under discussion showed a very small total number of deportations for radical activity, it is not surprising that none of the 612 cases studied was deported on any such ground. The fiscal year covering the first group of cases saw four deportations on grounds of anarchism or violation of the act of October 16, 1918, as amended, while the fiscal year covering the second group saw only one such deportation.

[1] For revocation of citizenship of radicals, *vide* United States *v.* Raverat, 222 Fed. 1018; United States *v.* Olsson, 196 Fed. 563; United States *v.* Swelgin, 254 Fed. 884; United States *v.* Stupiello, 260 Fed. 483.

In United States *v.* Wusterbarth, 249 Fed. 908, the man whose citizenship was revoked had been in the United States for thirty-five years.

[2] United States *v.* Tapolcsanyni, 40 Fed. (2d) 255, affirming 32 Fed. (2d) 383.

[3] *Vide infra*, p. ——, for discussion of nationality.

There was one man among the first group, however, whose record contained discussion of his radical activity, though no attempt was made to deport him on that ground. His illegal entry was sufficient to secure his deportation:

Robert Valdane (Case 49).

Robert Valdane was born in 1898 in Denmark, near Copenhagen. He emigrated to the United States in 1915 and, according to his own statement, " went to so many places they could fill a book," working as a laborer, oyster opener, machinist's assistant, etc. He secured his " first papers " in approximately 1918.

Mr. Valdane entered the United States army on November 8, 1919, serving for one year and eight months, at which time he received an honorable discharge.

In 1922 he went to Mexico, and reentered the United States in October, 1923 on foot across the border at Nogales, Arizona, continuing to Los Angeles. There he was soon arrested for distributing I. W. W. literature. In November, 1924, he served 13 days in jail for such distribution, but was released on bond of $100, paid by the I. W. W. He was almost immediately arrested again for distribution of I. W. W. papers, and served two months in prison for this offense; on its expiration, he was again arrested and served five months this time, being released from prison in May, 1925. Mr. Valdane then went to Michigan.

Someone reported him anonymously to the immigration authorities, who apprehended him in Michigan and took him to the St. Clair County Jail for detention, beginning September 3, 1925. The next day a telegraphic warrant of arrest was issued.

On September 9th, Mr. Valdane was given a hearing at the jail, but stated he did not wish legal representation. When questioned regarding his I. W. W. activity, his statements were as follows:

Q. How long have you been a member of the International Workers of the World?

A. Since June, 1924.

Q. Where did you join?
A. At Drumcamp, Cal. They were building a concrete dam there.
Q. Did you still belong?
A. Yes, I have my membership book here.
Q. Do you attend their meetings regularly?
A. Yes, when I get the chance.
Q. Do you believe in our present form of government?
A. No.
Q. What kind of government do you believe in?
A. A government ruled by the workingman.
Q. Do you believe in the overthrow of the United States Government?
A. Yes, but not by violence.
Q. How do you suppose the United States Government could be overthrown by means other than violence?
A. By general strike and election.
Q. How did you happen to join the I. W. W.?
A. One day I thought that it was not fair for some people to have everything while I had nothing. I heard of the I. W. W. and joined.
Q. What did you expect to gain by joining this organization?
A. To bring about a condition such as: Like Henry Ford, for instance, he should not have the money he has, it should be divided amongst all his help and they should equally share in profits. It is not right for the workingman to be made a tool of the capitalists, they should run everything themselves; for if everybody has the same money it would be better.
Q. Is the I. W. W. affiliated with the Third International and other organizations, such as the Soviet Government?
A. No, but we have the same views.
Q. Does the I. W. W. advocate the overthrow of the United States Government?
A. They advocate government by the workingman or labor rule and are opposed to capitalists.

Q. You say you were arrested in California and served two months in Lincoln Heights Prison for distributing papers?

A. Yes.

Q. What did those papers set forth?

A. It was radical literature, on how good the organization was and what it could do for the workingman, an effort to enlarge membership and a general means of keeping in touch with the members.

On October, 1925, Mr. Valdane was sent to Detroit, where he was held in the Wayne County Jail until November 1, and then sent to Ellis Island. On November 7th, a warrant of deportation was issued on the same grounds as the warrant of arrest, which were (1) " L. P. C." and (2) that he entered the United States at a place other than designated by the Commissioner General of Immigration. There was never any recommendation as to deportation on grounds of radical activity, as the testimony did not elicit information which would bring Mr. Valdane under the specific wording of the statute pertaining to deportation of radicals.

He was deported on November 27, 1925 at the expense of the government, as his entry by steamship had been more than five years previous, but his entry illegally across the border had been within five years.

PROSTITUTES

The *provisions* regarding deportation of radicals are definite. The difficulty lies in the indefiniteness of the *activity* for which they are deported. Another category of persons whose deportation is mandatory and for which the provisions in the law are also definite and explicit is the group connected in any way with prostitution. With them the offenses are, however, more definite than those involved in radical activity. Aliens connected in other ways with " immorality " are more dependent on administrative discretion in use of the term.

It had early become obvious that of all the possible " undesirables" who might strive to enter the country, those involved in prostitution and immorality akin to it were least worthwhile additions to the population and should be rigorously prohibited from entering or remaining here. The first of the federal immigration acts, that of March 3, 1875, forbade the importation of women for purposes of prostitution and made such importation a felony,[1] and by 1903 the practical application of this idea had been worked out in definite form, for it not only excluded prostitutes and persons who procure or attempt to bring in prostitutes or women for the purpose of prostitution,[2] but it provided that

> the importation into the United States of any woman or girl for the purposes of prostitution is hereby forbidden; and whoever shall import or attempt to import any woman or girl into the United States for the purposes of prostitution, or shall hold or attempt to hold, any woman or girl for such purposes in pursuance of such illegal importation shall be deemed guilty of a felony, and, upon conviction thereof, shall be imprisoned not less than one nor more than five years and pay a fine not exceeding five thousand dollars.[3]

Here too even citizens might be involved, and the penalty extended to aliens and citizens alike.

By 1907, a further effort was made to combat the prostitution evil by adding that

> whoever shall keep, maintain, control, support or harbor in any house or other place, for the purpose of prostitution, or for any other immoral purpose, any alien woman or girl, within three years after she shall have entered the United States, shall, in every such case, be deemed guilty of a felony, and on conviction

[1] Sec. 3. For discussion of the provisions of this act, *vide* Garis, *op. cit.*, pp. 86-7.

[2] Sec. 2.

[3] Sec. 3.

thereof be imprisoned not more than five years and pay a fine of not more than five thousand dollars; and any alien woman or girl who shall be found an inmate of a house of prostitution, or practicing prostitution, at any time within three years after she shall have entered the United States, shall be deemed to be unlawfully within the United States, and shall be deported.[1]

But even with so great an evil as that of prostitution, legislators were proceeding slowly and carefully and had not yet dared to authorize deportation at any time after entry, clinging conservatively to a period of three years after entry. By 1910, however, they had become more courageous, and they then[2] extended the exclusion provisions by adding "persons who are supported by or receive in whole or in part the proceeds of prostitution," and removed the three-year limit for deportation of

any alien who shall be found an inmate of or connected with the management of a house of prostitution or practicing prostitution after such alien shall have entered the United States, or who shall receive, share in, or derive benefit from any part of the earnings of any prostitute; or who is employed by, in, or in connection with any house of prostitution or music or dance hall or other place of amusement or resort habitually frequented by prostitutes, or where prostitutes gather, or who in any way assists, protects, or promises to protect from arrest any prostitute, shall be deemed to be unlawfully within the United States and shall be deported.

In these provisions, forming a part of the present law, the principle of deportation at any time after entry was introduced. So by them a small baby girl brought to this country by her parents and some twenty years later becoming a prostitute would be deportable to the country whence

[1] Act of February 20, 1907, sec. 3.

[2] By act of March 26, 1910 (36 Stat. 263).

she had come twenty years before, regardless of the social conditions in this country which might be responsible for her occupation.

The same 1910 act provided for punishment for anyone attempting to return after deportation, and for deportation after the expiration of sentence for violations of this provision. In the growing severity against prostitution, the same year brought forth the "White Slave Traffic" Act [1] which is still in force and which focuses attention on the interstate and international implications of the problem. Conviction of an alien under the Mann Act for transportation of a woman for an immoral purpose, within the United States, does not necessarily subject the alien to deportation.

It may be necessary in a particular case, for the government to prove that an alien has shared in the profits of a prostitute and that element may be entirely lacking in the case of a conviction under the White Slave statute. The conviction may not involve prostitution. In a given case, however, the evidence upon which the conviction was made may be appropriately incorporated in the record upon the warrant of arrest for deportation and considered in determining the deportability of the alien.[2]

The gradually increasing severity as regards those connected with prostitution and growing definiteness mark the development of the law to date. Under the 1917 act, without any exceptions, prostitutes, persons coming to this country for purposes of prostitution, those coming to the United States for an immoral purpose, or directly or indirectly procuring or attempting to procure or import prostitutes or persons for the purpose of prostitution or any other immoral purpose, or who receive any or all of the proceeds

[1] Act of June 25, 1910 (36 Stat. 825). This act is also called the "Mann Act". *Vide* esp. sec. 6 for immigration of prostitutes.

[2] Cook and Hagerty, *op. cit.*, p. 148, § 296.

of prostitution, are excludable from the country.[1] For such persons, exclusion is not deemed sufficient, and it has been provided, as indicated in the earlier law, that the person guilty of importation of an alien for an immoral purpose, or attempt to import, is guilty of a felony and is punishable by fine of not more than $5,000 and, in addition to the fine, imprisonment for not more than ten years,[2]—such penalty of course applies to alien and citizen alike and must be distinguished as such. It is an example of the provision of criminal penalties in connection with the deportation law. Although deportation itself is not a punishment for crime, criminal punishment may be added to deportation. If an alien connected with prostitution is ordered excluded or deported and returns to this country, he is not only subject to deportation but on conviction by a court shall be sentenced to imprisonment for not more than two years.[3] Here is foreshadowed the development of the 1929 law which makes it a felony for aliens deported after March 4, 1929 to return to this country, no matter why they may have been deported.[4]

Of course, the five-year limitation after entry on the excludable category of prostitution has been removed, and anyone who was excludable on grounds of prostitution or connection with it at the time of entry, may be deported, no matter how long that person has been in the country. Furthermore, should an alien enter the country legally and without taint and then become an inmate of or connected

[1] Immigration act of 1917, sec. 3; United States *ex rel.* Femina *v.* Curran, 12 Fed. (2d) 639; United States *v.* Bitty, 208 U. S. 399; *Ex parte* Pouliot, 196 Fed. 437.

[2] Immigration act of 1917, sec. 4.

[3] *Ibid.* The procedure under this section is by prosecution in a federal court. Every alien involved constitutes a separate offense. *Vide* Cook and Hagerty, *op. cit.*, p. 154, § 308.

[4] *Vide infra*, p. 464 *et seq.*

with the management of a house of prostitution or practicing prostitution in this country, he or she would be deportable, no matter when he or she had entered the country.[1] It is not necessary for any court to convict for committing prostitution or being connected with it in any manner requiring deportation;[2] if prostitution can be shown to have been practiced,[3] deportation follows. Conviction for "an offer to commit prostitution" is not sufficient to cause deportation in itself, for it is not "practicing prostitution."

Not only are those practicing prostitution deportable but any alien receiving any share in, or deriving any benefit from the earnings of a prostitute; or managing, or employed by, or in connection with, a house of prostitution, music or dance hall, or place of amusement or resort habitually frequented by prostitutes or where prostitutes gather; or who assist prostitutes or promise to protect them from arrest; or importing or attempting to import persons for the purpose of prostitution, or any other immoral purpose, is deportable irrespective of the length of his stay in this country.[4] As already indicated, any alien excluded and deported, or arrested and deported because of connection with prostitution, and returning to this country, or convicted for the importation of prostitutes or persons for any other immoral purpose, is also deportable.

As the law regarding prostitutes is so definite, most court decisions have been less concerned with interpreting the statute than with discussion of whether or not a certain alien should fall within the given categories of the law.

[1] Immigration act of 1917, sec. 19.

[2] Gambroulis *v.* Nash, 12 Fed. (2d) 49; *Ex parte* Pouliot, 196 Fed. 437.

[3] United States *ex rel.* Mittler *v.* Curran, 8 Fed. (2d) 355.

[4] Immigration act of 1917, sec. 19; *Ex parte* Loo Shew Ung, 210 Fed. 990; *Ex parte* Young, 211 Fed. 370; *In re* Psimoulos, 222 Fed. 118, 224 Fed. 1022; Katz *v.* Commissioner of San Francisco, 245 Fed. 316; United States *v.* Johnson, 7 Fed. (2d) 453.

Many cases regarding fairness of proceedings come before the court in regard to prostitution. As the law is definite, and the provisions regarding prostitution specific, if a person is apprehended for violating any of the specific provisions, the only feasible way by which he or she tries to avoid deportation is by trying to show that the proceedings were so unfair as to warrant interference by the court.[1]

Cases of prostitution are generally picked up by the police when caught soliciting or in disorderly houses. They are then taken to police headquarters and held. While being detained as witnesses or awaiting trial, they are reported by the police to the local immigration authorities, who come, as a general rule, to police headquarters, to take the "preliminary statement"[2] and then apply for a warrant of arrest from Washington. If there is a woman's bureau connected with the police department[3] this bureau usually does the reporting of the women's cases to the immigration officials and in some rare instances tries to get in touch with a relative or social agency in the place to which the prostitute will be sent if she is deported. At the expiration of her sentence, she is turned over to the immigration authorities for deportation, as are alien "panderers" when they have paid their fines and served their sentences.[4]

[1] *Vide* Toku Sakai *v.* United States, 239 Fed. 492; Weinbrand *v.* Prentis, 4 Fed. (2d) 778; Yip Wah *v.* Nagle, 7 Fed. (2d) 426; Svarney *v.* United States, 7 Fed. (2d) 515, for illustrations of the type of such cases.

For general discussion of fairness of proceedings, *vide infra*, ch. x, p. 369 *et seq.*

[2] *Vide infra*, p. 331.

[3] As in Detroit, Cleveland, Washington, etc.

[4] It is a criminal offense on the part of either alien or citizen to import an alien for an immoral purpose, or attempt so to import, and is punishable by Sec. 4 of the act of Feb. 5, 1917, by fine of not more than $5,000 and (in addition to the fine) imprisonment for not more than ten years. Every alien so imported for such purposes constitutes a separate offense. *Ex parte* Szumrak, 278 Fed. 803.

Immigration Rules of January 1, 1930, rule 19, subdivision M, par. 2.

AN "IMMORAL PURPOSE"

One provision of this section of the immigration act is as vague as the preceding part is definite. "Any alien who shall import or attempt to import a person . . . for any other immoral purpose" is deportable. But what, one asks, is an "immoral purpose"? The courts have been at some pains to find out, and have contented themselves with deciding on the merits of each particular case rather than attempting to lay down a general definition.[1] They have on occasion contented themselves with repeating the phraseology of the statute by saying that an alien entering the country for any immoral purpose is deportable, whether or not the purpose has any connection with prostitution.[2] Thus a foreigner resident here and bringing in his European mistress would be subject to deportation.[3] However, if he brought in his common-law wife from a place where common-law marriages are held valid he would not be considered to have brought his wife for an "immoral purpose" and so would not be subject to deportation.[4] Or if he had been married by a ceremony which might not be valid in the United States but was legal where performed, and if he then brought his wife to this country, he could not be held to have brought her for an "immoral purpose," for the validity of a marriage ceremony is to be determined by the law of the place where it was performed.[5] So also, an alien woman who came to

[1] *Ex parte* Morel, 292 Fed. 423; Morrel. *v.* Baker, 270 Fed. 577; Dorto *v.* Clark, 300 Fed. 568; United States *v.* Dorto, 5 Fed. (2d) 596; Yip Wah *v.* Nagle, 7 Fed. (2d) 426.

[2] Grkic *v.* United States, 3 Fed. (2d) 276; United States *ex rel.* Reinmann *v.* Martin, 193 Fed. 795.

[3] United States *v.* Bitty, 208 U. S. 393; Caminetti *v.* United States, 242 U. S. 470; United States *ex rel.* Femina *v.* Curran, 12 Fed. (2d) 639.

[4] *Ex parte* Morel, *supra*.

[5] *Ex parte* Suzanna, 295 Fed. 713; Kane *v.* Johnson, 13 Fed. (2d) 433.

this country to marry and lived with her fiancé on the representation by him that the contract of marriage was sufficient to constitute marriage, and then left him when she discovered his deceit and obtained judgment for breach of promise of marriage, would not be subject to deportation on the ground that she entered the United States for an " immoral purpose." [1] If an alien brings a woman into the United States for such a purpose he may be deported immediately without any necessity of being convicted of such importation.[2] It is conceivable that an alien might bring in an American woman, who had been abroad, for " an immoral purpose." In such a case, the alien would be deportable, while the American woman could of course remain here.

The position of the common-law wife is only one of the problems that have arisen in connection with the citizenship of " immoral women." Attempts were made before the passage of the " Cable Act " [3] to render it impossible to deport prostitutes who, after proceedings were started married American citizens and thus acquired American citizenship and could not be deported. To avert this, the law of 1917 specifically stated that

> the marriage to an American citizen of a female of the sexually immoral classes the exclusion or deportation of which is prescribed by this act shall not invest such female with United States citizenship if the marriage of such alien shall be solemn-

Here the question turned on the right of the wife of an American citizen to enter on a non-quota basis. The ceremony by which she and her husband had been married would have been void in the state in which he was domiciled, but the court held as above stated and also that the right of a woman to enter was a federal question, not dependent on the law of the particular state where the husband happened to be domiciled.

[1] United States *ex rel.* Reinmann *v.* Martin, 193 Fed. 795.

[2] *Ex parte* Pouliot, 196 Fed. 437.

[3] Act of September 22, 1922 (42 Stat. 1021).

ized after her arrest or after the commission of acts which make her liable to deportation . . . [1]

Of course since the Cable Act became effective a woman does not acquire the citizenship of her husband merely by reason of her marriage to him and so this provision of the law is in effect a dead letter, and a deportable woman may be either excluded [2] or deported [3] even though she is the wife of an American citizen. This is particularly true in the case of women of the immoral classes.[4]

Prostitutes among the Cases Studied

In the first group of cases studied, there were sixteen deported on various grounds connected with prostitution, such as managing a house of prostitution, or music or dance hall or other place of amusement, or resort, habitually frequented by prostitutes; or entering the United States for the purpose of prostitution; or being supported by or receiving in whole or in part the proceeds of prostitution. In the second group, with similar charges, there were two cases. In only six of the total number of cases was the charge " L.P.C." used. Even in the days when " L.P.C." was used more frequently than at the time of the second group, charges connected with prostitution were evidently " strong " enough by themselves. The two prostitution cases in the second group had entered the country illegally, and the additional charge was used that the person had entered the United States without an unexpired immigration visa.

[1] Sec. 19. *Vide Ex parte* Bigney, 285 Fed. 669.

[2] United States *ex rel.* Ulrich *v.* Kellogg, 30 Fed. (2d) 984.

[3] Gomez *v.* Nagle, 6 Fed. (2d) 520.

[4] Although the case of Dorto *v.* Clark, 300 Fed. 568, and 5 Fed. (2d) 596, ran contra to Gomez *v.* Nagle, *supra,* as far as the general run of alien wives of American citizens goes, even that case did not uphold the right of immoral wives to remain here.

Vilma Megyi (Case 50).

Vilma Megyi was born March 20, 1906 in Budapest, Hungary. She came to the United States with her father in 1913, but her mother stayed at home in Hungary. Vilma went to school in New York, graduating from the 8th grade of public school.

In 1922 Vilma returned to Budapest to visit her mother, but she did not remain long, returning to the United States on November 24, 1922, and being admitted on primary inspection as a returning resident alien. She soon secured work as a telephone operator, earning $18 a week. She stayed over 2 years and then was increased to a salary of $22 a week. During the time she was working she continued to live with her father and keep house for him.

On April 18, 1925, Miss Megyi was arrested, and 5 days later was committed to Bedford Reformatory by the Magistrate's Court, with a sentence of 1 day-3 years. The next day (?) the case was reported to the immigration office at Ellis Island by a probation officer of the Women's Day Court. A warrant of arrest was issued on June 4 and a hearing was held at the Bedford Reformatory on October 23. There Miss Megyi stated she had no money for a lawyer.

A warrant of deportation was issued on November 25, with the same charges as in the warrant of arrest, (1) "L. P. C.", (2) that she had been found practicing prostitution subsequent to her entry into the United States. Miss Megyi was deported on December 19, 1925, at the expense of the steamship company which had brought her back from her visit to Europe in 1922.

Giordano Vittorio (Case 51).

Giordano Vittorio was born in 1892 in the province of Salerno, Italy. He learned the trade of shoemaker at an early age and worked at it previous to his emigration to the United States with his father in 1910. His father had come to the United States before, and, so his son later claimed, had been naturalized in 1903, but returned to Italy for a visit and brought his son over with him. His son stayed two years in New York with his father, then returned to Italy and tried to return to the United

States in 1922. As he could not secure a quota number, he went to Canada and entered the United States illegally in 1923.

Mr. Vittorio was deported from New York to Italy on July 17, 1923, on the grounds of his illegal entry. He then took ship for Mexico, and landed on July 26, 1924 at Vera Cruz. He went to Mexico City for a few weeks, then entered the United States at Nogales, Arizona on August 2, 1925. He presented a birth certificate to the effect that he was born in the United States, but he had bought the certificate in Mexico.

When he entered he brought Marquita Velasquez with him. She had been born in the United States but had been living in Mexico, practicing prostitution and smuggling narcotics and aliens into the United States. She had employed Mr. Vittorio to help her.

A warrant for his arrest was issued on August 24, 1925, and he was detained in the county jail at Nogales. He was given a hearing 4 days later, and as no Italian interpreter was available, a Spanish one was used. A warrant of deportation was issued on October 6, with the same charges as those in the warrant of arrest, namely, (1) "L. P. C.", (2) that at the time of his entry he was supported by or received in part the proceeds of prostitution, (3) that he was not in possession of an unexpired immigration visa, (4) that he entered by land at a place other than a designated port of entry for aliens, (5) that he was brought to foreign contiguous territory by a transportation company which had not complied with the requirements of Sec. 17 of the immigration act of 1924 and had not resided in that territory for two years. He was deported from Galveston on October 22, sailing to Bremen.

Hélène Mousseau (Case 52).

Hélène Mousseau was born on December 24, 1902 in Le Havre, France. She came to the United States on December 1, 1921, being admitted as a temporary visitor. When she landed she secured work as a dressmaker in New York, then went to Chicago and finally to San Francisco.

On March 12, 1929, Miss Mousseau was arrested for prostitution in San Francisco, and was sent to the city hospital there for 7 weeks observation. On April 29, a preliminary statement was taken from her at the hospital, and a warrant was issued for her arrest on May 14. She was released on bond for $1000. A hearing was held on June 1, but was postponed until the 11th to secure a lawyer. The lawyer testified that the preliminary statement was taken entirely in English and that Miss Mousseau could not understand English sufficiently well to know what was being asked of her. A warrant of deportation was issued on September 1, 1929, on the grounds (1) that she had been found practicing prostitution subsequent to her entry into the United States, and (2) that she had remained longer than the time allotted her for a visit, with no permission to stay. The warrant of arrest had contained the further charge that she was not in possession of an unexpired immigration visa at the time of entry, but this was not recommended by the board of review or sustained.

Miss Mousseau was deported on January 5, 1930 from Galveston, at the expense of the steamship line which had brought her to the United States.

NARCOTIC LAW VIOLATORS

For many years the law pertaining to deportation of narcotic law violators was one of the least inclusive parts of the immigration law, for it was filled with loopholes which prevented numerous aliens involved in the traffic from being sent from the country.

The 1917 immigration act is silent on the subject, so in 1922 the early act of 1909 was amended providing that if any person fraudulently or knowingly brings any narcotic drug unlawfully into the United States,

or assists in so doing, or receives, conceals, buys, sells or in

[1] An act to prohibit the importation and the use of opium for other than medicinal purposes, approved Feb. 9, 1909, amended May 26, 1922.

any manner facilitates the transportation, concealment, or sale of any such narcotic drug after being imported . . . knowing the same to have been imported contrary to law.

he is to be fined, if convicted, nor more than $5,000 and imprisoned not more than ten years. An alien convicted under these provisions is deportable, without any statute of limitations on his going.[1]

This law was far from inclusive. For instance, *knowledge* was an essential element in securing conviction, for only fraudulent or knowing sale, or importation, or purchase with knowledge of illegal importation could be punished. So an alien engaged in narcotic buying who did not know that his purchases had been illegally brought into the country would not be punishable or deportable under the act. The statute was conceived as a revenue act and not as a statute declaring against the importation of narcotics[2] and so conviction under it would not involve "moral turpitude." Furthermore, the act defined only certain classes. An alien convicted of even knowingly buying or selling illegally imported narcotics not consisting of "opium, coca leaves, cocaine, or any salt derivative, or preparation of opium, coca leaves or cocaine" would not be liable under the act for punishment or deportation.[3]

Nor did conviction for violation of any other narcotic acts render the alien so convicted liable to deportation. The early Narcotic Drug Export and Import Act of May 26, 1901 could not be construed as grounds for deportation.[4]

[1] Chung Que Fong *v.* Nagle, 15 Fed. (2d) 789; United States *ex rel.* Grimaldi *v.* Ebey, 12 Fed. (2d) 922.

[2] Cook and Hagerty, *op. cit.*, pp. 149-150, § 299 and § 300.

[3] Violation of other sections of the same act than the one quoted [Sec. 2(c)] would not render an alien deportable.

[4] Weedin *v.* Moy Fat, 8 Fed. (2d) 448.

Violation of the so-called " Harrison Anti-Narcotic Law [1] was held to be violation of a revenue act only. So the person convicted under it would not have committed a crime involving moral turpitude, nor would he come under the provisions for deportation of those connected with narcotics,[2] as discussed above.

The deficiencies in the law for deportation of those involved in narcotic traffic were so many that Congress by act of February 18, 1931 provided for deportation of an alien convicted in violation of the Harrison narcotic law and amendments. The act states:

> that any alien (except an addict who is not a dealer in, or peddler of any of the narcotic drugs mentioned in his Act) who after the enactment of this Act, shall be convicted and sentenced for violation of or conspiracy to violate any statute of the United States taxing, prohibiting, or regulating the manufacture, production, compounding, transportation, sale, exchange, dispensing, giving away, importation, or exportation of opium or coca leaves, heroin or any salt, derivative or preparation of opium or coca leaves, shall be taken into custody and deported . . . [3]

[1] Of Dec. 17, 1914.

[2] Hampton *v.* Wong Ging, 299 Fed. 289; United States *ex rel.* Andreacchi *v.* Curran, 38 Fed. (2d) 498.

The revenue aspects of the law are shown by a recent case, where it was held that a man convicted of selling narcotics without being registered and without having paid the special tax required by the Harrison Act "could not be convicted of selling narcotics without requiring from the purchaser a written order issued in blank by the Commissioner of Internal Revenue, under another section of such law, since the criminal act under both sections is the sale, and as there was but one sale there was but one criminal act, although the defendant could have been prosecuted therefor under different sections of the narcotic law, and therefore convictions under both sections with only the one criminal act as the basis therefor would place the defendant twice in jeopardy in violation of the Fifth Amendment of the United States Constitution.—Ballerini *v.* Aderholt, Warden, C. C. A. 5, October 28, 1930, no. 5865, quoted in *U. S. Daily*, November 6, 1930.

[3] H. R. 3394, 71st Congress, 3rd Session.

Since the passage of that act, not only may an alien convicted of involvement in buying or selling narcotics may be deported but also one convicted of violating any United States narcotic law.

Narcotic Law Violators in the Cases Studied

In view of the numerous possibilities for involvement in various aspects of the narcotic traffic which have not been grounds for deportation, it is not surprising that there were only five cases out of the total number where narcotic law violation was given as one of the grounds of deportation. In all of these cases, the " L.P.C." charge accompanied the narcotic charge, as would seem logical. Several additional grounds for deportation were also involved, as two of the aliens had also entered illegally.

The following show the type of narcotic case:

Manuele Balbo (Case 53).

Manuele Balbo was born in 1902 in Sopramonte, Italy. He came to the United States in 1920, was legally admitted, and stayed five months. Then he went to Argentina for ten months and finally to Mexico, where he remained 2 years.

In May or June, 1923, Mr. Balbo entered the United States illegally, crossing the railroad bridge from Juarez to El Paso. He went to Nogales, Ariz., and lived there for a year and a half. Then he crossed the border to Mexico for a few hours, returning with a narcotic smuggler. They were not apprehended, and got as far as Denver, before they were caught on October 26, 1925 and taken to the county jail there. Mr. Balbo was found to have bought or sold one ounce of cocaine on August 19, 1925, and so he was sentenced to 4 months in jail, plus $500 fine, for violation of the " Jones-Miller " Narcotic Act. The sentence was to begin September 21, 1925.

A warrant was issued for Mr. Balbo's arrest in deportation proceedings on October 21, and a hearing was given him at the jail on November 3. On November 20, a warrant of deportation was issued with the same charges as in the warrant of arrest, (1) "L. P. C.", (2) that he was not in possession of an unexpired immigration visa at the time of entry, and (3) that he was an alien who had been convicted under subdivision C, Section 2 of the act approved May 26, 1922.

Mr. Balbo was sent to New York, January 1, 1926 and deported three days later, at government expense, destined direct to Italy.

It must be remembered that violation only of certain narcotic laws is a cause for deportation. The following shows conviction for violation of a narcotic law which was for revenue only and so could not cause deportation:

Carlo Pontormo (Case 54).

Carlo Pontormo was born in 1887 in Girgenti, Sicily, Italy. He came to the United States in 1911 and remained until 1916 when he returned to Italy and served in the war. In 1920 he again came to the United States, being admitted on primary inspection on April 30, 1920, and going direct to Cleveland, where he had previously lived.

Mr. Pontormo worked first as a bricklayer, then opened a grocery store. He was sentenced to the Federal Penitentiary at Atlanta for violation of the act of December 14, 1914, as amended by the Revenue Act of 1918. He was sentenced by the district court of the Northern District of Ohio on January 3, 1923. His sentence was to expire on September 1, 1926, but he could be paroled in May, 1924.

On August 11, 1924, the inspector in charge of the immigration service at Atlanta wrote the Commissioner General of Immigration, "This alien was convicted within 5 years after his entry into the United States and sentenced to the Federal Penitentiary for violation of the narcotic law. While he claims to have been innocent of the crime, and his statement if true would seem to bear out his claim, this office cannot go back of the findings and sentence of the court, and the evidence makes it clear that he has become a public charge within 5 years of entry." A preliminary statement had been taken at the prison on July 5, 1924, when Mr. Pontormo had stated: "I had a grocery store and 5 rooms above, all rented. One night they raided those rooms and found 7 ounces of morphine or cocaine, I do not know which as I haven't seen either. The Judge told me I could be sent back to Italy so I could take care of my mother who is sick with no one to care for her." A warrant of arrest was issued the same day.

A hearing was held on August 9, through an interpreter, at the prison. The case came before the board of review in Washington on August 22, 1924, and they recommended release on $500 bond on the expiration of the man's sentence, to close up his business, but he could not raise the money and was not released. Meanwhile, the President on March 18, 1925, commuted Mr. Pontormo's sentence on condition that he be immediately deported. Word of the commutation did not reach the penitentiary until March 24th, and a deportation party had left there for Ellis Island the previous day. So Mr. Pontormo had to wait until another party went through, on May 1, 1925. A warrant of deportation had been issued on March 23rd, on only the ground of "L. P. C."; despite the previous recommendation of the inspector, the charge that he had become a public charge within 5 years, etc. had not been used. As the narcotic law Mr. Pontormo had violated was a revenue one, he could not be deported on that ground. He was deported on July 1, 1925 at the expense of the steamship company which had brought him to the United States.

CONCLUSIONS

The laws pertaining to deportation of those aliens whose political and social beliefs do not coincide with ours were framed as being all-inclusive. In practice they have met with the approval neither of those who favor a drastic policy nor those who desire leniency, while those concerned with administration of the laws have objected from the viewpoint of execution. In contrast to the vague "L.P.C."

provisions, the sections of the law aimed at radicals " are framed with such infinitely detailed description of the offenses concerned that it has been found exceedingly difficult and often impossible to bring some obviously dangerous anarchistic activities within the scope of the law." [1]

Whether or not new legislation is adopted to modify the existing provisions of law in regard to deportation of radicals, it is certain that the tide of prosecution of radicals will continue to rise and fall as political and economic events shape a psychology of fear within the United States. It seems equally certain that the convictions of no anarchist or communist, be he alien or citizen, were ever changed by law and that it is possible that, as Commissioner Day indicated, for every one arrested five more will spring up. Perhaps some day men in general may have come to agree with Mr. Justice Holmes:

> when men have realized that time has upset many fighting faiths, they may come to believe even more than they believe the very foundations of their own conduct that the ultimate good desired is better reached by free trade in ideas,—that the best test of truth is the power of thought to get itself accepted in the competition of the market, and that truth is the only ground upon which their wishes safely can be carried out.[2]

Many of the remarks applying to criminals involved in " moral turpitude " apply equally well to prostitutes and narcotic traffickers. Merely to send from the United States a person involved in prostitution or in the narcotic traffic is no solution as far as the *problem* goes. Individuals as accustomed to evading the law, as are these two classes, are apt to be less frightened by the provisions forbidding reentry than the more desirable citizens of other countries, and so

[1] Abrams *v.* United States, 250 U. S. 616, 630, dissenting opinion.

[2] *Annual Report of the Secretary of Labor for,* etc., *1930,* p. 19.

are apt in many instances to return to the United States. Here too, then, there is need for international cooperation regarding care for such socially inadequate persons. But in these classes as with criminals care must be taken not to give a deported person the stigma of prostitution when "other immorality" may be far from prostitution.

CHAPTER VII

Illegal Entries

THE BORDERS

Long stretches of desert, mountain and easily wadable river on the Mexican border, mile after mile of farm-land, river and lake on the Canadian line, and thousands of miles of coast-line from Maine to Florida and from Washington to California, have offered all possible hospitality to the foreigner determined by fair means of foul to enter the United States, and to alien or citizen who for a consideration smuggles otherwise inadmissible aliens into the country. With increasing restrictiveness in American immigration laws, it has become more and more necessary to attempt to stem the tide of surreptitious entry; yet it has proved well-nigh impossible to make a water-tight compartment of these United States so that no inadmissible aliens may seep in. They may come by land in the never-ending ebb and flow of persons of all races and peoples across the borders of the United States; they may come by air; they may come by sea, in large boats or small,[1] stowing themselves away

[1] The following table shows the number of persons dealt with by the immigration service at land borders alone during the fiscal year 1930, to say nothing of those who enter by sea or air. It gives some idea of the problem of ascertaining the citizenship of those who cross the borders, from the numerical side alone.

Number of Persons Entering the United States via Land Borders, 1930

Each entry of the same person is considered a separate transaction.

among the cargo of incoming steamships, or serving as seamen and deserting the ships; they wade the Rio Grande, or row across the Detroit River, or walk across the bridges at

From the *Annual Report of the Commissioner General*, etc., *for 1930*, p. 16.

Inward movement	Aliens	United States citizens	Total
Via the Canadian border . .	14,498,083	17,753,465	32,251,548
Via the Mexican border. . .	15,536,218	11,488,873	27,025,091
Total	30,034,301	29,242,338	*59,276,639

* Estimated.

PERSONS, IN POSSESSION OF IMMIGRANT-IDENTIFICATION CARDS OR BORDER-CROSSING CARDS, HABITUALLY CROSSING THE CANADIAN AND MEXICAN LAND BORDERS

Country of residence	Aliens			United States citizens			All crossers		
	Intermittent	Active	Total	Intermittent	Active	Total	Intermittent	Active	Total
Residents of the United States:									
Crossing Canadian border	19,005	629	19,634	2,902	1,429	4,331	21,907	2,058	23,965
Crossing Mexican border	30,821	16,960	47,781	28,711	7,037	35,748	59,532	23,997	83,529
Total	49,826	17,589	67,415	31,613	8,466	40,079	81,439	26,055	107,494
Residents of Canada . . .	14,999	10,385	25,384	953	631	1,584	15,952	11,016	26,968
Residents of Mexico . .	51,289	51,049	102,338	615	843	1,458	51,904	51,892	103,796
Grand total	116,114	79,023	195,137	33,181	9,940	43,121	149,295	88,963	238,258

NOTE. — Intermittent crossers are those who cross the border not more than three times a week on an average; the active crossers are those who cross the border daily, or at least four times a week on an average.

such places as Niagara Falls and El Paso; they enter as visitors and disappear into the unknown, or as students who fail to register in the school to which they supposedly are destined or who leave before the termination of their periods of study, — the methods of their entrance are legion, but come they do. How many of them is not known, for

> basic information is so meager that any statement as to the number of aliens who have entered the United States unlawfully or who are now unlawfully resident here must of necessity be largely based on conjecture. . . . Various estimates have been submitted by immigration officers in the field . . . and by others interested in immigration matters, and after a careful consideration of these estimates and other factors . . . it would appear that a fair estimate or conjecture would be about 400,000.[1]

When the law provided for exclusion on the basis of economic, moral, mental, and physical disqualification, only such as feared rejection on one or more of those grounds were likely to enter surreptitiously. Then the addition of the literacy test in 1917 made many who were otherwise eligible fear they could not learn to read and so gave additional reason for trying to avoid examination on entry. The final impetus, however, was given by the addition of the numerical basis for exclusion in the so-called "quota acts."

If the whole system of restrictive immigration is to work, the arm of the immigration service must continue to stop the holes in the dyke through which the flood of illegal en-

[1] Report of the Secretary of Labor, January 6, 1931, in response to Senate Resolution No. 355, December 8, 1930, which had requested information regarding the number of aliens in the country illegally, and the percentage of those who are deportable. For methods by which the Secretary estimated the numbers, *vide U. S. Daily*, January 7, 1931.

The Secretary feels that of the 400,000, possibly 25% are deportable. *Vide infra*, p. 327.

tries strives to pour. The problem is to devise methods of preventing the leakage in the restrictive immigration wall. Obviously, immigration inspectors on the force were entirely insufficient in numbers and equipment to see that the miles of seacoast and land border were properly patrolled to exclude those who were not admissible. When it became impossible for an alien to secure one of the prized numbers within the quota, it seemed an easy way out of the difficulty to go to Canada, Mexico or Cuba and surreptitiously slip in from there. This method of ingress to the country was used not only by those seeking entrance for the first time, but also by those who had previously been in the country and found it impossible legally to return. It was soon realized that the miles of woods and open country and the line between the United States and its northern and southern neighbors, imaginary in every sense of the word, necessitated a border patrol to prevent easy illegal entry, and to check an embryonic flourishing trade in "bootlegging" aliens.

In 1924 an expenditure of $1,000,000 was authorized[1] for land border patrol and this has been augmented, so that the force of men engaged in the work increased from 472 in 1925 to 805 in 1930. These men attempt to watch over the extended coast line of the United States, with its extensive harbors, inlets and rivers; the Great Lakes and other international waterways; the 6,000 miles of land boundary. They engage in a multitude of activities, as may be seen from the following tables for 1925 and 1930:

[1] By appropriation act of May 28, 1924 (43 Stat. 240). Additional funds were provided the following year by act of Feb. 27, 1925 (43 Stat. 1049).

For discussion of the development of the border patrol, *vide Annual Report of the Commissioner General of Immigration for*, etc., *1930*, p. 34 *et seq.*

PRINCIPAL ACTIVITIES OF BORDER PATROL OFFICERS DURING THE FISCAL YEAR ENDED JUNE 30, 1925.[1]

Character of Work	*Number*
Persons questioned or investigated	1,252,379
Persons detained temporarily	9,321
Persons referred to local immigrant inspector for further investigation	14,078
Persons apprehended (or assistance rendered in their apprehension for violation of customs regulations)	1,185
Aliens arrested involving seizure of vehicles or contraband goods	536
Aliens arrested on warrants	2,847
Aliens attempting to enter the United States turned back without resorting to warrant procedure	14,711
Smuggled aliens captured	
Miles patroled (on foot, by vehicle and by boat)	2,288,000
Alien smugglers captured	331
Inspection of trains, motor vehicles, etc.	
Freight and passenger trains examined	104,094
Passengers on same (estimated)	1,553,500
Automobiles and motor busses stopped and examined	418,128
Boats and other means of transportation stopped and examined	33,485
Passengers on above	1,543,400
Seizures (including assistance given other officials) for violation of customs, prohibition and immigration laws	
Automobiles	253
Boats and other conveyances	195
Value of above, including seized contraband goods (estimated)	$475,600
Special investigations made, such as requests by immigration officers, to establish responsibility and willingness to support relatives applying at various ports of entry for admission to the United States	2,177

[1] *Annual Report of the Commissioner General of Immigration for the Fiscal Year Ended June 30, 1925*, p. 16.

Activities of immigration border patrol during the fiscal year ended June 30, 1930[1]

Miles patroled, total	7,038,785
By motor	6,375,024
By railroad	193,688
By horse	63,657
By boat	3,377
By aircraft	1,065
Afoot	401,974

Trains, busses, etc., examined and passengers thereon interrogated

	Number of conveyances	Number of passengers
Total	980,103	751,833
Freight trains	95,281	50,886
Passenger trains	82,264	94,733
Automobiles	723,536	510,878
Busses	52,325	57,806
Boats	17,031	12,839
Other conveyances	9,666	24,691

Pedestrians interrogated		348,319
Persons apprehended, total		22,448
For violation of immigration laws, total		21,149
Smugglers of aliens	269	
On warrant	65	
Endeavoring to enter the United States	20,815	
For violation of other laws		1,299

In the course of their work, any border patrol officer (or other bureau of immigration employee authorized to do so) has power without warrant

(1) to arrest any alien who in his presence or view is enter-

[1] *Annual Report of the Commissioner General*, etc., *for 1930*, pp. 42, 43.

ing or attempting to enter the United States in violation of any law or regulation made in pursuance of law regulating the admission of aliens, and to take such alien immediately for examination before an immigrant inspector or other official having authority to examine aliens as to their right to admission to the United States, and (2) to board and search for aliens any vessel within the territorial waters of the United States, railway car, conveyance, or vehicle, in which he believed aliens are being brought into the United States; and such employee shall have power to execute any warrant or other process issued by any officer under any law regulating the admission, exclusion, or expulsion of aliens.[1]

The border patrol and other immigration officers have be-

Delivered to	Persons apprehended	Seizures *						
		Automobiles		Other conveyances		Liquor		Miscellaneous contraband, estimated value
		Number	Estimated value	Number	Estimated value	Quantity (in quarts)	Estimated value	
Total........	22,448	633	$249,450	173	$142,699	229,099	$364,654	$9,239
mmigration......	21,149	20	15,775	10	650	....	....	10
stoms	745	484	172,995	146	130,489	188,789	280,310	2,611
ohibition	63	50	28,625	2	1,200	25,511	67,964	904
stice	19	1	400	.....	....	148	398	90
my and Navy...	44	.....	....	.....	....	....	....	344
rcotics	11	.....	....	.....	....	....	....	505
griculture.......	1	.....	....	.....	....	....	....	23
ast Guard......	....	.....	....	3	7,500	....	....	....
ate and municipal	416	71	31,255	12	2,860	14,651	15,982	4,637
vners	....	1	400	.....	....	....	....	115

* Total estimated value of seizures, $766,042.

[1] Act of Feb. 27, 1925 (43 Stat. 1049).

come so zealous in their pursuit of aliens and smugglers that they have sometimes crossed the invisible boundary they are set to guard. As no immigration officials are vested with any extraterritorial authority, the Secretary of State sent word to the Department of Labor in regard to " unfortunate incidents involving apparent trespasses by American officers on Canadian and Mexican soil while engaged in law enforcement work." The Department of Labor then issued an order requesting immigration officers " to refrain from any acts which might possibly be regarded as violating the sanctity of Canadian or Mexican soil." [1]

The activities of the border patrol are so multitudinous that it is small wonder they may have now and then wandered into foreign territory. Not only do they have to aid in enforcing the immigration laws but they are also called upon to enforce other than immigration laws. The bootlegger of aliens often travels in company with the liquor bootlegger, or traffic in one shields traffic in the other. It has therefore been decided that

> there appears to be no question but that it is the manifest duty of an officer of the Immigration Service to seize any and all intoxicating liquors being transported contrary to law, together with the vehicle or other conveyance, and to arrest any person found engaged in such illegal transportation. Violations of the Harrison Anti-Narcotic Act of December 14, 1914, and of the act entitled " an act to prohibit the importation and the use of opium for other than medicinal purposes " approved February 9, 1909, are felonies and it appears to be quite conclusively established that a private person may without warrant arrest any one who is committing a felony in his presence, or whom he has reasonable ground to suspect of having committed it. . . . When persons are apprehended who are found to be engaged in violation of laws herein referred to, and seizures made, they

[1] Bureau of immigration, General Order No. 82.

should be turned over to the nearest Federal Law Enforcement Agency primarily engaged in the enforcement of the respective laws.[1]

When officers of the immigration border patrol apprehend automobiles, boats or aeroplanes, whether for their own activities or those of other services, they may not seize and hold for forfeit any such conveyances. Other border organizations, such as the customs, have a right to seize such vehicles, and retain them, if they are ordered forfeited by the court. The Commissioner General of Immigration has repeatedly requested similar authority, asking

> that legislation be enacted authorizing the seizure and forfeiture of vehicles and vessels used to import aliens into the United States in violation of the provisions of the immigration laws, or to transport them thereafter pursuant to such illegal importation; and to permit the Immigration Service to make use of such vehicles and vessels after they have been ordered forfeited by the courts.[2]

In view of the patrols of the federal government in the customs, immigration, and prohibition services, and the possible conflict of jurisdiction between them, a unified border patrol has been suggested.[3]

It may be well to attempt to visualize the situation in a border district like that of Montreal, which stretches from

[1] Bureau of immigration, General Order No. 63.

[2] *Annual Report of the Commissioner General for*, etc., *1927*, p. 23; *idem* for 1929, p. 30, *et seq.*

[3] H. R. 11204, 71st Congress, 2d Session.

The American Federation of Labor at its convention, October 6-17, 1930, declared itself opposed to such unification because of the danger that immigration-law enforcement would be sacrificed to prohibition activity. *Foreign Language Service Interpreter Release*, vol. vii, no. 38, Nov. 5, 1930.

Houlton, Maine to Messina, New York.[1] Headquarters for the district are in Montreal, Canada, with a commissioner, assistant commissioner, inspector in charge of the inspection division, permanent chairman of the board of special inquiry to act in admission cases, inspectors, clerks, etc. As this office is outside the United States, there is no " picking up " of warrant cases there. When persons are deported from Montreal, en route to Europe from the United States, one or more of the inspectors are detailed to put the deportees on the boats.[2] The Montreal district is divided into four subdistricts for administrative purposes, — Rouses Point, N. Y., Newport, Vt., Houlton, Maine and Messina, N. Y. Each sub-district has an inspector-in-charge and a force of inspectors and officials of the border patrol to watch the miles of farm-land, the back country roads, and the woods, which compose the district. In this locality, aliens often cross the border on foot, and are apprehended wandering through the farm-lands; or else they cross the border on foot, and then just south of the line attempt to take a train.

[1] *Immigration Laws*, etc., *of January 1, 1930*, Rule 30.

It is impossible to maintain United States detention quarters in foreign territory. As against the disadvantages of having an immigration station in another country are to be weighed the advantages gained from location at a port of entry from Europe, and on direct railroad lines to chief points in the United States and Canada.

For discussion of the border situation in other districts, *vide* " Mexican Border Problems "; " The El Paso District "; " Florida Problems "— in *Problems of the Immigration Service*, papers presented at a conference of commissioners and district directors of immigration, Washington, D. C., January, 1929. *Vide* also, R. N. McLean, " Tightening the Mexican Border ", *Survey*, April 1, 1930.

[2] Attempt is made to avoid detention of deportees from the United States in Montreal, though when unavoidable, it is done by having the Canadian immigration authorities hold them in the Canadian immigration station at the expense of the American government. An alien unofficially detained by Canadian officials might sue out a writ of *habeas corpus* in Canada.

The immigration inspectors examine persons on the train *at* border points, but not south of that; often, therefore, officers of the border patrol go through trains to see if any illegal entries have boarded the train south of the border. A similar situation prevails in regard to the heavy tourist traffic on the direct roads from New York to Montreal. Cars are examined at the border at such towns as Rouses Point, Champlain, Moers, Malone, etc. by immigration inspectors, but it is not impossible for a car to cross the border by a back road and elude examination, nor is it impossible to prevent entry of aliens in cars, for, unless the person looks suspicious, his word is taken as to his citizenship. Furthermore, at small towns there is usually only one immigration inspector, and when he is absent from his post his work is done by the customs inspector, who might be too concerned about liquor smuggling to worry about aliens.

The subdistrict immigration office at Rouses Point has only temporary detention facilities of the roughest sort. If a person is to be detained over night, he may be kept there, but also may be sent to the village "lock-up"[1] or, if he is of a type the inspector in charge feels will not escape and can afford it, he may go to the hotel over night. Most commonly, if detention is to be more than for a very brief period, the alien is taken by train or car to Plattsburg, twenty-six miles away, and there held in the Clinton County Jail.

Trains, motor cars and boats go by Rouses Point each day. There is, furthermore, daily aeroplane service in summer between Montreal and New York. So the immigration

[1] The "lock-up" has four cells of the old type. Men and women are sometimes locked up here at the same time, with no woman attendant in charge. *Vide* Report of Commissioner Cecelia D. Patton, Aug. 20, 1930, approved by the New York State Department of Correction, Sept. 25, 1930, quoted in *Plattsburg Sentinel,* Sept. 26, 1930, p. 3.

officials must look out for trains, automobiles, aeroplanes, boats and foot passengers.

A somewhat different situation presents itself in a place such as Detroit, where a narrow stretch of river separates the Canadian city of Windsor from the American city of Detroit. Detroit was destined by nature, economic conditions and immigration laws to be a focal point in the administration of immigration affairs. The Detroit River between the United States and Canada is only 2,530 feet wide at Detroit. The phenomenal growth of the city of Detroit from somewhat over a quarter of a million in 1901 to almost a million and a half in 1926, and the rapid expansion of the automobile industry there showed a person on the Canadian side of the river the desirability of crossing to the American side.[1] Until the unemployment depression of 1929 and 1930 set in and caused havoc in the automobile industry, it was ordinarily not difficult to secure work in Detroit, and naturally foreigners as well as others were attracted to the city.

Detroit is easy of access to travelers from Canada, for in addition to ferry lines there are a bridge and tunnels across the river. In addition to the River Rouge, where people do not ordinarily cross, there are thirty-two miles of waterfront at Detroit, thus affording temptation to the alien to enter illegally from Canada. The possibilities for entering without inspection have been so great that a flourishing trade of "bootlegging aliens" began soon after the first "quota act" went into effect in 1921. The business proved so profitable that rings of smugglers were soon formed. These alien smugglers usually bring from seven to twelve men in a party, and cross the river in small motor boats or

[1] In the spring of 1926 the average daily wage in all branches of industry in Detroit was $6.09, while in Windsor it was $4.12. Figures from the Detroit Chamber of Commerce in letter to the author, June 11, 1926.

rowboats, landing often at night in an obscure corner of the river-front. They often have an accomplice on the American side to warn them of possible danger as they approach. The rates paid for such entry vary widely, from $10 to $200. A smuggler awaiting trial in the Wayne County Jail in Detroit told the author that he averaged about $70 per alien, with higher amounts for Chinese.

When a party of aliens is apprehended on landing, the smuggler makes every effort to get away, because he will, if convicted, have to serve a heavy criminal sentence. The 1917 immigration act provides that

> any person . . . who shall bring into . . . the United States . . . or shall conceal or harbor . . . or assist or abet another to conceal or harbor in any place . . . any alien not duly admitted . . . shall be deemed guilty of a misdemeanor and upon conviction thereof shall be punished by a fine not exceeding $2,000 and by imprisonment for a term not exceeding five years, for each and every alien so landed or brought in or attempted to be landed or brought in.[1]

Failure by owners, agents, etc. of a vessel to prevent illegal entry of an alien from their vessel is punishable by fine of $200 to $1,000 or a maximum imprisonment for one year or both.[2] Action may be brought against a smuggler or against the vessel which brought the illegally entering alien

[1] Sec. 8. Hackfeld & Co. *v.* United States, 141 Fed. 9; Sototios Targakis *v.* United States, 12 Fed. (2d) 498. *Vide* Cook and Hagerty, *op. cit.*, § 312, and immigration act of 1917, sec. 10.

H. R. 17152, 71st Congress, 3rd Session, contains a provision (sec. 4) that any person who conceals or harbors, or attempts to conceal or harbor an alien entering illegally in violation of the act of March 4, 1929, or employs such alien (provided the person harboring or employing the alien knew of the illegal entry) shall be fined not more than $1,000 or imprisoned for not more than one year, or both.

[2] The Nanking, 290 Fed. 769.

into the United States.[1] There are various other penalties against smugglers, such as for assisting alien anarchists, illiterate aliens, etc.[2] A smuggler may, of course, be an alien or an American citizen. If he is an alien, however, the fact that he attempted illegally to smuggle other aliens into the country is in itself no reason for his deportation under the law.[3]

An alien smuggled into the country is of course deportable, but in many cases his presence is necessary for securing testimony in the criminal prosecution of his smuggler. Therefore it is provided[4] that the Department of Labor may stay the deportation of any alien who entered illegally if his testimony is necessary on behalf of the United States. He may be paid a witness fee of $1.00 a day while detained waiting to testify, or he may be released on bond of at least $500, conditioned for his production when required as a witness or for deportation.[5] Detention charges, witness fees, or authorization for release under bond are furnished by the Department of Labor only when at least one cause for the proposed deportation arose prior to entry. If no cause existed prior to entry, as when a woman has become a prostitute *since* landing, the alien can be held as a witness only when arrangements are made with the appropriate United States attorney for payment of detention and witness expenses by the Department of Justice. In some districts immigration officials make it a practice to supply

[1] If action is taken against the vessel by libel, the penalty of $1000 for each violation is to be paid by the master, owner, agent or consignee of the vessel or other object libelled.—United States *v.* One Airplane, etc., 23 Fed. (2d) 500.

[2] *Vide* Cook and Hagerty, *op. cit.*, ch. vi.

[3] *In re* Wysbach; *Ex parte* Lewis, 292 Fed. 761.

[4] Immigration act of 1917, sec. 18; *Immigration Laws*, etc., *1930*, Rule 21.

[5] *Ibid.*

United States attorneys with a statement of the essential facts in cases where proceedings have been instituted, together with the names of witnesses.[1]

THE PENALTY FOR ILLEGAL ENTRY

Even with the passage of the restrictive "quota acts," there was no criminal penalty attached to illegal entry as such, and aliens apprehended for entering the country illegally were held for deportation but nothing further, unless detained as witnesses. However, toward the end of the war, by the provisions of the act of May 22, 1918[2] passports were required of aliens entering the United States. This act was continued in force by Act of March 2, 1921.[3] Failure to have a passport on entering the country entailed criminal prosecution[4] and fine or imprisonment or both as the penalty therefor. Thus a foreigner entering illegally without a passport was liable to deportation, a non-criminal procedure; he was furthermore liable to criminal prosecution under the "passport act." He was subject to two proceedings, one criminal under the Department of Justice and one non-criminal under the Department of Labor. An alien who threw his passport into the Rio Grande or left it in Windsor, Canada would be held at the expense of the Department of Justice until indicted by the grand jury for violation of the passport acts, then after serving his sentence for such violation, would be turned over to the immigration authorities and detained,—often in the same jail in which he had served his sentence for violation of the passport act,—on the non-criminal charge of deportation.

Such cases were common indeed, for the practice of

[1] Bureau of immigration, General Order No. 897.

[2] And by executive order of August 18, 1918.

[3] 41 Stat. 1255, 1217.

[4] Provided by act of May 22, 1918, sec. 3.

smugglers often was to have the smuggled aliens throw their passports away as incriminating evidence of their illegal entry. Even those not smuggled but entering by themselves realized that a passport might show the illegality of entry. All these persons entering illegally and found on apprehension to be without passports were liable to prosecution as well as deportation. In sections of the country where there was a great deal of illegal entry the docket of the grand jury was so crowded that at times the prosecution was often omitted, and the deportation procedure alone carried out. Prosecutions under the passport law varied according to the part of the country in which the person was detained. In Detroit, jails were so overcrowded with illegal entries that attempts were made to hurry matters as much as possible and violations of the passport law were not always prosecuted. In different states and even in different counties of the same state the length of sentence imposed varied greatly, sometimes being six months, sometimes less. It was a common practice to date the sentence back, if for one reason or another the alien had been detained in jail for a period approximating that of the sentence, and then immediately turn him over to the immigration service for deportation.

Prosecutions continued under the law until in 1924 Stefan Flora was held for violation of this war-time passport act. The court held, when the matter came before it, that

it has never been the policy of this Government to punish criminally aliens who come here in contravention of our immigration laws. Deportation has been the remedy. A reversal of that policy ought to be based on clear legislative declaration and not on judicial construction of statutes which leave the subject in such uncertainty and doubt as do the statutes here under consideration.[1]

[1] Flora v. Rustad, 8 Fed. (2d) 335. *Vide* also United States Department of Labor Record, 55394/448; United States *ex rel.* Porter *v.* Yale, 14 Fed. (2d) 682; United States *v.* One Airplane, 23 Fed. (2d) 500.

Criminal prosecutions ceased for the time being, and deportation again became the only "penalty" for illegal entry.

In 1929 legislative intent to punish such entry manifested itself in the act of March 4 of that year, which provided that

any alien who enters the United States at any time or place other than as designated by immigration officials, or obtains entry to the United States by a wilfully false and misleading representation or wilful concealment of a material fact, shall be guilty of a misdemeanor, and upon conviction, shall be punished by imprisonment for not more than one year and by a fine of not more than $1000, or by both such fine and imprisonment.[1]

Thus the war-time "passport act" has not only been revived by legislative enactment but also extended, for now *any* illegal entry, whether with or without passport, is a punishable offense. It was thought that such enactment would in large measure stop the border leakage of aliens.

Under this act, an alien apprehended sneaking into the country by one means or another is reported to the local United States Commissioner (or turned over to the United States marshal for report to the Commissioner), who in turn may dismiss the alien or hold him for the grand jury for indictment, and then if he is indicted, for the next session of the federal district court. If the Commissioner dismisses the man, he might nevertheless still be deportable under one of the provisions of the immigration law, and so might be detained by the Department of Labor. However, this is seldom the case. After the report of the illegal entry to the Commissioner, the alien is a prisoner of the Department of Justice, held in jail on the criminal charge involved in illegal entry, with prosecutions instituted by the Department of Justice.[2]

[1] Act approved March 4, 1929, 45 Stat. 1551, sec. 2, as amended by act of June 4, 1929 (Public No. 21, 71st Congress).

[2] *Annual Report of the Commissioner General of Immigration*, etc.,

Such criminal prosecutions are entirely separate from deportation proceedings. But on the termination of the criminal prosecution the alien may continue to be held in the same jail, now detained by the Department of Labor, if deportation proceedings have not been completed. The Department of Justice may require a bond for liberation of the alien on the criminal charges, and it is possible for the Department of Labor to require a bond for his liberation on the non-criminal deportation proceedings. Thus two bonds may be required of him. Whereas the Department of Justice will not release an alien without bond, the Department of Labor will in certain instances release him on his own recognizance if the bond to the Department of Justice is satisfactory.[1]

In prosecution of aliens unlawfully entering the United States, the offense is the *entry*. So according to the Sixth Amendment to the Constitution, trial for that offense must take place in the district where it occurs. Persons often enter surreptitiously and are not apprehended until later, when they may be in a district of the country far distant from that of their entry. A man entering illegally across the border in Maine, for instance, might have gone to California before it was found that he had entered illegally. So he would have to be taken back to the Maine district where he entered in order to be tried there for his illegal

1930, p. 21. *Vide* also *Annual Report of the Attorney General* for the same year, "Report of the Assistant Attorney General in Charge of the Criminal Division," pp. 36-7. The latter report notes the marked increase in criminal prosecutions (including both misdemeanors for illegal entry and felonies for reentry after deportation) since the passage of the 1929 act. Including both classes, 1,568 prosecutions were commenced for the fiscal year ending June 30, 1929, while in 1930, 7,001 were commenced; 1,458 were terminated in 1929 as compared with 6,910 in 1930.

[1] For discussion of bonds, *vide* ch. ix, p. 341 *et seq.*

entry. The Secretary of Labor suggested [1] a way out of the constitutional difficulty. His suggestion was later embodied in a bill proposed in Congress, to the effect that remaining in the United States after such unlawful entry would itself constitute an offense as well as the original entry. If such provision were adopted, the offense of remaining could be punished by imprisonment for not more than one year or by a fine of not more than $1,000 or both.

The sentence arrangements under the 1929 act are similar to those under the "passport act," for under the new as under the old interpretation of law, an alien is often sentenced to the time he has already served in jail before his arraignment took place. For instance, an alien who was apprehended and taken to jail on January 15, 1930 had to stay there until May 13 of that year before the federal district court was in session. When arraigned and sentenced, he was sentenced on that day by the court to the time already served in jail. The sentences imposed under the law vary widely in different jurisdictions. In Seattle, cases have been noted of a sentence of twelve months in the county jail, with the proviso that the sentence be suspended unless the alien subsequently entered unlawfully; such entry would abrogate the suspension. In a southern California district sentences for thirty days in the county jail have been imposed, while elsewhere four months is a common length of sentence. John Jones, for example, entered in violation of the act of March 4, 1929 [3] and in violation of the customs law in regard to smuggling liquor. The case was called at a special session of the federal court in Brownsville, Texas, and there the man plead guilty to the charge of

[1] Report made Jan. 6, 1931 on Sen. Res. 355, Dec. 8, 1930, quoted in *U. S. Daily*, Jan. 7, 1931.

[2] H. R. 17152, sec. 3 (a) and (b), 71st Cong., 3rd Ses.

[3] Sec. 2.

entering illegally and was sentenced to the forty-four days already served in jail, from March 24, 1930 to May 6, 1930. On the liquor charge he was sentenced to 60 days in jail beginning May 6, 1930, and to one year and a day in Atlanta Penitentiary, suspended subject to good behavior.

In cases where the alien is held as a witness against his smuggler, it is common for the case against the alien for illegal entry not to be prosecuted, or else for it to be so arranged that the sentence is dated back to when he entered jail.

STUDENTS AND VISITORS

Two fertile sources of illegal entry are found in the provision of the 1924 immigration act allowing persons to enter outside the quota as students and as temporary visitors. For immigration purposes, a student is defined as a foreigner at least fifteen years old who enters solely for the purpose of studying at an American educational institution approved by the Secretary of Labor as a school for immigrant students and must have been accepted as a student by that institution previous to entry.[1] He is supposed to have sufficient funds with him to support himself while he is attending the educational institution.[2]

[1] Immigration act of 1924, sec. 4 (e). *Vide Foreign Language Information Service Interpreter Release,* vol. ii, no. 21 (Supplement), and vol. v, no. 55; Cook and Hagerty, *op. cit.,* §§ 96-108; *Ex parte* Tsiang Hsi Tseng, 24 Fed. (2d) 213; *Ex parte* Menaregidis, 13 Fed. (2d) 392.

[2] "Subdivision D of Rule 9 of the Immigration Rules promulgated by the Department of Labor under the provisions of the Immigration Act, that a non-quota immigrant student 'who engaged in any business or occupation for profit, or who labors for hire, shall be deemed to have abandoned his status as an immigrant student, and shall on the warrant of the Secretary of Labor be taken into custody and deported,' must be construed as applying to those who definitely give up their studies, and instead engage in business of work for profit or hire but not to students otherwise bona fide, who during their studies gain their maintenance and tuition by self-supporting labor."—United States *ex rel.* Antonini *v.* Curran, 15 Fed. (2d) 266.

The school where the foreign student goes must report to the Secretary of Labor the termination of attendance of the student, for whatever reason it occurs, whether by voluntary leaving, expulsion or inability to keep up. If the student does not immediately leave the country after the end of his period of study he is deportable. Many persons entering as students either never go to or else leave the educational institutions they have come to attend. Thus they too slip into the country; many of them are never caught. Since the passage of the immigration act of 1924, 10,831 persons have been admitted as students, and of this total only 4,825 had completed their studies and left the country before July 1, 1930. Warrants of arrest have been issued looking to deportation of 335 students who failed to comply with the requirements [1] and are illegally in the country.[2]

In cases of doubt of the status of the student applying for admission to the country, he must be held pending investigation. The burden of showing his admissibility is placed upon him, and if he cannot remove any doubt in the minds of the immigration officials, the matter is decided against his admission. The Commissioner General and the Secretary of Labor have for several years recommended the requirement of bonds of students on entering, if there is any doubt as to the *bona fides* of their desire to study here,[3] for

[1] *Annual Report of the Commissioner General of Immigration,* etc., *for 1930,* p. 27.

[2] Among the number are some Russian émigrés who came on League of Nations passports, are ending their studies and so must leave the country. They cannot secure passport for return to any other country, as they are persons without a country. Warrants of deportation are outstanding against them, but these cannot be served unless some place can be found to which to send these people. *Vide infra,* p. 408.

[3] *Annual Reports of the Commissioner General of Immigration for 1927* (p. 22), *1928* (p. 29), *1929* (p. 30), *1930* (p. 46); of the Secretary of Labor, i. e. for 1928, p. 152.

the immigration act of 1924, while requiring bonds in many classes temporarily admitted to the United States, has no such requirement as to students.

While aliens may secure illegal admission by entering as professors, ministers, etc and then failing to do the work for which they were admitted, such cases are uncommon. However, the great class of persons entering temporarily for business or pleasure or as tourists and "who, having a fixed domicile in some other country which they have no intention to abandon, come to the United States to remain for a temporary period only,"[1] provide another prolific source of illegal entry. Unless the terms of such employment are specified in the terms of application for admission, such temporary visitors lose their right to remain if they accept employment here or remain beyond the time allotted them, permission to remain longer not having been granted by the Department of Labor. Nor can an alien residing across the border in Canada or Mexico commute daily to employment in the United States, unless he has been regularly admitted to this country as an immigrant.[2] If the immigration officials doubt whether or not an applicant for admission to the country is a *bona fide* visitor, bonds guaranteeing departure within a given time may be required.[3] Such bonds may also be required for extension of stay, but may not be required prior to the arrival of the visitor in this country. There are many "temporary visitors" who use this means as a way of avoiding quota difficulties. For instance, a man in a country where the qota is full for some years ahead might succeed in being admitted temporarily to the United States for a six months' visit; then he might, as many do, disappear into the country, leaving no trace of

[1] Immigration act of 1924, sec. 3.

[2] Karnuth *v.* United States *ex rel.* Albro, 279 U. S. 231.

[3] Immigration act of 1924, sec. 15.

himself. There were 23,442 "temporary visitors for business" and 47,381 "temporary visitors for pleasure" admitted to the United States during 1930.[1] The administrative difficulties involved in keeping track of such large numbers may be imagined. The Commissioner General of Immigration has called attention to the problem of overstayed visitors, saying that "the number is sufficiently large to warrant a more careful check-up on them than is possible at the present time with the force available." [2]

STOWAWAYS

Perhaps the most numerous source of illegal entries is that of seamen deserting their ships in port in the United States. These, however, are beyond the scope of this book. Another numerous group who enter by sea are those who stow themselves away in the cargo of incoming vessels and then steal ashore unseen. Stowaways, however, if discovered on the voyage and otherwise admissible, may be admitted in the discretion of the Secretary of Labor.[3] Most of them, however, do not have an unexpired immigration visa as required by law, and so are not admissible. And doubtless many of them leave the ship and are never found.

THE STATUTE OF LIMITATIONS IN CASES OF ILLEGAL ENTRY

As there are many and devious means by which an alien may sneak into the country, so there have been various provisions in the law regarding the length of time within which he may be deported if later discovered to be here illegally.

The 1917 immigration act provided that:

[1] *Annual Report of the Commissioner General,* etc., p. 148.

[2] *Annual Reports,* etc., for 1919 (pp. 31-32) and for 1930, p. 48.

[3] *Vide Immigration Laws,* etc., Rule 2, Subdivision B, Par. 1 and Rule 3, Subdivision O. *Vide* also *Annual Report of the Secretary of Labor for,* etc., *1927,* pp. 179-180.

> at any time within three years after entry, any alien who shall have entered the United States by water at any time or place other than as designated by immigration officials, or by land at any place other than one designated by a port of entry for aliens . . . or at any time not designated by immigration officials, or who enters without inspection[1]

shall be deported. But for all practical purposes the three-year limitation has been abandoned, for several reasons. Another provision of the same act states that at any time within five years after entry "any alien who shall have entered or who shall be found in the United States in violation of this act, or in violation of any other law of the United States" shall be deported. For instance, if a man slipped across the border in the year 1922 at a time when the quota was exhausted of the country of which he was a native, he would have been deportable within five years of that entry, despite the fact that he entered illegally by land. The charge against him would be that he was not admitted and charged to the quota of his native country, for the quota year in which he entered. Suppose that instead of slipping across the border, a person had been admitted as a visitor but had remained beyond the time allotted him for visit. Even had the quota of his country not been exhausted when he entered, it would have made no difference had he stayed beyond the year in which he was admitted, as the availability of quota numbers ceased at the close of the particular year for which they were issued.[2] It would have been impossible to supply a quota number after the expiration of the quota year.[3]

[1] Sec. 19.

[2] United States *ex rel.* Filippini *v.* Day, 18 Fed. (2d) 781.

[3] However, if an error was made in not charging the alien to his quota, a correction of the record to harmonize with the correct facts may be permitted, even after the expiration of the quota year.—Cook and Hagerty, *op. cit.*, § 266.

Before the passage of the 1924 immigration act, it was impossible to secure the deportation of anyone for illegal entry after the expiration of the time limit set by law. Obviously, many aliens entering illegally before that year slipped unnoticed into the population and remained here, and there was no way of securing their deportation.

That second "quota act" made further provisions in regard to the time limit for deporting "illegal entries" of all sorts, by the adding to the deportable categories anyone who at the time of entry did not have an unexpired immigration visa or was born subsequent to the issuance of the visa of the accompanying parent. Such deportation might take place within five years after entry only if the 1921 immigration act was still in force when the person entered the country. If he came in after July 1, 1924, he may be deported at any time he is discovered, no matter how long he has been here.

The matter of practical importance since 1924 is the fact that under the act of that year all statute of limitations is removed from deportation for illegal entry. The man who enters the country without permission has been added to the list of "undesirables" who can be sent from the country no matter how long they have been here.

No sooner had the provisions of the 1924 law come into effect than a difficult situation immediately arose. Before the days of quota legislation, many an alien for one reason or another slipped unnoticed into the country. In those days mere entry without inspection was insufficient to render a person deportable. Furthermore, many persons entered legally, but due to inaccurate records at the ports of entry or to the fact that numerous people could not remember when or where they entered, a strange situation arose. Because of the expiration of the time limit within which deportation could occur for those people who entered illegally long ago or whose entry could not be verified, they were not subject to deportation. On the other hand, they could not become American citizens, as it is necessary in naturalization proceedings to show lawful admission for permanent residence. Nor could such persons secure immigration return permits in case they wanted to leave the country temporarily, as lawful entry must be established to secure such return permit; without a return permit, they would have to wait their turn to secure quota places, and this in effect would in many countries permanently bar their return.

To relieve this anomalous situation in regard to a large class of persons who might live in the United States and yet not be eligible for either citizenship or deportation, Congress by act of March 2, 1929 [1] provided that a record of registry may be made on payment of $20 for any alien in whose case no immigration record of arrival exists, if he entered the United States before June 3, 1921, has resided in the country continuously since then, and is a person of good moral character, and is not subject to deportation.[2] But no statutory relief is offered to those aliens who, discouraged by the difficulty of securing quota numbers after the passage of the 1921 immigration act or ignorant of its application, slipped unknown into the country during the years from 1921 to 1924; they remain in the position that all illegal entries were in previous to the passage of the act, for they can neither be deported nor naturalized. The Secretary of Labor has called attention to their unfortunate situation and the Commissioner General has recommended that the act of March 2, 1929 be amended "so as to provide that the registry of

[1] Public No. 962, 70th Congress (H. R. 49). *Vide Foreign Language Information Service Interpreter Release,* vol. vi, no. 11.

[2] During the first year of its operation, 18,800 applications for registry were filed, and of these 8,098 were granted, 1,125 denied, 114 withdrawn and 9,463 pending at the close of the year.—*Annual Report of the Secretary of Labor for,* etc., *1930,* p. 77.

aliens as therein provided may be made as to those aliens who entered the United States prior to July 1, 1924, instead of prior to June 3, 1921.[1]

Illegal Entries among the Cases Studied

Illegal entries provided by far the largest number of cases of both groups. Out of the first group, 362 entered illegally, while from the second group the number was thirty. Approximately 59.15% of the total of 612 entered the United States by other than legal means.[2]

The means of entry were varied among both groups, and the places where entry occurred were scattered over the whole country.

The greatest number walked across the border, while another favorite way of entering was in a rowboat at Detroit. The number of ways of entry were legion, from stealing in "in the car with the animals in a circus" to entering as a visitor and staying indefinitely. Two cases were noted of men in Canada who had paid to be taken "where there was work," and who had been brought into the United States without knowing where they were coming.

Out of the first group of cases, 98 had been in the United States previously for varying lengths of time, and had left the country for a visit home or to another country without proper credentials for return to the United States. Unable to secure places in the quotas to which they belonged and impatient to return to this country, they sneaked in illegally. The records stated that 56 of this number had close[3] rela-

[1] *Annual Report*, etc., *for 1930*, p. 47.

[2] In the *Annual Report of the Commissioner General*, etc., *1930*, p. 243, it is stated that in 1926 "miscellaneous classes", which included illegal entries, formed 76.8% of the total deportations. In 1930 they included 79% of the total. But "miscellaneous classes" include seamen, Chinese, geographically excluded cases, and "L. P. C."

[3] Wives, children, parents, brothers or sisters.

WHERE ILLEGAL ENTRIES CAME INTO THE UNITED STATES

	Group 1	Group 2
Canadian Border		
Idaho	4	
Michigan		
Detroit	52	9
Other places	6	3
Minnesota	13	2
Montana	10	
New York		
Buffalo	7	
Niagara Falls	29	4
Rouses Point	8	1
North Dakota	8	
Vermont	57	3
Washington	24	1
Indefinite	20	
Mexican Border		
Arizona	13	1
Texas		
El Paso	31	3
Matagorda	10	
Rio Grande City	12	
Indefinite	27	1
Seaboard		
South Carolina	1	
Florida	12	
New York	4	2
Unknown	4	
Total	362	30

tives in the United States to whom they desired to return. So the illegal entries studied contained a large group of returning residents who because of administrative difficulties and limitation of quota could not return. The second group studied contained only 6 who had previously been resident in the United States. This might indicate that the procedure of securing return permits had by 1930 become more thoroughly known than at the earlier date, and that aliens leaving the country recently have realized the necessity of securing such permits; furthermore, those who had left before the system of such permits came into use have probably either returned or given up the idea by the latter date.

Aside from the various illegal entry charges, a number of others are found in all these cases, for it is of course possible for a man entering illegally to be convicted of a crime involving moral turpitude, to become a public charge, or in numerous other ways to come under a deportable category.

One case was noted of a man entering illegally and becoming a public charge, where the hospital did not state that the onset of the trouble was due to causes not arising subsequent to entry. So deportation took place on the grounds of illegal entry rather than of being a public charge within five years after entry, from causes not affirmatively shown to have arisen subsequent to entry:

Patrick Casey (Case 55).

Patrick Casey was born in 1897 in County Kerry, Ireland, and lived there and in Dublin until his emigration to Canada in 1924. He landed in Halifax on April 13th of that year, and then went to Montreal in search of work, but failed to find any, so went on to Toronto where he began to work on a farm.

Mr. Casey had an uncle in New York who had advanced him $50 toward his emigration expenses. So. Mr. Casey decided to go to visit that uncle, and was brought across the ferry at Detroit by an American soldier. (Whether he paid anything for the smuggling is not stated on the record, or who the " soldier " was.) He entered on October 3, 1924, and was not apprehended.

Going to New York immediately, Mr. Casey decided to remain there. He began to work in the basement of a department store, bailing waste papers at a salary of $20 to $22 a week. He lived with his uncle, but decided not to remain, as he had not been well since coming from Canada, and as his aunt did not wish him. In March, 1925, Mr. Casey was operated on at the Harlem Hospital for mastoiditis.

After he had recuperated sufficiently to travel, he decided to return to Canada but was apprehended as he reached the border and questioned by an official of the immigration service. Mr. Casey was then taken to the immigration office at Rouses Point, and the next day, May 21, 1925, was taken to the nearest county jail, that of Clinton County, in Plattsburg, N. Y. He said he had about $80 with him, but this was taken for safe-keeping by the jailer.

After Mr. Casey had been in jail one day he became alternately depressed and excited and so was immediately committed to the St. Lawrence State Hospital. That same day, a warrant was issued for his arrest and a hearing was given him at the hospital on May 28th. The hospital refused a definite diagnosis on that date as it was felt Mr. Casey had not been there long enough to be properly diagnosed. Several weeks later, the hospital gave a diagnosis of dementia praecox, paranoid type, and the superintendent stated possible the onset was about November, 1924, but that he would not definitely state the trouble was due to causes existing prior to entry. The warrant of arrest had been issued only on grounds of (1) "L. P. C.", (2) entering without inspection, (3) not being in possession of an unexpired immigration visa. No attempt was made to re-open the hearing and add "public charge" to the causes of possible deportation, for, although Mr. Casey had become a public charge within five years of entry, there was a possibility that his illness had arisen subsequent to entry.

The warrant of deportation was issued September 18, 1925, on the same grounds as the warrant of arrest. By December 11, Mr. Casey could leave the hospital and was sent to Ellis Island. The following day the British Consulate in New York was notified of his deportation, which took place December 19th, at the expense of the steamship company which had brought him to Canada. He debarked at Queenstown and was sent to his home accompanied by a custodian. At his home he was signed for by his father on December 28th.

The following cases show the type of illegal entry found in this study, with some of the many methods of entry to the country, the various charges, and the procedure in such cases:

James Rogers (Case 56).

James Rogers was born in 1864 in London, England. He came to the United States in 1928, being admitted temporarily as a visitor on January 10th, to take part in a cross country race. The race failed, so Mr. Rogers was planning to go home but was offered work at Coney Island. He was afraid to ask for an extension of his visitor's permit, but remained anyway. That work failed too, and so Mr. Rogers attempted to secure a partner for a marathon dance in an endurance contest.

He did not know by whom he was reported to the immigration service, but his funds were running low at the time he was reported. A warrant was issued for his arrest on April 1, 1930, on the ground that he remained longer than the period allotted him for a visit. He was taken to the county jail at Los Angeles, and detained pending the securing of bond. He was unable to secure bond, so a hearing was given him at the jail on April 14. There he requested to be allowed to depart voluntarily, but the record states of him that " although his history since his arrival does not indicate that he can be depended upon to depart in accordance with any plans he may have, it is doubted if he is anything but a bona fide visitor. " At the hearing, when he was warned that he could never reenter the United States under the act of March 4, 1929, without being guilty of a felony, if deported, he said: " I feel that were public opinion to rule, many thousands who have seen me would accord an extension and also avoid any stigma of deportation. . . . I want to return in 1932 to the Olympic Games."

A warrant was issued for Mr. Rogers' deportation on May 1, 1930, on the same ground as that of his warrant of arrest. He was deported at government expense on May 12th.

Blair McAlister (Case 57).

Blair McAlister was born in 1901 in Scotland. He emigrated to Canada at the age of 26, landing at St. John, N. B. on April 3, 1927. He went west to Winnepeg, where he worked in the wheat fields of different farms for two years, then he decided to enter the United States. As he could not secure legal admission on April 16, 1930, he walked over the border at Blaine, Wash., without inspection, but he was apprehended by the border patrol and taken to the immigration station at Seattle.

On April 30, 1930, Mr. McAlister was arraigned before the United States District Court at Seattle, charged with violation of the act of March 4, 1929, Sec. 2. He pled guilty and was sentenced to 12 months in the county jail, the sentence to be suspended with the proviso that when deported, a subsequent unlawful entry would abrogate the suspension.

A warrant had been issued for his arrest on April 17. A hearing was given him on the warrant, and a warrant of deportation issued on May 12, 1930, on the same grounds as in the warrant of arrest, namely, (1) "L. P. C.", (2) that he was not in possession of an unexpired immigration visa (3) that he entered without inspection.

Mr. McAlister was deported on June 1, 1930, at the expense of the line bringing him to Canada.

Janet Haynes (Case 58).

Janet Haynes was born in 1906 in London, Eng., as one of a family of 10 children. She lived in London until 1927 when she emigrated to Canada, landing in Halifax on April 16 of that year, together with John Strong, who had paid her passage to Canada.

She quarrelled with him and so decided to come to the United States, crossing the border on April 30, 1928. She went to New York and worked in a store, then moved to Atlantic City. There she met an American by whom she became pregnant. She decided to return to Canada and have the baby there. On her attempt to cross the border to Canada, she was refused admission by the Canadian immigration service, on April 30, 1929. The American immigration officials took her to the detention quarters of the service at St. Albans, Vt.

The next day a warrant was issued for Miss Haynes arrest, on the grounds (1) "L. P. C.", (2) that she entered without inspection, (3) that she was not in possession of an unexpired immigration visa, and (4) that she admitted the commission prior to entry of a crime or misdemeanor involving moral turpitude prior to entry, to wit, concubinage.

A hearing was given Miss Haynes on May 10th, but there she stated that three weeks from that day the baby was due. A warrant of deportation was issued the following day, on the same grounds as those indicated in the warrant of arrest, except for the admission of the crime involving moral turpitude, as the board of review said "the record does not show that concubinage was a crime where it was committed." However, as Miss Haynes could not be deported to Canada, it was felt unwise to attempt to deport her elsewhere because of her physical condition.

As the detention quarters at St. Albans were not equipped even for more than temporary detention, it was of course impossible to keep Miss Haynes there. So bids were submitted to the Department of Labor by a private sanitarium and the St. Albans Hospital. It was decided to use the private sanitarium as its bid was less expensive. The local surgeon of the United States Public Health Service took the case, and was paid a fee of $25, as confinement cases were not considered in the regular routine of his public health duties.

On her recovery, Miss Haynes and her American-born child were sent to Ellis Island. She paid the expenses of her child to New York from St. Albans and on the boat. She was deported on January 1, 1930, at the expense of the steamship line which had brought her to Canada.

Alfred Diedrich (Case 59).

Alfred Diedrich was born in 1890 in Moscow, the son of parents born in Riga. He studied music and political science, and then became an opera singer, going to Holland to sing. Then he turned to portrait painting and journalism.

In 1924 Mr. Diedrich applied for a visa to come to the United States as a member of a delegation of the "All Church Peasants' Association," to "discover and counteract Bolshevik activities and to combat the growing Soviet influence over the church." His passage was paid by the organization.

Mr. Diedrich arrived on May 28, 1924 and was admitted as a temporary visitor. On February 14, 1925 he was reported to the immigration service by the Department of State. It had received word from the American Consul General in Paris that he had heard through the legation of Latvia in Paris that Mr. Diedrich was an adventurer.

A warrant was issued for his arrest on February 16, 1925, with the charges (1) "L. P. C.", (2) that he entered the United States by means of false and misleading statements, (3) that his passage was paid for with the money of another, (4) that his passage was paid for by a foreign body.

Mr. Diedrich was detained at Ellis Island from March 8 to July 2, 1925, while an attempt was being made to secure a passport for him. A warrant for his deportation was issued on June 10th, on the same grounds as those in the warrant of arrest. He was deported on July 2, at the expense of the steamship line, destined to Latvia.

Maria Goya (Case 60).

Maria Goya was born in 1900 in Cordova, Spain, and was married to Manuel Henriques, in 1917. In 1920 he emigrated to the United States and went to New Orleans to live. When he was established, he tried to send for his wife, but found he could not arrange to secure her admission in the quota. He bought her a ticket for Cuba, and she landed in Havana in July, 1924. Then she sailed from there to Mexico, where Mr. Henriques met her. On February 11, 1925 they went to Tiajuana, crossed the border, and went on to San Diego, where they rented a house.

They had barely settled, when they were reported, on

March 24th, by an unknown source to the immigration authorities, and were apprehended at their home by an immigrant inspector. Mrs. Henriques was taken to the Girls' Vocational Home, while her husband was sent to the county jail. A warrant of arrest was issued the same day for Mrs. Henriques (the record does not state what happened to her husband, except that he was held for criminal prosecution, for bringing her into the country, and was not deported with her), on the grounds (1) "L. P. C.", (2) that she was not in possession of an unexpired immigration visa at the time of her entry, (3) that she was brought to foreign contiguous territory by a transportation company which had not submitted to the requirements of section 17 of the act of 1924, and had not resided in such territory for two years prior to her application for admission to the United States, and (4) that she entered without inspection.

Three days later, Mrs. Henriques was transferred to the same county jail as her husband for detention. A hearing was given her at the jail the day of her transfer, but was postponed for her to secure a lawyer; however, the hearing was finally given on March 30, but she had decided legal representation would be useless.

A warrant of deportation was issued on April 21, 1925, on the same grounds as those in the warrant of arrest. Mrs. Henriques was deported on July 7, 1925 at the expense of the government.

John McIntyre (Case 61).

John McIntyre was born on July 6, 1905 in Glasgow, Scotland. When he was 16 years old, he went to sea, and then deserted the steamer in Victoria, B. C. He did odd jobs and so crossed Canada and entered the United States in 1925 across the bridge at Niagara Falls, without inspection.

He went immediately to New York, shipped to Havana as a seaman, hurt his leg on the boat and was taken off at Colon, where he remained three days. Then his passage was paid back to the United States by the American consul there. He arrived in New York on September 7, 1925.

His leg not being yet well, Mr. McIntyre began to beg, and was arrested on September 14, in Roselle, N. J., for vagrancy. That day he was reported to the immigration service and a warrant for his arrest issued. He was taken immediately to Ellis Island.

Mr. McIntyre was given a hearing on October 29. A certificate was presented from the United States Public Health Service surgeon there, stating " he is afflicted with osteomyelitis in the third lower tibia," which " might affect his earning capacity." Mr. McIntyre stated he could work, in spite of the certificate. A warrant of deportation was issued on November 17, with the charges (1) " L. P. C.", (2) that he was not in possession of an unexpired immigration visa at the time of entry, (3) that he was physically defective at the time of entry, (4) that he entered by water at a time other than designated by the immigration officials.

He was deported on December 19, 1925 at government expense, destined to Scotland.

Erich Hauser (Case 62).

Erich Hauser was born in 1894 near Athens, Greece, the son of a Swiss father and Czech mother. He was registered at the Swiss consulate as a Swiss citizen, and retained that citizenship. He was educated in Switzerland, becoming a physiological chemist. He read and wrote eight languages.

In 1914 Mr. Hauser came to the United States and lived here continuously after that. In late 1924 he went for a trip to Mexico, and in June, 1925 returned across the New Mexican border, reporting himself to the immigrant inspector who questioned him, as a resident of the United States for many years.

After his return, someone immediately reported him to the immigration service, and a warrant was issued for his arrest on July 8, 1925. That same day he was taken to the city jail at Douglas, Arizona. Two days later he was given a hearing at the jail, and he was detained there until a warrant of deportation was issued on August 20. The charges were the same as on the warrant of arrest, namely, that he was (1) "L. P. C.", (2) not in possession of an unexpired immigration visa, and (3) that he entered by land at a place not designated for entry.

Two weeks later, Mr. Hauser was sent to Galveston where he was held in the county jail until September 12, when he was deported to Switzerland, at government expense.

Giuseppe Raeta (Case 63).

Giuseppe Raeta was born in 1877 in the province of Caserta, Italy, and was married there in 1904. He lived there for 27 years after his marriage, working as a hack driver. Then he decided to emigrate, but as he was illiterate he could not secure a visa, he stowed himself away on a steamer, and paid 2000 lire to a man on the boat to get him into the United States. He landed in New York without apprehension in March, 1921.

He went to Boston, where he began to work in a rubber factory, then moved to Somerville, Mass. On July 2, 1925, he was sentenced to 1 month in the House of Correction at East Cambridge, plus $150 fine, for arrest in connection with a prohibition raid. His sentence expired on August 13.

Meanwhile, Mr. Raeta was reported to the immigration authorities by the House of Correction and a warrant was issued for his arrest on August 28, 1925. On August 8, he was given a hearing there, through an interpreter. On August 13, the date of the expiration of his sentence, Mr. Raeta was turned over to the immigration authorities and immediately released on $1000 bond.

On September 20, a warrant of deportation was issued, on the same grounds as in the warrant of arrest, (1) "L. P. C.", (2) that he entered in violation of the "passport law", (3) that he was unable to read English or some other language or dialect at the time of entry, (4) that he came as a stowaway. He was deported on October 14, 1925, from Boston, at the expense of the government, and destined to Italy.

It is difficult to ascertain much concerning smugglers from the cases read, for in addition to the fact that many smugglers either remain across the border or escape when they see the immigration officers appearing, a number of aliens are unwilling and afraid to testify or give any information against their smugglers. Of the total number of 362 in the first group, 68 reported that they paid smugglers amounts of money varying from $1.00 to $200 for aid in entering the country; it is probable that others in the group were smuggled in but did not say so. Out of the thirty in the second group, seven reported that they paid from $15 to $80 for help in entering. Of the sixty-eight in the first group, only twenty-one were held as witnesses against their smugglers, and three from the second group were so held.

Josef Petrovi (Case 64).

Josef Petrovi was born in 1903 in Lenni, Czechoslovakia and lived there until 1929. He married in 1926, but when he decided to emigrate in 1929 left his wife at home until he should become established in a new home. He landed in Halifax, Canada on March 13, 1926, and remained there some time before going to Quebec.

Mr. Petrovi was dissatisfied with the type of work he secured, so he went to Windsor about the beginning of 1930 and stayed there several weeks. He paid $75 to a smuggler, who approached him on the street one day, and was brought across the river to Detroit in a rowboat at 5:30 on the morning of March 29, 1930. He and the smuggler were apprehended by the border patrol and taken to the Wayne County Jail in Detroit.

On the same day a warrant was issued for Mr. Petrovi's arrest, on the grounds that he was (1) "L. P. C.", (2) not in possession of an unexpired immigration visa, and (3) that he entered without inspection. On April 8, he was turned over to the Department of Justice for prosecution, but detained in the same jail as before. On the report to the United States

District Attorney by the immigration service, it was requested that Mr. Petrovi be detained as a witness against his smuggler. The smuggler, who was an American citizen, was being prosecuted before the local federal court for violation of Section 8 of the 1917 immigration act.

On April 5, he was given a hearing at the jail.

On May 17, Mr. Petrovi was released under bond of $1500, which had been recommended by the board of review in Washington a few days previous. The case against Mr. Petrovi for violation of the act of March 4, 1929, was not prosecuted, as he had been held in jail so long as witness, and had then testified against his smuggler. A warrant was issued for his deportation on May 21, on the same grounds as those in the warrant of arrest, and he was sent to Ellis Island with a party of deportees on May 27th, and deported three days later at the expense of the steamship company which had brought him to Canada.

During the period of time covered by the first group, the so-called "passport act" was still being enforced in some places, while the time of the latter group embraced the beginning of administration of the act of March 4, 1929, with its penal features. The similarity in those features is shown by the following:

Ivan Galitzi (Case 65).

Ivan Galitzi was born in 1892 in Varna, Bulgaria. He left home in 1913 and went to France, where he stayed until 1916, working as a cook. In that year he went to Holland, then Belgium, continuing the same occupation.

In 1925, Mr. Galitzi went to Mexico, landing at Vera Cruz in March of that year. He began to work near there as cook and bartender. One evening, according to his story, he was drunk, and walked until he arrived in the United States, without knowing what he was doing. He entered on July 7, 1925, and was immediately caught by the border patrol. They took him to the county jail at Nogales, Arizona for detention. A warrant for his arrest was issued on July 11, and a hearing was held at the jail ten days later.

A warrant for Mr. Galitzi's deportation was issued on August 22, on the grounds (1) "L. P. C.", (2) that he entered the United States by land at a place not designated as a port of entry for aliens, (3) that he was not in possession of an unexpired passport on entry, (4) that he was brought to foreign contiguous territory by a steamship company which had not complied with all the requirements of Sec. 17 of the immigration act of 1924. The grounds were the same as those on the warrant of arrest.

Meanwhile, Mr. Galitzi was being held by the Department of Justice, pending trial for violation of the "passport law." He was sentenced, and served the sentence, to a term in the county jail at Tucson, from September 17 to November 7 of that year.

He held a League of Nations passport, but on November 10, after request through the Department of State, the Bulgarian Legation in Washington issued a new passport for Mr. Galitzi. He was sent to Galveston that day, in an attempt to have him "reship foreign one way," but it was not possible to secure a berth for him, so he was deported at government expense, on November 30, to disembark at Bremen.

Hermann Schulze (Case 66).

Hermann Schulze was born in 1889 near Hamburg, Germany. In 1913 he came to the United States, living here constantly until 1920, and working as a painter. The latter year he returned home, but was detained there by the illness of his mother.

Mr. Schulze decided after his mother's death to return to the United States, but was unable to secure a quota visa, so he sailed to Mexico, and walked across the border at Laredo, Texas. He was apprehended by the border patrol just as he was entering, on September 20, 1929, and was taken to the Webb County Jail at Laredo. A warrant was issued for his arrest on September 24.

Mr. Schulze was detained at the expense of the immigration

service until October 3rd, when he was reported to the local United States attorney. Although he continued in the same jail, he was transferred to the jurisdiction of the Department of Justice on that day and held at their expense. Mr. Schulze pled "not guilty," but the commissioner found the evidence sufficient to hold him over until the next term of the federal district court. A bond of $500 was fixed, but Mr. Schulze could not afford it, and so remained in jail. The court met on November 11, and sentenced him to the time already spent in jail. That day he was returned to the custody of the immigration service.

On November 20, a hearing was given him at the jail, and on December 1, a warrant was issued for his deportation, on the same grounds as those contained in the warrant of arrest, namely, that he (1) was "L. P. C.", (2) entered the United States without inspection, (2) was not in possession of an unexpired immigration visa at the time of entry.

Mr. Schulze was sent to Galveston on December 6, and there an attempt was made to "reship" him "foreign one way," but as this could not be accomplished, he was deported on January 9, 1930, at government expense.

Mary Hanna (Case 67).

Mary Hanna was born in 1908 in Finland, and lived there until 1929, when she emigrated to Canada. Three sisters had already come to the United States, to live in New York, Michigan, and Massachusetts, so she went to Canada as she could not secure admission to the United States. She landed in Halifax on August 24, 1929, and went to Windsor, Ont. There she made arrangements to be smuggled into the United States. She and a friend who also wanted to come in to the country paid $150 to a smuggler, who put them in an empty box car on November 9, 1929. They left the train at Port Huron, Mich., but were immediately apprehended by the border patrol and taken to the St. Clair County Jail at Port Huron, Mich., pending prosecution of their case.

A warrant of arrest was issued for Miss Hanna on the same

day she was arrested (a separate case was made for the other girl, not included in this study), on the grounds (1) "L. P. C.", (2) that she was not in possession of an unexpired immigration visa, and (3) that she entered by land other than at a designated place of entry for aliens.

Miss Hanna was referred to the local federal district attorney on November 13, for prosecution of the case against her for violation of the act of March 4, 1929. On that day she was sent to the Wayne County Jail in Detroit to await the outcome of the prosecution. She was given a hearing on November 16th, at the jail. The case then came before the board of review in Washington, and there it was stated that Miss Hanna was willing to work, had had experience as a domestic servant, and so the charge of "L. P. C." was not sustainable.

Meanwhile, Miss Hanna's sister, who had lived in Fitchburg, Mass., for 18 years, applied through the Family Welfare Association of Fitchburg to allow her sister to remain here, as she was afraid deportation to Finland would seriously affect their mother's health, which was none too good. She and another sister would be willing to give bond. As no action had been taken, the Association on February 2, 1930 telegraphed the bureau offering to give a bond for a six months visit to the sister in Fitchburg.

The same day Miss Hanna was sentenced to six months in the Detroit House of Correction, but the sentence was deferred two years, to become effective if Miss Hanna returned to the United States, after deportation.

The board of review in Washington reopened the case on February 4th, and recommended that Miss Hanna be not allowed to visit here but that a warrant of deportation be issued. This was done on February 9, on the same grounds as those on the warrant of arrest, with the exception of "L. P. C.", which had been deleted on recommendation of the board.

On February 10, a wire was received at the bureau in Washington, offering $1500 bond for release of Miss Hanna for a visit. Her sister from Fitchburg had been unable to leave her small children to go to Detroit and wanted to see Miss Hanna before she left the country. The bureau wired that request for a bond must be made locally.[1] The record contains nothing further of the matter. Miss Hanna was deported on March 8, 1930, at the expense of the steamship company bringing her to Canada.

The following cases are of particular interest in so far as the social problems involved are concerned:

Henry Beard (Case 68).

Henry Beard was born on January 24, 1911 in London, as one of five children. His parents are living in Godalming, Surrey, but felt it would be a good opportunity for Henry to go to his maternal grandparents who lived on a farm near Vancouver, B. C. So when he was nine years old, he was sent to Canada, first class, and was admitted and immediately sent on to his grandparents.

Henry continued school where he had left off in England. Several times, however, he ran away from his grandparents, as his grandfather would come home drunk and hit him. Once he was caught by the police in Vancouver and sent back to the farm, but another time he was not found, and began to work as a farmer's helper at Rosedale, B. C. He was afraid he would have to return to his grandparents, so he moved on, to get further south, in the hope of earning "enough money to get back to his mother." On September 3, 1924, he arrived in the United States, crossing the border in the train, with a ticket to Blaine, Wash., and was not inspected, as far as the record shows.

From Blaine he went to Portland, but there he could not get anyone to give him work, and since his money had given out, he took a purse from a woman in a store. He was caught and taken to the juvenile ward of the Multnomah County Jail in Portland on September 15, 1925. Ten days later a warrant was issued for his arrest in deportation proceedings. The

[1] Authority for granting a bond must come from Washington.

charges were that he was (1) "L. P. C.", (2) that he entered the country without inspection, (3) that he was not in possession of an unexpired immigration visa, and (4) that he was under 16 years of age. A warrant for his deportation was issued on October 9, on the same grounds.

The charge against Henry for taking the purse was to be dropped, if deportation occurred. He was deported on November 3, 1925, destined to his father in England. The record does not show whether or not he arrived safely.

Henry Hammer (Case 69).

Henry Hammer was born on October 8, 1902 in London. His father died when he was seven months old and his mother soon after, so he was placed in a school for orphans. When he was ten years old he was sent to St. George's Home in Ottowa, Canada, and about a month after his arrival was placed by the home with a French Canadian family in Napierville, P. Q., near Montreal.

He remained there until he was 18, in 1920, and was often visited by the sisters from St. George's Home. As Napierville was very near the border to the United States, he decided to visit this country, and entered in 1921 for a short time. After working on various farms, he returned to Canada, about a year later.

On July 1, 1925, Mr. Hammer again entered the United States, crossing the border at Alburg, Vt. He was apprehended by the border patrol, and sent immediately to the St. Lawrence County Jail at Canton, N. Y., as the county jail at Alburg was full. A warrant was issued for his arrest but the hearing was not given him until November 16, 1925, at the jail, and a warrant of deportation was issued for him on December 12, 1925, with the charges (1) "L. P. C.", (2) that he entered without inspection, and (3) that he was not in possession of an unexpired immigration visa.

On January 9, 1926, Mr. Hammer was sent to Rouses Point, was detained in the immigration station there over night, and was sent to Ellis Island the next day. He was deported to England on January 14, 1926, at government expense.[1]

St. George's Home had its last contact with him on January 14, 1924, when he wrote them from Vergennes, Vt., asking them for the allowance they had saved for him and had banked to his account. This amounted to $60, and it was forwarded to him. On January 23, they had a letter of thanks from him for it. The matron of the home said Henry "was an exceptionally nice little boy, and they became very fond of him, and would be willing to do anything to help him if he is in difficulties. Mother F. would be grateful if you would let her know whether he was deported to Canada or back to England, as in your letter you mention that some of these people were returned to the Europan countries from which they originally came. Mother F. hopes that (Henry) was not returned to England as she says that he has no relatives there and he looked upon Canada as his home." [2]

CONCLUSIONS

To build a wall around the United States so high and so broad that no alien may climb over has been a difficult and at times it has seemed an insuperable task. As the border patrol increases in numbers and efficiency, however, and as American restrictive immigration policy becomes better known in other countries, it seems probable that illegal entries will diminish. Economic conditions will have their important part in keeping aliens out or in increasing the thin but steady trickle that inevitably will seep in illegally. Every effort should be made to spread knowledge of our quota and other restrictions and every effort should be made to tighten up on border enforcement. The problems involved in the enforcement of immigration laws are so great

[1] Report to the author from the Ottawa Welfare Bureau, February 11, 1927.

[2] *Ibid.*

that unless a unified border patrol is established, officials involved in the immigration task should not be responsible for other enforcement activities, such as liquor prohibition.

President Hoover in his message to Congress on December 2, 1930 called attention to the "thousands of persons who have entered the country in violation of the immigration laws" and stated that "the very method of their entry indicates their objectionable character." On the other hand, the Secretary of Labor in his annual report for the fiscal year ending the previous June[1] had said that this same group of illegal entries included, among others,

> many persons of a very desirable type, a large number being composed of persons who had been in the country for years, entering before the present day restrictions were known; those who came as visitors, liked the country and remained; those who came as seamen and did not rejoin their vessel upon its departure.

The Secretary's statement takes into account a large number who entered before restrictive immigration became a part of American immigration policy, as the President's does not. Furthermore, there are still others who through ignorance of the law and its implications, desire to see relatives, pressing need for work, or a number of other reasons, might enter the United States illegally. Method of entry may not be a proper criterion for determining objectionable character.

[1] P. 77.

CHAPTER VIII

ADMINISTRATIVE STANDARDS AND METHODS[1]

HISTORIANS of the law, tracing the slow course of legal development in the United States, are becoming aware of "the rise of delegated legislation, the shifting of leadership in political life from legislatures and courts to the executive, the setting up of administrative commissions with mixed powers, and the steady growth of boards and commissions with jurisdiction over what were once taken to be matters of judicial cognizance."[2] The increasing complexity of modern life has shown that justification for a path of development of the law must be sought elsewhere than in the mere fact that our forefathers followed it. Despite our best Federalist traditions, it is no longer possible to divide the provinces of the executive, judicial and legislative into separate water-tight compartments.[3] With this change has come the abandonment of the age-old subjection of all questions to controlling decision by the judiciary, at least where there is need for speedy and flexible decision and where

[1] This chapter has appeared in part in the *Political Science Quarterly*, vol. xliv, no. 2, June 1929, p. 193 *et seq.*

[2] Roscoe Pound, "Social and Economic Problems of the Law", *Annals of the American Academy of Political and Social Science*, vol. cxxxvi, no. 225, March 1928, p. 6.

[3] *Vide* John Dickinson, *Administrative Justice and the Supremacy of Law in the United States* (Cambridge, U. S. A., 1927), ch. i; R. M. MacIver, *The Modern State* (Oxford, 1926), Bk. III, ch. xii, 1. A different view is taken in Frederick Green, "Separation of Governmental Powers," *Yale Law Journal*, vol. xxix, pp. 371 *et seq.*

public interest may be regarded in a manner impossible between two parties to a litigation. Thus administrative law has arisen. In the United States, administrative law may mean the law applicable to controversies between the individual and the state or the representatives of the state respecting administrative power to affect private rights and the remedies available to the individual affected; it may also mean the law applicable to the organization, procedure, and operations of the executive branch of the government; and finally, it may include the rules of law developed and announced by administrative agencies.

In few questions involving public policy has this administrative growth been more strikingly shown than in the activities of the bureau of immigration of the United States department of labor. The courts, regarding immigration in the same way as taxation and defense as a problem vital to the existence of government, have confined within narrow limits the scope of their review of the administrative decisions of immigration officials.

Progressive thinkers, otherwise alive to the futility of attempting to decide problems of modern life by century-old judicial methods, are often loath to concede the right of administrative action in immigration cases, which turn on questions of interference with personal liberty, and which may involve issues individually more tragic than those of property rights. Lawyers and humanitarians alike have joined in decrying the wide latitude allowed immigration officials, particularly in cases of deportation. It has long been settled that the power to exclude or expel is vested in the executive department of government and may be exercised entirely through executive officers, for it was established in the Fong Yue Ting case that the "power of Congress to . . . expel, like the power to exclude aliens, or any specified class of aliens, from the country, may be exercised entirely through executive officers ";[1] the principle has been constantly reiterated in a steady stream of cases.[2] The question immediately arises as to how far the administrative fiat of deportation allows the alien " due process of law " in the proceedings against him, and how far it is used in accordance with legislative delegation of power to administrative officials. It must be remembered that

> an alien as well as a citizen, is protected by the prohibition of deprivation of life, liberty and property without due process and the equal protection of the law. This principle is universal. It applies to " all persons within the territorial jurisdiction of the United States, without regard to any difference of race, or color, or of nationality."[3]

It is to this question of constitutional right that the courts most frequently turn and which will be mentioned in connection with court cases.[4] Here attention is focussed rather on the development of the administrative agency within the Department of Labor by which departmental discretion is applied to specific cases, and the development of administrative standards by rule and regulation of the department.

ORGANIZATION OF THE BUREAU OF IMMIGRATION IN THE DEPARTMENT OF LABOR

Let us turn our attention to the organization of the administrative hierarchy within the Department of Labor, by

1 Fong Yue Ting *v.* United States, 149 U. S. 698, 714. *Vide supra*, p. ——.

2 Buttfield *v.* Stranahan, 192 U. S. 470; Oceanic Steam Navigation Co. *v.* Stranahan, 214 U. S. 320; Murray's Lessee *v.* Hoboken Land and Improvement Co., 18 Howard 272; Hilton *v.* Merritt, 110 U. S. 97. For deportation cases, *vide* esp. United States *ex rel.* Brazier *v.* Commissioner of Immigration, 5 Fed. (2d) 162; Skeffington *v.* Katzeff, 277 Fed. 129; Ng Fung Ho *v.* White, 259 U. S. 276.

3 Whitfield *et al.* *v.* Hanges *et al.*, 222 Fed. 745, quoting Yick Wo *v.* Hopkins, 118 U. S. 356, 369.

4 *Vide infra*, pp. 312 *et seq.*, and 369 *et seq.*

which decisions are reached in immigration matters. The procedure is rigidly centralized within the Department, in a pyramidal structure, with the Secretary of Labor at the top as a kind of court of last resort. All phases of administrative judgment are vested in him. The immigration acts within themselves contain no rules as to proceedings for deportation but merely state that a member of one of the deportable classes " shall, upon the warrant of the Secretary of Labor, be taken into custody and deported." Furthermore, in every case where any person is ordered deported from the United States . . . the decision of the Secretary of Labor shall be final." [1] In one group of cases, however, such is not the case. An alien ordered excluded at the time of entry would have his case originally decided by a board of special inquiry, whose decision is final, " unless reversed on appeal to the Secretary of Labor: *Provided,* That the decision of a board of special inquiry shall be based on the certificate of the examining medical officer, and . . . [2] shall be final as to rejection of an alien affected with tuberculosis in any form or with a loathsome or dangerous contagious disease, or with any mental or physical disability " which would make him excludable; there would be no appeal from the certificate of the examining medical officer. If the alien

[1] Immigration act of 1917, sec. 19. Other sections of the act confirm the finality of the Secretary's decision, i. e., judges sentencing alien convicts may " recommend to the Secretary of Labor " that such convicts be not deported (sec. 19); places to which deportation may be made are at the " option of the Secretary " (sec. 20); personal care is to be provided for such deported persons as need it " in the opinion of the Secretary " (sec. 20); bail in deportation cases is to be provided with security approved " by the Secretary "; etc.

[2] Except as provided, " that any alien liable to be excluded because likely to become a public charge or because of physical disability other than tuberculosis in any form or a loathsome or dangerous contagious disease may, if otherwise admissible, nevertheless be admitted in the discretion of the Secretary of Labor upon the giving of a suitable and proper bond."

were admitted and it was not found until after his arrival that he belonged to such classification, and if the discovery were made within five years, he could be deported. Such aliens are among those "mandatorily deportable," and even the Secretary of Labor cannot prevent their deportation, according to law.

In all other cases, the decision of the Secretary is final. However, the statutory enumeration of the grounds for deportation prohibits deportation on grounds not covered by the statute,[1] and so the administrative authorities cannot add to the list of deportable categories by mere interpretation of the statute. Thus Regina Kornmehl reached the United States with a child who was excluded because of disease and so she too was excluded as liable to become a public charge at the time of entry as one "of a class of aliens excluded by law, in accordance with department circular No. 172, dated Oct. 19, 1897." The court in its decision[2] remarked that the clause "would seem to indicate that the inspectors rendered their decision, not because the examination of the facts led their minds to such conclusion, but because they felt themselves constrained to render such decision because of some instructions from the treasury department" which said, "if any minor alien suffering with said loathsome disease is accompanied by its parents, one parent should be returned with such alien." The court then held the order unwarranted by the statute, which contained "no phraseology which can be construed as leaving the exclusion of immigrants to the mere arbitrary discretion of the Secretary of the Treasury or the commissioner general of immigration" and "no mere rule can operate to exclude a person not excluded by the statutes." It is of note that the rule

[1] *Ex parte* Guest, 287 Fed. 884.

[2] *In re* Kornmehl, 87 Fed. 314; *vide* Sibray *v.* United States *ex rel.* Plichta, 282 Fed. 795.

which the court refused to allow here was later incorporated into the statute, as administrative rules so often are embodied in later statutes.

The volume of work for the Secretary is manifestly far beyond the strength and capacity of one individual; so statutory provision has been made for two Assistant Secretaries of Labor [1] two Assistants to the Secretary,[2] and for the hybrid combination of administrative official and court known as the "Secretary and Commissioner General's Board of Review." [3] As "the head of an executive department of this government cannot himself sign every official communication emanating from his department and a proper notice signed by the Assistant Secretary has the same force as though signed by the Secretary," [4] so "a warrant for the deportation of an alien charged to be unlawfully in the United States . . . is not insufficient because signed by an Assistant Secretary instead of the Secretary." [5] This is true, whether the warrant be signed by the First or the Second Assistant Secretary [6] or by one of the Assistants to the Secretary,[7] provided of course it is duly authorized by the Secretary. However, the Commissioner General of Immigration has no authority to sign such warrants, and the

[1] An Assistant Secretary of Labor was provided by the Act of March 4, 1913, creating the Department of Labor (37 Stat. 766) and the Second Assistant Secretary of Labor was provided by the act approved June 30, 1922 (42 Stat. 766).

[2] Provided by the act approved March 4, 1927 (44 Stat. 1415).

[3] *Vide infra*, ch. x, p. 377.

[4] Hannibal Bridge Co. *v.* United States, 221 U. S. 194.

[5] United States *ex rel.* Calamia *v.* Redfern, 180 Fed. 506; *In re* Jem Yuen, 188 Fed. 350.

[6] United States *ex rel.* Chin Fook Wah *v.* Dunton, 288 Fed. 959; MacKusick *ex rel.* Pattavina *v.* Johnson, 3 Fed. (2d) 298; Lew Shee *v.* Nagle, 22 Fed. (2d) 107.

[7] Hajdamacha *v.* Karnuth, 23 Fed. (2d) 956.

Secretary may not delegate the authority to him. Only where there is a personal interest of the Secretary or where there are very exceptional circumstances does the Secretary himself take action.[1] Of course, if there is disagreement between the lower officials of the Department, the Secretary himself is the final authority.

Next lower in the administrative hierarchy comes the Commissioner General of Immigration. As already indicated, he has charge of administration of all laws regulating immigration, but he has no authority to make *decisions* in deportation or other immigration cases. He may make recommendations, but if the Secretary of Labor should adopt them it would be on his own undivided responsibility, precisely as is his adoption of the recommendations of the board of review. During the World War, the line of demarcation in authority was sometimes more noted in the breach than the observance. Mr. Louis Post, Assistant Secretary of Labor during the Presidency of Mr. Wilson, called attention to this situation:

Notwithstanding the Commissioner General's lack of authority to make primary decisions, the Bureau of Immigration in the Department of Labor long assumed to act, both in exclusion appeals and upon expulsion warrants, with a pronounced air of . . . authority. This assumption of jurisdiction took the form of recommendatory memorandums to the Secretary for his formal approval. Had those memorandums been prepared for the purpose of rendering ministerial or clerical or expert assistance to the Secretary, there could have been no more serious objection than their inevitable tendency toward such a climax. For instance in recommending a warrant of deportation in an expulsion proceeding, the Bureau of Immigration declared that "the Bureau finds," etc. many other Bureau memorandums in

[1] The First Assistant Secretary of Labor deals less frequently with immigration matters than the Second Assistant Secretary.

expulsion proceedings used the same or similar adjudicatory language for the manifest purpose of assuming, and of securing the Secretary's formal approval of the assumption, that the Commissioner General's authority in such cases went to the extent of making primary decisions. Nor were such verbal instances the only indications of a tendency both in expulsion and in exclusion cases, toward the transformation of the Bureau of Immigration into a court of first instance. The extent to which this tendency went may be inferred from the further fact that records in both expulsion and exclusion proceedings were frequently detained for long periods for the stated purpose of enabling the Commissioner General to pass judgment upon the cases and to make primary decisions in them; and this notwithstanding that it was the official duty of the Bureau of Immigration as a ministerial branch of the Department of Labor in such cases, to deliver . . . records promptly to the office of the Secretary for authoritative action.[1]

The development of the board of review and work of the Assistants to the Secretary have meant a concentration of authority in the direct line of secretarial responsibility. There are an Assistant Commissioner General and an Assistant to the Commissioner General to aid and advise the Commissioner General. The actual working of the bureau of immigration is done by the ten divisions which conduct the daily routine of business. These divisions are as follows:

1. Mail and files
   all mail, telegrams, etc. coming to the bureau are sorted and distributed to the proper person; files are made up of individual cases, etc.
2. Information
   all inquiries are answered or referred to the proper person for answer.

[1] Post, Louis J., Unpublished MS., p. 131 *et seq.*

3. Correspondence
   letters are answered, and notices, orders, etc. sent to the officials "in the field."
4. Visa and petition
   correspondence is carried on relative to the issuance of immigration visas, and petitions of American citizens, etc. for non-quota or preference admission of relatives.
5. Permit
   applications are received and permits issued for alien residents to leave the country and return exempt from the quota.
6. Chinese
   cases of Chinese exclusion, deportation, etc. are handled.
7. Statistical
   statistics are gathered pertaining to emigration from and immigration to the United States. The work of the bureau of immigration is tabulated.
8. Warrant, formerly the "law division"
   warrants of arrest and deportation are issued, telegraphically and by letter.
9. Deportation
   arrangements for deportation are made, after the issuance of the warrants.
10. Accounts and personnel
    employees' records, expense accounts, supplies, transportation, etc. are cared for, general accounts of the bureau made up, funds allocated, etc.

Aside from the officials in Washington, there are those "in the field." For administrative purposes, the United States is divided into thirty-five immigration districts, in each of which there is either a district director or commissioner of immigration as administrative officer. The district directors and commissioners of immigration have similar functions, but the latter are appointed by the President and Senate under the act of August 18, 1894[1] to serve

[1] 28 Stat. 372.

for four years unless sooner removed and until their successors are appointed; the district directors are appointed by the authority of the Secretary of Labor [1] on recommendation of the Commissioner General of Immigration, according to the Civil Service Act of January 16, 1883. The Immigration Act of 1917 provides [2] that nothing shall be done to change the method of appointing commissioners of immigration, which is to continue as provided in 1894. The district directors are usually promoted from the ranks of inspectors.[3]

The duties of both commissioners of immigration and district directors and other immigration officials in charge of districts, ports, or stations are of an "administrative character." [4] They or their assistants must visit each port, subport and station within their respective districts at least once every six months and report it to the bureau.[5] Inspectors in charge, directly responsible to the district directors, are in charge of the sub-district headquarters. Throughout the various districts there are immigrant inspectors, responsible to the district director if stationed at the district headquarters and responsible to him through the inspector in charge at other points in the district.

An important arm of the immigration service "in the field" consists of the border patrol, established primarily to prevent and detect the illegal entry of aliens into the United

[1] Immigration Act of 1917, sec. 24.

[2] Sec. 24.

[3] There are commissioners at Montreal, Boston, Ellis Island, Philadelphia Immigration Station at Gloucester City, N. J., Baltimore, New Orleans, Seattle, San Francisco, San Juan, Porto Rico—nine in all; there are district directors at the 26 other headquarters of immigration districts.—*Immigration Rules and Regulations of January 1, 1930*, Rule 30.

[4] Immigration Act of 1917, sec. 23. *Vide* also *Immigration Laws*, etc., *of January 1, 1930*, Rule 29, Subdivisions A-D.

[5] *Ibid.*, Subdivision D.

States, and operating along the land and sea boundaries of the United States.[1] From the beginning of its organization in 1925, the territory in which the border patrol operates for administrative purposes has been divided into "border patrol districts," of which there are now eleven, located largely along the land boundaries of the country.[2] These eleven districts are divided into thirty-three subdistricts, and these in turn are each divided into four patrol stations, with from two to eleven employees each.[3] The entire patrol force of each district operates under the supervision of the respective district head.[4]

The patrol force consists of the following:

Supervisors (Border Patrol);
Officers in charge of districts;
Assistant Superintendents, who shall be qualified immigrant inspectors;
Chief Patrol Inspectors, who shall be qualified immigrant inspectors;
Senior Patrol Inspectors;
Patrol Inspectors;
Clerks, and Motor Mechanics.

A kind of liaison service between the field and the bureau in Washington is found in the supervisory staff of three immigration officials who act as the special representatives of the bureau to investigate, report on and make recommendations concerning immigration activities in the field direct to the Commissioner General.[5]

[1] *Vide supra*, p. 254 *et seq.*

[2] Except that they include South Carolina, California, Washington, Florida, Louisiana and Texas.

[3] Conversation of the author with Major Davenport, supervisor of the border patrol organization in the bureau in Washington, in May, 1930.

[4] *Annual Report of the Commissioner General for the Fiscal Year Ended June 30, 1925*, p. 23.

[5] Bureau of immigration General Order No. 61 as amended. Subdivision C. "No arbitrary power or authority is conferred upon such supervisors."

POWERS AND FUNCTIONS OF THE BUREAU OF IMMIGRATION

Let us consider for a moment how this organization functions in dealing with deportation cases. As far back as 1827 the courts decided that "in the construction of a doubtful and ambiguous law the contemporary construction of those who were called upon to act under the law, and were appointed to carry its provisions into effect, is entitled to very great respect";[1] and again, "the construction of these statutes is that given them in their practical administration by the treasury department even since their enactment."[2] Such is especially the case in regard to the immigration acts, replete as they are with a plethora of vague terms, from "liable to become a public charge" to "moral turpitude." Instances of administrative interpretation of such terms could be multiplied *ad infinitum*. The courts often tend to follow the interpretation of the immigration officials, as they will not interfere with administrative interpretation of "matters of fact." For instance, the court cannot inquire into a finding and certificate that an alien is physically defective,[3] and a decision of the Secretary, though clearly erroneous, cannot be reviewed by the courts,[4] if there was evidence on which the decision was based. In the famous Gottlieb case, the lower court departed from the construction adopted by the immigration officials, but the Supreme Court returned to it.[5] On the other hand, the

[1] Edward's Lessee *v.* Darby, 12 Wheaton 206.

[2] Smythe *v.* Fiske, 23 Wall 274; United States *v.* Philbrick, 120 U. S. 52; United States *v.* Pugh, 99 U. S. 265; Brown *v.* United States, 113 U. S. 570.

[3] United States *ex rel.* Duner *v.* Curran, 10 Fed. (2d) 38.

[4] *In re* Ota, 96 Fed. 487.

[5] Commissioner of Immigration of the Port of New York *v.* Gottlieb *et al.*, 265 U. S. 310. This was a case of exclusion, not deportation.

immigration officials tend strictly to follow the court interpretation of terms. Even so, there is still considerable variation in the use of terms, especially as between one immigration district and another. Thus, as already seen, one district will use the term "public charge" for a person sentenced to the county jail for a short term and another district will reserve the same nomenclature for only those aliens in public institutions because of lack of pecuniary resources. The immigration inspectors usually know the district judges and are apt to use such definitions as they feel would meet with the judge's approval, should the case be taken to court. The bureau of immigration in Washington occasionally sends out notices attempting to standardize to a degree at least the use of such vague terms as "liable to become a public charge," and modifies its use of terms in accordance with the trend of the courts, as in the instruction to use "liable to become a public charge" on one case where it was stated, "the trend of court decisions in 1928 is that aliens who enter surreptitiously are 'L.P.C.'" [1]

An interesting illustration of administrative interpretation is found in the case of a man with a wife and four children in Canada and a wife and one child in the United States. When held for deportation, he was charged with being likely to become a public charge at the time of entry, despite the fact that he was a prosperous automobile salesman. The charge was upheld "as the record in the case shows him to be quite a worthless fellow, one who recognizes no responsibilities. If he were to meet his legal and moral obligations to those for whose existence on earth he is responsible, he would have little or nothing on which to support himself." Another instance is the case of an insane woman in a public institution where she had been examined by an expert medi-

[1] Bureau File 55628/706.

cal witness, introduced at her own expense, in accordance with statutory authority. In view of the conflicting diagnoses made by him and the officials in charge of the institution, it was decided by the bureau of immigration that "the official certificate of the institution in which the alien is confined should be accepted." The question arises as to the usefulness of the provision allowing private diagnosis, at least from the point of view of the alien.

Departmental discretion applied in a series of individual cases develops administrative standards which are later embodied in rules and general orders, or else calls attention to the misapplication of administrative standards, with the consequent issuance of a rule ordering cessation of a certain practice.

The powers given the Secretary of Labor, then, are quasi-judicial in the discretion allowed him to make final decision in individual cases. Precedent in those cases paves the way for a general rule and calls attention to its need. Thus we come upon the second kind of power given under the immigration statutes, that of quasi-legislative authority. "What distinguishes legislation from adjudication is that the former affects the rights of individuals in the abstract and must be applied in further proceedings before the legal position of any particular individual will be definitely touched by it; while adjudication operates concretely upon the individuals in their individual capacity." [1] Thus the authorities of the immigration service act judicially in designating the concrete instances which the statute describes in general terms; they also act legislatively, for the statute gives them power to fill in the details of the act by making rules and regulations. The Commissioner General of Immigration

shall perform all his duties under the direction of the Secretary

[1] John Dickinson, *op. cit.*, p. 12.

of Labor. Under such direction he shall have charge of the administration of all laws relating to the immigration of aliens into the United States, and shall have the control, direction and supervision of all officers, clerks and employees appointed thereunder; he shall establish such rules and regulations, prescribe such forms of bond, reports, entries, and other papers, and shall issue from time to time such instructions not inconsistent with law, as she shall deem best calculated for carrying out the provisions of this act. . . . The duties of commissioners of immigration and other immigration officials in charge of districts, ports, or stations shall be of an administrative character, to be described in detail by regulations prepared under the direction or with the approval of the Secretary of Labor . . . [1]

The numerous rules and regulations made in pursuance of statutory authority show in clear relief the problem of a statute, supposedly complete when it left the law-making body, but yet with a mass of detail to be filled in by legislative action of the administrative authorities. Indeed, the immigration statutes seem to fall between the horns of the dilemma pointed out by Professor Powell [2] referring to the case of Blue *v.* Beach, where the anomalous rule is laid down: " While it is necessary that a law, when it comes from the law-making power, should be complete, still there are many matters relating to methods and details which may be by the legislature referred to some designated ministerial officer or body." The comparatively simple wording of the immigration act of 1917 concerning the power of the Secretary of Labor to issue his warrant for the deportation of

[1] Immigration act of 1917, sec. 3. In practice, such rules and regulations are often written by the solicitor or a subordinate member of the Department of Labor, signed by the Commissioner General, and approved by an Assistant Secretary of Labor.

[2] Thomas Reed Powell, *Separation of Powers: Administrative Exercise of Legislative and Judicial Power,* Political Science Quarterly, vol. xxvii, p. 215.

aliens and to make final decision as to questions of deportability, and the power of the Commissioner General of Immigration to issue rules and regulations for carrying out the provisions of the act, have caused the development of a highly complex system of regulations and general orders promulgated by administrative officials under the quasi-legislative authority conferred on them.

The rules and regulations as printed do not furnish the complete story of departmental regulations in immigration cases, for it is provided in the rules that the rules and regulations " may from time to time be amended, supplemented, or repealed by general orders duly issued by the Commissioner General of Immigration with the approval of the Secretary of Labor." Such general orders are issued in mimeographed form to the immigration officers in the Department of Labor and throughout the field, and bear the mimeographed signature of the Commissioner General, " approved " and signed with the mimeographed signature of the Second Assistant Secretary. When such general orders are amendments to the rules, the next printed edition of the rules of course contains the amended rather than the original form; other orders pertain to matters of departmental administration and are not printed. For instance, the act relating to the border patrol is defined in a published rule, but is explained as to organization and duties in General Order No. 61, which is not published.

JUDICIAL REVIEW

The complex mass of rules, regulations, general orders and supplements gives rise to the question how far they are rules of law. These executive rulings have come before the courts in but few instances, for it must constantly be borne in mind that a comparatively small number of deportation cases ever reach any court, much less the Supreme Court.

The act invests the District Courts with jurisdiction of all causes, civil and criminal, arising under it. The cases come before the court on petition for a writ of *habeas corpus* when the alien or his friends can afford the expense of litigation. The poverty of many of the aliens held for deportation, and the degree of latitude allowed the administrative officials in interpretation of such terms as "liable to become a public charge," and the consequent unwillingness of the courts to overrule administrative interpretations, account for the small number of cases that come before the courts.

When cases do arise in which court action is taken, the question of finality of the administrative regulation involved may be before the courts. As the administrative officials have authority under the statute to make rules, the court will not perform the task of the immigration officials by substituting its own determination for that of the administrative authorities. In general,[1] it has been held that executive regulations made in pursuance of an express authority of Congress become part of the body of laws of the country of which the courts will take judicial notice, and regulations made under such authority have the full force of a statute upon a private individual as well as upon a public official.[2] In this connection it is of interest to note the 1925 New York "Window Cleaners' Case," where Judge MacLaughlin presented the point of view that the legislative declaration that a rule has the force and effect of law does not make it equivalent to or equal to legislative enactment.[3] The Labor Law of New York, involved in the case, conferred on the

[1] In this section I am indebted to "The Supreme Court on Administrative Construction as a Guide in the Interpretation of Statutes", note in *Harvard Law Review*, vol. XL, pp. 469-472, and to Thomas Reed Powell, *op. cit.*, *Political Science Quarterly*, vol. xxviii, p. 46.

[2] Caha *v.* United States, 152 U. S. 211.

[3] Louis Schumer, Respondent *v.* Harry Caplin, Appellant, 241 N. Y. 346.

Industrial Commission power to make rules governing the administration of its own affairs *only*. A violation of the rule of the commission, as it did not have the force of a statute, did not constitute negligence. This line between provisions whose violation does and those whose violation does not constitute negligence is adverted to in the immigration case of Mahler *v.* Eby,[1] where it is stated that greater precision is required of a statute defining and punishing crimes than of those delegating legislative power to executive boards and officers.

The few cases in which the administrative regulations of the bureau of immigration have come before the courts have held that the rules will be noticed judicially[2] and "departmental rules governing deportation procedure in so far as themselves consistent with law are themselves law and binding on the government as well as the aliens and compliance with them is essential to due process of law."[3] In accordance with the doctrine of the New York case, however, violation of such rules could not constitute negligence. Last of all, such rules obviously could not go beyond the power delegated by the statute.[4]

With the detailed administrative organization provided within the Department of Labor and with the provisions in the immigration statute that the decision of the Secretary shall be final, how do deportation cases ever reach the courts? If an alien held in deportation proceedings can show that he has exhausted all available administrative remedies within

[1] 264 U. S. 32.

[2] Colyer *et al.* *v.* Skeffington, 21 Fed. (2d) 376.

[3] *Ex parte* Radivoeff, 278 Fed. 227.

[4] Gegiow *v.* Uhl, 239 U. S. 3; The Parthian, 276 Fed. 903; United States *ex rel.* Jefferian *v.* Curran, 297 Fed. 470; United States *v.* Stump, 292 Fed. 354.

the Department [1] and is being unlawfully restrained of his liberty he is entitled to a writ of *habeas corpus,* for "the privilege of the writ of *habeas corpus* shall not be suspended, unless when in cases of rebellion or invasion the public safety may require it." [2] This privilege extends to aliens and citizens alike. The object of the writ, of course, is "to determine whether a prisoner can be lawfully detained, to protect against unwarranted encroachments upon personal liberty; and the proceedings under the writ are to be deemed civil rather than criminal, in which the civil right of personal liberty is asserted." [3] *Habeas corpus* challenges the right of a person to detain the subject of the writ, is addressed by the court to the officer in whose keeping the alien is,[4] and so can be obtained only when the alien is actually *in* custody of the immigration officials or others.[5] But cause must be shown for the issuance of the writ, and it cannot be involved when the imprisonment is voluntary only.[6]

In determining the question of cause, the courts are faced with the problem of how far they will review the determinations of the administrative authorities.[7] In other

[1] If he neglected opportunities under the administrative procedure to question the rightfulness of the action, a court will not hear the question. —United States *v.* Sing Tuck, 194 U. S. 161.

[2] United States Constitution, sec. 9, art. i.

[3] Constitution of the United States, Annotated, quoted Cook and Hagerty, *op. cit.*, p. 112, § 228.

[4] Cook and Hagerty, *op. cit.,* p. 126, § 252.

[5] Application for the writ must be made to a federal court, for a state court cannot issue a writ to secure release of a person held under authority of federal laws.—Duncan *v.* Darst, 1 How. 301; Robb *v.* Connolly, 111 U. S. 624; *In re* Wood, 140 U. S. 278.

[6] *Ex parte* Miller, 110 Pac. 139 (13 Cal. App. 564); *Ex parte* Ford, 116 Pac. 757, 160 Cal. 33.

[7] The situation regarding judicial review is merely outlined here, as it involves many problems of administrative and constitutional law. *Vide*

words, what circumstances will allow an alien the right of judicial determination of his right to remain in the country, in view of the wording of the statute that "the decision of the Secretary of Labor shall be final"? The courts have tended to restrict the scope of their review very rigidly in immigration cases, for they have recognized that immigration is a problem of importance in the very existence of government and as one which falls within the province of the political department of the state.[1] The question always arises as to where the line is to be drawn between questions which the courts in the exercise of their reviewing powers insist on discussing themselves and questions whose decision by the administrative authorities they recognize as final.

Even in the narrowly restricted field which they have allowed themselves, the courts have interfered to prevent bureaucratic denial of an alien's rights. They have held, in the first place, that matters of *fact* are for the Secretary of Labor to decide and may be reviewed only if the hearing was not full or fair or based on the evidence.[2] "Where there is jurisdiction, the finding of fact by the executive

J. Dickinson, "Administrative Law and the Fear of Bureaucracy", *Journal of the American Bar Association,* Oct. and No. 1928, vol. xiv, no. 9, and vol. xv, no. 10. F. Frankfurter, "The Task of Administrative Law", *University of Pennsylvania Law Review,* May, 1927; E. Freund, *Administrative Powers Over Persons and Property* (1928); pt. iii, chs. xiii, xiv, and esp. xv; N. Isaacs, "Judicial Review of Administrative Findings", xxxx *Yale Law Journal,* p. 781 *et seq.*; S. Wiel, "Administrative Finality", xxxviii *Harvard Law Review,* p. 447 *et seq.*

[1] They have acted according to the doctrine of Murray's Lessee *v.* Hoboken Land Co., 18 How. 272, and Hilton *v.* Merritt, 110 U. S. 97.

[2] Yamataya *v.* Fisher (the Japanese Immigrant Case), 189 U. S. 86; Whitfield *v.* Hanges, 222 Fed. 745; *Ex parte* Hidekuni Iwata, 219 Fed. 610 (affirmed without opinion Iwata *v.* Cornel, 244 U. S. 643); *Ex parte* Watchorn, 160 Fed. 1014; United States *ex rel.* Berman *v.* Curran, 13 Fed. (2d) 96; Dominici *v.* Johnson, 10 Fed. (2d) 433. *Vide* also Cook and Hagerty, *op. cit.*, p. 127, § 53-4.

department is conclusive[1] and the courts have no power to interfere unless there was denial of a fair hearing[2] or the finding was not supported by the evidence[3] or there was an application of an erroneous rule of law."[4]

On matters of *law*, the courts will always review. But the distinction between law and fact is nebulous and goes off into the shadowland of "mixed questions of law and fact." Indeed, there is no fixed distinction between the two, for

> matters of law grow downward into roots of fact, and matters of fact reach upward, without a break, into matters of law. The knife of policy alone affects an artificial cleavage at the point where the court chooses to draw the line between public interest and private right. It would seem that where the courts are unwilling to review, they are tempted to explain by the easy device of calling the question one of "fact"; and when otherwise disposed, they say it is a question of "law."[5]

It is then useless to attempt to embark on the stormy sea of clarification of what is law and what is fact.[6] The true test in a given case seems to be the practical consideration of what the court considers to be the best procedure for the public welfare. If the courts feel that matters of public policy and interest are particularly involved, they are less scrupulous to insist that the administrative authorities uphold the rights of the alien than if no questions of public

[1] United States *v.* Ju Toy, 198 U. S. 253.

[2] Chin Yow *v.* United States, *supra.*

[3] American School of Magnetic Healing *v.* McAnnulty, 187 U. S. 94.

[4] Gegiow *v.* Uhl, 239 U. S. 3; Ng. Fung Ho *v.* White, 259 U. S. 276.

[5] John Dickinson, *Administrative Justice and the Supremacy of Law*, p. 55.

[6] *Vide* Wigmore, *A Treatise on the System of Evidence* (Boston, 1905), vol. i, pp. 1-3.

welfare are at issue. As deportation cases usually involve such questions, the tendency is to insist on only the loosest kind of procedural safeguards. As already indicated, the hearing must be full and fair; furthermore, the courts regard themselves as bound by the administrative finding only where the evidence on which the immigration officials acted was at least reasonably adequate to support the decision [1] or where the immigration officials did not act in excess of their jurisdiction, or did not act on erroneous conclusions of law.

If any evidence is brought out tending to support the immigration authorities in their decision, the court will not say that in interpreting the evidence a wrong conclusion was reached. If no evidence was obtained, the court will remand the alien to the custody of the immigration service for a new hearing or discharge.[2] In brief, if the hearing was unfair, the court in general will direct a new hearing; if the law was misapplied so as unjustly to deny freedom to the alien, the writ of *habeas corpus* will be sustained and the alien immediately released; if the alien has been held with an unreasonable amount of bond demanded as a requisite for release, pending disposition of the case, the court may direct reduction in the amount of the bond.[3]

If the court finds the alien to be properly in custody its duty is to return him to the immigration authorities for deportation according to law. However, if the court finds him illegally detained, and that due process has been denied him, there is a question as to procedure. Should the court

[1] Zakonaite *v.* Wolf, 226 U. S. 272; Lewis *v.* Frick, 233 U. S. 291; Healy *v.* Backus, 221 Fed. 358; United States *ex rel.* Rennie *v.* Brooks, 284 Fed. 908.

[2] Hughes *v.* United States, 295 Fed. 800; *Ex parte* Joyce, 212 Fed. 282.

[3] Mahler *v.* Eby, *supra*; United States *v.* Uhl, 266 Fed. 929; Colyer *v.* Skeffington, 265 Fed. 17; Frick *v.* Lewis, 195 Fed. 693; United States *v.* Brooks, 284 Fed. 908.

take jurisdiction and decide the case on its merits or should the court turn the case back to the appropriate administrative authorities with an order for a new hearing?

The practice approved by the Supreme Court and generally prevailing . . . seems to be that the court which takes jurisdiction and custody of the alien under the writ of habeas corpus and finds that this hearing has been unfair retains custody and jurisdiction of him and of the case and tries on the merits *de novo* on evidence introduced before that court the question whether or not the alien is guilty of the charges made against him in the warrant of arrest before making his discharge absolute.[1]

Having decided that the writ of *habeas corpus* shall be issued, the court then takes up the question of fact and so acts in the same way the administrative officer had, in hearing the facts and determining the matter accordingly.[2]

Immigration officials object particularly to this tendency of the courts, for they feel their administrative prerogatives are being supplanted. The Secretary of Labor feels the situation to be a serious one from the administrative viewpoint, for he thinks the tendency is growing on the part of the courts and calls attention to it:

Recourse to the courts is the undenied right of an alien in the event the Secretary exceeds the authority given him by the immigration law, but certainly it was never intended that his legitimate administrative acts should be subject to review by the courts. The law, which vests the administration of the immigration laws in the Secretary of Labor, seems plain enough, and there is a long line of judicial decisions supporting it, but

[1] Whitfield *et al.* *v.* Hanges, *supra*, citing Chin Yow *v.* United States, 208 U. S. 813; United States *ex rel.* D'Amato *v.* Williams, 193 Fed. 228; Sibray *v.* U. S., 282 Fed. 795; Howes *v.* Tozer, 3 Fed. (2d) 849; United States *ex rel.* Rosen *v.* Williams, 200 Fed. 538.

[2] McCandless *v.* United States *ex rel.* Rocker, 30 Fed. (2d) 652.

unless the principle involved can be firmly reestablished by the Supreme Court, it is my opinion that it ought to be reasserted in the law in terms which cannot be misunderstood or misinterpreted. Otherwise there is grave danger that the regulation of immigration . . . will be taken over by the courts, and when it is considered that in the course of a year about 40,000 decisions of various kinds are made by or for the Secretary of Labor, the growing danger of substituting judicial for administrative control becomes regrettably apparent.[1]

There are no statistics available on the prevalence of the practice alluded to by the Secretary of Labor, nor so far as it is known has anyone studied the matter thoroughly. Some district courts follow the procedure of returning the case to the proper administrative authorities to rehear if necessary.[2] In so doing there is opportunity for exercise of the same administrative discretion which before may have denied due process.

As immigration officials are administrative officers and their decisions are those of the executive department of government, an order discharging an alien in deportation proceedings cannot operate as *res adjudicata* in subsequent proceedings against the same alien.[3] So there is therefore no bar to new proceedings for deportation, even though release has been secured by the alien or his counsel through a writ of *habeas corpus*.[4]

A small proportion of the total number of deportation cases ever get to even the lowest federal court. During the fiscal year 1930, when 16,631 aliens were deported from the

[1] *Annual Report*, etc., *for 1929*, p. 18.

[2] United States *v.* Petkos, 214 Fed. (2d) 978; Damon *ex rel.* Loon Goon Wong *v.* Johnson, 13 Fed. (2d) 284.

[3] Sire *v.* Berkshire, 185 Fed. 967; Ladaux *v.* Berkshire, 185 Fed. 971.

[4] Colyer *v.* Skeffington, 265 Fed. 17; United States *ex rel.* Waldman *v.* Tod, 289 Fed. 761.

United States, only the following cases were before the courts on writs of *habeas corpus:*

WRITS OF HABEAS CORPUS IN DEPORTATION CASES, FISCAL YEAR 1930.[1]

	Cases
Cases pending beginning of year	199
New cases during the year	302
Pending close of year, before	
District Courts	95
Circuit Courts	57
Supreme Court	2

	Sustained	*Dismissed*	*Withdrawn*
Cases disposed of during the year on immigration charges:			
Criminal	11	23	12
Immoral	7	12	3
Act of 1924	30	171	24
Mental or physical defect and public charge	..	9	6
Chinese exclusion law		12	1
Citizenship, excess quota, anarchist, and others	8	11	7
Total	56	238	53

It is not surprising that so few of the total number of cases ever get to court, as many aliens have not financial resources to fight their cases, and furthermore, since the law regarding deportation is so inclusive, they seldom have sufficient grounds to secure release under the writ.

In view of the small number of cases reaching court, it is not cause for wonder that of the total of 612 cases included in this study, none came to court, but all were deported entirely by administrative process.

[1] *Annual Report of the Commissioner General,* etc., p. 20.

CONCLUSIONS

Whether judicial review should be narrowly restricted or liberally applied depends on the procedure by which aliens are deported, and the rights guaranteed the aliens as " persons " under the United States Constitution. Answer cannot be given until the methods are examined by which the Department of Labor secures the deportation of an alien. Let us then turn to see the procedure and how it works.

CHAPTER IX

The Initial States of Procedure

THE REPORT AND INVESTIGATION—THE PRELIMINARY STATEMENT—THE WARRANT OF ARREST—THE POSSIBILITY OF RELEASE

THE REPORT AND INVESTIGATION

The simple and direct wording of the statute, that any deportable alien " shall, upon the warrant of the Secretary of Labor, be taken into custody and deported " [1] gives but little hint of the complexities that have developed in administration. Indeed, the present procedure for the deportation of aliens is a hybrid mixture of statutory rule, delegated administrative regulation, and administrative interpretation of statutory construction, so that questions are raised concerning points of both constitutional and administrative law.

Although the process is highly centralized, it begins in the various immigration districts, and the local immigrant inspectors are responsible for the first steps. Possible deportation cases are usually reported to the local immigration office [2] and only on rare occasions are cases reported direct to the bureau of immigration in Washington. When that does occur, the bureau in turn sends the information to the

[1] Immigration act of 1917, sec. 19.

[2] Theoretically all cases are reported to the district director but in practice they are often reported to an individual inspector, who then consults the inspector in charge if necessary before making the investigation.

district where the suspected person is located. Reports come in sundry ways. First of all, alien public charges and such aliens as are serving prison sentences may be reported to the local immigration office by official notification from the state or by investigation in state institutions made by an immigrant inspector. Then naturalization examiners in investigation of citizenship petitions may discover and report persons found illegally in the country. Police or local officials may report cases. Aliens trying to slip in illegally may be apprehended by the border patrol or immigrant inspectors. Last and probably most numerous [1] of all are those reported because of personal grudge. A man may tell someone how he crossed the Canadian border at night without inspection. Then the story travels until it reaches one of his enemies and is reported to the immigration service, who must determine whether or not the tale has any foundation in fact. All cases reported are supposed to be investigated, for:

officers shall make thorough investigation of all cases when they are credibly informed or have reason to believe that a specified alien in the United States is subject to arrest and deportation on warrant. All such cases, by whomsoever discovered, shall be reported to the immigration officer stationed nearest the place where the alien is found to be.[2]

Even anonymous reports are accepted, whether by letter or telephone, though there is some question as to whether such reports either "credibly inform" the officer or give him "reason to believe" that an alien is subject to possible deportation proceedings. In border districts or cities with large alien population, it is often impossible for all reported

[1] A district director told the author that in his opinion 90% of the cases reported were of this category of "spite cases".

[2] *Immigration Laws and Rules of January 1, 1930*, Rule 19, Subdivision A, par. 1.

cases to be investigated immediately.[1] In view of the pressure of cases, it seems unlikely that "stool pigeons" are used by the immigration service, at least to any great extent.

On the other hand, times of stress and panic may lead to a tightening up of administration. At such times a wave of deportation develops and inspectors are apt to lay dragnets among the alien population and find cases of possible deportation by raids on alien or supposedly alien gatherings. Thus the economic depression of 1930 and 1931 served to revive the practice of "deportation raids," abandoned as a matter of general practice by the Department of Labor since the raids of 1919 and 1920. On February 4, 1931, a group of immigrant inspectors and the "alien squad" of the New York police raided the Seamen's Church Institute where seamen congregate in large numbers.[2] Ten days later a second raid was made by the same group at 10:30 o'clock on the evening of February 14th. As told by the *New York Times* on February 16th,

> twenty Department of Labor agents . . . and ten policemen . . . converged upon the Finnish Workers' Education Association . . . where a dance was in progress.
>
> The raiders blocked the doors and told the musicians to cease playing. The 1,000 dancers were ordered to show credentials or offer other evidence proving they were in this country legally. In an atmosphere of hysteria tinged with indignation, the dancers came forward singly and offered their proof. All but sixteen men and two women passed the test. These were taken to the West 123d Street Police Station and then to Ellis Island for deportation.

Secretary of Labor Doak has explained his intention to round

[1] For instance, in Detroit there were in the spring of 1926 from 130 to 200 reported cases awaiting investigation.

[2] *Vide Minority Views to accompany H. R. 17152*, 71st Congress, 2nd Session, pp. 9-10, for description of this and the following raid.

up aliens who are here illegally in a series of nation-wide drives. . . .

Inspector Kaba, whose flying squadron has raided the Seamen's Mission and the Municipal Lodging House among other favored resorts of smuggled immigrants, says New York has thousands of illegal residents. He intends to continue his raids, he said, until the city is cleared of all of them. The Police Department has announced its "fullest cooperation" in this drive and President Hoover has offered additional Federal support if it should become necessary.[1]

In this connection it should be borne in mind that officials of the Department have authority only in cases of persons proved to be aliens, and even then may be acting without authority. No law, except the Chinese registration laws, requires either alien or citizen to produce a certificate either of admission to the country or of birth or naturalization, even if demanded. So much for the authority of the immigrant inspectors. However, they did not act alone in conducting the raids, but were accompanied by officers of the newly established alien bureau in the New York City Police Department. Yet local police are without authority to act under federal immigration law. Again it must be reiterated that deportation is not punishment for crime and that the method of illegal raid is of more than dubious validity even in criminal matters.

Raiding calls to mind the problem of investigation with and without search warrants. In investigating a case immigrant inspectors often search the house and person of the alien in an effort to obtain passports, papers or other evidence leading to possible deportation. This is sometimes

[1] The same article tells of more than 500 persons illegally in the country who had been rounded up in Greater New York within the five preceding weeks and "deported as rapidly as immigration officers could arrange their transportation."

done without a warrant and is a practice felt even by some inspectors to be indefensible.[1] Even if there is well-founded belief that an article sought is concealed in a dwelling house, there is no justification for the search of that place without a warrant, and this notwithstanding facts unquestionably showing probable cause.[2] Yet it must be remembered that evidence obtained in such unlawful search in violation of constitutional rights is admissible [3] as competent evidence in the hearing.[4] An officer may not use such drastic measures against an alien as to throw him, handcuffed, and under solitary confinement, into a room for investigation, and there, with weapon in hand, question him in a threatening manner.[5] If, on the other hand, an alien consents to an official search of his premises, he may not then complain if the inspector unearths evidence prejudicial to him.[6] It is allowable for an inspector to search the person of an alien to look for dangerous weapons; in that search it is often possible to secure evidence on his person.

With deportation as with criminal cases, it is the unlucky individual whom the arm of the law happens to find, for who slips undiscovered into the country and who, once here, is reported to the immigration authorities is a matter of chance. No one can estimate with any degree of accuracy the number of deportable aliens in the community.[7] Even

[1] Statement of an inspector to the author.

[2] Agnello *v.* United States, 46 U. S. 4.

[3] *Ex parte* Caminita, 291 Fed. 913.

[4] But *vide* United States *v.* Wong Quong Wong, 94 Fed. 832. There it was held that an inspector may not unlawfully seize papers and then use them against an alien, nor may he open private letters and make them the basis of the government's case.

[5] United States *ex rel.* D'Amato *v.* Williams, 193 Fed. 228.

[6] Kush *v.* Davis, 3 Fed. (2d) 273.

[7] *Vide supra*, p. 253.

the often-advocated registration system would not solve the problem unless a complete system of registering both aliens and citizens alike were attempted, for those not registered as aliens could disappear into the mass of citizens of whom no accurate record is kept. It is particularly difficult to trace all cases of possible deportation unless the immigration force is materially increased. There is evidence that immigrant inspectors often work far into the night because of the inadequacy of their force.[1]

Similarly, the reporting of deportation cases by state institutions varies widely from state to state. New York and Illinois, for instance, each has a Bureau of Deportation which regularly reports deportable cases. Some other states have deportation officers in charge of such work. Still others, especially those with a small foreign-born population, rarely trouble to report a single case. If the state authorities, therefore, do not report possible cases, immigrant inspectors visit state hospitals, prisons, and jails to ascertain the number of possibly deportable aliens in the institutions. The law directs them to make such calls, when detailed to do it by the Commissioner General of Immigration,

> to secure information as to the number of aliens detained in the penal, reformatory and charitable institutions (public and private) and to inform the officers of the institutions of the provisions of the law regarding the deportation of aliens who are public charges.[2]

Furthermore, officers in charge of immigration districts are

[1] During the fiscal years 1925 and 1926, the inadequacy of the force to cope with the problem of investigation so limited effective enforcement of existing deportation provisions that investigation of cases was confined to those within the five-year statutory period for deportation and of those of immorality beyond the five-year period. The situation has been alleviated by additions to the force, and (since 1931) provisions for overtime pay.

[2] Immigration act of 1917, sec. 23.

to notify the nearest immigration officer in charge promptly concerning all aliens sentenced to the various United States penitentiaries and against whom deportation proceedings have been instituted in other districts,[1] while the district director at Kansas City is to be furnished information about all cases sent to Leavenworth, the district director at Atlanta given similar information relating to aliens sentenced to Atlanta, and the commissioner of immigration at Seattle concerning aliens sent to McNiel Island Penitentiary.[2]

Several states require that all criminal aliens sentenced to prison be reported to the immigration service. In other states, it is merely the practice to report such cases, while in still others it is necessary for inspectors of the service to visit institutions and find the deportable aliens serving sentence. Here, as in public-charge cases, there is wide variation between different states or even within the same state, depending on the state laws and the organization of correctional institutions. For instance, the Illinois state penal institutions report with considerable regularity through the state deportation agent. Local institutions like the Chicago House of Correction do not report, probably because of the short term in many instances and the fact that such short terms often do not lead to deportability. The Chicago immigration office, therefore, sends inspectors to ascertain the possibility of aliens serving sentence there.

Immigration officers prefer to have a report as soon as possible after the commitment of an alien, even though the sentence may be for some years. An early report makes it

[1] *Immigration Laws*, etc., *op. cit.*, Rule 19, Subdivision A, par. 2. Furthermore, they "shall furnish that officer with copies of preliminary statements and other papers necessary to the completion of warrant proceedings which may have been instituted."—*Ibid.*

[2] *Ibid.*, par. 3.

possible to locate relatives, passports, etc., and so obtain the information necessary for deportation while there is more likelihood of securing it than there may be months or years later. Also, when difficulties are encountered, if time is allowed while the alien is still serving sentence, there is less likelihood of delay on the expiration of sentence than if it is about to expire when the information is sought.

As in public-charge cases, there is small danger of the criminal escaping while serving sentence; so there is usually no immediate hurry in reporting cases of possible deportability or applying for a warrant of arrest unless the sentence is about to expire. The prison usually furnishes sufficient information on which to apply for a warrant of arrest, but when it does not an inspector must visit the prison or other institution to obtain such information before applying for a warrant.

Foreigners whose entry is surreptitious, by land, sea, or air, present a special problem, for immediately upon their being caught, steps must be taken toward their detention to prevent escape. A special statute [1] has provided that

> any employee of the bureau of immigration authorized to do so under regulations prescribed by the Commissioner General of Immigration with the approval of the Secretary of Labor, shall have power without warrant (1) to arrest any alien who in his presence or view is entering or attempting to enter the United States in violation of any law or regulations . . . and take such alien immediately for examination before an immigrant inspector . . . (2) to board and search for aliens any vessel, conveyance or vehicle, in which he believes aliens are being brought into the United States . . . [2]

[1] Act of February 27, 1925 (43 Stat. 1049).

[2] This act relates especially to the border patrol. It has been provided by regulation that "any immigrant inspector, Chinese inspector acting as an immigrant inspector or patrol inspector may without warrant arrest any alien who in his presence," etc. — *Immigration Laws*, etc., Rule 29, Subdivision F, par. 1.

So it is possible to take into custody almost all aliens without formal warrants of arrest, unless they are held in public institutions or other places allowing little possibility of escape while awaiting the issuance of formal warrants of arrest from Washington. In exceptional cases where the inspector has reason to believe the individual alien will remain at home or elsewhere and make no effort to escape, the inspector awaits the issuance of a formal warrant before making the arrest.

THE "PRELIMINARY STATEMENT"

As soon as an alien is taken into custody, it is the custom, not provided for by either statute or regulation, for the inspector to take a "preliminary statement." This is done wherever the person in custody happens to be, whether at his home, at work, in an institution, or in the immigration office. As taking a "statement" does not constitute even a hearing, it is done in the most informal manner possible, without safeguards for the rights of the alien. He may not have opportunity to secure counsel; this has been held not to be an invasion of his rights.[1] Even lack of an interpreter when one is needed will not render the statement of the alien legally void.[2] Nor does the alien need to know how the statement is to be used.[3] Because the inspector is

[1] *Ex parte* Ah Sue, 270 Fed. 366; Chan Wong *v.* Nagle, 17 Fed. (2d) 987; Plane *v.* Carr, 19 Fed. (2d) 470; *Ex parte* Emastu Kishimoto, 32 Fed. (2d) 991.

[2] "Although it be conceded that a witness both understood and spoke the English language imperfectly, it does not follow that the statement elicited from her before she secured counsel, and without the aid of an interpreter, must be rejected entirely, or that its consideration constitutes jurisdictional error."—*Ex parte* Garcia, 205 Fed. 53, 55.

[3] It has been held, however, that the admission by an alien prisoner of a crime when the prisoner was without counsel and not informed of his rights, does not afford grounds for deportation.—Gomes *v.* Tillinghast, 37 Fed. (2d) 935.

so little restricted at the time of this preliminary statement, it has become customary to secure all necessary information from the alien at that time, so that the hearing, where there is a certain amount of legal safeguard, will be a mere routine procedure. If all necessary information is secured before the alien has opportunity to secure a lawyer, there is less chance of a hitch in the proceedings, and there is more chance that the alien will answer all the questions put to him.

Often several such statements [1] are taken at the same time in an immigration office, sometimes with several going on at the same time in the same room, and with other stenographers and inspectors at work nearby. The inspector and the alien sit near the stenographer's desk, if there is a stenographer, and she takes the notes in shorthand or directly on the typewriter. The inspector may act as either stenographer, or interpreter, or both, if properly qualified.[2] However, failure by the government to furnish a competent interpreter is reviewable by the court.[3]

Before questions are put to the alien, he is " sworn " and the penalty for perjury explained. Then the inspector says:

as a United States immigrant inspector it becomes my duty to

[1] The author has listened to a number of such statements in various immigration offices, such as Detroit, Cleveland and Rouses Point.

[2] Because of arrangement of the civil service examinations for immigrant inspectors, credit is given the candidates for qualification as interpreter or as secretary who can take testimony in shorthand, and then type it afterward. If the inspector cannot qualify as interpreter and one is necessary, another government employee may be requested to serve. A government employee is bound by his oath of office and does not need to be " sworn ", but anyone outside the government employ must be duly sworn to interpret faithfully and accurately. Sometimes neighbors, relatives or other patients in the same institution, outsiders, representatives of social agencies, etc., act as interpreters. Theoretically all persons not government employees must be paid for their work, but this charge is often waived, especially in the case of representatives of social agencies.

[3] Gonzales *v.* Zurbrick, 45 Fed. (2d) 934.

inquire into your right to be and remain in the United States and it is desired to give you an opportunity to give a statement in that regard. You are advised that should the facts warrant, any such statement you may make will likely be used against you.[1]

Further that the law

places on you the burden of proving your right to be and remain in the United States. Under these conditions, are you willing to make a sworn statement?

Or,

I wish to inform you under authority of the United States Immigration Laws and Regulations, I desire at this time to question you under oath as to your right to be and remain in the United States. Are you ready and willing to be so examined?

In answering the questions, the alien is likely to include irrelevant matter, and the inspector may rephrase that part of it which is relevant and ask if the re-wording is correct before the stenographer takes it down.[2] If the questions are not clear, the inspector attempts to clarify them, but is often unable to do so, as for instance, when the alien does not know what is meant by "race" as used in immigration definition.[3] In case the person interrogated will not talk or is too ill to say anything, the inspector may send a report of such facts as are known to him personally, or can secure

[1] It used to be the practice in some instances in taking formal statement in criminal proceedings for the immigration officers to warn the persons examined that the statements to be made might be used either *for* or against them. This was erroneous, and it was called to the attention of the officers (General Order No. 83, 1927) that statements could not or at least would not be used *for* the alien by the government.

[2] That this is done is apparent from reading records of deportation cases, for there the information as recorded is concise, and straight to the point, with no extraneous matter.

[3] A Canadian-born person of Polish parentage would be listed as Canadian by birth and nationality but Polish by race.

the affidavit of some reputable person known to him, as to the facts warranting request for a warrant of arrest.

In public-charge cases, the inspector does not usually take a preliminary statement from the person being held in the institution, for the certificate [1] which the superintendent or other official in charge of the institution [2] must fill out gives the necessary evidence as to the maintenance of the alien at public expense, and there is no need for questioning or seeing him before the hearing. The application for the warrant of arrest must be accompanied by this certificate,[3] and by any available evidence tending to show that the alien has become a public charge from causes not affirmatively shown to have arisen subsequent to entry.[4] Sometimes the transcript of the clinical history is sent with the application, but usually it goes later with the record of the hearing.

Whether or not the inspector interviews the possible deportee personally, he may obtain sworn statements of friends, relatives, employers, or others, if such statements will materially aid in establishing the status of the person being detained. It is most important to establish that position correctly, for on it depends the whole question of jurisdiction. Such jurisdiction in deportation proceedings exists only if the person arrested is an alien,[5] and the burden of proof to show his alienage is upon the government.[6]

[1] Form 534.

[2] In states where there is a centralized system for reporting cases such as Washington and New York (in most institutional cases), the report comes from that agency. It cannot be too strongly emphasized that there is no uniformity between states in the matter of reporting public charges, and often the procedure between different institutions in the same state varies widely. *Vide* Edith Terry Bremer, "The Jobless Alien," *Survey*, lxv, December 15, 1930.

[3] *Immigration Laws*, etc., *of January 1, 1930*, Rule 19, Subdivision C.

[4] *Ibid.*

[5] Ng Fung Ho *v.* White, 259 U. S. 276.

[6] The act of 1924 as originally passed by the House stated (sec. 23): "In

THE WARRANT OF ARREST

The local inspector makes such investigation as will show the probability of securing deportation before he applies for a warrant of arrest.[1] If he thinks he has grounds for applying for such a warrant, and if he thinks the alien may escape, he telegraphs in code to the bureau in Washington for the issuance of a *telegraphic* warrant of arrest. If the alien has been apprehended late in the day, or if there is other reason to think that the telegraphic warrant will not arrive at the local office until the following day, the inspector may arrange for detention in the immigration station (if there is one equipped for detention), or by the local police or other local authorities, who by this unofficial arrangement will hold the person in the county jail or police headquarters as a "suspicious character" without a warrant of arrest. The inspector may also ask a social agency to detain the person apprehended, or may release him on his own recognizance, if he thinks there is no danger of escape, or if women or children are involved. The rules state:

> telegraphic application may be resorted to only in case of necessity, or when some substantial interest of the Government would be subserved thereby, and must state (a) that the usual written application is being forwarded by mail and (b) the date and place of entry and the substance of the facts and proof contained in such application. The code supplied by the department shall be used wherever practicable.[2]

every proceeding under the immigration laws, the burden of proving the right of any *individual* to enter or remain in the United States shall be upon such individual." As finally enacted, *alien* was substituted for *individual,* thereby placing the burden of proof of his right to remain in this country only upon aliens *first proved to be such. Vide* Louis Post, Unpublished MS., p. 128.

[1] The form varies in which the summary of the investigation is sent to the bureau in Washington, but usually one copy of any interview is forwarded for the bureau files while another is retained locally.

[2] *Immigration Rules,* etc., *op. cit.,* Rule 19, Subdivision B.

In practice, such telegraphic application is used in almost all cases except those of public charges or criminals serving sentence. In such cases, the federal authorities think there is no need for hurry in obtaining warrants unless the person is about to be released.[1]

Because of the inevitable delay caused by applying to the bureau in Washington for a warrant of arrest, it has been urged that the Secretary of Labor be authorized to delegate to certain others the power of issuing warrants of arrest, now centralized in him. Since local officials have no power to issue the warrants, they often resort to extra-legal methods of detention, or else lose track of the alien. A proposal for vesting authority lower in the administrative hierarchy of the Department of Labor in regard to issuance of warrants of arrest was made in the 70th Congress [2] and revived during the 1930-1931 increased emphasis on deportation. At the suggestion of the Secretary of Labor [3] it was proposed in Congress that authority be vested in the Secretary of Labor to authorize " any official of the Department of Labor or the United States Immigration Service " to issue warrants of arrest in deportation cases. As a matter of fact, the Secretary of Labor himself never signs a warrant, for the work of signing such warrants is done by an Assistant to the Secretary. However, the signing of warrants is confined to the bureau of immigration in Wash-

1 The fact that cases where the cost of maintenance is borne by the states are not hurried, has occasioned criticism of the immigration service by state officials. However, the service feels that as application for several hundred warrants of arrest a day reach the "warrant division" of the bureau, it is essential first to issue warrants for those persons who may escape into the community or for whose detention there are no facilities, or who for some other reason must be released without delay.

2 H. R. 10078.

3 In his report on Sen. Res. No. 355, of Dec. 8, 1930, made Jan. 6, 1931.

4 H. R. 17152, sec. 1, 71st Congress, 3rd Session. *Vide* also *Minority Views to accompany H. R. 17152*, Feb. 24, 1931, pp. 3-5.

ington. Opponents of the proposed change hold that seldom, if ever, even in the most urgent cases, would it take substantially longer to make telegraphic application to Washington than to have the actual warrant issued locally. They say, furthermore, that local officials are more likely to " want to make a record " in numbers of deportation cases than the officials in Washington, that such local officials are more apt to be swayed by local and passing mob psychology against aliens than bureau officials, and last of all that detention facilities are already overtaxed and that without departmental restraint jails would be even more overtaxed than at present. Those who favor the change say that actually there would be no difference in administration, for as circumstances exist, aliens are taken into detention now without warrants, and are unofficially held by local police or county authorities. The advocates feel the changed procedure might be of advantage even to the alien, in that it might hurry proceedings for him and so release him from custody sooner than at present.

Under present procedure, the telegraphic application is acted on in Washington the same day it is received in the bureau. It goes immediately to the " mail and files " division of the bureau, where it is given a file number and a card is made for the card catalogue; then it proceeds without delay to the " warrant division " where the charges are looked over and those that obviously cannot be sustained[1] are deleted. Finally a clerk prepares a telegraphic warrant of arrest in code, so that it may receive the signature of an Assistant Secretary of Labor before sending. It goes out the same day.[2]

[1] If the wire were sent noting that the alien had entered illegally by water and illegally by land, of course one of those charges could not be sustained.

[2] By army wires if these are available, otherwise by a commercial company, which grants a reduction in rate to the department.

Even though an application for a warrant of arrest be sent and the warrant received by telegraph, the inspector "in the field" must follow his telegraphic application by formal application for a warrant and this must be issued. "The application must state facts showing *prima facie* that the alien comes within one or more of the classes subject to deportation after entry, and . . . should be accompanied by some substantial supporting evidence."[1]

The inspector must attempt to obtain verification of landing, at the time of application for a telegraphic warrant of arrest. This verification may show whether or not the alien is in the country legally[2] and also whether the government or the steamship company is to bear the expense of deportation.[3] The field officials obtain the verification without sending a request through the bureau in Washington. If a foreigner, for instance, landed in New York but is detained in Chicago, the director of the Chicago district writes for verification to the commissioner at Ellis Island, who replies

[1] *Immigration Laws*, etc., *op. cit.*, Rule 19, Subdivision B. Also, "if the facts stated are within the personal knowledge of the inspector reporting the case, or such knowledge is based upon admissions made by the alien, they need not be in affidavit form. But if based upon statements of persons not sworn officers of the Government (except in cases of public charges . . .), the application should be accompanied by the affidavit of the person giving the information or by a transcript of a sworn statement taken from that person by an inspector. Where deportation proceedings are predicated on convictions of crime involving moral turpitude subsequent to entry or conviction under section 2(c) of the act approved May 26, 1922, the application for a warrant should, in the absence of a transcript of a statement covering a preliminary examination accorded the lien in which it is conclusively shown that the offense and conviction will support a deportation order if issued, be accompanied by a copy of the *mittimus* or a certificate of the clerk of the court in which conviction occurred."

[2] This is not absolute proof because of possible inaccuracies in recording.

[3] *Vide infra*, ch. xii, p. 459 *et seq.*

direct to him, enclosing verification if it is obtainable. It is then sent to the bureau in Washington, together with the application for the formal warrant of arrest, or else follows immediately afterward.[1]

If the alien has no passport and one cannot easily be obtained locally,[2] an application for a passport accompanies or follows the original application for warrant of arrest. If the person is in an institution, such as a state hospital, a health certificate and proof that he has become a public charge [3] are also enclosed.

In public-charge cases, or where an alien is held in a state or other public institution, application for a warrant of arrest is made by letter instead of wire, for there is no danger of escape. Furthermore, detention in a public institution is at the expense of the state, county, or municipal

[1] "In all cases subject to a time limitation or in which deportation will, if directed, be at the expense of the responsible steamship company, the application must be accompanied by a certificate of landing obtained from the immigration officer in charge of the port where landing occurred, unless entry without inspection within such limitation is confessed, or a reason given for its absence. In the absence of such certificate, effort should be made to supply the principal items of information mentioned in the blank form provided for such certificates." — *Immigration Laws*, etc., *op. cit.*, Rule 19, Subdivision B.

[2] *Vide infra*, p. 406 *et seq.*

[3] It is interesting to note that there has been change in the wording of the form. The wording used to be that proof must be secured that "the alien has become a public charge from causes existing prior to landing", while the more recent copies of the form take cognizance of the fact that the law of 1917 does not read that way, but "from causes not affirmatively shown to have arisen subsequent to landing". The newer copies also have space for answer to the question whether or not demand was made upon the detained alien or his relatives for payment of hospital expenses and the result of the demand. Neither old or new form has any place to show whether or not the alien has been discharged from the hospital, after "having become a public charge within 5 years", etc. *Vide Immigration Laws*, etc., *op. cit.*, Rule 19, Subdivision C.

authority and not of the federal government. Therefore the immigration service has felt,—as the immigration appropriation is small for the amount of work to be done,—that it is more urgent to secure deportation for aliens detained at its expense than for others. It is possible too that passports may not be issued so quickly for people receiving care in public institutions, particularly hospitals for the insane, as in other cases. State authorities constantly complain of the length of time required for deportation of public-charge cases,[1] while on the other hand, the immigration service often bewails the negligence of many state institutions in reporting public-charge cases.

The formal warrant of arrest is issued by an Assistant Secretary of Labor, when all necessary information is secured. There are no provisions in either law or regulations as to just what the warrant must state. The courts have held that "a warrant for the arrest and deportation of an alien need only comply substantially with the law and need not conform to all the niceties or technicalities of criminal pleading."[2] Furthermore, "neither the Immigration Act nor the promulgated regulations require that a warrant of arrest in deportation proceedings shall state the alleged grounds on which deportation will be demanded."[3] So there may be certain irregularities in the warrant of arrest without making the proceedings void. When it reaches "the field," an immigrant inspector takes it to the hospital or wherever the alien is located and gives him a hearing to show cause why he should not be deported.

1 *Vide supra*, p. 330.

2 *Ex parte* Pouliot, 196 Fed. 439.

3 United States *ex rel.* Freeman *v.* Williams, 175 Fed. 274; Guiney *v.* Bonham, 261 Fed. 582.

THE POSSIBILITY OF RELEASE

When an alien is taken into custody the problem arises of detaining him so that he will not escape pending deportation proceedings. The statute provides:

Pending the final disposition of the case of any alien so taken into custody, he may be released under a bond in the penalty of not less than $500 with security approved by the Secretary of Labor, conditioned that such alien shall be produced when required for a hearing or hearings in regard to the charge upon which he has been taken into custody, and for deportation if he shall be found to be unlawfully within the United States.[1]

The question arises as to whether or not bond must be granted as of right, or whether aliens may be released on bond only if the Secretary of Labor in his discretion recommends it.[2] The court has held that the Secretary has no discretion either to grant or refuse bail to an alien pending disposition of his case,

" may be released " being used in the sense of " may have " and mandatory. It is important to notice that the provision under consideration states that " he may be released under a bond," but it does not state "at the discretion" of anybody. The difference thus noted, together with the natural and ordinary construction of the words thus grouped in the sentence raises the presumption that Congress intended to grant to the alien a right and that its failure to follow with some such phrase as " at the discretion of the commission " vests the discretion to avail himself of the opportunity afforded the alien, and not the discretion to allow bail in the commissioner or director . . . if it is said that the official *may give* a privilege to an applicant, the words are presumptively permissive only, while if it is said that the

[1] Immigration act of 1917, sec. 20.

[2] For early discussion of right to bond, *vide* United States *v.* Lipkis, 56 Fed. 427.

applicant *may have* the privilege, the words are, presumptively, mandatory upon the official.[1]

Under the construction adopted by the court, an alien has the possibility of securing bond as of right. In practice, however, the Department of Labor puts a different construction on the statute. The local immigrant inspector in his telegraphic or written application for a warrant of arrest recommends that the alien be or be not released on bond of a certain amount.

The statute provides the amount of bond shall be not less than $500 but further than that does not specify. It states that the security is to be approved by the Secretary of Labor, but does not say in whose discretion the amount shall be determined. The rules in addition provide:

the amount of bond under which any arrested alien may be released will be indicated by the department in the warrant of arrest. The approval of the local United States attorney, or the commissioner of immigration, or the district director, or the inspector in charge of the subdistrict as to the form and execution shall be sufficient to warrant the release of such alien pending approval of the bail bond by the Secretary of Labor. United States bonds or Treasury notes may be accepted, or sureties may deposit such securities instead of justifying in real estate.[2]

The application for a warrant of arrest suggests the amount to be required in the particular case in hand. The Department has a schedule showing the amount of bond to be specified in particular types of cases. Thus narcotic cases, criminals or illegal entries would all require differing amounts of bond varying within limits set on the Department of Labor schedule. The amount required in different types of case varies with the social seriousness of the possi-

[1] Prentis *v.* Manoogian, 16 Fed. (2d) 422, *passim.*

[2] *Immigration Laws,* etc., *op. cit.,* Rule 19, Subdivision E.

bility of losing the bonded individual in the community. The recommendations as to the amount of bond required in a certain case are usually accepted but not always so. The telegraphic and formal warrants of arrest state the amount of bond on which the alien in question may be released.

It often takes the alien some days to secure the necessary amount of the bond, and he stays in jail until he can produce the money. Frequently the granting of bond is not originally recommended by the inspector, but at the hearing he does recommend it and then when the board of review considers the case, it recommends whether or not the privilege of bond be granted.

Special bond forms are issued for the purpose by the Department of Labor and sent to the office of the immigration inspector for the district in which the relative of the alien or other bondsman lives, usually in the same district where the alien is detained, but not always so. The bond is executed at the direction of the inspector in charge of the local office; if there is no such local office, the relatives receive official instruction in a letter accompanying the bond forms.

Sometimes confusion arises; for a person held first by the Department of Labor and then by the Department of Justice for criminal violation of the immigration acts (or as a witness) and for deportation, may have to give two bonds, one to each department, though, as already indicated, the Department of Labor sometimes allows the bond given in the criminal proceedings by the Department of Justice to suffice and allows the alien to go on his own recognizance.

When an alien ordered deported is required as a witness and released on bond during the period of his detention, the bondsman is responsible for producing the alien when required as a witness or for deportation.[1]

[1] *Immigration Laws*, etc., *op. cit.*, Rule 21, Subdivision A, par. 1.

To minimize the temptation to breach the bond, the immigration officials retain any documentary evidence of nationality while the alien is released from custody.[1] Yet in a number of instances, the alien still breaches his bond and disappears into the void.

During the fiscal year 1929-1930, bonds in deportation cases were exacted and forfeited as follows:

BONDS EXACTED AND BONDS FORFEITED, 1929-1930[2]

	No. aliens bonded	*Bonds forfeited; Payment:* *Voluntary*	*Enforced*
Involving bail bonds, total	2,032	144	19
Under warrant of arrest	1,923	36	2
Under warrant of deportation	109	108	17

Failures to appear and escapes	*While under warrant of* *Arrest*	*Deportation*
Failures to appear when wanted after release on own recognizance	54	44
Escapes from		
Immigration officers	31	20
Others	59	48

The immigration act of 1917 makes no mention of the possibility of release on "one's own recognizance," but provides only for release on bond. However, a rule of the Department states:

Pending determination of the case, in the discretion of the immigration officer in charge, the alien may be taken into custody or allowed to remain in some place deemed by such officer secure and proper, except that in the absence of special instructions an alien confined in an institution shall not be removed therefrom until a warrant of deportation has been issued and is about to be served.[3]

[1] Bureau of immigration, General Order No. 132.

[2] *Annual Report of the Commissioner General for the Year Ended June 30, 1930*, p. 20. The numbers under warrant of deportation as quoted add incorrectly.

[3] *Immigration Laws and Rules*, etc., Rule 19, Subdivision D, par. 1.

The Department of Labor has construed the provision in the act as declaratory of what the law always has been as to release under bond, except that the Act specifies the amount of the bond where required and makes clear that a bond is to be required where the alien is able to furnish it.[1]

No statistics are available to show the numbers of arrested aliens in deportation proceedings who are released on their own recognizance. However, if the investigator thinks the alien is trustworthy and responsible, he recommends that he be so released, and this recommendation is usually concurred in by the inspector in charge or the district director and then by the bureau in Washington.[2] Such release is often allowed in the case of women and children, when the husband is in jail, although this is not always the case. Such release is also allowed in the case of a person who wishes deportation and will surely appear when wanted, or in the cases of people of such obviously high standards that their word may be entirely trusted.

Release may be made at different stages of the procedure. Thus an alien may be offered bond at the first stage of proceedings, but he may not be able to secure it immediately, and so may remain temporarily in custody.

The Report and Investigation in the Cases Studied

Many varied sources of report to the immigration authorities appear in the cases studied, particularly in the cases of illegal entry and of "L.P.C." 119 of the 392 cases of illegal entry were apprehended on entering by officers of the border patrol or immigration service, five were apprehended

[1] Memorandum from the Second Assistant Secretary of Labor to the author.

[2] Application for release on bond or "own recognizance" is first sent in the telegraphic application for a warrant of arrest, and replied to in the same way, to save detention expense.

by customs or prohibition enforcement officers, and 57 were reported by such various means as letters, telephone calls, or personal visits from relatives, ministers, fellow-employees, etc. One of these cases, for example, was reported by the American consul in Manchester, England, one by a Greek-American Republican Club, and one by a divorced wife. In 214 cases the report was from unknown sources. This means either that the report was anonymous or that its source might be found only in the local district record and not in that of the bureau in Washington.

Eleven of the "L.P.C." cases were reported by social agencies, and one by the alien himself, who wished deportation. The 136 people who had actually become public charges were reported through hospitals or institutions, state hospital commissions, or state deportation agents. In one of those cases, however, a relative anxious for deportation reported the person before the hospital did, although the hospital later reported it too. In one case, reporting was accidental; an immigration officer happened to be in a southern state in the neighborhood of a hospital where it was thought no deportable aliens were public charges. On looking over the hospital registrations he found one who was deportable.

The forty-one criminals were reported by prison or some one connected with the state commissions of correction, while the eighteen persons connected with prostitution or narcotic law violation were reported by prisons, court officials, or police. Two were reported by relatives who wished to hasten deportation.

Some of the varying sources of report are shown in the following:

John Crocker (Case 70).

John Crocker was born in 1892 in Cambridge, England. He lived there and in London during his early life, and married in 1919. He had four children by this marriage.

In 1923 Mr. Crocker left his wife and children to emigrate to Canada. He landed in Quebec on August 12 of that year, and just three months later was admitted to the United States at Detroit, entering as a professional singer, exempt from quota. He was examined by a board of special inquiry, but admitted. He then secured work singing three nights a week in a variety performance, and as an oiler in an electric concern during the day time.

On May 18, 1925 he was reported to the bureau of immigration in Washington by letter from an inspector of the poor of the Parish Council in Bathgate, England, who stated that since leaving England Mr. Crocker had supported his wife and children only at irregular intervals. The letter further said that nothing had been received from Mr. Crocker since July 11, 1924, and so his family had been receiving relief from the Parish Council; request was therefore made to ascertain the possibility of making Mr. Crocker provide means for his wife and children or else be deported.

The bureau was not able to locate Mr. Crocker for some time, but finally found him and issued a warrant for his arrest on November 12, 1925. He was taken to police headquarters in Detroit and detained there for 6 days. Then because of the crowded conditions in Detroit, he was sent to the Philadelphia immigration station at Gloucester City, N. J. for detention. Just before leaving Detroit, Mr. Crocker was given a hearing at police headquarters, but there no mention was made of the source of the report to the immigration service, nor of the family situation in England.

On December 16, 1925 a warrant of deportation was issued for Mr. Crocker, with the same charges as those in the warrant of arrest, namely, that he was (1) "L. P. C.", (2) entered the United States by means of false and misleading statements, (3) entered the United States in violation of the "passport law." He was deported on January 1, 1926, New York, a at the expense of the steamship company which had brought him to Canada. He had barely arrived home, when, on January 13, 1926 he wrote a letter to the bureau of immigration in Washington asking for permission to reapply for admission to the United States before the expiration of a year from the date of his deportation. On February 23 the bureau wrote him stating that permission to re-apply had been granted.[1]

Joan Schachtel (Case 71).

Joan Schachtel was born in 1902 in London, the daughter of a Polish Jewish father and Russian Jewish mother. Her father emigrated to the United States (date unknown), became naturalized in 1919 and died in 1921. Just before Mr. Schachtel's naturalization, his wife had come over to join him, and so she too became an American citizen through her husband's naturalization.

The daughter remained in London with relatives, and at the age of 14 left school and began to work in a factory as an operator on waists. In 1923 she came to the United States to join her mother, arriving in New York on June 8. She almost immediately began to work in Woolworth's 5 and 10 Cent Store, earning $14 a week. On April 27, 1924 Miss Schachtel was married to an American-born paper-hanger. Soon after her marriage, she secured her own declaration of intention to become an American citizen.

On December 26, 1924 she was reported to the immigration office at Ellis Island by her brother-in-law with whom she had a quarrel. A warrant was issued for her arrest on April 25, 1925, and she was taken to Ellis Island, where her husband gave $500 bond to secure her release, which was accomplished three days later. The hearing had originally been scheduled for April 26, but was continued until May 12, so that a lawyer might be secured.

A warrant of deportation was issued on June 24, with the

[1] As this was before the passage of the act of March 4, 1929, this was of course possible.

same charges as in the warrant of arrest, namely (1) "L.P.C.", (2) that she entered the country by means of false and misleading statements, (3) that the country from which she came had an exhausted quota at the time of her entry, (4) that her passage was paid for with the money of another. It seems that when she entered, the statement had been made that she had lived in the United States previously and was returning here.

Deportation took place on July 9, 1925 at the expense of the line bringing her to the United States.

The Warrant of Arrest in the Cases Studied

There was wide variation in the type of case as to the length of time between the report to the immigration authorities and the issuance of the warrant of arrest. In 221 cases of illegal entry, the source and date of the report is not given in the record; therefore it is impossible to ascertain the length of time that elapsed between the report and the warrant in these particular cases. The other illegal entries, with only two exceptions, had the warrant of arrest issued within two days after apprehension. The criminals and prostitutes had a variation in length of time from one day to six months, with a modal period of approximately three months, while the public charges varied from one day to nine months, with a modal period of approximately two months.

Preliminary Statement

These were taken in the various places where the aliens were detained—jails, hospitals, homes, immigration detention stations, and one was even noted at the place where a man was working. In most of the statements, an attempt was made to secure all necessary information at that time, so that merely supplemental information was obtained at the final hearing. In only eleven cases was the alien warned at this time that anything he said could be used against him, and in no case was he told his statements were to be entirely voluntary. In two cases, lawyers appearing at the hearings protested that the information used against their clients had been obtained in preliminary statements, and in one of those cases, the lawyer stated his client had not understood English sufficiently to know what was being done, and that no interpreter had been used.

In the following case, a man refused to say anything at the time of the preliminary statement, and it was later continued:

Giorgio Mascagni (Case 72).

Giorgio Mascagni was born in 1897 in Palermo, Sicily, Italy. He came to the United States on May 15th, 1918 as a stowaway, and was not discovered. He worked as a laborer, then as a barber.

On November 30, 1920 he was sentenced to 10-20 years for robbery in Maryland. He was paroled on August 30, 1929 after 10 years, less time off for good behavior. He tried to get work as a barber but did not succeed in getting anything permanent. In November, 1929 he was arrested for vagrancy and sentenced to three months in the Maryland House of Correction.

A warrant of arrest was issued for Mr. Mascagni's arrest on January 9, 1930 and a hearing was given him the next day. The day before the warrant was issued, a preliminary statement had been taken, but Mr. Mascagni refused to testify. He said " I am not going to say anything and see what you can do." He also refused to testify at the hearing on January 10 and was continued in the House of Correction, but at government expense after his sentence expired on February 9. On February 10 another preliminary statement was taken, where sufficient information was secured on which to proceed. At the hearing accorded Mr. Mascagni the next day, he merely stated he was not able to afford a lawyer, and accepted the preliminary statement as accurate.

A warrant of deportation was issued on February 25, 1930

on the same ground as in the warrant of arrest, that Mr. Mascagni had been sentenced to a year or more for a crime involving moral turpitude committed within 5 years after entry. He was deported from New York on March 22, 1930, at government expense.

Interpreters in the Cases Studied

As 82 of the total number of cases spoke English, there was no need for interpreters in those cases, at either the preliminary statement or hearing. It is impossible to tell, when the records state "as the alien spoke English, no interpreter was employed," how well the alien spoke the language, and whether or not he understood all the proceedings. In some cases, the records would seem to indicate that the person held in deportation proceedings failed to understand all the questions put to him. One hundred and thirty-nine persons had their cases carried on in English, besides the 82 from Great Britain.

Four hundred and one persons used interpreters. In 171 of these inspectors qualified as interpreters, but various others were used in other cases, such as social workers, neighbors, relatives, members of other government services, other patients or other prisoners in institutions. Even one other insane patient was used as an interpreter. Also, one case was noted where no Italian interpreter was available and a Spanish one was used.

The Warrant of Arrest in the Cases Studied Continued

In all cases where there was need for rush, telegraphic warrants of arrest were applied for and issued, followed by formal ones. However, in four cases the record contained no formal warrant after the telegraphic one was issued. In cases such as public charges and criminals, there was no telegraphic but merely the formal warrant, save in one instance where the time limit for deportation proceedings was to expire the day after application was made for a warrant of arrest.

The Possibility of Release in the Cases Studied

The number and amounts of bond are as follows:

Release on Bond in Cases Studied

Number of Cases (*1925*)	(*1930*)	*Amount of Bond*
18	4	$ 500
31	4	1000
1	1	1500
	1	3000
50	10	

Two men apprehended in Montana as illegal entries were allowed to go at large because of lack of funds in the appropriation at the time, but after a month and three days at large, detention funds became available and they were held in jail five months and twenty-four days and four months and twenty-eight days respectively before deportation. Another interesting case is that of a man released on his own recognizance, who "had no place to go" and so requested detention. He was consequently held on Ellis Island a month pending deportation.

The following show the type of cases released on bond:

Ioannis Demetri (Case 73).

Ioannis Demetri was born in 1893 near Corinth, Greece. He came to the United States in 1911 and remained until 1925, living in Savannah, Ga. That year he went to Greece for a visit, and returned to this country in July, 1926. How and where he entered is not known.

On November 18, 1928, he was sentenced to the United States Penitentiary for the possession of stolen goods under the Act of February 13, 1913. His sentence was to expire on July 25, 1930.

A warrant was issued for Mr. Demetri's arrest on February 14, 1929, and a hearing was given him at the penitentiary on April 20, but was postponed for him to secure counsel. The hearing was continued on June 27, with a lawyer present to represent Mr. Demetri. He requested 30 days to finish up his affairs, and this request was granted by the board of review, $3000 were given as bond. This was done, and Mr. Demetri was released on that bond on the same day. On August 3 a warrant was issued for his deportation, on the ground that he had been sentenced to prison for a year or more for a crime involving moral turpitude, committed within 5 years after entry.

Mr. Demetri requested three months' further extension, as his business was not yet completed. He was deported on January 4, 1930, at the expense of the government.

George Mariu (Case 74).

George Mariu was born in Costanza, Roumania in 1900. He landed in Quebec on May 13, 1929, and went west. On September 17, 1929, he entered surreptitiously across the border near Portal, N. D., brought in by a smuggler.

It is not known by whom he was reported to the immigration authorities, but he was apprehended while living in Minneapolis a few months later. He was taken immediately to the Hennepin County Jail there, and a warrant of arrest was issued for him the next day, November 19. It was recommended by the bureau on suggestion of the local inspector in charge, that Mr. Mariu be released on $500 bond. As he was also being held as witness against his smuggler, it was recommended that such release be effective when he was released under court bond as a witness to appear at the March, 1930 term of the federal district court.

A warrant of deportation was issued for Mr. Mariu on March 3, on the grounds that appeared in the warrant of arrest, namely, (1) "L. P. C.", (2) that he entered without inspection, (3) that he was not in possession of an unexpired immigration visa on entry. He was deported from New York on April 26, 1930, at government expense, to land in France and go by train to Roumania.

The following case illustrates the type where bond was breached. There were only four such cases among all those studied:

Stanislaw Zuroska (Case 75).

Stanislaw Zuroska was born in 1904 in Kracow, Poland. He emigrated to Canada on April 26, 1927, and entered the United States illegally on April 6, 1928, at Detroit. He was apprehended and a warrant was issued the next day for his arrest, and he was taken to the Wayne County Jail for detention. On April 9 he was given a hearing at the jail, and it was suggested to the board of review that he be released on $500 bond. This was done. However, he disappeared as soon as released, and the board of review declared the bond breached.

Mr. Zuroski was apprehended in Cleveland on December 10, 1929, and a warrant of deportation was issued on the 20th of the month, on the same grounds as in the warrant of arrest, (1) that he was not in possession of an unexpired immigration visa on entry, (2) that he entered without inspection. He was deported on January 10, 1930.

Breach was prevented in this case:

Karl Schmidt (Case 76).

Karl Schmidt was born in 1904 in Stettin, Germany. He came to the United States in 1928 on a visitor's permit for 6 months, but failed to leave at the end of that time.

He was reported to the immigration service by an anonymous letter, and was caught in Philadelphia on November 1, 1929. His release on $500 bond was recommended and accepted on November 10. ——— days later his bondsman appeared at the immigration office at Gloucester City and advised that Mr. Schmidt was planning to decamp, so he was taken into custody when surrendered by the bondsman the same day.

A warrant for his arrest had been issued on November 2, and

for his deportation on January 1, 1930, on the ground that he had overstayed the time allowed him for visit and was not in possession of an unexpired immigration visa. He was deported on January 30, 1930, at the expense of the steamship company which had brought him to this country.

Of the total number of cases released on bond, the records show that seven were required to furnish two bonds, one to the Department of Labor, and one to the Department of Justice. This double furnishing of bond occurred under both the "passport law" and the 1929 immigration act.

Josip Petrovich (Case 77).

Josip Petrovich was born on Oct. 28, 1888, in Cettinje, Jugoslavia. He was married and his wife is still living there. On April 24, 1924, he decided to emigrate, landing at Halifax and going to Toronto. He remained a little less than 2 months, for he crossed the border in an automobile, paying $35 for the trip and coming with three others so smuggled. They were not apprehended.

Mr. Petrovich went to live near Duluth, and began to work as a miner. He was reported to the immigration service anonymously, and a warrant for his arrest was issued on April 4, 1925. He was taken to the St. Louis County Jail in Duluth and held at the expense of the Department of Justice, pending action for violation of the "passport law." He was released on $2000 bond in their proceedings. On April 7, Mr. Petrovich was given a hearing at the immigration office, but he wished legal representation, and the hearing was postponed three days. However, he had been told a lawyer would do no good at the hearing, so had not secured one.

In November, the indictment for violation of the "passport act" was dismissed, and Mr. Petrovich was turned over to the custody of the immigration service, but was released on December 4, on $1000 bond. A warrant of deportation had meanwhile been issued (exact date unknown) on the same grounds as in the warrant of arrest, namely, (1) "L. P. C.", (2) that he entered without inspection, (3) that he entered in violation of the passport law, (4) that the quota of the country from which he came was exhausted at the time of entry.

He was deported on December 24, 1925, at the expense of the steamship company which had brought him to Canada.

Two cases were released on $500 bond each, but were held under court order as witnesses against the smugglers who had brought the men into the country.

Had the aliens been able to arrange it, fifty-nine of the 1925 cases and three of the 1930 group could have been released on bond, but as it proved impossible for them to get the money, they remained in jail. On the other hand, from the total number of cases, there were eight requests for release on bond which were not granted, as illustrated by the following:

Mario Nocchi (Case 78).

Mario Nocchi was born on June 10, 1901 in Palermo, Sicily, Italy. He left home in January, 1922 and went to France, where he remained four months. Then he took ship from St. Nazaire to Cuba, where he remained for over two years.

On September 14, 1925, Mr. Nocchi took passage on an alien-smuggling schooner, bound for Florida, but the boat was captured just off the Florida coast the next day by a vessel of the United States Coast Guard. A warrant of arrest was issued that day for Mr. Nocchi, and he was taken to the Hillsborough County Jail at Tampa, Florida.

He was given a hearing at the jail on September 22, through an interpreter. On October 5, the district director suggested release on bond but the board of review denied the application. Five days later, the district director sent a wire stating that the man would offer bond in any necessary amount. Nothing was done until November 4, when the board of review denied the application. At the board, the secretary of a congressman appeared and requested permission for Mr. Nocchi to remain

2-6 months, or at least to be allowed to depart voluntarily, but this request was also denied.

On October 8, a warrant of deportation was issued on the same grounds as those in the warrant of arrest, namely, (1) "L. P. C.", (2) that he entered by water other than at a time or place designated by the immigration service, (3) that he was not in possession of an unexpired immigration visa at the time of entry. Mr. Nocchi was deported at government expense on November 28, 1925, destined to Italy. He had been sent to the Philadelphia Immigration Station at Gloucester City, N. J., on October 24, and then was sent to Ellis Island via motor bus to Jersey City on November 23.

Release took place at various stages of the proceedings—from immediate release the day of detention up to three months after the person had entered jail.

A smaller number were released on their own recognizance than on bond, as can be understood. Of the total number, eleven were so released, as shown by the following type of case:

Richard Stevenson (Case 79).

Richard Stevenson was born on May 8, 1887 in Glasgow, Scotland, and lived there all his early life. He was married in 1910, and has two children, one born in 1911 and another in 1922. He taught violin as a profession.

Mr. Stevenson left his wife and children and emigrated to Canada to seek better work, landing in Quebec on November 7, 1924. He found great difficulty in securing work and later said of it, "I was desperate for money as I could get nothing to do there." So he walked across the border near Champlain, N. Y., and was not seen.

He went to Mansfield, Ohio, and there secured work as a violin teacher, but had not been there many months before he was anonymously reported to the immigration authorities. A warrant for his arrest was issued on July 25, 1925, but he was released on his own recognizance, as the inspector in charge had urgently recommended it, stating Mr. Stevenson to be "a clean, nice type of man with mild manners and full willingness to co-operate and a realization of the risk of illegal entry, and willingness to make any amends." Mr. Stevenson was given a hearing at his home on August 13. A warrant of deportation was issued on October 3, with the charges (1) "L. P. C.", (2) that he entered without inspection, (3) that he was not in possession of an unexpired immigration visa.

He was sent to Ellis Island on November 1, and the next day to Montreal. Three days later he was deported from Montreal at the expense of the steamship company which had taken him there.

Henrik Carlson (Case 80).

Henrik Carlson was born in 1899 in Gothenberg, Sweden. He had a university education, followed by technical school, so that he became a graduate civil engineer.

In 1924, Mr. Carlson came to the United States, being admitted for a six months visit to his uncle, and landing in New York on February 1st of that year. Soon after being admitted, Mr. Carlson secured a position as a draftsman, earning $250 a month. On November 6, 1924, he filed his declaration of intention to become an American citizen and was reported to the immigration officials on that date by the district director of naturalization in New York.

However, no warrant of arrest was issued for him until April 21, 1925. He was immediately released on his own recognizance, as the commissioner recommended it, because Mr. Carlson was "educated and intelligent and presented a fine appearance." A hearing was given him on May 20, at Ellis Island. Afterward, the commissioner recommended that the "L. P. C." charge which had been in the warrant of arrest be not sustained.

A warrant of deportation was issued August 14, 1925, with the "L. P. C." charge, and with the others (1) that he entered by means of false and misleading statements, (2) that he entered in violation of the quota act. The board of review had recommended that the "L. P. C." charge be sustained, despite the recommendation of the local commissioner.

Mr. Carlson asked for six months to settle his affairs here, but this was not granted. He was deported on September 19, at the expense of the steamship line.

The record notes that Mr. Carlson could have been admitted as a member of a learned profession at the time he entered, despite the status of the Swedish quota, but that he did not at that time seek permanent admission. As the quota act had expired at the time deportation proceedings were pending, it was impossible to make his admission here on a permanent basis.

The following case shows violation of release on a man's own recognizance:

Ian Mestrovic (Case 81).

Ian Mestrovic was born on June 27, 1901 near Prague, Czechoslovakia. He went to Canada in 1923, landing in Halifax on December 2, 1923, and going direct to Toronto, where he began to work as a tailor.

He had no intention of coming to the United States until he heard that his sister's husband had died in Pittsburg, Pa., leaving her with seven children. On February 25, 1925, Mr. Mestrovic walked across a bridge at Niagara Falls and went immediately to Pittsburg. He went to live with his sister and secured work as a tailor to support her family. Mr. Mestrovic had applied for a visa before he left Montreal, but all the Czech quota places available there had been given out. He did not wait for a visa as he felt his sister's need was immediate but paid $36 to be shown across the bridge.

It is not known by whom he was reported to the immigration authorities, but a warrant for his arrest was issued on October 3, 1925. He was released on his own recognizance on the assurance of himself and his sister that he would appear. Four days later a hearing was given him at the immigration office in Pittsburg, but was postponed to secure a lawyer for him. He was again allowed to go on his own recognizance on his plea and that of his sister. However, he disappeared, and was apprehended in Detroit en route back to Canada on October 8. The hearing was continued in the Detroit immigration office the same day, without a lawyer. Mr. Mestrovic said that as he could not remain in the United States, he did not wish to return to Czechoslovakia and so was trying to return to Canada when apprehended. The Canadian immigration service had refused to allow him to enter, and on his return across the ferry from Windsor he had been apprehended by the American immigrant inspectors.

Mr. Mestrovic was detained in the Detroit police headquarters from the day of his apprehension. On October 23, a representative in Congress wrote the bureau of immigration asking that Mr. Mestrovic be allowed to depart voluntarily rather than be deported, and the next day the Associated Charities of Pittsburg wrote the bureau that he was "intelligent, a good worker, and had good standards of living." They requested that if deportation were unavoidable he be sent to Canada where he could more easily continue to contribute to the support of his sister's family.

On October 24, Mr. Mestrovic was sent to the Philadelphia immigration station at Gloucester City, N. J., because of overcrowding in the Detroit detention facilities. Six days later a lawyer in Pittsburg wrote the bureau of immigration the same request that the Associated Charities had previously made. The next day the case came before the board of review, but they refused to consider deportation to Canada, as they felt Mr. Mestrovic would not stay but would return to his sister. A warrant of deportation was issued on November 10, with the same charges as in the warrant of arrest, namely, (1) "L. P. C.", (2) that he entered without inspection, (3) that he was not in possession of an unexpired immigration visa at the time of entry, (4) violation of the "passport law," and (5) that the country from which he came had an exhausted quota at the time of his entry.

On December 1, the Second Assistant Secretary of Labor wired the Philadelphia immigration station to find out about Mr.

Mestrovic's detention, as thus far it has proved impossible to secure a new passport for his return to Czechoslovakia. Two days later, the same Secretary suggested the possibility of granting extension of time, and the same day Mr. Mestrovic's sister stated she had been able to secure money for a bond but he was not released. The record does not state why. He was deported on December 12, 1925, at the expense of the steamship line which had taken him to Canada. He was destined to his home in Czechoslovakia.

CONCLUSIONS

It is certain that the present procedure in accepting and following up reports of possible deportations, in making investigations and in taking "preliminary statements" offers opportunity for grave violation of personal rights. It seems clear that the method of raid should not ever be permitted, and that individual investigations should be made only upon probable cause and not merely in response to anonymous reports. In making such investigations, immigrant inspectors should be eternally vigilant not to subject aliens to illegal search and seizure and to remember that their purpose as inspectors is to investigate the facts rather than to press for an increased number of deportations. Better for some aliens to slip through than for fundamental constitutional rights to be disregarded in regard to either aliens or citizens.

The "preliminary statement," without legal or other representation, need not necessarily be unfair, but it too bears within itself the germs of possible abuse, unless scrupulous regard is had for constitutional rights. It seems only fair that the alien be notified of the nature of the proceedings against him in such terms that he can understand them, and given opportunity to refuse to say anything at all should he so desire it, until he appears at the hearing which is later given him. He should always be provided with an adequate interpreter where necessary. Here again there is need for emphasis on the method of administration, continued realization by immigration officials that they are acting as investigating and not prosecuting officials. The trend of public opinion in regard to deportation activity is in the last analysis responsible for a desire to press deportations with all possible speed, which may disregard fundamental rights.

Until the attitude of unbiased investigation becomes general on the part of *all* officials of the service, it seems wise to continue the issuance of the warrants of arrest by the bureau in Washington rather than in the field, where local prejudice may influence wholesale issuance of such warrants more than in the more objective and distant atmosphere of the bureau in Washington.

In view of the overcrowding of detention facilities and the possibility of mingling criminals and non-criminals in jails [1] it seems necessary to investigate the possible extension of release of more aliens on bond and on their own recognizance than are so released at present. This matter will be touched upon later on, but for the present let us continue the discussion of the actual procedure.

[1] *Vide infra*, ch. xi, pp. 389 *et seq.*

CHAPTER X

The Procedure Continued

THE HEARING—THE BOARD OF REVIEW

THE HEARING

Upon receipt of the warrant of arrest, a hearing is held to allow the alien to show cause why he should not be deported. This hearing, while surrounded by more legal safeguards than the "preliminary statement," is nevertheless of an informal character. As has been repeatedly emphasized, deportation is not punishment for crime;[1] therefore the hearing is not in the nature of a criminal trial. If the alien is located in a county jail, hospital, prison[2] or at his own home, he may be given the hearing where he is, or at the convenience of the inspector may be taken elsewhere. If the hearing is held at a hospital or other institution, the superintendent receives a copy of the warrant of arrest, is notified of the time of the hearing, and is sometimes called to testify. If it is thought that relatives of the alien might help clarify the situation, they may be asked to appear at the hearing. Sometimes they send statements or affidavits without appearing in person.

As soon as the hearing is called, the alien and the interpreter, if one is necessary, are "sworn." Government offi-

[1] Fong Yue Ting *v.* United States, 149 U. S. 698 *passim*; Siniscalchi *v.* Thomas, 195 Fed. 701; Zakonaite *v.* Wolf, 226 U. S. 272; Bugajewitz *v.* Adams, 228 U. S. 585; Bechard *v.* Ebey, 300 Fed. 558.

[2] It has been held that the hearing is not unfair even if conducted in a state prison. United States *ex rel.* Ciccerelli *v.* Curran, 12 Fed. (2d) 394.

cials acting as interpreters do not need to take the oath. The alien no longer has any constitutional right to refuse to answer even incriminating questions, if germane to the subject of the inquiry.[1] His fingerprints are immediately taken, to be sent to the bureau of investigation of the Department of Justice.[2] Then he is allowed to inspect the warrant of arrest, though he may not understand either the English or the nature of the proceedings against him. The inspector now proceeds with the hearing. It is assumed that the jurisdictional fact of alienage has already been satisfactorily established, for the burden of proof is on the government to show that the person taken into custody is an alien. Just what the burden of proof is on the alien is not entirely clear from the wording of the statute:

in any deportation proceeding against any alien the burden of proof shall be upon such alien to show that he entered the United States lawfully, and the time, place and manner of such entry into the United States, but in presenting such proof he shall be entitled to the production of his immigration visa, if any, or of other documents concerning such entry, in the custody of the Department of Labor.[3]

Does this provision place the burden of proof on the alien with respect *only* to the lawfulness of his entry? Such is the interpretation of the Department of Labor and of the Supreme Court.[4] But the Department at least is not satis-

[1] United States *ex rel.* Rennie *v.* Brooks, 284 Fed. 908.

[2] The same bureau wishes notification when and if deportation occurs, of the date, port through which deportation takes place, and the country to which the alien is to be deported, in all "moral turpitude", prostitute, anarchist, narcotic, etc. deportations. — Bureau of immigration, General Order No. 151, 55603/264, March 1, 1930, and first supplement to it, February 11, 1931.

[3] Immigration act of 1924, sec. 23. *Vide supra*, p. 334.

[4] United States *ex rel.* Vajtauer *v.* Curran, 273 U. S. 103.

fied with this explanation, as indicated by a statement made by the Secretary of Labor on January 6, 1931.[1] It has been suggested that the burden of proof be more definitely laid on the alien [2] but this has not been done; if it were the question of lawfulness of entry would not be a criterion.

In order to help establish his right to remain here, the alien is allowed legal representation in the hearing. Much difficulty has been caused by the question, *at what stage* in the hearing can the person held under warrant proceedings know of his right to obtain counsel. During the post-war deportation activity, the hearing was often nearly over before opportunity was given for a lawyer to be secured.[3] Under present procedure, the alien is categorically advised, usually at the beginning of the hearing, that he has the right to be represented by counsel [4] and asked the direct question: " Do you desire to be represented by counsel?" If he does desire a lawyer, the hearing is postponed for a period varying from a few hours to several days, to allow opportunity to find a lawyer. Then if the detained person has decided he does not wish a lawyer, or, as is often the case, that he

[1] Report on Sen. Res. 355 (Dec. 8, 1930), quoted in *U. S. Daily*, Jan. 7, 1931.

[2] " In any proceeding in which an alien is taken into custody upon warrant issued by the Secretary of Labor . . . and charged with being subject to deportation upon a specified ground . . . and such charge is supported by *prima facie* evidence adduced at the hearing accorded the alien on such charge, the charge shall be held to be established unless the alien shall establish to the satisfaction of the Secretary of Labor that the charge is not true." — H. R. 17152, 71st Congress, 3rd Session, sec. 5. *Vide* also *Expedite the Deportation of Certain Aliens*, Minority Views to accompany H. R. 17152, Feb. 24, 1931, p. 17.

[3] In Bilokumsky *v.* Tod, 263 U. S. 149, 155, the Supreme Court held the Department of Labor must at least observe its own rules in allowing the right of representation by counsel. *Vide also* Whitfield *v.* Hanges, 222 Fed. 745.

[4] *Immigration Laws*, etc., *op. cit.*, Rule 19 Subdivision D, par. 2.

cannot afford one, or thinks one superfluous, he is asked at the beginning of the resumed hearing: "Do you then waive all right to counsel?" and the hearing is continued without an attorney. However, if the alien is persuaded or intimidated against exercising his right to counsel, the proceedings are irregular and the order for deportation void, if issued.[1] The government will not provide an attorney and the alien himself or his friends must bear the expense of legal representation.

It must be borne in mind that under present procedure much if not all of the testimony as to the deportability of a foreigner from this country may be obtained at the time of the preliminary statement, and at the hearing he would simply be shown a copy of the statement, asked if he agrees with it, and given an opportunity to secure a lawyer. Such a hearing would disclose no new facts, and in actuality the preliminary statement would have constituted the hearing. The courts have held that

> the absence of counsel when they (the aliens) were being interrogated by the arresting officers is immaterial, nor does it make a hearing . . . unfair . . . that the alien may not have had the benefit of counsel at the beginning of the proceedings; but it is sufficient if, during the hearing, he is advised of his rights and accorded counsel, and no part of the evidence previously taken or used against him is concealed or withheld from his counsel, and he is not thereby deprived of the privilege of bringing forward any explanatory or rebutting evidence.[2]

[1] United States *ex rel.* Bosny *v.* Williams, 185 Fed. 598; Roux *v.* Commissioner of Immigration, 203 Fed. 413; *Ex parte* Lam Pui, 217 Fed. 456; *Ex parte* Chin Loy You, 223 Fed. 833; Guiney *v.* Bonham, 261 Fed. 582.

[2] *In re* Kosopud, 272 Fed. 330; *Ex parte* Garcia, 205 Fed. 53; *Ex parte* Chin Quock Wah, 224 Fed. 138; Guiney *v.* Bonham, 261 Fed. 582; *Ex parte* Ah Sue, 270 Fed. 356. *Contra:* Whitfield *v.* Hanges, 222 Fed. 745.

Even if a lawyer is present at the hearing, he may only present his objections in his brief, and the bare fact that he has objected is entered in the record,[1] with no statement of the reasons for objection. The attorney may not by his objection prevent any question of the inspector; he may of course question the alien himself. He often does not have a right to cross-examination [2] and on one occasion had not submitted his brief before the administrative decision had been reached.[3] The attorney is then allowed a certain length of time—usually from a week to ten days, in which to prepare his brief, if he wishes to present one. This brief, embodying the objections at the hearing and the reasons why the client should not be deported or else should be granted a stay of deportation, is forwarded to the bureau of immigration in Washington, together with the record of the hearing. In order to complete his case, the lawyer may review the record in its entirety until deportation has actually taken place.[4]

Others besides lawyers may represent aliens; sometimes social agencies [5] interested in a particular alien send someone

[1] *Immigration Laws*, etc., *op. cit.*, Rule 19, Subdivision D, par. 2.

[2] Gonzales *v.* Zurbrick, 45 Fed. (2d) 934, held such right a constitutional one.

[3] United States *ex rel.* Sinclair *v.* Smith, 33 Fed. (2d) 914.

[4] *Immigration Laws*, etc., *op. cit.*, Rule 28, Subdivision B. It is of note that attorneys desirous of practising before the department of any immigration station must be attorneys in good standing in the courts of the state to which they belong. Furthermore, all appearances must be entered in writing, and anyone claiming to represent the alien may be required to show he is entitled to appear.—*Ibid.*, Subdivision A, pars. 1, 2. An attorney is theoretically not allowed to charge more than $25 for his services, according to departmental regulation (*ibid.*, Subdivisions C-D), but this regulation is not followed.

[5] Such as the *National Catholic Welfare Conference*, the *Department of Service for the Foreign-Born* of the *National Council of Jewish Women*, the *Foreign Language Information Service*, "Hias", etc. Apparently

to represent him. Congressmen are sometimes represented, but usually they save their political influence to bring to bear when the record is in Washington before the board of review.

The alien's lawyer "shall be permitted to be present during the conduct of the hearing and to offer evidence to meet any evidence presented or adduced by the Government." [1] There is nothing in the law or regulations which prevents the inspector in charge of the case from collecting evidence or testimony outside the hearing, so the presence of the alien's lawyer at the hearing may not of necessity be an opportunity for him to hear evidence and see witnesses [2] against the alien. On the other hand, it is sometimes necessary for relatives or friends of the person in custody to testify; [3] particularly when the alien is in such mental or physical condition as to be unable to testify himself.

Often a full hearing is given to an insane person in the same manner as to anyone else, except that the insane man or woman is not "sworn." Despite the fact that the court has held a hearing was not fairly conducted if an insane man testified and waived counsel in his behalf, such waiver

appeals for aid to legal aid societies are somewhat rare in deportation cases. The author addressed a questionnaire to the 1927 Conference of the National Association of Legal Aid Organizations and found that there was no uniformity of practice among the legal aid societies as to whether or not they will provide lawyers for aliens in deportation proceedings. The attitude of the particular society is determined by the facts in individual cases.

[1] *Immigration Laws, op. cit.,* Rule 19, Subdivision D, par. 2.

[2] *Vide* the following cases where the court intervened to protect the alien in such cases: United States *ex rel.* Huber *v.* Sibray, 178 Fed. 144; McDonald *v.* Siu Tak Sam, 225 Fed. 710; United States *ex rel.* Chila *v.* Hughes, 24 Fed. (2d) 707; *Ex parte* Jackson, 263 Fed. 110; *Ex parte* Radivoeff, 278 Fed. 227; Ungar *v.* Seaman, 4 Fed. (2d) 80.

[3] These names may be secured from Form 534 if the alien is in an institution; otherwise they may be obtained from him himself.

being insufficient in that case,[1] the general practice is to give an insane person a hearing unless he is in a very serious mental condition. His relatives and friends have opportunity to offer expert testimony as to his condition and particularly as to whether or not his disability arose subsequent to his residence here. If such testimony is not received the hearing is not fair.[2]

At the close of the hearing, no matter where it is held, the person held under warrant proceedings is warned that if he is deported and then attempts to re-enter the United States, he will be guilty of a felony under the act of March 4, 1929, and upon conviction will be liable to imprisonment or fine or both. "This warning shall be entered upon the minutes of the hearing in a separate paragraph." [3]

The most moot question in all deportation procedure and one to which discussions in and out of court most frequently turn [4] is that of fairness of hearing. An alien, once in the

[1] United States *ex rel.* Diognardi *et ux. v.* Flynn, 15 Fed. (2d) 576.

[2] *Ibid.* In practice, relatives often do not wish to give such testimony if they wish the deportation of the insane or ill person. If no relatives or friends testify, the superintendent of the institution where the alien is confined is asked to testify and show reason why deportation should not take place. Such testimony is usually a matter of form only, as the superintendent would be apt to desire to rid his institution of ill or insane aliens.

[3] *Immigration Laws, op. cit.*, Rule 19, Subdivision D, par. 5.

[4] Edith Abbott, "Federal Immigration Policies", *University Journal of Business*, vol. ii, nos. 2, 3, 4, March, June, September, 1924; Zechariah Chafee, *Freedom of Speech*, ch. v; Kate Holladay Claghorn, *The Immigrant's Day in Court*, chs. ix, x; Albert J. Beveridge, *Law and Order and the Administration of Justice*, Report of Sub-Committee, Republican National Committee, 1920; John Lord O'Brian, "The Menace of Administrative Law", *Proceedings*, 25th Annual Meeting, Maryland State Bar Association, 1920, p. 153 *et seq.*; Ernst Freund, "Deportation Legislation in the Sixty-ninth Congress, *Social Service Review*, vol. i, no. 1, March 1927, p. 47 *et seq.*; Louis F. Post, "Administrative Decisions in Connection with Immigration", *Political Science Review*, vol. x, 1916, p. 251 *et seq.*, and *The Deportations Delirium of 1920.*

United States, is entitled to the benefit of the provisions of the Constitution that no person—be he alien or citizen—shall be deprived by the federal government or the states of life, liberty, or property without due process of law.[1] But as it is difficult to determine what constitutes "due process," so it is difficult to determine in what a fair hearing consists, and such hearing in good faith is essential to "due process."

Before touching on the question of fairness of hearing, we must dwell for a moment on the problem of due process in itself.[2] In order to have due process of law, there must be jurisdiction of the administrative authority over the person held for deportation. Jurisdiction includes, in the first place, the requirement that the immigration authorities must conform to the statutes.

Aliens must be deported according to law and not according to men. This statute must be administered according to its terms and the rules established by the Commissioner General of Immigration. Those charged with the enforcement are not at liberty in any particular case, and for reasons that may appeal to them at the moment to set aside any one of the rules on which the rights of aliens depend.[3]

In the second place, as already indicated, alienage is essential to the jurisdiction of the administrative authorities, for it is up to the government to show that a person held in deportation proceedings is an alien.

Another and most important essential to due process is fairness of hearing. In the line of decisions holding deportation to be a civil and not a criminal proceeding, the courts

[1] *Vide* Japanese Immigrant Case, 189 U. S. 86. *Vide* also Corpus Juris, vol. i, p. 1046.

[2] For more adequate discussion of this problem on the constitutional side, *vide* Norman Alexander, *Rights of Aliens* (Montpelier, Vt., 1931), ch. ii.

[3] Sibray *ex rel.* Plichta *v.* United States, 282 Fed. 795.

Norman Alexander, *op. cit.*, holds that "the proceedings cannot be constantly state the lack of necessity for the safeguards of a criminal trial. Even though the reasons assigned for the deportation of an alien may constitute a crime under local laws, these do not make " the deportation hearing a trial in a criminal case, to be conducted under the rules of evidence that apply to such a trial." [1] So the hearing may be summary in form [2] and hearsay evidence, anonymous reports, or other evidence inadmissible in a judicial trial is acceptable.[3] So much for what a fair hearing does *not* require.

What, on the other hand, are the positive requirements? The court has laid down the rule that

> a full and fair hearing on the charges which threaten his deportation and an absence of all abuse of discretion and arbitrary action by the inspectors are indispensable to the lawful deportation of an alien, where by the abuse of the discretion or the arbitrary action of the inspector, or other executive officer or without a full and fair hairing an alien is deprived of his liberty, or is about to be deported, the power is conferred and the duty imposed upon the courts of the United States to issue a writ of habeas corpus and relieve him.[4]

The opinion of the court in the Whitfield case is so important in giving the essentials of a fair hearing that it may be quoted *in extenso:*

classed as civil or criminal." Technically, however, the proceedings are civil. However, the fact that the alien is restrained of his liberty under a warrant authorizing the seizure of his person, that he may be released on bail bond, etc. call to mind the similarity of this procedure to that in criminal cases.

[1] Skeffington *v.* Katzeff, 277 Fed. 129; United States *ex rel.* Rennie *v.* Brooks, 284 Fed. 908.

[2] Chin Yow *v.* United States, 208 U. S. 8.

[3] Lewis *ex rel.* Lai Thuey Lem *v.* Johnson, 16 Fed. (2d) 180.

[4] Whitfield *v.* Hanges, 222 Fed. 745, citing The Japanese Immigrant Case, 189 U. S. 86; Chin Yow *v.* United States, 208 U. S. 8; Low Wah Suey *v.* Backus, 225 U. S. 460; *Ex parte* Petkos, 212 Fed. 275; United States *v.* Chin Len, 187 Fed. 544; United States *v.* Williams, 185 Fed. 598, 193 Fed. 228.

The indispensable requisites of a fair hearing . . . are that the course of the hearing shall be appropriate to the case and just to the party affected; that the accused shall be notified of the nature of the charge against him in time to meet it; that he shall have such opporunity to be heard that he may, if he chooses, cross-examine the witnesses against him; that he may have time and opportunity, after all the evidence against him is produced and known to him, to provide evidence and witnesses to refute it; that the decision shall be governed by and based upon the evidence in the hearing, and that only; and that the decision shall not be without substantial evidence taken at the hearing to support it. . . . That is not a fair hearing in which the inspector chooses or controls the witnesses, or prevents the accused from procuring the witnesses or evidence or counsel he desires.[1]

A rule of the department gives no authority to the inspector, secretly, in the presence of no one but himself and his police officer, whose presence and power unavoidably places the defenseless alien under fear and restraint, to examine and question him. It is limited to giving authority to the inspector to give the alien a hearing to enable him to show cause why he should not be deported, and by its terms it excluded a secret examination of the alien to extort a confession or evidence unfavorable to him. The provision of the rule that the inspector shall grant the alien a hearing, that during the hearing he shall be permitted to inspect the warrant, and that at such stage thereof as the officer deems proper he shall be permitted to have counsel, were made for the benefit of the alien for the purpose of giving him a fair trial. The liberty, and the property also, for if he is imprisoned and deported he must lose his business and sacrifice his property, of a permanently resident alien like the appellees, as well as their deportation, are involved in the issue, and these provisions of the rule should be liberally construed to accomplish their plain purpose. To the same end the discretion of

[1] Chin Yow *v.* United States *supra*; United States *v.* Williams, *supra*; United States *ex rel.* Huber *v.* Sibray, 178 Fed. 144; Roux *v.* Commissioner of Immigration, 203 Fed. 413.

the inspector in determining when the alien shall inspect the warrant and when he shall have counsel should be explicit, so that his hearing shall be full and fair. A denial of permission to him to see the warrant and to give counsel within five minutes of the close of the hearing would be a clear abuse of this discretion, and would render the provision of the rule as administered "inconsistent with law" and void. Although a law or rule to be fair and just in appearance yet it is applied and administered by public authority with an evil eye and an oppressive hand so as to deprive a person of his fundamental rights it cannot be sustained.[1]

One of the objects of this rule is to give, not to deprive, the alien of the benefit of counsel. The time when an alien, who is ordinarily ignorant of legal procedure and of his rights, may derive the most benefit of counsel is when he is arrested and his hearing begins. It would have been no abuse of the discretion of the inspector to have permitted the appellees to have counsel, to advise them immediately upon their arrest, and to have permitted them and their counsel to inspect the warrant of arrest, and to be present and to take part in the procedure at and after the first state of the examination and hearing of the aliens. Such a course would have been in accord with the fundamental principles of English and American jurisprudence consistent with the law, and it should have been pursued. The refusal of the inspection of the warrant of arrest and the refusal to permit the aliens to see and consult their counsel before, and then to permit them to participate in the proceedings at their examination directly tended to prevent a fair hearing upon the charges against them.

Whether or not the weight of the evidence, in substantial conflict at the hearing, sustained the charges against the appellees is a question of fact,—within the exclusive jurisdiction of the officials of the Department of Labor, and the courts, in the

[1] Yick Wo *v.* Hopkins, 118 U. S. 336; Henderson *v.* Mayor of New York, 92 U. S. 259; Chy Lung *v.* Freeman, 92 U. S. 275; *Ex parte* Virginia, 100 U. S. 339; Neal *v.* Delaware, 103 U. S. 370; Soon Hung *v.* Crowley, 113 U. S. 703.

absence of fraud or misconstruction, are without jurisdiction to reverse their findings thereon.

But whether or not there was any substantial evidence at the hearing in support of those charges and of the findings of the inspector that they were proved, and of his recommendation that the aliens be deported under which the appellees were being deprived of their liberty, is a question of law, the power and duty to determine which are vested in the courts, and any injurious error in deciding that question by any executive or quasi-judicial official or tribunal is reviewable and remediable by them. Administrative orders and findings quasi-judicial in character are void if the finding is contrary to the " indisputable character of the evidence " . . . [1]

That was not a fair hearing in which the inspector after the hearing imported into the case and based his findings and record of deportation on hearsay and rumors of alleged facts which there was no evidence to support, and which the accused had no notice of and no opportunity to refute at the hearing.[2] In this case (Interstate Commerce Commission *v.* Louisville and Nashville Ry.) it was held. . . . "There is no hearing when the party does not know what evidence is offered or considered and is not given an opportunity to test, explain, or refute." . . .

Despite the fact that the hearing may be summary in form, the decision made as a result of it must be supported by evidence and there must be no application of erroneous rules of law.[3] Nor must the regulations of the Department of Labor fail to be followed.[4]

[1] Whitfield *v.* Hanges, 222 Fed. 745, 746; School of Magnetic Healing *v.* McAnnulty, 187 U. S. 94; Interstate Commerce Commission *v.* Cincinnati, N. O. and T. P. Ry. Co., 167 U. S. 479.

[2] Interstate Commerce Commission *v.* Louisville and Nashville Ry., 227 U. S. 88.

[3] Chin Yow *v.* United States, 208 U. S. 8; American School of Magnetic Healing *v.* McAnnulty, 187 U. S. 94; Gegiow *v.* Uhl, 239 U. S. 3; Ng Fung Ho *v.* White, 259 U. S. 276.

[4] *Ex parte* Radivoeff, 278 Fed. 227.

Let us summarize the most important requisites of a fair hearing.[1]

1. The course of proceeding shall be appropriate to the case and just to the party affected.
2. The accused shall be notified of the charges against him in time to meet them.
3. He shall have such opportunity to be heard that he may, if he so desires, cross-examine the witnesses against him.
4. He may have time and opportunity, after all the evidence is produced and known to him, to produce evidence and witnesses to refute it.
5. The decision shall be governed by and based upon *only* the evidence at the hearing.
6. The decision shall not be without substantial proof taken at the hearing to support it.
7. The inspector conducting the hearing may not choose or control the witness, or prevent the accused from procuring the witness or evidence or counsel he desires.
8. Whether or not the weight of the evidence sustains the charge is a question of fact which the courts may not review.[2]
9. Whether or not there was any substantial evidence at the hearing to support the charges and the findings of the inspector that the alien be deported is a question of law, the power to determine which is vested in the courts.

The hearings are supposedly transcribed *verbatim*,[3] for

[1] It is beyond the scope of the present study to attempt a thorough discussion of constitutional right on the administrative side, or of the problem of administrative power to affect private rights, and the remedies available to the individual affected.

[2] *Vide supra*, p. 312.

[3] As with the "preliminary statement", the testimony as recorded often indicates condensation. For instance, a person may give his whole life history in the briefest and most logical form, stating just the salient facts, with no digressions. The difficulties under which an inspector labors must be remembered, especially if he acts as clerk or interpreter or both while attempting to secure an accurate record.

the record is all-important in the determination of deportability. Thus the courts have demanded a full and accurate [1] record, for "it is the province of the courts in proceedings for review to prevent abuse of this extraordinary power (over the fundamental rights of men), and this is possible only when a full record is preserved of the essentials on which the executive officers proceed to judgment." [2] So the record must have a full statement of the hearing and also a summary of the case, together with the charges against the alien and the recommendation as to the issuance of the warrant of deportation.[3]

When the hearing is over, the immigrant inspector conducting the case makes a brief summary, and forwards it with the record and any brief submitted by a lawyer to the inspector in charge or to the district director. If he does not agree with the cases as stated by the inspector or inspector in charge, the matter is straightened out between them. Then the district director forwards the record to Washington, together with a yellow page of summary, restatement and recommendation.[4] Since the decision "of

[1] *Immigration Laws*, etc., *op. cit.*, Rule 19, Subdivision D, par. 3.

[2] Kwock Jan Fat *v.* White, 253 U. S. 454. Here the testimony of important witnesses favorable to a Chinese applicant to enter the country was omitted from the record sent to the Commissioner General of Immigration. On the basis of this record he affirmed a decision denying the petitioner's right to enter the country. So the court directed a writ of *habeas corpus* to issue.

[3] Additional charges to those contained in the original warrant of arrest may be lodged during the hearing, or it may be recommended that others previously lodged are not sustainable. *Immigration Laws*, etc., *op. cit.*, Rule 19, Subdivision D, par. 2.

[4] *Immigration Laws*, etc., *op. cit.*, Rule 19, Subdivision D, par. 6. The record of the hearing concerning any alien suffering from physical or mental disability must also contain a medical certificate from the officer in charge of the institution in which the person is detained or from a United States Public Health Service official showing (1) whether such alien is in condition to be deported without danger to life and (2) whether he will require special care and attention on the ocean voyage.—*Ibid.*, par. 4.

the Secretary of Labor " as to whether a warrant of deportation shall be issued is made on the basis of the written record, it is essential that the record be complete and that the *full* record be forwarded to the bureau.[1] If there is discrepancy in the record, the courts will not uphold the proceedings.[2] However, it is up to the Secretary of Labor to give his own weight to the evidence in that record.[3]

THE BOARD OF REVIEW [4]

This decision " of the Secretary of Labor as to whether a warrant of deportation shall issue " is reached in a noteworthy manner, not provided by either statute or regulation. As already noted, under authority granted by statute, deportable aliens " shall upon the warrant of the Secretary of Labor be taken into custody and deported "; furthermore, " in every case where any person is ordered deported from the United States, under the provisions of this act, or of any law or treaty, the decision of the Secretary of Labor shall be final." To aid in this adjudication, the department of labor has developed within itself a kind of administrative court known as the " Secretary and Commissioner General's Board of Review."

The board of review is the lineal descendant of an advisory committee in the office of the Secretary which was organized during the administration of Secretary Wilson in

[1] *Ibid.*, par. 6.

[2] Kwock Jan Fat *v.* United States, 253 U. S. 454.

[3] Sibray *v.* United States, 282 Fed. 745. The Secretary may accept as of the most probative value the first statement of the alien, made before the selection of a lawyer and before consultation with him.—Ghiggeri *v.* Nagle, 19 Fed. (2d) 875; Plane *v.* Carr, 19 Fed. (2d) 470. *Vide* Cook and Hagerty, *op. cit.*, p. 125, § 249.

[4] Part of this section appeared in the *Political Science Quarterly*, vol. xliv, no. 2, June 1929, under the title of " Administrative Standards in Deportation Procedure ".

consequence of a controversy over the administrative jurisdiction of the commissioner general of immigration with reference to exclusion and deportation cases. With the change of presidential administration in 1921 this committee was dissolved, but it was reestablished in January, 1922, and now functions as a kind of clearing house for the thousands of exclusion and deportation cases. At first there were five members, with Assistant Secretary of Labor Robe Carl White as chairman; now there are ten, two of whom are immigration inspectors assigned for duty on the board, with special reference to Chinese cases; the remaining ones are appointed without reference to civil service rules, under the provisions of "Section 24" of the immigration act of 1917. It had been provided by act of March 4, 1915[1] that an officer and clerk be detailed to enforce the contract labor provisions, while the 1917 act in its often-mentioned "Section 24" provides that the Secretary of Labor

in the enforcement of that portion of this act which excludes contract laborers and induced and assisted immigrants, may employ, for such purposes and for detail upon additional service under this act when not so engaged, without reference to the provisions of the said civil-service act, or to the various acts relative to the compilation of the Official Register, such persons as he may deem advisable, and from time to time fix, raise, or decrease their compensation. He may draw annually from the appropriation for the enforcement of his act $100,000, or as much thereof as may be necessary, to be expended for the expenses of persons so employed and for expenses incident to such employment; and the accounting officers of the Treasury shall pass to the credit of the proper disbursing officer expenditures from said sum without itemized account whenever the Secretary of Labor certifies that an itemized account would not be for the best interests of the Government.

[1] 38 Stat. 1151.

The decline in volume and importance of contract labor work has meant the assignment of inspectors appointed under the provisions of this section for other duties, notably for work on the board of review.

The record of the local hearing goes to the board, one member of which reads the entire record, adds his opinion, then forwards it all to the chairman for re-reading and signature, although with great pressure of cases the chairman does not read them. If there is any disagreement, informal discussion is held and the majority opinion recorded for the advice of the Assistant to the Secretary, to whom the record goes after it has left the board.

The alien has opportunity to have a lawyer or friend represent him before the board, or he may even appear himself. It is at this stage of the proceedings that Congressmen or their secretaries most often appear, to attempt to exert political pressure. Sometimes their appearance is routine and nominal, but if the pressure behind them is great or if they have personal interest in the alien being held, they exert greater efforts to prevent, or at least to stay, deportation.

When representation is desired before the board of review, three members of the board sit for the hearing. Labelled *Court Room* on the door, the room in which they sit has an official appearance, with its elevated platform and bench for the members of the board, and its railing separating those presenting cases and spectators. Supposedly the hearing is based entirely on the record. If the record shows the need for additional testimony, the whole matter is remanded to the local immigration district, where the hearing is reopened and additional information taken. The application for a rehearing should be presented to the local immigration authorities and a court has no control of the department of labor in the exercise of its discretion in passing on such application.[1]

When the decision of the board is reached, either with or without hearing in the court room, it is forwarded with the record to one of the two Assistants to the Secretary for decision as to deportability. It must be remembered that the board is purely advisory in capacity and its decision is advisory only, for the power of final decision must rest in the hands of the Secretary of Labor. However, in point of fact, the Secretary of Labor rarely sees or hears of a case of deportation or exclusion.

Because of the vast increase in deportation cases, it became utterly impossible for the Secretary or even one of his assistants to read so many records, much less digest and decide upon them. The practical result is that the decision rests in the hands of the extra-legal advisory board of review, for the assistant to the Secretary usually accepts the recommendation of the board. However, he does not always abide by their "decision" and in rare instances discusses the matter with them and either is converted to their point of view or overrules them with his power of decision.

The importance of the "decisions" of the board may be seen from the number of cases which they read and on which they render an opinion. The figures given in the reports of the Secretary of Labor[2] do not separate exclusion from deportation cases, but the total number of both kinds gives an indication of the work of the board:

[1] Maniglia *v.* Commander of the Giuseppe Verdi, 5 Fed. (2d) 680. "The Secretary of Labor's denial of a rehearing to an alien is not reviewable by the court."—United States *ex rel.* Ickowicz *v.* Day, 18 Fed. (2d) 963.

[2] *Sixteenth Annual Report of the Secretary of Labor for the Fiscal Year Ended June 30, 1928*, pp. 71-72; *1930*, p. 78.

SOME WORK OF BOARD OF REVIEW, 1928-1930 [1]

	1928	*1929*	*1930*
Number of warrant cases reviewed	12,512	14,235	18,258
Number of cases reconsidered	19,469	21,284	14,436
Number of oral hearings	1,844	1,798	2,174

Neither the act nor the regulations as printed give any instructions concerning the organization or operation of the board of review, and it is referred to only in the unprinted general orders and amendments. The first mention of it in an *Annual Report of the Secretary of Labor* was in 1923. The courts have taken scant notice of it and have merely upheld its general position by stating that "the hearing before the board of review is merely in aid of the Secretary of Labor and is a lawful method of administering the duties of the department," [2] the United States Supreme Court has not passed on its position, nor has there been court discussion even in the lower federal courts of the *details* of its procedure.

Whether this embryonic administrative court will receive statutory authority or not is an open question, and one to be watched by those interested in the development of administrative adjudication and legislation in the United States. Thus far the opinions of the board have not been thought to extend beyond the powers allowed, in that the Secretary may appoint those whom he desires for consultation and advice regarding decision of immigration cases; yet the tendency is for the board to become more formal and for more weight to be given to its opinions than at first, and the development from an advisory committee to a body with its own "Court Room" and definite personnel is worthy of notice. There is no tendency, however, to give the board of review definite statutory authority.[3]

[1] *Annual Report of the Secretary of Labor*, etc., *1930*, p. 78.

[2] United States *ex rel.* Chin Fook Wah *v.* Dunton, 288 Fed. 959.

[3] For further discussion of the board of review, *vide* Louis Post, un-

In cases where there is rush,[1] such as when a deportation train is immediately going through the place where the alien is held, a telegraphic warrant of deportation is issued, but this must be followed by the formal warrant and sent to the local immigration office where the alien is held. Official copies of the warrant are also forwarded to the port from which deportation is to take place and where arrangements for sailing are made, if travel is to be by sea.

The Hearing in the Cases Studied

The hearings were held in widely varying places, from public hospitals and prisons to private homes, but in none of them was any objection noted as to the place of hearing.

The cases differed as to whether or not lawyers were secured by the aliens, according to their financial status and according to the reasons for deportation. In all the cases, the alien was asked at the *beginning* of the hearing whether or not he desired legal representation, and if he replied that he did not, the question was put: " Do you then waive any right to counsel?" If the alien replied " Yes " with no further statement, it was impossible to determine whether or not he could afford a lawyer. This happened in 326 cases, but in 109 others the alien further replied that he could not afford counsel.

In the group of 25 "L.P.C." cases, there were two families who were anxious to return to their home country, and would not have desired legal representation in any event. Furthermore, the whole group was composed of people who could not by their own unaided efforts get along in the

published MS. on *Immigration and Labor Problems*, p. 153 *et seq.*; also, *The Immigrant's Day in Court*, speech by Hon. John L. Cable, of Ohio, in the House of Representatives, January 27, 1925, *Congressional Record*, Appendix, January 28, 1925, pp. 2684-2686.

[1] *Vide infra*, ch. xii, p. 452 *et seq.*

United States and were therefore more willing to return home than they might otherwise have been. Most important, they had no money for lawyers, even had they wanted them. Only one of the group said he desired counsel, but even he changed his mind. Seven of the 136 public charges had lawyers. In two of these, medical testimony was also secured.

Another group where deportation was often desired was in the 41 criminal cases. The feeling seemed to prevail among them that deportation would cause a shorter prison term. However, out of the total in this group, 22 said they wished to secure a lawyer, though only sixteen actually did. These numbers are larger than might be expected, due, perhaps, to the fact that the individual criminals had had previous contact with the law and so felt legal representation a matter of routine necessity. Criminals with underworld connections might have financial resources or legal connections not available to others.

This last statement seems to apply with particular force to the prostitute category. Of the total number of prostitutes and narcotics, only three did not have lawyers.

The illegal entry group varied widely. As many had come across the border and been immediately apprehended, they knew little of their whereabouts or situation. Unless they had been in the United States before, or had friends here, they did not have counsel. Sixty-one out of the total of 392 secured legal representation.

In two of the total number of all cases, lawyers went to Washington after the hearing to appear before the board of review if necessary. In 57 out of the 99 cases with legal representation, briefs were presented, showing family, business, or other social reasons for requesting that deportation be prevented or at least that a stay be granted.

None of the whole group of cases came to court, and so

the question of fairness of hearing was not discussed before any judicial tribunal. In two of the cases, however, counsel made the charge of unfairness of procedure, on the ground that the rules of evidence were not followed.[1] In one case, the lawyer gave the additional ground that the alien had no interpreter and failed to understand English sufficiently to know the nature of the proceedings against her.

In only six cases did representatives of social agencies appear.

The Cases Included in this Study before the Board of Review

Aside from the two lawyers appearing before the board of review in behalf of their clients, nineteen Senators or their secretaries and 58 Representatives in Congress or their secretaries appeared or wrote letters requesting cancellation of proceedings or stays of deportation. It is not possible to judge the effect of such appearances from the cases studied, as they were all cases where deportation *actually occurred,* and deportation was not prevented at all by such appearance. In four cases, however, an extension of time was granted, probably as a result of such intercession. Several of the appearances were merely requests for information, rather than efforts to prevent deportation, and so were merely perfunctory.

In nine cases, the board of review felt the testimony given at the hearings was insufficient to sustain the original charges in the warrant of arrest, and requested the hearing to be re-opened, as in the following case:

Michele Nero (Case 82).

Michele Nero was born in 1892 in the province of Calabria, Italy. He emigrated to the United States in 1920 and was

[1] There is no need to follow them as to particulars. *Vide supra*, pp. 371, 374.

married in Chicago that year. Six months later he returned to Italy for a visit, but remained longer than he had intended. Meanwhile he had lost trace of his wife in the United States.

In October, 1923, Mr. Nero, finding it impossible to enter the United States legally went to Canada and lived in Quebec. In 1930 he took a trip to see Niagara Falls and on January 19, walked across the Falls View Bridge. He was questioned by an inspector but said he intended to return to Canada after a few hours. When he tried to reenter Canada that afternoon, the Canadian inspector refused to admit him. He was turned over to the American immigration officials and detained in the Niagara Falls police station.

A warrant was issued for Mr. Nero's arrest on January 22, 1930, on the grounds (1) that he entered the United States by means of false and misleading statements, and (2) that he was not in possession of an unexpired immigration visa. Two days later, Mr. Nero was transferred to the Niagara County Jail at Lockport, as a prisoner of the immigration service. On January 25, he was given a hearing at the jail.

When the case came before the board of review, they felt that the testimony at the hearing did not show that Mr. Nero entered the United States by means of false and misleading statements, and furthermore, that as Mr. Nero had shown his intention of returning to Canada that day, there was no need for his having an immigration visa. As the board of review did not feel that the charges on the warrant of arrest were sustained, they requested the hearing to be re-opened. This was done, at the jail, on February 28. Mr. Nero stated he had told the inspector on entering that he was a Canadian whereas he was still an Italian citizen; also, he had no passport visaed for entry, even though for temporary purposes only. The district director felt that this testimony at the re-opened hearing sustained the charges and recommended accordingly, and the board of review agreed.

The warrant of deportation was issued on March 10, and Mr. Nero was deported on April 19, 1930, at the expense of the government.

There is no discussion in the record of prosecution for violation of the act of March 4, 1929.

In no case did the Assistant to the Secretary or Assistant Secretary disagree with the case as stated by the board.

CONCLUSIONS

A method of guaranteeing safeguards more completely than by an entirely executive process has often been advocated—namely, that of jury trial for the person held in deportation proceedings.[1] The advocates of jury trial feel that it is the method for giving the alien his day in court in the fullest sense of the word. On the other hand, in these times when jury trial is not always regarded as a panacea, the possibility arises of developing increased safeguards on the administrative side.

Are such safeguards possible? Several come to mind. First of all is the problem involved in an adequately trained and qualified personnel, for often the whole administrative decision depends on the type of person who makes the investigation and recommendations. The inspector who has a judicial attitude of mind and who regards his job as that of ascertaining facts rather than of pressing for the deportation of the alien under investigation, is the first rung in a ladder of administrative safeguards for the alien.

In the second place, administrative procedure should take into account the lessons learned from the procedure of the ordinary courts of justice. Even executive justice administered in a spirit of fairness and equality of treatment may afford its measure of due process of law. A judicial attitude in the administrative system is then all-important. Should it be lacking, an appeal is necessary from the administrative body on all questions where proper consideration has not been given to the alien and to the facts in his cause.

[1] *Vide supra*, p. 369, esp. Chafee, *op. cit.*, and Post, "Administrative Decisions", *op. cit.*

More adequate representation of the alien by counsel or representatives of social agencies is needed. It often seems that social agencies are ready to criticize the administrative procedure but loath to provide representation for the alien either at the hearing or the board of review. In a summary administrative procedure, rights may be better safeguarded by legal or social representatives than without.

There is need for establishment of a more definite principle than now exists as to the right of review of administrative decisions. This review may be by ordinary courts of law or by a higher specially constituted administrative tribunal. It is perhaps less important that the review be entrusted to an ordinary court than that it should be entrusted to some definite authority. The board of review, with its court room and embryonic judicial procedure, seems a step in that direction, but there is need for legal training on the part of its members and of publicity for its hearings. If statutory authority were granted to the board, and if it were given powers of review and a personnel duly qualified to conduct judicial proceedings, it might serve as a kind of administrative court instead of an aid to the Secretary in deciding cases. In that case, the organization of the Department of Labor would have to be revamped so that other aid might be given the Secretary in the making of decisions. In connection with the possible development of the board of review, one must bear in mind the development of other administrative bodies, such as the Interstate Commerce Commission, for

more and more these bodies are becoming assimilated to the courts, employing truly judicial processes and hedged about with proper judicial safeguards. The same development may be expected to take place in other administrative tribunals. . . . The result will be the formation of a great system and its own practice, but truly judicial in character and methods, and all subject in matters of general law to the ultimate control of the traditional courts.[1]

The safeguards, however, must be particularly carefully made in any procedure involving such fundamental personal rights as does that of deportation.

[1] J. Dickinson, "Administrative Law and the Fear of Bureaucracy", *American Bar Association Journal*, Oct. and Nov. 1928, vol. xiv, nos. 9 and 10.

CHAPTER XI[1]

THE MIDDLE OF THE PROCESS

THE DETENTION PERIOD—COUNTRY TO WHICH DEPORTATION TAKES PLACE—THE AMERICAN-BORN CHILDREN OF DEPORTEES

DETENTION

THE road is indeed long to travel before the alien is finally "upon the warrant of the Secretary of Labor" taken into custody and deported. What happens to him while his fate is being determined, if for lack of available funds or other reason he is unable to be released on bond or on his own recognizance? Let us turn for a while to the circumstances and conditions of detention.

No statistics are available as to how and where the 16,631 persons deported during the fiscal year 1930 were detained, over what periods of time they were held, and how many were released to social agencies.[2] Approximately 14.8% of the number were members of the criminal and immoral categories and were probably held in penitentiaries and jails; 3.9% were public charges and so held temporarily or permanently in public or semi-public institutions; 2.3% were mentally or physically defective at the time of entry, and were possibly held in similar institutions or in jails; 79% were of the "miscellaneous classes," consisting for the most

[1] Part of this chapter was given as an address at the National Conference of Social Work, Boston, June 10, 1930.

[2] For release on bond or their own recognizance, *vide supra*, pp. 341 *et seq.*

part of illegal entries,[1] and were detained in county jails, the few port immigration stations equipped for detention,[2] or released on bond or their own recognizance until deportation. Here again no statistics are available of the total number of these "miscellaneous classes" held in county jails or released.

The bureau of immigration has no complete figures available as to how many deportees it is detaining in county jails.[3] Indeed, not until December 1930 did the United States prison bureau have any idea of the *total* number of federal prisoners of all sorts detained in county jails,[4] and even then the immigration cases were not separately enumerated. Nor are statistics available regarding other places of detention for deportation cases.

Although deportation is merely the removal of an alien

[1] For comparison of these percentages with those from 1916-1929 *vide Annual Report of the Commissioner General*, etc., *for 1930*, p. 244.

[2] Ellis Island at New York, Philadelphia Immigration Station at Gloucester City, N. J., Angel Island at San Francisco, Boston and Seattle.

[3] The accounts and personnel division of the bureau of immigration was good enough to run through its pay vouchers to sheriffs, etc., from May 1, 1929 to May 1, 1930 for the author. It found that 134 different county jails, 13 social agencies, and the homes of 32 individuals were used for detention of deportees during that period, in addition to 2 penitentiaries, used for want of any detention facilities whatsoever.

[4] On that date it announced the result of its study of detention of such prisoners during the fiscal year ended June 30, 1930. In city and county jails during that period there was an average daily population of 10,324 for all offenses.—*New York Times*, Dec. 21, 1930.

The figures obtained by Dr. Hastings Hart are interesting in this connection. He states in *United States Prisoners in County Jails* (Russell Sage Foundation, 1926) that in 1924 more than 900 jails were used by the federal government for its prisoners. In May, 1930 Dr. Hart told the author that he had found more than 1100 county jails in use at that time for detention of federal prisoners. These, of course, include places where persons are held for all types of federal offense, and include various interior points. Most immigration cases are detained at or near border points.

from the country without any punishment being imposed, the alien in jail awaiting deportation must, like the person detained as witness, feel strangely like a criminal.[1] Unlike the witness, however, he finds the line between being a criminal and not being one hard at times to find. Under the former war-time "passport act" and now under the act of March 4, 1929, criminal prosecution may accompany deportation proceedings. As already indicated,[2] any alien entering the country illegally is guilty of a misdemeanor, punishable by fine or not more than $1000 or imprisonment for not more than one year or both. So an unfortunate Czech, stranded in Canada without employment and paying ten dollars to a man who promised to take him "to get work," found himself unwittingly in Detroit, there apprehended, and, unlike Ko-Ko in *The Mikado*, taken *to* "the county jail by a set of curious chances," and at the same time a criminal and a non-criminal.

An alien apprehended by the border patrol, for instance, is detained in the county jail by arrangement with local authorities until the warrant for his arrest is issued by the Department of Labor. The warrant is issued almost immediately,[3] and the alien is turned over from his unofficial detention by the local authorities to be held — usually in the same jail—at the expense of the immigration service, while the non-criminal deportation proceedings are carried on. Meanwhile his illegal entry is reported to the local United States Commissioner, who may, if the evidence warrants, hold him for the grand jury. If an indictment is made, the jury in turn holds him for the next session of the federal

[1] Such detention in jail is proper, however.—United States *ex rel.* Ross *v.* Wallis, 279 Fed. 401; United States *ex rel.* Schlimm *v.* Howe, 222 Fed. 96. *Vide* Cook and Hagerty, *op. cit.*, § 246.

[2] *Vide supra*, p. 267 *et seq.*

[3] *Vide supra*, p. 335 *et seq.*

district court. After the report to the United States Commissioner, the alien is held as a prisoner of the Department of Justice, in the same jail as before, but this time on the criminal charge of violation of the act of March 4, 1929. He may be sentenced by the court to a term in the same jail, and on its expiration again be turned over to the custody of the Department of Labor. It, meanwhile, has issued a warrant of deportation for him. If the Department of Labor has been unable during the period of criminal prosecution to procure a passport, secure passage and complete other deportation arrangements, the detained person may continue to be held in the same jail, but he is back in his original state of detention on a non-criminal charge. If the man who smuggled him into the country has also been caught, the alien may be held in jail on the further non-criminal charge of witness against his smuggler. In practice, as already noted,[1] where anyone is held in jail over a period of time to testify against his smuggler, his own violation of the law may not be prosecuted. Also,—especially at border points where many illegal entries take place,—the grand jury and federal district court may sit at rare intervals. Thus the alien may be held in jail so long before he is sentenced, that when sentence is given it is dated back to the day he first entered jail. Another practice of some judges is to suspend sentence for a certain period, with the proviso that if the foreigner so sentenced reenters the country after deportation, the sentence will automatically begin. Of course, some persons under warrant proceedings are released on bond. Two bonds may be required in cases of illegal entry, one to the Department of Justice and one to the Department of Labor, though the latter department often allows a person under bond to the other department to go

[1] *Supra*, p. 270.

on his own recognizance as far as deportation proceedings are concerned.[1]

Let us illustrate the situation. A Finnish girl of twenty-two went to Canada to become a domestic servant. With no relatives in Canada but with three sisters in the United States, she soon decided at all hazards to try to enter here. She paid $75 to a smuggler to bring her across the Michigan border one night under the straw in a railroad box-car. Apprehended by the border patrol, she was taken to the local county jail where she stayed four days before being transferred to the Wayne County Jail in Detroit. There she waited three months before being sentenced to serve six months; the judge, however, suspended sentence for two years, to become effective if she returned to the United States. She was then turned over to the immigration authorities and detained in jail pending the issuance of her passport. Her sisters in Massachusetts offered a bond of $1500 through the local family welfare association for a six months' visit to them, but this was refused and she was deported just four months from the night she was smuggled into the country.[2]

Aliens illegally sneaking into the country and caught by the activities of the border patrol or other officials are causing conditions of indescribable overcrowding in local jails along the border. Indeed, the situation has become so serious that the Secretary of Labor has called attention to it:

The detention of aliens held under warrant proceedings has long been one of the serious problems of the Immigration Service, especially in localities that are remote from such immigration stations as are provided with detention facilities. There are almost no such stations except at the principal seaports, and for obvious reasons these are not available for the detention of

[1] For discussion of bonds, *vide supra*, pp. 341 *et seq.*

[2] Case from the files of the bureau of immigration.

aliens who are apprehended along the land boundaries or in the interior of the country and who must be detained in jails. This already deplorable situation has been made immeasurably worse since the passage of the immigration act of March 4, 1929 . . . the detention of aliens awaiting prosecution and their imprisonment upon conviction of illegal entry has in several instances overcrowded available jails along the land boundaries to an alarming extent.[1]

The situation of inadequate detention facilities and overcrowding repeats itself constantly on both the northern and southern borders, but perhaps one report of a jail of the "better" kind will suffice, leaving the reader to imagine for himself conditions in a worse type of jail:[2]

Report of inspection of the Clinton County Jail by Commissioner Cecelia D. Patten to the New York State Department of Correction, Inspection on August 16, 1930, Report approved by State Department of Correction, Sept. 25, 1930.

This old jail . . . is approaching the expiration of its usefulness and the county officials . . . must bear in mind that within a short period they will be called upon to provide a new jail adequate in size and equipment, with modern facilities for the housing of prisoners. The jail should be located in the country where time prisoners may be given work and the deadly and harmful idleness, now the rule here, may be wiped out. . . .

At the present time, this jail is used for the detention of county prisoners, federal prisoners and those arrested in the city of Plattsburgh and held for trial in the city police court.

The jail is provided with 24 cells of which four are double, one women's room, two rooms for boys and one for the Plattsburgh city police. The women's room is inadequate in size and

[1] *Annual Report of the Secretary of Labor for the Fiscal Year Ending June 30, 1929*, p. 46.

[2] The author has visited county jails where aliens are detained in Detroit, Cleveland, Buffalo, Plattsburg (N. Y.), Charleston, S. C., Jacksonville, Fla.

furnishings and the boy's rooms are unfit for the purpose for which they are used. The practice of locking from two to four boys in each of these rooms without sufficient light and ventilation—in addition to the dangers of locking more than two prisoners in one cell—is fraught with many dangers and condemned in every instance by the Commission.

Notwithstanding the wretched physical plant which goes to make up this jail, the sheriff had it in as clean condition as possible . . . .

The jail, so far as cell space is concerned, is only adequate enough to take care of county prisoners. . . . (The secretary of the Board of Supervisors) in conference with the sheriff, has agreed that he will refuse to accept Federal prisoners under the authority of Chapter 216, Laws of 1926, at all times when he is unable to properly segregate and classify prisoners as required by the New York state law.

On the date of this inspection there were 13 county prisoners and 23 federal prisoners. . . . The highest number at any time during the fiscal year ending June 30, 1930 was 49 males and 3 females; lowest, 16 males and the average daily population, 32 males and 1 female. The jail has 24 cells.

Of those admitted during the year, 299 males and 29 females were aliens. . . . Periods of detention ranged from one day to 180 days . . . 540 males and 30 females were confined in the institution for the first time; 20 males and 2 females for the third time; 13 males for the fourth time; and 2 males for the fifth time. . . .

On the date of this inspection the room for boys on the north side contained 3 minor male aliens awaiting deportation. The south side boys room contained 2 minor males serving time. The women's room had one adult occupant charged with violation of the immigration law . . . the south lower tier had 10 federal prisoners, in six cells doubled, and the south upper tier had 9 immigration male adults in six cells.

. . . the doubling of prisoners in cells is a dangerous practice and strongly disapproved by the Commission and should not be permitted under any circumstances. The sad thing about the federal prisoners found here was that most of them were seemingly a desirable type and very few, if any, ever having come in contact with the law before, and whose only offense was attempting thru ignorance of the law or otherwise, to enter this country. Some federal prisoners are held here from three to five months without any opportunity for outside exercise or any freedom of movement except within the cells, or at best in the cell corridors where the light and ventilation are not of the best. One man was held here nine months and then released to go where he saw fit. It was learned afterwards that he died soon after in New York. It is recalled that some years ago a prisoner held here for a long period became so depressed over the disposition of his case that he committed suicide.[1]

In talking with the prisoners confined here, hardly any of them had any idea of the status of their cases, as to how long they were going to be kept, what the next step was or when they could expect that their cases would be disposed of. It is understood that on the day after this inspection some of the aliens were taken from this jail to other jails in the state. It is further understood that the delay in handling a number of immigration cases which seem to be troublesome ones, is due to securing of passports so that prisoners may be deported, but inasmuch as no passports are required in Canada, it would seem that Canadians arrested and confined here should have their cases speedily disposed of and the jail thus relieved of a number of prisoners promtply. From January 1 to July 31, 1930, 195 immigration cases were held in this jail; a considerable proportion of them were Canadians.

It is recommended that the sheriff keep in regular contact with the immigration officials as to the status of immigration prisoners held in this jail and that an explanation of it be made to them from time to time. . . . [2]

[1] Author's note.—The case occurred in 1925 and was a case of "illegal entry" where it was difficult to obtain a passport. Another case in the same year occurred where a man detained here became insane and had to be removed to a state institution.

[2] *Plattsburg Sentinel*, September 26, 1930, p. 3.

The story might be repeated in many other places.[1] In-

[1] "Housing of federal prisoners in the various county jails of the State continues to present a troublesome problem in several counties, particularly those located nearest the Canadian border. During the year ending June 30, 1929, the number of federal prisoners received by . . . county jails . . . was . . . 3151.

FEDERAL PRISONERS IN NEW YORK STATE COUNTY JAILS
YEARS ENDING JUNE 30.

1926	*1927*	*1928*	*1929*
3384	3412	2752	3151

"County jails were not intended, and many of them are not adequate, to care for this class of prisoners. It was to prevent over-crowding in the county jails that there was enacted a law, effective March 1, 1927, empowering jail officials to refuse to accept federal prisoners if by their acceptance it would be necessary to violate the provisions of section 92 of the County Law relative to classification of inmates of county jails. It has been found, however, that jail staffs in some counties, in an endeavor to cooperate with the federal authorities, sometimes accept prisoners when the population of their jails would warrant them in refusing to do so. When admitted, it is sometimes difficult to secure their early removal, particularly in immigration cases some of which are held in the jails for months. . . .

"An act of Congress approved March 4, 1929, makes mandatory the commitment of aliens convicted of entering the United States illegally. The usual practice in the past has been to hold such aliens in the county jails until the necessary steps to effect their deportation could be completed. With mandatory sentences discretionary with the court of 'imprisonment for not more than one year or by a fine of not more than $1000, (etc.) . . . ,' it is assumed there will be additional demands on the facilities of the county jails, due to the longer terms of imprisonment.

"The Commission has urged upon Congress to provide a federal prison in this State to relieve the situation caused by the detention of United States prisoners in the county jails. . . ."—*Third Annual Report of the State Commission of Correction for the Year 1929.* State of New York. Legislative Document (1930) No. 90, pp. 13-14. In other states a similar situation prevails. The *Twenty-Ninth Biennial Report of the Michigan State Welfare Commission,* 1927-1928, p. 7, states: "That, whereas the care of Federal prisoners in the county jails of the State of Michigan has become a problem, and since the Federal Government has no jails or other institutions in this State in which to care for its offenders, this Commission would suggest that the U. S. Congress be petitioned to provide the necessary quarters in the State of Michigan for the care of its prisoners."

deed the story of the county-jail everywhere has been made old by the telling, but conditions continue with little improvement. The lack of segregation is notorious. Persons whose only offense may consist in attempting to "find a job" across the border, or in illegally entering to see relatives here, are allowed to mingle freely in jail with narcotic addicts and prostitutes. "Illegal entries" are confined in probably the worst of the county jails, small, ill-equipped places at far-off border towns, where social agencies are lacking and jail is the only detention place for adults and children, insane and ill. The immigration officials sometimes try to keep women and children from jail if there is chance of releasing them, but there are cases of women and children in jail for illegal entry only.[1] The situation is immeasurably worse at border points. In 1924 Dr. Hastings Hart found that counties in the 14 states bordering directly on Canada and Mexico had a ratio of 77 federal prisoners for each million inhabitants, while the ratio for the remaining 34 states was 53 per million, the border state ratio being 45% greater than that for the other states.[2] Since the

[1] In the Franklin County Jail at Malone, N. Y., in 1929, "a woman with three small children has been detained for over a month. The husband is in the men's jail and both are charged with violation of the Immigration Law. A federal agent . . . stated that everything possible was being done to expedite the removal of this family from the jail and he expected this would be accomplished in a few days. It is to be regretted that these small children must be held in jail and that the sheriff is obliged to violate the provision of the Children's Court Act in admitting them. . . ."—*Third Annual Report of the Commission of Correction, New York State*, p. 277.

[2] *United States Prisoners in County Jails.*—Report of the Committee of the American Prison Association on Lockups, Municipal and County Jails (Russell Sage Foundation, 1926), p. 29.

Transportation of aliens causes further trouble. For instance, "an inspection of the city jail at Lackawanna in December revealed the fact that seven federal prisoners awaiting deportation for violation of the Immigration Law were being held at the request of federal officers.

passage of the act of March 4, 1929 the disproportion is doubtless even greater.

Considerable difficulty arises from lack of responsibility for aliens detained, for they are held by various county jails as " boarders " of the federal government. The rates paid for them vary widely from one place to another; in 1930 the range was from 37½ cents to $2.00 a day.[1] Often the counties receive less than the actual cost of maintaining prisoners.[2]

While arrangements vary as to paying local authorities, the cost of maintaining aliens during deportation proceedings is borne by the Department of Labor, unless the aliens are public charges in institutions. In such cases the states where the institutions are located defray expenses until removal occurs.[3] Furthermore, if aliens are being held for

They had been arrested in the west and had been brought east to await the formation of a party to be deported either from Montreal or New York. While it is desirable that local officials cooperate with United States officers when possible, city jails are not intended for such use, and a continuation of the practice would mean that eventually the city would have to enlarge its jail. . . ."—*Third Annual Report of the State Commission of Correction,* New York, *op. cit.*, p. 14.

[1] Statement secured from the accounts and personnel division of the bureau of immigration.

In 1924 Dr. Hastings Hart found 44 different rates paid during one quarter of the year, and a number of different rates paid within certain states. He ascertained that rates paid are determined by contract between the federal government and local officers. In some instances sheriffs are paid by fees, or by a *per diem* allowance for feeding the prisoners.—*United States Prisoners in County Jail, op. cit.*

[2] *Vide* Dr. Hart's *Report of the Committee on Jails of the American Prison Association* on the Distribution of the Cost of Maintaining United States Prisoners between the Federal Treasury and the Taxpayers of the local counties. Pittsburgh, Pa., Oct. 20, 1926.

[3] Previous to 1913, the Department of Commerce and Labor paid detention expenses of aliens in state institutions, after warrants of arrest were issued in deportation proceedings.

prosecution for violation of the act of March 4, 1929 or as witnesses against their smugglers,[1] they are detained at the expense of the Department of Justice.

COUNTRY TO WHICH DEPORTATION TAKES PLACE

A fact often too little appreciated by those anxious to rid the country of "undesirables" with all possible speed is that the United States can deport no one unless some other country is willing to receive the deportee. No matter how deportable a foreigner may be under our laws or how entirely unwelcome here, we must keep him here unless some other country is willing to take him in, for he cannot eternally wander the seas. It often takes a long time to find just what country will accept him, and in such a case detention in jail seems endless.

The 1917 immigration act states:

> that the deportation of aliens provided for in this act shall, at the option of the Secretary of Labor, be to the country whence they came or to the foreign port at which such aliens embarked for the United States; or if such embarkation was for foreign contiguous territory, to the foreign port at which they embarked for such territory; or, if such aliens entered foreign contiguous territory from the United States and later entered the United States, or if such aliens are held by the country from which they entered the United States not to be subjects or citizens of such country, and such country refuses to permit their reentry, or imposes any condition upon permitting reentry, then to the country in which they resided prior to entering the country from which they entered the United States.[2]

The verboseness of the provision does not add to its clarity. Indeed, one court at least has noted it and referred to the

[1] In such cases the aliens are also paid $1.00 a day witness fee.

[2] Sec. 20.

" single, ill-drawn sentence of this section." [1] Does " country whence they came " mean the country in which the persons were born or whence they originally came, or does it refer to a country where they had *resided* previous to entry into the United States? The Supreme Court has done little to clarify the statement by saying " ' country ' means the State which, at the time of deportation, includes the place from which an alien came." [2] Lower courts too have made confusion worse confounded. Thus it has been held that " ' return to the country whence he came ' unquestionably requires his deportation to the country of his nativity or citizenship," [3] or on the other hand that it means " return to the country in which he last had domicile " prior to an unlawful entry into the United States.[4] Thus if a man is domiciled in Canada with the intention of becoming a *bona fide* resident there, he is deportable to Canada.[5] Still another court has held that the departmental rule or custom identifying the country whence an alien came as the land of which he is a citizen or subject is plainly wrong and that the " exact meaning of coming from a country cannot be stated in general and accurate terms. The meaning depends on the circumstances." [6] One particular case shows the difficulties of interpretation. On October 29, 1914 a man was ordered deported to Austria, but together with the order went the statement: " In view of the fact that a state of war exists in Europe at this time, the alien should not be conveyed to New York for deportation until he can be re-

[1] United States *ex rel.* Karamian *v.* Curran, 16 Fed. (2d) 958, 960.

[2] United States *ex rel.* Mensevich *v.* Tod, 264 U. S. 134.

[3] United States *ex rel.* Lisafeld *v.* Smith, 2 Fed. (2d) 90.

[4] *Ex parte* Gytl, 210 Fed. 918.

[5] United States *ex rel.* Borowiec *v.* Flynn, 22 Fed. (2d) 302.

[6] United States *ex rel.* Karamian *v.* Curran, *supra.*

turned with safety. In the meantime he may remain at large on bond." In 1920, the bondsmen were called on to surrender the alien for deportation, but after six years at large, he did not appear. In 1923 he was found and, on petition of his counsel, was allowed a stay of deportation for one year. Then he surrendered and was allowed to go at large on a new bond, but on May 27, 1924—almost ten years after the original arrest—the Department of Labor directed that deportation proceed. After two months more, the warrant of deportation was amended so as to direct deportation to Poland instead of Austria, as the province of Galicia, whence the man had originally come, was now part of Poland. The man protested against the change but the court held:

there was no error in the order amending the warrant of deportation to require deportation to Poland instead of Austria. The statute provides that the alien shall be returned to the country whence he came, which mans deportation to the country of his nativity or citizenship. . . . In August 1925, the government of Poland issued the necessary passport.[1]

The same sentence contains still other provisions, so deportation may be " to the foreign port at which the aliens embarked for the United States." According to this, an Italian starting from France could be deported to France and not necessarily to the place in Italy from which he originally came. Unless he were ill, insane, or discovered to be

[1] Seif *v.* Nagle, 14 Fed. (2d) 416. It was also argued in the case that the right to deport had been waived by the long delay in carrying out deportation after the Department of Labor had assumed jurisdiction of the man. The court found no merit in the point. " When the original order of 1914 was made directing deportation to Austria, because of the war, the alien could not have been deported to that country. Since the war, even as late as 1924, the alien himself has exerted efforts to prevent deportation and has been successful in obtaining several stays."

a serious criminal, he might slip unnoticed into the population of France.[1]

In an attempt to summarize the somewhat vague situation, the provisions may be divided into three divisions, as follows: (1) The general provisions that aliens deported under the statute shall go to their foreign port of embarkation or the country whence they originally came, at the Secretary's option; (2) the special provision for such as embarked originally for foreign contiguous territory. At the option of the Secretary, such aliens are to be deported to the foreign port at which they embarked for such foreign contiguous territory;[2] (3) the provision concerning (a) those who entered from foreign contiguous territory *after* having entered that territory *from* the United States, and (b) those refused unqualified readmittance by the country from which they entered the United States. Both of these subclasses

are to be sent by virtue of the power given in the first subdivision (there is no other) to the country of their citizenship *or* that of their residence before going to the country from which they entered. . . . The Secretary is (to decide which). So that the cause as to his optional power affects every subdivision of the clumsy sentence.[3]

Let us illustrate by concrete cases. An Italian coming to the United States in 1904, remaining four months, and then going to Canada for three years before returning to the

[1] France has received so many "undesirables" that she is trying to insist that deportees be routed directly through the country and out again to their country of destination.

[2] The court stated in United States *ex rel.* Karamian *v.* Curran, 16 Fed. (2d) 958, p. 960: "no reason can be seen for sending those who come *directly* to the United States to either the port of embarkation or the 'country whence they came' but sending those who came *indirectly* only to the embarkation port."

[3] *Ibid.*, p. 961.

United States on becoming deportable would be liable to deportation to Italy rather than Canada, in the discretion of the Secretary.[1] Take another illustration. A Swedish subject might land in New York in transit to Canada, where he went immediately. If he subsequently entered the United States illegally without inspection he would be deported to Sweden rather than Canada, again in the discretion of the Secretary. So if a person uses Canada or Mexico as a doorstep by which to enter the United States, he is thought to enter not from Canada or Mexico but from the country of his citizenship or the country in which he lived previous to entering Canada or Mexico.

Non-Canadians and non-Mexicans perpetually wandering across the border into the United States have caused untold difficulties in the border situation. A "reciprocal agreement" with Canada attempts to alleviate the situation by providing that an alien, not a Canadian or citizen of Great Britain, domiciled in Canada, who applies for admission to the United States and is rejected by the immigration officer to whom he applies and then illegally tries to enter the United States, is not readmissible to Canada.[2]

The statute, as already indicated, gives the Secretary of Labor option as to where he wishes to deport an alien. He makes the decision, not subject to court review,[3] for the authority and "weight of responsibility for possible human woe"[4] are placed on his shoulders. In cases involving

[1] Lazzaro *v.* Weedin, 4 Fed. (2d) 704, affirming 293 Fed. 475; United States *v.* Testolini, 14 Fed. (2d) 76.

[2] As the agreement is reciprocal, the United States would refuse readmission to an alien arriving from Canada under similar circumstances, and he would be deported from Canada to the place from which he had come or of which he was a citizen rather than the United States.

[3] Lazzaro *v.* Weedin, 4 Fed. (2d) 704; MacKusick *v.* Johnson, 3 Fed. (2d) 398.

[4] United States *ex rel.* Karamian *v.* Curran, 16 Fed. (2d) 958, 961.

political or religious difficulties, the " option " of the Secretary becomes of especial humanitarian importance. A deportable anti-Fascist faces serious consequences if returned to Italy. Guido Serio is an example of a person in just such a situation. Arrested in May, 1930, after a speech in which he was alleged to have denounced Mussolini and the Pope, and to have declared his willingness to lead American workers against the government in the event of another war, when he was given a hearing he was held to be an anarchist and ordered deported to Italy. He then appealed to the federal district court to be allowed to leave the country voluntarily to go to Russia. Judge Bondy deferred judgment and returned the case to the Department of Labor for further consideration by the Secretary. The Department did not change its decision, and the order of deportation to Italy remained, for the Department felt " Whatever may be the result of the alien's deportation to Italy is beyond the scope of this inquiry." [1]

The power of the United States in deportation cases cannot legally extend across the seas. However, serious questions of policy arise on humanitarian grounds. Furthermore, representatives of foreign governments might easily discover one of the many causes of deportation against one of their citizens whom they wished returned to stop the spread of subversive ideas against their country. They might report him for deportation, anonymously or otherwise, and if he were found deportable on any charge, could be returned to them. It has always been against United States policy to allow extradition for political crimes, but unless investigation is made of the source of reports to the immigration authorities, there is grave danger that deportation where political activity is concerned might become a kind of back-handed extradition process.

[1] Quoted in the *Nation*, November 19, 1930, p. 541.

Whether or not a given country accepts a deported person depends on its willingness to recognize him as a citizen. In other words, if he has a valid, unexpired passport of that country, it cannot refuse to receive him. If he has no passport of that country and the country issues one for him, he is thereby denoted acceptable in that country. Hence an important stage of deportation proceedings is that of obtaining passports for possible deportees where necessary.

The United States cannot ordinarily deport aliens without passports, except to Japan, China and foreign contiguous territory,[1] and in cases of "reshipment foreign" as seamen, for then only seamen's papers, issued by the masters of the vessels, are necessary. Such reshipment is usually available only to seamen, as it is not impossible to secure nearly enough such positions for even the deportable seamen, but sometimes other "men without a country" succeed in reshipping.[2] In other deportation cases, depor-

[1] *Immigration Laws*, etc., *op. cit.*, Rule 19, Subdivision H, par. 1. During the winter of 1931 the Chinese Consul General in New York stated that China no longer would accept deportees without passports, but on February 5, 1931 the deportation division of the bureau of immigration wrote the author that deportees were still being sent to China without passports.

[2] In 1929, 802 persons were allowed to ship one way foreign as members of crews in lieu of deportation, and of these 801 had had experience as seamen.—*Annual Report of the Commissioner General*, etc., *for 1929*, p. 20. The following year the economic depression was reflected in the situation, for only 555 men left the country as members of the crews of departing vessels, and of these it is not known how many had had previous experience as seamen.—*Idem* for 1930, p. 22.

Aliens who leave the United States by "reshipment foreign" are technically considered deported and are in no better position as regards return to this country than other deportees, unless they have been allowed to "reship foreign" as voluntary departure before the issuance of warrants of arrest.—*Vide ibid.*, p. 23. The advantage of "reshipment foreign" to the alien lies in being paid the wages of a member of the crew during the trip; the advantage to the United States consists in considerable financial saving. Assuming the cost of deportation to Europe to be $100 per deportee, the savings during 1930 to the appropriation were $55,500.

tees must be provided with valid, unexpired passports,[1] and with proper transit visas for countries through which they must pass *en route,* if such visas are required. Apparently, however, deportees are sometimes allowed to slip through without passports, transit visas or papers, so that such countries as France and Germany are making efforts to protect themselves against the "dumping" at their doors of undesirables not even of their nationality.[2]

If the alien to be deported is in possession of a valid, unexpired passport and does not need to secure transit visas, he may be sent out of the United States as soon as he has completed any sentence he may have to serve, and when deportation arrangements are complete. If, on the other hand, he has a valid but expired passport, as is often true in the case of a person long absent from home, he must have the passport renewed before he may return to his own country. If he has expatriated himself by too long residence abroad, as, for instance, in the case of a German residing abroad more than ten years,[3] he may not return to his home country at all.

If the person whom the United States seeks to deport never had a passport or lost it or threw it away, he must usually be provided with a new one before he may leave this country. And it is often impossible to secure one. As the United States has no diplomatic relations with Soviet Russia, there are no facilities for securing Russian passports here, and, except in the rare instances where a Russian

[1] Of course deportation to Canada and Mexico is not discussed here.

[2] The requirement of transit visas is one means of accomplishing this. France is attempting to discover, for example, what deportees are to be routed directly *through* the country and not allowed to remain.

[3] Law of June 1, 1870, sec. 21, *Imperial Law Gazette* of Germany, p. 355, quoted by R. W. Flournoy and M O. Hudson, *A Collection of Nationality Laws of Various Countries* (New York, 1929), p. 311.

has a valid, unexpired Soviet passport, no deportations can take place to Soviet Russia. The difficulties in discovering whether or not a Soviet passport would still be valid are so great that the bureau of immigration has issued instructions [1] that Soviet citizens, even if possessed of such passports "should not be conveyed to seaports for deportation except by express authority of the bureau." The hundreds of other Russians with outstanding deportation warrants against them must, for the present at least, remain in this country.[2] A similar situation obtains with regard to Armenians. As a general rule, an Armenian who has once left Turkey may not return there,[3] and so may not be deported to that country. The situation of an Armenian whose birthplace is now Soviet territory is similar to that of Russians. Sometimes Armenians are deported to Greece or Syria, but this is rare, and if their birthplace is now Turkish or Soviet territory, deportation must be indefinitely postponed.

Other difficulties arise in obtaining passports because of varying nationality laws. Nationality may be acquired by the method of *jus solis* or of *jus sanguinis* or a combination of the two. Thus a child born in the United States and "subject to the jurisdiction thereof," excluding children of ambassadors, etc., and enemies in war-time, is an American

[1] Bureau of immigration, General Order No. 152, March 27, 1930.

[2] For instance, many Russian refugees are in the United States (legally or illegally), bearing certificates of identity issued by the League of Nations. These certificates would not serve as passports in cases of deportation, for no other country would be required to accept the deportees.

[3] "Ottoman subjects who during the War of Independence took no part in the National movement, kept out of Turkey and did not return from July 24, 1923 to the date of the publication of this law, have forfeited Turkish nationality."—Law No. 1042, of May 23, 1927, quoted by Flournoy and Hudson, *op. cit.*, p. 569. Furthermore, the return to Turkey of all persons deprived of their Turkish citizenship is prohibited."—Law of May 28, 1928, quoted *ibid.*, p. 571.

citizen according to American law, as is also a child born of American parents in another country. Combinations of law according to the *jus solis* and the *jus sanguinis* may result in the acquisition at birth of two or even more nationalities. A child born during the stay of a French family in the United States would be an American under American law and French according to French law. Furthermore, a child may be born without any nationality, or a child born with one nationality may later lose it without gaining another, and so become "stateless." It is the stateless individual who causes particular difficulty in deportation, for he can claim no country as his own which will receive him.[1]

The varying national complications play infinite variations on the citizenship theme. Obviously no country is anxious to receive a deportee unless it firmly establishes the fact that such person is its citizen. Indeed, international difficulties may arise if deportation occurs to a country of which the deported person is not a citizen. Thus the Polish government presented a claim of $152.35 to the United States government for reimbursement of expenses incurred by the community of Rzsczyczany in repatriating an insane person who turned out to have been erroneously deported there from the United States. The money was paid by Congressional authorization.[2] To avoid the situation of receiving "undesirable" people who turn out not to be

[1] For discussion of the problems of dual and multiple nationality and statelessness, *vide* Edwin Borchard, *Diplomatic Protection of Citizens Abroad*, esp. §§ 11 and 319. *Vide* also D. H. Miller, "Nationality and Other Problems Discussed at the Hague", *Foreign Affairs*, vol. viii, no. 4, July, 1930.

For legislation in regard to repatriation and deportation in other countries, *vide Migration Laws and Treaties, op. cit.*, vol. ii, ch. x, and vol. iii, ch. iv, § 4.

[2] H. R. 12037, 71st Congress, 2nd Session, April 30, 1930. Authorized February 14, 1931.

citizens, countries usually make assurance doubly sure before issuing passports in deportation cases.

In some instances countries refuse to receive back people who have been their citizens but who have expatriated themselves. Thus a German who by ten years' residence abroad might have lost his German citizenship or a Hungarian who might have lost his by the same means,[1] even if never naturalized elsewhere, would not be received unless he had taken steps to retain his citizenship. Some countries refuse to issue a passport when on investigation it is shown that the person for whom a passport is desired left the country "forever." [2] If a Canadian naturalized citizen comes to the United States and remains, Canada regards him as having left permanently and refuses to permit his return under ordinary circumstances, for " when any citizen of Canada who is a British subject by naturalization, or any British subject not born in Canada having Canadian domicile shall have resided for one year outside of Canada, he shall be presumed to have lost Canadian domicile and shall cease to be a Canadian citizen." [3] So a person born in England but living in Canada since early childhood would lose his domicile there if he resided a year in the United States. If he should become deportable from the United States he would be sent to England, whence he had come many years before.

The World War added not a little to the difficulties in determining citizenship, because of the many changes in terri-

[1] *Hungarian Law of Dec. 20, 1879*, art. 31, quoted Flournoy and Hudson, *op. cit.*, pp. 340-1.

[2] According to the bureau of immigration, this is the practice in Scandinavian countries.

[3] *Immigration Act of 1910*, sec. 2, quoted by Flournoy and Hudson, *op. cit.*, p. 74. The same act provided that Canadian domicile could be acquired only by a person having his domicile for at least five years in Canada.

tory and governments.[1] Some of the difficulties are found in the case of a man, of Greek tongue, born in Veria, Macedonia, which was formerly part of the Turkish Empire and after the war became part of the Greek Republic. Although the man's citizenship had been Turkish, he was ordered deported to Greece. The Greek government refused to issue a passport for him or to allow him to enter. The man requested his discharge in *habeas corpus* proceeding, but the court held him not entitled to immediate discharge, for

> under the broad discretion vested in him by law the Secretary of Labor may find other means to carry out the order of deportation and the utmost the courts can or will do is to discharge the appellant from further imprisonment if the government fails to execute the order of deportation within a reasonable time.

The lower court allowed two months for the Secretary of Labor to get around the international difficulties involved in exercising his " option," and the Circuit Court of Appeals upheld it.[2] Instances of post-war difficulty might be multiplied. A Baltic state will not take back natives of what is now its territory but was formerly Russia unless those people have opted for the citizenship of the new Baltic state since its independence.

Every effort must, however, be made to obtain a passport for an alien detained in deportation proceedings, despite the legion of difficulties which may be involved. Local immigration officials make the first attempt through the nearest consul of the deportee's nationality.[3] If the local consul is without authority to issue passports, or doubts the citizenship of the applicant, or for any other reason refuses to

[1] It will be noted in the cases quoted in this study that all names of countries are given as they are since the war.

[2] Caranica *v.* Nagle, 28 Fed. (2d) 955.

[3] *Immigration Laws*, etc., *op. cit.*, Rule 19, Subdivision H, par. 1.

issue a passport, the bureau of immigration in Washington is requested to have the matter taken up through diplomatic channels.[1] In such cases, the deportation division of the bureau usually sends a letter to the particular foreign embassy or legation, submitting the necessary documentary evidence and requesting the issuance of a passport.

If the citizenship of the deportee is in doubt, the matter is often referred abroad for investigation. The delays consequent to securing a report from Europe are so great that two to three months is usually necessary. In an attempt to hurry matters, whenever an alien is detained in jail or anywhere else at federal government expense, a cabled reply is requested, the expense of such cable to be paid by the bureau of immigration.[2] Experience has shown that detention cost is much greater than cable cost, to say nothing of the alleviation of the situation for the person awaiting decision. Even if no cabled reply is requested, notice is sent the foreign diplomatic agent that "whatever action you may find it convenient to take with a view to expediting the issuance of passport facilities will be greatly appreciated." [3]

In some cases, request for the issuance of a passport cannot go direct from the bureau of immigration of the Department of Labor but must travel entirely through diplomatic channels. So a letter may go from the local immigration district to the deportation division of the bureau of

[1] Then "two extra copies of the record of hearing, two copies of Passport Data for Alien Deportees, six photographs of the alien, and all documentary evidence of nationality and citizenship shall be promptly forwarded to the bureau of immigration for appropriate action."—*Ibid.*

[2] This has been done only since 1928. If the alien is held in a public state institution or in a prison serving sentence, such procedure is not followed. In many instances states have been vehement in their protests at the federal government's attempt to save its own funds but its lack of hurry where detention is at state expense. *Vide* ch. iv, p. 121 *et seq.*

[3] Mimeographed form letter.

immigration of the Department of Labor, to the Department of State, to the embassy or legation of the foreign country from whom passport is requested, to the Foreign Office *in* that country, to the local officials in the town where the person was born whose citizenship is laboriously being established, and then back through the same devious channel, before authority is given the embassy or local consul in the United States to issue the passport. Now and then an even more roundabout procedure is followed, of having the foreign embassy notify the bureau of immigration that authorization has been granted for the issuance of a passport; then the local commissioner or district director of immigration is notified; he in turn notifies the local foreign consulate of authorization for local issuance of a passport.

Sometimes a deportee turns up his old passport while the bureau is negotiating to obtain a new passport through diplomatic means, or else the local immigration office succeeds in getting the much-desired passport. Of course the bureau is immediately notified in all such cases.[1]

The exact procedure of securing passports varies from country to country, and changes with the times and officials in charge.[2] The passport division of the bureau must attempt to obtain speed amid the difficulties of diplomatic convention.

[1] Bureau of immigration, General Order No. 152.

[2] The following are illustrations of the varying types of procedure, though change occurs rapidly and the situation may change overnight from when this was written.

Countries of South and Central America, Bulgaria, Czechoslovakia, Denmark, Roumania, Austria, Belgium, Spain, France, Greece, Norway, Sweden, Holland, Finland and Persia issue passports direct from the legation to the bureau of immigration, after authorization is granted to issue a passport. On the other hand, Germany and Poland request cases to be handled through the Department of State if a question of establishing citizenship is involved. So if the local German consul refuses to issue a passport, the case is referred by the deportation division of the

Diplomatic red tape and delay in investigation may cause interminable slowness in the issuance of passports. Then deliberate procrastination by representatives of foreign governments is not unknown. The result has been that the United States has shown signs of impatience over the difficulties of obtaining passports. In 1927 the Secretary of Labor called attention to the situation:

In a number of instances the department has been unable to effect deportation of undesirable aliens because of passport complications and the refusal of foreign Governments to accept from the United States aliens who should be deported to those countries. These refusals involve criminal and mental defective cases, as well as those who for other reasons have become a burden upon public beneficence. Frequently the foreign Governments decline the responsibility solely on the grounds that by absence from the homeland the alien has become expatriated.

bureau of immigration to the Department of State to the German legation, who communicate with the German foreign office for authorization. Until May, 1930, all Polish cases were handled similarly, but since then the bureau of immigration refers cases to the Department of State, which in turn reports them to the Polish legation in Washington. The Department of State then instruct the local Polish consul in the district where the alien is detained to cable the home authorities for verification of citizenship. The Irish Free State has different procedure at different times, for sometimes it wishes letters requesting issuance of passports to be sent to it direct from the Department of Labor and sometimes through the Department of State. Sometimes word is sent directly from the Free State legation to the Department of Labor that the Free State "passport control officer" in New York has been instructed to issue a passport and forward it to the local consul where the alien is held; sometimes this word is sent through the Department of State.

Some countries, such as Roumania and Greece, issue certificates of travel to deportees in lieu of passports.

The United States government paid approximately $3300 for passports for deportees during the fiscal year ending June 30, 1930. Some countries allow the government reduced rates, but few do this. If an alien is deported at steamship company expense, it pays for his passport.

In all such cases, however, it should be pointed out, the alien has not actually acquired any other nationality; if he had, naturally the deportation order would be to the country of such alien's allegiance.

The situation seems to me to require legislative action, and it is suggested that suitable enactment be made whereby immigration shall be suspended or further restricted from countries which refuse to accept back deportable aliens or unreasonably delay issuance of passports for those whose last allegiance was to their Governments. This action is recommended also as to nationals of such countries from which it is impracticable to obtain passports through the usual channels.

While referring to these cases of difficulty in effecting deportation, I believe it only fair to call attention to a somewhat analogous situation existing in some of the States of the United States as regards citizens of this country, former residents of those States, who become deportable from other countries to this because of becoming public charges or of insanity. Because of absence from those States they refuse to accept back from other nations former resident citizens of their Commonwealths. As a matter of experience, this difficulty arises only as to American citizens who become public charges in near-by foreign territory, and the complication does not frequently present itself, but is of sufficient consequence to cause friction in the enforcement of our own deportation laws . . . if a particular state refuses to accept former residents, the only course left open to the country seeking to return a citizen is to convey him into the United States and abandon him at some point. . . . [1]

[1] *Annual Report of the Secretary of Labor for*, etc., *1927*, pp. 191-2.

By act approved March 2, 1929 (45 Stat. 1495) it was provided "that upon application of the Secretary of State, the Secretary of the Interior is authorized to transfer to Saint Elizabeth's Hospital, in the District of Columbia, for treatment, all American citizens legally adjudged insane in the Dominion of Canada, whose legal residence in one of the States, Territories or the District of Columbia it has been impossible to establish. Upon the ascertainment of the legal residence of persons so trans-

During the economic depression of 1930, a proposal was made in Congress to embody the Secretary's recommendation in legislation,[1] but nothing was done about it because of the international repercussions of such a retaliatory policy and because of the lack of relationship between the particular offenders and victims of the policy if carried out.

On the other hand, if a person has the citizenship of more than one country he may be accepted by either country. Here the Secretary of Labor may decide where the deportee is to be sent, and in such choice the "responsibility for possible human woe" may be great.

In many instances persons are deported to countries in which they have never been. For instance, a woman from Czechoslovakia, married to a Cuban and living in the United States, became ill here and was deported to Cuba, where she had never been, because by marriage she had acquired her husband's citizenship, according to the laws of both Czechoslovakia and Cuba. A case involving a similar situation came to court concerning a woman born in Russia and married to a Pole. The court held that the woman, unable to secure a passport for Russia, might be deported to Poland, notwithstanding the fact that she had never been there, be-

ferred to the hospital, the superintendent of the hospital shall thereupon transfer such persons to their respective places of residence. . . ."

The act does not provide for repatriation of others than insane or from places other than Canada. The number of American citizen public charges in other countries than Canada is not known, nor the number of otherwise "undesirable" Americans in other countries, but this matter merits attention.

[1] S. J. Res. 207, 3rd Session, 71st Congress, originally provided (sec. 4), "if any country refuses to admit or readmit aliens subject to deportation under the law of the United States, and who are citizens or subjects of such country, the Secretary of State may, in his discretion, decline to issue a visa to any national of such country seeking to enter the United States." The provision was dropped in committee.

cause she had become a Polish citizen by her marriage.[1] A German girl of Austrian parentage on becoming insane in the United States was deported to Austria, where she had never been, as by German and Austrian law she had acquired the citizenship of her parents.

A somewhat anomalous situation exists regarding those naturalized American citizens who lose their citizenship in the United States. Could they then become deportable from this country? If they expatriate themselves from the United States by naturalization in another country in conformity with its laws their situation seems clear, for they could be deported to the country of their new citizenship. If they take oaths of allegiance to any foreign states in connection with military service, those states might doubtless recognize them as citizens and so be willing to receive them back if deported from this country. If they take up residence in the country of their nativity and remain there two years and so lose their American citizenship, they might on returning to the United States and becoming deportable be accepted back by the country of nativity, but probably would not. If they lost their American citizenship on the ground of having fraudulently procured it, they might be received back by their own country but probably would not.[2] If they took up permanent residence abroad within five years of naturalization, their citizenship might be revoked, and they might be received by their own country if later deported

[1] Weglinsky *v.* Zurbrick, 38 Fed. (2d) 985.

[2] This might become of practical importance during a wave of anti-radical agitation.

For interesting cases of revocation of citizenship, *vide* United States *ex rel.* Canfora *v.* Williams, 186 Fed. 354; United States *v.* Wusterbarth, 249 Fed. 908; United States *v.* Stupiello, 260 Fed. 483. *Vide supra*, ch. viii, pp. 227 *et seq.*

from the United States. At least one may say there is possibility of deportation of *former* American citizens.[1]

The "dumping" of deportees, particularly criminals, seriously ill, and insane, into other countries from the United States, with little or no warning, made those countries gradually realize that a social duty devolved upon them in such repatriation. Consulates of various countries in the United States began to request notification of the date and steamer on which deportees of certain "undesirable," or even of all classes, were being sent, so that arrangements might be made for their reception and care on arrival, if such care were necessary. In 1925 a general order was issued by the bureau of immigration that the proper consular representative of the country of which a deportee is a subject be notified at the earliest possible moment of the date and steamship upon which deportation takes place, and the port of debarkation, in cases of subjects of Great Britain, Austria, Poland, and Denmark.[2] But the next year the British embassy, through the United States Department of State,

> requested that notification be given to the appropriate consular officer in advance in all cases where British subjects of insane or criminal tendencies are to be deported from the United States, in order that timely arrangements may be made for meeting the deportee at the port of debarkation. Such advices should be given in cases of this nature when making application for passports for aliens of this class. The term "criminal tendencies" will be understood to apply to all aliens who are known to have been engaged in crime either in the United States or Great Britain.[3]

[1] For discussion of expatriation, *vide Foreign Language Information Service Interpreter Release,* vol. ii, nos. 41 and 46, Nov. 13 and Dec. 15, 1925.

[2] Bureau of immigration, General Order No. 10, 8th supplement, Aug. 5, 1925.

[3] *Idem,* No. 70, June 29, 1926.

About a year and a half later, the British government further extended its interest by requesting that advance detailed records of all destitute and insane British subjects to be deported to British territory be furnished consular officers, even in cases where the deportees already possessed proof of nationality.[1] It took two years more for Great Britain to take note of all deportees, by requesting that advance detailed records of *all* British subjects to be returned to British territory be furnished by the district in which the case originates to the nearest British consular office, even in cases where deportees have valid passports.[2] Other countries have less comprehensive arrangements, but they too are beginning to realize the international implications that deportation has for them.

For instance, in 1927 the Irish Free State began to request notification of deportation to that country of persons afflicted with tuberculosis.[3] Three years later they added insane persons to the list, with request that notification be given " in sufficient time " for the Free State passport control officer to communicate with Dublin in order that appropriate steps may be taken for the care of such deportees on their embarkation."[4] Poland wishes the Polish consul in New York to be notified long enough before deportation of insane Polish citizens so that he may designate the port of entry for such persons into Poland, while Denmark wants notification of deportation of such of their citizens as are criminal or insane. Czechoslovakia has the unique system of notifying the Ministry of Social Welfare and the Ministry of Foreign Affairs in Prague when informed that de-

1 First supplement to General Order No. 70, Feb. 3, 1928.

2 Second supplement to General Order No. 70, March 26, 1930.

3 Bureau of immigration, General Order No. 99.

4 *Idem*, Third supplement to General Order No. 70.

portation of one of their citizens is to take place; if health is involved, the Ministry of Health is also notified.[1]

Since 1930, the representative of a foreign country in the United States has known when one of its citizens is to be returned, regardless of whether or not the deported person has a valid passport. The bureau " and the proper consular representative of the country of which the deportee is a subject shall be notified at the earliest possible moment (by telegraph if necessary) of the date and steamship upon which the alien is to be deported, and the port of debarkation." [2]

Thus a beginning has been made toward preventing indiscriminate dumping of deportees from the United States, and toward international cooperation in social care. Yet it is only a beginning and the practice is still limited by lack of real social viewpoint between nations. It is worthy of more than passing note that in the last analysis American deportation procedure is not merely an administrative problem of American government but also one of international importance.

AMERICAN-BORN CHILDREN ACCOMPANYING DEPORTEES

Further implications of the *jus solis* are to be noted in connection with deportation. Often aliens residing in the United States have children born in this country, and these children are American citizens under the law of the United

[1] In May, 1929 the author was told at the Ministry of Social Welfare in Prague that Czechoslovakia has "repatriation subsidies" in the national budget, to aid returned deportees. It was also stated that if a man has been deported from the United States for illegal entry, he is not allowed to emigrate again to North America. If it is discovered that many illegal entries are going to the United States from one particular district in Czechoslovakia, passports are refused to all residents of that district for a certain period of time.

[2] Bureau of immigration, General Order No. 152.

States. Even a girl who entered the country without anyone realizing her pregnant condition and gave birth to an illegitimate child soon after her arrival would be the mother of an American citizen.

Obviously no child born in the United States could be deported from the country, as this country cannot deport its own citizens. However, because of the possibility of dual citizenship, a child born here of foreign parents might by the *jus sanguinis* acquire the citizenship of his father or mother, or both. Such a child could be entered on the passport of his deported parents or on that of the one from whom he derived his non-American citizenship.[1] Then the parents who are being deported, if they are willing and able, may pay the cost of the child's transportation back to the country to which they are being deported. Otherwise a social agency may defray expenses, as the government will never do so; should the government pay transportation costs, it would to all intents and purposes be deporting its own citizens. If the parents do not pay for the child's trip and no relatives or social agency can be found to do it, the child must remain in this country.

The child also remains here if the country to which the parents are being deported refuses to accept it, as is often the case in regard to illegitimate children. The Irish Free State will not, under ordinary circumstances, allow an American-born illegitimate child of an Irish mother deported to the Free State to accompany her. On the other hand, Germany accepts such children, for they are German citizens, according to German law. Many interesting and sad cases arise under this possibility of separating deported parents and their American-born children.

[1] If the child is legitimate, it takes the citizenship of his father, should that citizenship be different from that of the mother; if the child is illegitimate, it takes the citizenship of the mother.

During the winter of 1930, the Department of Service for the Foreign Born of the National Council of Jewish Women called my attention to a particularly tragic case. In deporting a Canadian Jewish woman to Canada, it was thought her illegitimate baby, born in the United States, could accompany her. As there was no need for a passport for the mother, the question of whether or not the baby would be accepted by Canada did not arise until mother and baby reached the border. There the mother was accepted, but the child was left in the United States. For want of other detention facilities, the baby was taken to a border jail and kept there for a month by the sheriff's wife. Then the Council of Jewish Women got the baby and arranged for its care.

The International Migration Service calls attention to the fact that sometimes when another country refuses to accept an American-born child accompanying its parents or one of them, it is possible later to secure the child's admission to that country.

DETENTION AGAIN

Let us return to the person being held in jail or out on bond, awaiting the disposition of his case. Usually he has no idea of the interminable investigations necessary to secure a passport and cannot understand why he may wait in jail for weeks or months. His being in jail does not indicate that he is a criminal, and yet his stay there may be greatly prolonged. The courts have repeatedly held that indefinite imprisonment while awaiting deportation is not authorized by the immigration act or regulations, and that a deportee must be sent out of the country within a "reasonable time." [1]

[1] United States *ex rel.* Ross *v.* Wallis, 279 Fed. 401; *Ex parte* Mathews, 277 Fed. 857; United States *v.* Howe, 222 Fed. 96; Petition of Brooks, 5 Fed. (2d) 238. The Brooks case held that an alien cannot be imprisoned indefinitely pending recognition of the Soviet Government by the United States. The Mathews case had previously held that an alien

What a " reasonable time " is seems to vary with the speed in carrying out proceedings, the difficulties of obtaining a passport, and the availability of judicial relief. No statistics are available as to the length of detention in general, but it varies over wide periods.

The social consequences to the deportees of long detention in jail may be imagined,—of being kept from work and the support of a family,[1] of associations formed with all sorts of characters during long periods of idleness in jail, of the possible effect on health. The situation of detention of federal prisoners became so serious that finally New York City notified the Department of Justice they could no longer handle federal prisoners in the New York City jail, so a garage was converted into a jail and on March 15, 1929 all federal jail prisoners in the southern and eastern districts of New York were moved to the new institution.[2] Congress began to realize the situation and by act of May 12, 1930[3] a bureau of prisons was established in the Department of Justice and given authority " to provide suitable quarters for the safekeeping, care and subsistence of all persons " for any reason held as federal prisoners.[4] The director of the bureau of prisons

in confinement for months on a warrant of deportation which the government was unable to execute because of uncertainty as to the country of his nativity or the absence of a recognized government was entitled to discharge on *habeas corpus*.

[1] Federal prisoners in county jails rarely have any work.

[2] *Annual Report of the Attorney General for the Fiscal Year Ended June 30, 1930*, p. 77.

Of course all types of federal prisoners could be held in such a jail, but in New York the proximity of Ellis Island as a detention station means that usually only immigration cases where criminal proceedings are involved are held in the federal jail.

[3] H. R. 7832, 71st Congress, 2d Session.

[4] The Commissioner General of Immigration and the Secretary of Labor in their annual reports had for several years recommended the need for such detention facilities as might be necessary either for immigration purposes alone or in connection with the enforcement of other laws.

may contract, for a period not exceeding three years, with the proper authorities of any State or Territory or political subdivision thereof, for the imprisonment, subsistence, care and proper employment of any person held under authority of any United States statute. . . . The rate to be paid for the care and custody of said persons shall take into consideration the character of the quarters furnished, sanitary conditions, and quality of subsistence. The taxes to be paid may be such as will permit and encourage the proper authorities to provide reasonably decent, sanitary, and healthful quarters and subsistence for persons held as United States prisoners. . . . Hereafter all persons convicted of an offense against the United States shall be committed, for such terms of imprisonment and to such types of institutions as the court may direct, to the custody of the Attorney General . . . who shall designate the places of confinement. . . . The Attorney General may designate any available, suitable, or appropriate institutions, whether maintained by the Federal Government or otherwise, or whether within or without the judicial district in which convicted. The Attorney General is also authorized to order the transfer of any person held under authority of any United States statute from one institution to another if in his judgment it shall be for the well-being of the prisoner or relieve overcrowded or unhealthful conditions in the institution. . . . [1]

Appropriations were asked for when the bill was passed to establish two federal jails, one on the northern and one on the southern border. Even when they are completed "it will still be necessary and advisable to continue to house in local institutions the greater portion of Federal short-term prisoners and persons awaiting trial." [2] This includes, of

[1] The procedure of transfer had already been followed in some deportation cases when conditions of overcrowding made it imperative. Thus when conditions in the Wayne County jail and other detention quarters in Detroit made it necessary, deportation cases were transferred to the Lucas County jail in Toledo, Ohio.

[2] *Annual Report of the Attorney General, op. cit., for 1930*, p. 91.

course, many immigration prisoners awaiting deportation.[1] During the deportation raids and round-ups in the winter of 1930 to 1931 the same conditions of overcrowding and detention prevailed as before in county jails.[2]

Detention of the Cases Studied

Three hundred and forty-three of the 612 individuals studied were held in county jails for periods varying from one day to thirteen months, with the modal length of detention falling at two and one-half months.

The records contain many requests for early release from jail, chiefly on account of need for work to support families. A letter from the Erie County Jail in Buffalo says:

The only crime ever indicted (sic) against me is that I wanted work to provide my family with sustenance. . . . For over twelve solid months I fought against the industrial depression I found so rampant in Canada but employment was not be had. Under circumstances like mine wouldn't you yourself have done the same and felt yourself justified? When I left England I hadn't the slightest idea of entering America but when I experienced the state of trade in Canada, I wrote your representative in London, Ontario, but my efforts to get in on a sound legal basis proved useless. I eventually took a chance and entered your country illegally. I was not desirous to rob, embezzle or forge, all I wanted was work. . . . To me my detention means little, to my dependents all. I have no qualms of

[1] Public No. 440, June 28, 1930, provides for better border accommodations for the immigration service. This may alleviate the situation somewhat.

[2] The bureau of prisons in the Department of Justice in 1930 established regular inspection service for federal prisoners in county jails, and began to work out a new form of contract devised to meet the suggestions of the statute that the character of accommodations furnished be taken into account in setting the rate of payment for board of federal prisoners in jails.—*Annual Report of the Attorney General*, etc., *1930*, p. 91.

conscience in this matter, under the same conditions I would do it again. Seven eighths of my fellow prisoners are fundamental law-breakers, some habitual. All these grades of criminals will after a short period be allowed to dwell again in your midst, whereas I will probably receive the most severe sentence of all, I shall be ostracised by this country.

One case of a young Swiss boy contained a request for early release from jail on grounds of health:

Heinrich Koch (Case 83).

Heinrich Koch was born, October 10, 1905, in Paris, France, the son of a Swiss father and French mother. He lived in Paris and Switzerland during his early life, learning French, English, German, and Spanish; then he was trained as a machinist.

He landed in Quebec on June 6, 1924 and secured work there, first as a gardener, then in a foundry and machine shop, but changed again to farming after some months there. On November 4 of that year he walked across the border with some friends at Hallock, Minn. They stopped at a restaurant for some food and were immediately taken into custody by an immigration officer who happened to be there. Two days later a warrant of arrest was issued for Mr. Koch [1] and he was taken to the Kittson County Jail for detention. On November 20, a complaint was filed with the United States commissioner charging Mr. Koch with violation of the "passport law." He was given a hearing 10 days later at the jail, but he did not wish a lawyer. A warrant of deportation was issued on December 6, 1924, with the charges, the same as in the warrant of arrest, (1) "L. P. C.", (2) that he entered without inspection, (3) that he was not in possession of a valid unexpired immigration visa on entry.

Mr. Koch was indicted by the grand jury at Minneapolis on April 16, 1925, having remained in jail until that time. His case was to come up for trial at Fergus Falls, Minn., but by that

[1] The friends form separate cases.

time he was confined in the hospital at Hallock, Minn., with tuberculosis. The next term of the court in that district was not until November, 1925, so the case was held over until then. While awaiting trial, Mr. Koch wrote as follows:

> I am here in the county jail for ten months for crossing the border unlawfully at Hallock, Minn. I could not appear before the court of May 5th on account of sickness. I am now discharged from the hospital where I was suffering for four months pleurisy and tuberculitic influenza. I am not as strong physically as they have expected at the beginning and I feel uneasy, having to wait another two months for trial. In view of my present condition while I still could stand the transportation, does not the law allow that I might be tried earlier, and in view of my tuberculitic condition could I not be sent home earlier? Kindly accept in advance my gratitude.

He had a passport which expired during his detention, and which was renewed by the bureau with no delay.

While he was waiting, the bureau had a letter from the American Consul in Paris on behalf of the mother of the boy. This letter stated: "Apparently (he) is a youth of somewhat undisciplined nature who left Canada without his parents' consent and probably without papers and quite certainly with the intention of smuggling himself into the United States."

He was deported on January 15, 1926 from Montreal, where he had been sent two days previously. The warrant of deportation read "to Switzerland." His parents, however lived in Paris.

The following cases may shed some light on problems of detention:

Karl Anderson (Case 84).

Karl Anderson was born on May 10, 1880 in Ostervale, Sweden, one of nine children. He came to the United States in 1903 and remained until December 1, 1924, "begging and bumming."

On that day he went to Mexico for two hours, and returned across the border from Tiajuana. He was not seen, and begged his way back to San Diego, then to Los Angeles. He was arrested in Fullerton, Cal. for begging and sentenced to serve 30 days from December 26, 1924. As soon as he was released, he went to Arizona, was there taken into custody by the immigration service, and detained in the Pima County Jail at Tucson from February 6, 1925, the date of taking him into custody. A warrant for his arrest was issued on that day.

Three days later, a hearing was held at the jail. There Mr. Anderson stated he had been in jail some 15 times in the United States for begging, with sentences ranging from two weeks to two months. The inspector stated at that time that he would not be criminally prosecuted for violation of the "passport law," as the offense, if there was one, had not occurred in the judicial district in which Tucson was located.

A warrant of deportation was issued on March 10, on the grounds, (1) "L. P. C.", (2) that he entered by land other than a designated port of entry for aliens, (3) that he was a professional beggar at the time of entry.

It took from March 19 to May 5 to obtain a passport for the man through the Swedish legation in Washington. Meanwhile he was detained in jail, and an attempt was being made to "reship" him "foreign." This attempt was continued until July, when he was sent to Galveston. One of the federal judges in the district had meanwhile stated the possibility of a judicial investigation of the length of the detention period.

As it had not been possible to secure "reshipment foreign," Mr. Anderson was deported on July 7, 1925 from Galveston, at government expense. He was to land in France, and go to Sweden.

John Marmich (Case 85).

John Marmich was born on December 22, 1895 near Agram, Jugoslava. Six brothers and sisters still live there but two are in the United States at Newark, N. J.

Mr. Marmich came to the United States in June, 1913 and

remained until September 19, 1922, living in Newark, and working as a laborer. He was married in Newark in 1915 and has four American-born children. In 1922 he and his wife went to Austria to visit his wife's family, but found they could not get in, and when they attempted to return in 1924, Mr. Marmich went to Hamburg and sailed for Cuba from there, to see if he could enter the United States and then arrange to bring his family in.

He waited five months in Cuba and tried to secure permission to return to the United States but could not, so he went to Mexico and landed at Vera Cruz on April 7, 1925. There he decided he could not wait any longer, and waded the Rio Grande River on June 4th, near Villa Acuna. He chose that place, as he had ascertained the country to be sparsely settled there. He was apprehended a few days later near Del Rio, Texas and was taken to the Val Verde County Jail.

Mr. Marmich was detained in jail, but no warrant was issued for his arrest until June 27, 1925, and the hearing was not held until just one month later. At the hearing, he stated he wanted to return to Austria, not Jugoslavia, as he had left the latter country many years ago, and as his wife and American-born children were now in Austria.

A warrant of deportation was issued on July 30, on the same grounds as in the warrant of arrest, i. e., (1) "L. P. C.", (2) that he entered without inspection, (3) that he entered by land at a time or place not designated for entry.

Mr. Marmich was held in jail until November 4, 1925, at the expense and in the custody of the Department of Justice for violation of the "passport act." On that day the case was withdrawn by the United States attorney from the grand jury and the matter was turned over to the immigration authorities for action. On November 23, Mr. Marmich wrote the bureau of immigration saying that his family already needed support and he had been in jail for six months awaiting release, and awaiting a passport. When the bureau in Washington investigated the matter, it was found that a Jugoslavian passport had been sent him on November 19, but that it bore no Austrian visa.

As a party was ready to pass through the town, Mr. Marmich was joined to it and left at Galveston, as a boat was leaving from there for Germany. In view of the facts in this special case, the agents of the departing boat accepted the responsibility for obtaining an Austrian visa after Mr. Marmich arrived in Germany, but did so with the understanding that this was not to constitute a precedent and was a very particular arrangement.

Mr. Marmich was deported on November 30, at the expense of the government, and was to land in Bremen and be sent from there to Vienna.

It was found that both men and women were detained in jail, and even in two cases children. It may be well at this juncture to point out the sex of the persons in the cases studied:

Sex of Persons in Cases Studied

	Male	*Female*	*Total*
Illegal Entries	354	38	392
Likely to become a Public Charge	12	13	25
Public Charges	78	58	136
Criminals	39	2	41
Prostitutes and Narcotics	5	13	18
Total	488	124	612

As is to be expected, the men outnumber the women, for a number of reasons, chiefly because the possibilities of securing illegal entry to the country are far greater for men than women. Furthermore, in the stream of immigration in general the men go first, and the women follow. The American quota laws caught the process in mid-stream. Among the criminals and illegal entires, the men outnumber the women. However, in those connected with prostitution, the women obviously outnumber the men. The women also predominate in the "L.P.C." category; probably because a man on the verge of becoming a public charge might pass unnoticed in the community more easily than a woman.

Among the thirty-eight public charges, twenty-seven were held in county jails for varying periods of time. This number included two women who were pregnant.

Anne Graham (Case 86).

Anne Graham was born on December 31, 1903 in Plymouth, England, one of five children. As soon as she finished school, Anne began to work as a waitress, and then in a tailoring shop.

In 1921 she had an illegitimate child by a Canadian who was temporarily in England but who had a wife and six children in Vancouver, B. C. He left and returned to Canada, and the family paid Miss Graham's expenses at the hospital. The child was placed out by a social organization.

As soon as she was well, Miss Graham decided to go to Canada. She was assisted by the Canadian government in the payment of her passage money, and landed in Halifax on December 2, 1922. She went to work in the Canadian immigration office in Montreal. There she decided to go to the United States and was admitted as a visitor at Buffalo on October 4, 1923.

She immediately began to work as a waitress in a lunchroom. She was reported to the immigration service by an unknown source on April 12, 1925. The following day a warrant was issued for her arrest, and she was taken to the Erie County Jail for detention. A hearing was held at the jail on April 14. There Miss Graham admitted that she was pregnant, and said the man responsible for her condition was an English citizen living in Buffalo. Nine days later, Miss Graham was transferred from the jail to a hospital, suffering from a miscarriage. The same day the man was apprehended and taken to the jail, to be held in deportation proceedings.

A warrant of deportation was issued on May 4, with the same charges as in the warrant of arrest, i. e. (1) "L. P. C.", (2), that she entered without inspection, (3) that she was not in possession of an unexpired immigration visa at the time of entry. On May 30, Miss Graham was returned to the jail, and held until June 25, when she was sent to Montreal. She was deported on July 3, at the expense of the steamship line which had brought her to Canada.[1]

Edward Carey (Case 87).

Edward Carey was born on December 17, 1897. He stated later that he was born in Adelaide, Australia, and then said his birthplace was Birmingham, England. He was trained as a show-card writer and window-dresser.

He came to the United States on October 23, 1924 at Galveston, Tex., as a stowaway on a boat from Mexico, where he had been for a short time. On November 7 he was taken by the police at Galveston as a " suspicious character " and sent to the jail in the custody of the immigration service. A warrant of arrest was issued the next day. Mr. Carey was transferred to the Tarrant County Jail at Fort Worth, where a hearing was given him on November 13.

At the hearing he reported that he had been in Houston working as a sign-painter for a few days, and had then gone back to Galveston where he was arrested. He stated he had been born in Adelaide, and had lived in Melbourne and Sidney. He was evasive about answering questions concerning his family, and said his father had died when he was seven and his mother when he was only a year older, and that he had been brought up by " different families.

An attempt was made to secure a passport for his return to Australia, and it was recommended by the board of review that he be deported to Australia from San Francisco. The passport had to be secured through the British Embassy and on Decem-

[1] Miss Graham was known to the Church Mission of Help of Buffalo, although the record in the bureau of immigration does not so state. The Church Mission reported to the author that Miss Graham desired to return to England and had been reported by them to the immigration service. They had had a mental study made of the girl, with the report: " Mental Age of 13 years, 9 months; I. Q. 86; a borderline case. Psychiatrist's recommendation: 'Considering her tendency to drift, and her general lack of judgment, would advise that every effort be made to return her to England as soon as possible before she gets into any further trouble.' "

ber 24, 1924, they sent word to Australia for verification of the man's birth there so that a passport might be issued. On April 22, 1925, they wrote the Department of State that word had come from Australia that it was impossible to verify Mr. Carey's birth there and so no passport could be issued. This was reported to the Department of Labor, who in turn tried to secure further information from Mr. Carey about his birthplace but he could give none.

On April 23, an official of the American Federation of Labor wrote the bureau that Mr. Carey had been held in jail for five months and that he was intelligent and worth-while. On May 20, the inspector in charge wrote the bureau: "The alien does not appear to be in very good health. He is thinner than he was when he first was apprehended. His complexion and eyes are very sallow, he is almost yellow in color."

A warrant of deportation was issued on June 23, 1925, with the charges the same as in the warrant of arrest, i. e. (1) "L. P. C.", (2) that he was brought to foreign contiguous territory by a transportation company which had not complied with all the requirements of Sec. 17 of the 1924 immigration act, and had not resided in that territory more than two years before entry into the United States, (3) that he entered by water at a time or place other than designated by immigration officials, (4), that he was a stowaway at the time of entry. Deportation was directed to Australia in the warrant.

Mr. Carey was detained in jail until August 19, 1925, when he was sent to San Francisco, in an attempt to "reship" him "foreign," if deportation could not be effected to Australia. He was taken to the immigration station at Angel Island for detention. While held there, Mr. Carey admitted he was an illegitimate child who had been born in Birmingham, England, but that he had been so ashamed of the fact that he changed his name and would never admit who he was. He enlisted in the British army under his assumed name, and served eleven months overseas. After his discharge from the army, he went to England for a short time, and then went to Cuba as a stowaway.

On November 21, 1925, the British Embassy issued a British

passport for Mr. Carey so that he might return to England. On November 24, the warrant of deportation was amended to read that deportation would take place to England instead of Australia. On December 12, 1925 Mr. Carey was sent to New York through the Panama Canal. On January 2, 1926 he was deported from New York to England, at government expense.

Country to which Deportation Took Place in the Cases Studied

As already indicated, the difficulties of detention may be made great by the length of time and complications involved in securing passports. The table on the next page indicates the countries in which the persons were born, in the cases covered by this study.

Of the total number of cases, " first papers," or declarations of intention to become citizens of the United States had been secured in 14 of the total number. Eight of these persons had served in the American army with honorable discharge and one was in the army when taken for deportation.

Gertrud Baumer (Case 88).

Gertrud Baumer was born in Halberstadt, Germany on May 3, 1883, one of seven children. Miss Baumer attended school in her home until 14, then began to work in a factory. She was ill off and on, and always very nervous, as were several of her brothers and sisters.

She came to the United States with her mother, landing in New York on December 7, 1923 and being held for the board of special inquiry but admitted to a sister of Miss Baumer, who lived in Chelsea, Mich. Soon after arriving at her sister's home, Miss Baumer began work as a domestic servant, but soon became depressed and imagined people were talking about her.

On April 6, 1924, she was admitted to the Pontiac State Hospital at Pontiac, Mich., where a diagnosis of *dementia*

COUNTRY OF BIRTH [1] AND MAJOR CAUSE OF DEPORTATION IN CASES STUDIED

Country	"L. P. C."	Public Charges	Criminals	Prostitutes and Narcotics	Illegal Entries	Total
Albania				1	1	2
Austria		5	1		3	9
Belgium					2	2
Bulgaria			1		9	10
Czechoslovakia		10	5	1	41	57
Denmark	1	2	3		4	10
Finland		3	1		11	15
France		3	2		2	7
Germany	2	14	3	3	14	36
Great Britain	8	11	9	3	44	75
Greece		4	4	4	13	25
Holland		1			4	5
Hungary		3		1	12	16
Irish Free State	5	22	2		21	50
Italy (north)[2]	1	12	1	2	42	58
Italy (south)[2]	4	13	4		53	74
Jugoslavia		3	1		35	39
Latvia		1			1	2
Lithuania		2			4	6
Mexico					1[3]	1
Norway	1	4			3	8
Poland		2	1		15	18
Portugal		3	1		10	14
Rumania		1		1	10	12
Spain		1			26	27
Sweden	2	11	2		5	20
Switzerland	1	5		1	5	12
Syria					1[4]	1
United States				1[5]		1
Total	25	136	41	18	392	612

[1] Country of birth is used to mean the country in 1925 and 1930, not as it was the year a person was born. For purposes of this table, a person born in territory that used to belong to Germany but is now Polish would be listed here as coming from Poland.

[2] Anything north of Naples; south here means anything south of Naples.

[3] Married to a German and deported with him to Germany.

[4] Born in Syria but deported to France.

[5] A woman born in the United States and married previous to 1922 to an Englishman and deported with him to England.

praecox was made, with a possibility of *manic depressive insanity*. Miss Baumer had a sister who was also a patient in the same hospital, with the same diagnosis. She had been admitted on October 21, 1921.

A warrant of arrest was issued on May 17, 1924 for Miss Gertrud Baumer.[1] A hearing was held on May 29, and the sister from Chelsea testified that she was willing to have Miss Baumer deported. On June 30, a warrant of deportation was issued, on the same grounds as those in the warrant of arrest, i. e., (1) "L. P. C.", (2) that she had become a public charge within 5 years of entry, etc. The warrant directed her deportation to Germany, but on February 6, 1925 it was found through the German embassy that Miss Baumer was not a German citizen and that no German passport could be obtained for her. She had been born in Germany, but as her father had been born in Austria, she was an Austrian citizen. So after report from Vienna, an Austrian passport was secured for Miss Baumer on May 27, 1925. The warrant of deportation was amended on December 15, 1925, directing deportation to Austria, instead of Germany, although she had never been in Austria.

She was deported on December 26, 1925 at the expense of the steamship line which had brought her to the United States. She landed in Antwerp on January 8, 1926 and was sent via Luxemberg and Basle to Schwarzenburg, Austria, where her father had been born, and was signed for by the local police there.

There was also a German woman married to a Czech and deported with him to Czechoslovakia.

The difficulties of obtaining passports are indicated by the following cases:

[1] It is not known whether or not her sister was deported, as her case formed a separate record.

John Smith (Case 89).

John Smith was born in 1900 and went to Canada in 1922. Going west to work, he met an English girl whom he married and by whom he had one child, born in Calgary, Alberta. When the baby was about six months old, the family illegally crossed the border to the United States and went to live in a small Nebraska town. There the man tried to run an art school, but with no success, so the local charity board helped the family. Soon thereafter the man was arrested for indecent exposure on the street, released, and reported to the immigration authorities. He was committed to the county jail on the warrant of arrest of the immigration service, pending investigation of citizenship. His wife and child were paroled to the custody of the police matron and their care paid for by the county.

Investigation in Canada showed he had lost his Canadian domicile by residence in the United States of more than two years, that the family had received financial assistance before and after the birth of the child in Calgary, and that the man had been arrested in Canada for the same reason that he was arrested in this country, but had been released. So Canada refused to accept the family. The Canadian investigation took four months. Meanwhile, the Nebraska county protested to the immigration service that the woman and child were being cared for by the county, while the man was being paid for by the immigration service. Finally, after five months in jail, Mr. Smith was released to the custody of the police officer of the town.

Meanwhile, Mr. Smith had stated that he had been born in Australia and had been temporarily in an institution for mental disease there after the war. The Commissioner General of Immigration in Washington then wrote the British Embassy there, and they in turn referred the matter to the Prime Minister of Australia. Five months later a report came that Mr. Smith's birth could not be verified in Australia and immediately the Commissioner General wrote the British Embassy regarding deportation to England. The Embassy wrote the Secretary of State for Foreign Affairs in London, but after a two months investigation in London he reported no trace of the man's birth there. After the lapse of another month, report came that a second investigation in Australia had failed to bring results. The Assistant Secretary of Labor then wrote the Department of State in the United States requesting them to communicate with the American Consul General in London who would then have someone interview the solicitors of Mr. Smith's mothers estate in London.

Meanwhile the family, because of entire inability to support themselves, had been "warned out" of the Nebraska town. They moved to another small town in Colorado and disappeared. Now, a year and five months after the original warrant of arrest, Mrs. Smith wrote the Department of Labor, stating that her husband had been arrested for "difficulty with a young girl," that she had obtained a divorce from him, and wished to be deported to England, together with her Canadian-born son. She was being assisted by the town authorities, who were refusing to care for her and her child any longer.

A month after the receipt of this letter, the American Consul General in London wrote the Department of State concerning the interview with the law firm in London, who reported Mr. Smith's unregistered birth in London as the illegitimate son of an English mother and a German father.

Mrs. Smith now secured her own birth certificate from England, and a year and nine months after her husband's original warrant of arrest in deportation proceedings, she and her child were deported to England without him. The same month saw Mr. Smith committed to the Colorado State Hospital for the Insane, but a few weeks later the superintendent of the hospital reported Mr. Smith entirely sane and ready for release. On April 10, 1930, the British Embassy wrote it was impossible to issue a passport as Mr. Smith's birth could be verified in neither England nor Australia, so he remained in the United States.

Jose Horta (Case 90).

Jose Horta was born in 1882 near Seville, Spain. He lived there throughout his youth, but never went to school and so was illiterate. He was married there and had 4 children by this marriage. In 1923 Mr. Horta left home and went to Malaga, then to Cuba, where he stayed for 15 months. He then went to Mexico, landing at Tampico on January 10, 1925.

Four days later, Mr. Horta entered the United States by wading the Rio Grande River near El Paso. He was not discovered but went to Santa Fé and near there was apprehended as a suspicious character. He was taken to the Bernalillo County Jail, Alberquerque, N. M. and was detained there in the custody of the Department of Justice, awaiting prosecution for violation of the "passport act." He was given a hearing at the jail on February 26.

On March 4, Mr. Horta was sentenced by the United States District Court in Santa Fé to serve 60 days in jail for violation of the "passport act." A warrant of deportation was issued on April 9, on the same grounds as those in the warrant of arrest, i. e., (1) "L. P. C.", (2) that he was illiterate at the time of entry, (3) that he entered by land at a time or place not designated for entry, (4) that he was not in possession of an unexpired visa at the time of entry, (5) that he entered foreign contiguous territory by a transportation company which had not complied with all the requirements of section 17 of the immigration act of 1924, and had not resided in that territory more than two years before entry into the United States.

Mr. Horta had no passport, so one was requested from the Spanish consul in New Orleans. He issued a passport for return to Cuba, with the statement that he was authorized to issue return passports only to those Spaniards who had made through trips to the United States from Spain, and if they had come through Cuba or Mexico they were to have made stops only of sufficient length of time to reach the Mexican border or obtain a sailing to a United States seaport. The immigration office at Ellis Island secured a passport from the Spanish consul in New York.

Mr. Horta was sent to the immigration office at Houston, from where he was deported on July 7, 1925, at government expense, and destined to Le Havre, with a ticket to Spain.

Edith Frye (Case 91).

Edith Frye was born on February 6, 1904 in Newton, Norfolk, England, and lived there throughout her school life. She went through what would be the equivalent of III High School and then taught children in a kindergarten.

Miss Frye went to Canada to marry a man she had met in England, and landed in Quebec on November 4, 1923. She was married the same day to Walter Stevens, whom she had come to join. He had been permanently admitted to the United States for residence but merely went to Canada to meet his fiancee. He had been unable to arrange for her admission, so he told her he would return to the United States and that she was to come across the bridge at Niagara Falls to join him. He told her to say that she had been in Canada three years, but as she was crossing on November 7 she was questioned and said she had just reached Canada. So she was sent back. She stayed a week and then crossed the bridge without inspection.

Mr. and Mrs. Stevens rented rooms in Niagara Falls, and she began to work as a waitress. In August, 1924, her husband went to Florida on business, and during his absence she had an illicit love affair with a man she had recently met. Mr. Stevens discovered it and on his return from Florida reported her to the immigration service, on December 4, 1924.

A warrant was issued January 9, 1925 for Mrs. Stevens' arrest. She was taken that day to the Erie County Lodging House for detention. A hearing was given her on January 19. A warrant of deportation was not issued until May 23. The grounds were the same as in the warrant of arrest, i. e., (1) "L. P. C.", (2) that she entered without inspection, (3) that she was not in possession of an unexpired passport at the time of entry, (4) that the quota of the country from which she came had expired at the time of her entry, (5) that she entered the United States within one year from the date of exclusion, permission to apply not having been granted.

The British Embassy protested the length of Mrs. Stevens' detention, but the Department of Labor replied through the Department of State that request had been made for a passport, but that it had taken over three months to secure it. At the time it arrived, no party was going through Buffalo en route to a port, so Mrs. Stevens had to be detained another month until a party could take her to a port for sailing. The letter to the British Embassy stated, "Alien deportees are seldom, if ever, transported singly from points inland to the point of departure, for the reason that such procedure is too costly to justify it."

Mrs. Stevens was deported on July 13, 1925 from Montreal, at the expense of the steamship company which had brought her to Canada.

Lars Antikanen (Case 92).

Lars Antikanen was born in 1902 near Helsingfors, Finland. He went to Canada in 1924, arriving at Halifax on May 2 of that year. Then he went west to work in the harvest fields.

On June 20, 1925, he came to the United States in a rowboat at Detroit, paying $30 to be brought across. He was apprehended by the border patrol, and taken to police headquarters, where he was held in the custody of the Department of Justice as a witness against his smuggler. A warrant of arrest was issued for him on June 25, and a hearing was given him the next day, through an interpreter.

A warrant of deportation was issued for Mr. Antikanen on August 15, 1925, with the same charges as in the warrant of arrest, i. e., (1) "L. P. C.", (2) that he entered without inspection, (3) that he entered without an unexpired immigration visa.

Mr. Antikanen had no evidence of his nationality, and the Finnish consulate in New York refused to issue a passport when an attempt was made through the Ellis Island authorities to secure one on June 2, 1925. He was sent to the Philadelphia immigration station at Gloucester City, N. J., on October 23, to await either the issuance of a passport or "re-shipment foreign." On November 3 an attempt was made through the Finnish legation to secure a passport, but they replied that the report of the hearing, in which Mr. Antikanen had stated he was a Finnish subject did not constitute evidence as to his nationality. He was requested to secure affidavit from two persons who knew him to be a Finnish subject, and who had known him over a certain period of time. This he could not do, as he had no friends or relatives here.

Finally, the record of Mr. Antikanen's arrival in Canada, giving the name of his father and his address in Finland, was sent the Finnish legation and they issued a passport for him on December 11, 1925. On January 2, 1926, he was sent to Ellis Island and was deported three days later, at the expense of the steamship line which had brought him to Canada.

John Stanislas (Case 93).

John Stanislas was born in 1884 in the province of Kaunas, Lithuania, as one of six children. He was married in his home town and came with his wife to the United States in 1911. They went to Chicago, and here two children were born, one in 1915 and one in 1917.

Mr. Stanislas, became involved in a bootlegging scheme, and then left the United States, while his wife and children remained here. He remained in Europe from 1921 until 1924, when, failing to secure possibility of readmittance to the United States, he sailed to Mexico, where he landed at Vera Cruz on March 24, 1924. He went from here to Juarez and paid $100 to a man in the hotel where he was staying, to aid in smuggling him into the United States. On June 18, the attempt was made, but he and the smuggler were caught and were taken to the El Paso immigration station. Mr. Stanislas was held in the custody of the Department of Justice for violation of the passport act" and as witness against his smuggler. On July 1, he came before the United States commissioner in proceedings for violation of the "passport act," and was committed to the county jail in default of $750 bail. On July 29, he was sentenced to 30 days in jail. He was given a hearing at the jail on July 30, on the warrant of arrest, which had been issued on June 20. At the hearing Mr. Stanislas stated he was on his way back to the United States to try to find his wife and 2 American-born children.

A warrant of deportation was issued for him on August 27, 1924, with the charges, (1) " L. P. C.", (2) that he was brought to foreign contiguous territory by a transportation company which had not complied with the requirements of Sec. 17 of the immigration act of 1924, and had not resided in such territory more than 2 years before entry, (3) that he entered by land at a time or place other than designated as a port of entry for aliens, and (4) that the quota of the country from which he came was exhausted at the time of his entry, (5) that he entered in violation of the " passport act."

On September 25, 1924, the bureau of immigration in Washington wrote the Lithuanian legation requesting the issuance of a passport. They replied that the report of the hearing which had been sent them stated Mr. Stanislas had left his passport in the hotel in Juarez, Mexico, and that the bureau of immigration should secure that passport from there. The bureau then wrote the immigration office at El Paso, who replied that it was impossible to secure that passport. Then the bureau in Washington again wrote the legation, who in turn wrote the home government in Lithuania requesting permission to issue the passport.

As no bond was available for Mr. Stanislas' release, and as he had been held in jail for so many months, the district director at El Paso recommended release on his own recognizance, but the board of review refused to recommend this. On March 17, the Department of Labor addressed the Department of State for aid in securing a passport. On May 27, 1925, after the man had been in jail almost a year, a passport was issued by the Lithuanian legation. On June 3, Mr. Stanislas secured a lawyer who was able to provide bond, and offered $1000 bond for the release of his client, but as the passport had been issued by now, this was not granted. On June 17, Mr. Stanislas was sent to Galveston, and was deported on July 2, at government expense, destined to Lithuania.

Wladislaw Bacswicz (Case 94).

Wladsilaw Bacswicz was born in 1896 in Tarnoff, Poland. He had two brothers and sister who emigrated to the United

States while he was young. They are now living in Chicago. His father is dead, and his mother is an inmate of an old people's home in Tarnoff.

On August 11, 1923, Mr. Bacswicz entered the United States, to join his brothers and sister and was admitted on primary inspection as a quota immigrant. On April 23, 1927, he was admitted to the Elgin State Hospital at Elgin, Ill., where a diagnosis was made of *dementia praecox, hebephrenic type.*

A warrant was issued for his arrest on April 16, 1928, and a hearing was given him at the hospital five days later. His brother testified he had no objection to deportation. A warrant of deportation was issued on May 22, 1928, on the same grounds as in the warrant of arrest, (1) "L. P. C.", (2) that he had become a public charge, etc. At the hearing it had been stated that at the time of entry, Mr. Bacswicz had not been in possession of financial means for his maintenance and so was "L. P. C."

He had in his possession an old Polish passport, but the Polish Consul General in Chicago said that passport must be referred to Warsaw for verification. It took until July 30, 1929 before the man's citizenship was definitely established, despite his possession of the old passport. Then it took until February 27, 1930 before a new passport was issued. Permission had also to be secured for Mr. Bacswicz to enter Poland through the port of Danzig. He was deported on April 18, 1930, at the expense of the steamship company bringing him to the United States.

The report of his arrival is not contained in the record.

The following case shows a choice of countries to which deportation might take place:

Armido Torelli (Case 95).

Armido Torelli was born in 1907 in Ancona, Italy. He worked in a sulphur mine as soon as he was old enough (age unknown). In 1923 he and his father went to Belgium and stayed nine months, then went to Le Havre, where they took ship for Cuba and remained there three months. Next they went to Mexico, landing at Tampico on November 8, 1924 and going directly to Juarez, where they tried to enter the United States. When Mr. Torelli, Sr., found he could not enter legally, he refused to try to come in, but remained in Juarez, while his son paid $50 to the owner of a car to drive him across the border into the country. The attempt was made on January 27, 1925, but Mr. Torelli and his smuggler were apprehended by the border patrol and taken to the immigration station at El Paso, where they were detained.

A warrant of arrest was issued on February 16, and the next day a complaint was filed by the United States Commissioner for violation of the "passport law." He entered a plea of guilty and was held for the next session of the grand jury. He was offered release on $500 bond to the Department of Justice, but was unable to furnish it and was committed to jail. However, his smuggler was detained in that same jail, so Mr. Torelli was changed back to the immigration station to keep them apart.

Mr. Torelli was given a hearing at the immigration station on March 13, through an interpreter. Several days later a lawyer presented a brief urging deportation to Mexico to Juarez, where Mr. Torelli's father still was. This request was not recommended by the board of review. The lawyer then urged deportation to Belgium, not Italy, to avoid military service in Italy, as Mr. Torelli was then liable to it. His father came to see him in jail, returning to Mexico immediately, he disapproved greatly of his son's illegal entry, and the district director reported he felt sure the disapproval was sincere.

A warrant of deportation was issued on June 4, with the charges the same as in the warrant of arrest, i. e. (1) "L. P. C.", (2) that he entered without inspection, (3) that he was not in possession of an unexpired immigration visa, (4) that he entered foreign contiguous territory by a steamship line, etc., and did not remain there at least two years previous to entry. Ten days later, the board of review acceded to the request of the lawyer at least in part, and recommended that Mr. Torelli be allowed to depart at his own expense to Belgium, instead of Italy, and that the warrant of deportation be amended to that effect. However, he did not have money to pay his own expenses, so the warrant was again amended, and he was deported July 7, from Galveston, at government expense. He landed in Le Havre, and it is not known whether he returned to Belgium or Italy.

AMERICAN-BORN CHILDREN

Of the total number of people in the cases studied, there were twenty-nine who had American-born children, who either remained here when deportation took place or else accompanied their deported parents. Of these eighteen accompanied their parents when deportation occurred. It is not known what happened to eight of them. Six of the total number were illegitimate, with the citizenship of the father unknown in four of the six, American in one case and British in another. The ages of the children varied from twelve years in one case to a baby of two months in another—the modal age being under a year.

Clarence Adams (Case 96).

Clarence Adams was born in 1896 in Newcastle, England. He left school at the age of 15 and began to work as a painter, continuing this trade until his emigration. He was married in Glasgow to Margaret Williams, who had been born there in 1898. They had one daughter born in Newcastle in 1920.

The family went to Canada in 1924, landing in Quebec on May 18 of that year. As Mrs. Adams had a sister and brother in the United States, they decided to come to this country. So Mr. and Mrs. Adams and the little girl applied for admission in Montreal, but were refused admission to the United States by the board of special inquiry on May 20. Ten days later, they entered at Lewiston, N. Y., by boat from Toronto, and were admitted as visitors.

They went immediately to Sharon, Pa., where Mrs. Adams had a sister. There Mr. Adams began work as a painter, earning $8 a day. He found this position one week after arrival there, and worked steadily at it until he was reported to the immigration authorities by an unknown source on September 7, 1925.

Meanwhile, another daughter had been born in Sharon, on August 16, 1925. Furthermore, Mr. Adams had $400 worth of furniture with the installments completely paid, $110 in the savings bank and a $2000 insurance policy on Mr. Adams' life, with the payments paid up to date.

Warrants of arrest were issued for Mr. and Mrs. Adams and the older child on September 16, 1925. Mr. Adams was released on $500 bond, and his wife and child on their own recognizance. They were given a hearing at their home on October 6, where the family stated they wished to depart voluntarily and take their American-born child with them. The inspector who took the testimony stated they were "sincere, hard-working people." Warrants of deportation were issued on October 27, with the same charges as in the warrants of arrest, i. e., (1) "L. P. C.", (2) they entered the United States by means of fase and misleading statements, (3) the country from which they came had an exhausted quota at the time of their entry, (4) they entered the United States in violation of the passport law, (5) they entered within one year from the date of their exclusion from the country, permission to reapply not having been granted.

The family were sent to Ellis Island on November 19, and were deported on December 5, 1925, at the expense of the steamship company taking them to Canada. Mr. Adams paid the complete transportation expenses of his American-born child himself. She had previously been entered on the passport of her parents.

The following case had another almost exact replica among the group studied, save that in the second case there were three (one set of twins) American-born illegitimate children involved:

Mary Murphy (Case 97).

Mary Murphy was born on July 12, 1902 in County Donegal, Ireland. She was placed in a convent school when she was 9 years old and remained there until she was 17.

She came to the United States direct from Ireland, landing in New York on January 1, 1925 and going to Roxbury, Mass. to be with her aunt. Then she began to work as a chambermaid in the Hotel Statler and other hotels in Boston.

On August 30, 1927 Miss Murphy gave birth to a son of an unknown father. The child was born in the Boston City Hospital and was taken by a social service organization for placement or adoption. Miss Murphy returned to work, but on March 20, 1929 was admitted to the State Infirmary at Tewksbury, where the following day she gave birth to a girl. She was reported by the infirmary to the immigration authorities, and a warrant of arrest was issued for her on August 2, 1929, after she had left the institution. The report from the infirmary stated: " With the Stanford-Binet intelligence test, there is a mental age of 10 years and 4 months, I. Q. 71% (using 14½ years as the average normal). Delivered of an illegitimate child two years ago and thirteen weeks ago. With low mental age and inability to care for herself from the sex standpoint, she is not desirable material for citizenship. The mental deficiency is probably basic, not educational, since she attended school in Ireland for 8-9 years."

A hearing was given Miss Murphy at her aunt's home on August 19, with a woman inspector taking the testimony. When the case later came before the board of review in Washingon, a letter was received from a Massachusetts representative saying the father of the child had been found and was willing to marry Miss Murphy and that he would like her to stay in this country. The bureau replied that marriage would not affect her status, as she was deportable anyway.

A warrant for her deportation was issued on September 5, 1929, on the same grounds as in the warrant of arrest i. e., (1) " L. P. C.", (2) that she had become a public charge within five years of entry, etc., (3) that she was mentally defective at the time of her entry to the United States.

Meanwhile the Department of Labor had written the Department of State asking them to request the issuance of a passport for Miss Murphy, and allowing her to take her second child with her, which she wanted to do. After verifying her citizenship, the legation of the Irish Free State wrote the Department of State authorizing the issuance of a passport through their New York consul in charge of passports, but refusing to accept the American-born child with Miss Murphy. The Department of State reported this information to the Department of Labor.

Miss Murphy was deported from New York on January 2, 1930, at the expense of the steamship company which had brought her to this country. Her two American-born children were left in this country.

CONCLUSIONS

Several remedies should be considered for the relief of the detention situation. There is need for more adequate statistics concerning numbers detained, points of greatest congestion, length of detention of all deportees, facilities available for proper detention and care for those who need it, and statistics of those released on bond, on their own recognizance, or to social agencies. Second, many difficulties of detention could be obviated if more aliens could be safely released on their own recognizance or to social agencies, and an effort should be made to see if this practice could not practicably be extended to cases of differing types. Third, the matter of providing bonds should be carefully examined, with a view to the possibility of their wider use. The question of the financial ability of aliens held in such proceedings should be investigated, to discover all possible honest sources of securing bond. Fourth, a means should be devised by which those who are merely likely to become public charges should never, no matter where they are located, have to go to jail for lack of other detention facilities. Fifth, the problem of support for the dependents of those detained during deportation proceedings should be considered. Sixth, some further thought should be given the possibility of providing separate immigration detention quarters instead of detaining deportees with other federal prisoners. The development of federal jails as provided by the act of May 12, 1930, is a helpful step forward from the catch-all of the county jail. When jails are built, it is important to provide that deportees who have committed no offense other than illegal entry are properly segregated from such other federal prisoners as narcotic law violators. If such segregation is not accomplished, the need for separate detention quarters becomes apparent for persons held by the bureau of immigration. In any provision for detention of deportees, it must be remembered that deportation itself, as so often stated, is not punishment for crime. Different treatment should be accorded those deportees who have committed no crime other than illegal entry from the treatment accorded to incarcerated criminals. The reason for separate detention of alien deportees would be to save them from possibly worse associations.

Most difficult of solution is the problem of establishing foreign citizenship and securing passports for aliens who are to be deported from the United States. A plan should be worked out in cooperation between the Departments of Labor and State and the representatives of other countries by which such countries may be assured that they are receiving only their own deported citizens, and by which, for the sake of their citizens and the United States, a minimum of delay and red-tape may be had in obtaining passports for such of their citizens as are deported from the United States.

Such a road is a long one to travel, as is indicated by the difficulties and slim results of the first Conference for the Codification of International Law called by the League of

Nations in March, 1930, to codify the subjects of nationality, responsibility of states for injuries to aliens, etc. The goal of the conference was to eliminate, as far as possible, cases of statelessness and of dual nationality arising from conflicting national laws regarding nationality. It was impossible to agree on any convention in regard to the responsibilities of states for injuries to aliens and the conference agreed upon only a limited convention (against which the United States voted) in regard to nationality. A special protocol was finally adopted, which provides:

> If a person, after entering a foreign country, loses his nationality without acquiring another nationality, the State whose nationality he last possessed is bound to admit him, at the request of the State in whose territory he is:
>
> (1) if he is permanently indigent either as a result of an incurable disease or for any other reason; or
>
> (2) if he has been sentenced, in the State where he is, to not less than a month's imprisonment and has either served his sentence or obained total or partial remission thereof.
>
> In the first case the State whose nationality such person last possessed may refuse to receive him, if it undertakes to meet the cost of relief in the country where he is as from the thirtieth day on which the request was made. In the second case the cost of sending him back shall be borne by the country making the request.[1]

The matter of nationality is far from solution. It is the crux of the whole problem of deportation, and only when the responsibility of states is in clearer position will solution even be approached.

[1] *Conference for the Codification of International Law*, Report of the First Committee (Nationality), Série de Publications de la Société des Nations, V, Questions juridiques. 1930. V 8, p. 3, Article 2.

CHAPTER XII

Deportation and Afterwards

THE WARRANT OF DEPORTATION—THE DEPORTATION PARTY AND THE TRAIN—THE PERMANENT BAR AGAINST RETURN

THE WARRANT OF DEPORTATION

While the alien is waiting and the board of review discussing and the foreign country investigating, no decision has yet been reached in regard to deportation. Finally an Assistant to the Secretary of Labor, with advice of the board of review, reaches a decision which either rings the knell of the alien's stay in the United States or allows him to go free.[1] In other words, a warrant of deportation is issued or else the outstanding warrant of arrest is cancelled and the alien released from custody. The Secretary or his Assistant has no discretion or option, so if an alien is clearly within a deportable category, the warrant of deportation must be issued. The provisions of the law in regard to deportation of particularly undesirable aliens, such as prostitutes, anarchists, criminals, insane, etc. are held to constitute a mandatory class where under all circumstances a warrant of deportation must be issued. The only chance for the alien is to prove that he does not fall within the deport-

[1] As already indicated, *supra*, p. 302, if authority has been delegated for an Assistant to the Secretary or Assistant Secretary to sign a warrant of deportation, his decision and signature are as legally binding as that of the Secretary himself. The Secretary seldom sees a case or signs a warrant in person. A commissioner of immigration or district director is without authority to issue a warrant.—Low Kwai *v.* Backus, 229 Fed. 481.

able class, for once he is shown to be in it, deportation follows. The decision of the Secretary or Assistant, as the case may be, is final as to the sufficiency or the facts warranting deportation.[1]

Since a warrant of deportation usually ends [2] a foreigner's stay in this country, it is important that it be accurately and carefully made out. The finding as to deportability must appear clearly in the warrant, else it is void.[3] Furthermore, the grounds for deportation given in the warrant must be the same as those on which a hearing was given the alien,[4] for it would obviously deny a person due process of law if he were heard on one set of grounds and deported on others. The warrant must be an order to leave the country and not a mere statement of departure.[5] Last but by no means least, there is great necessity for strictness in defining "destination." Otherwise there could be considerable abuse on the power to deport, and "undesirable foreigners" might be dumped from the United States into almost any other country that did not object." Hence "a warrant ordering deportation of an alien 'to the country whence he came' but not naming it does not order deportation to any country and is therefore fatally defective." [6] The warrant must provide for deportation to the port required by law,[7] and if an alien is ordered deported to the country of which the Department

[1] Mon Singh *v.* White, 274 Fed. 513; Sibray *v.* United States *ex rel.* Plichta, 282 Fed. 795.

[2] Even after the issuance of a warrant of deportation, it is still possible to show the alien's right to remain here. Then the warrants of both arrest and deportation would be cancelled.

[3] Mahler *v.* Eby, 264 U. S. 32.

[4] Throumoupopolou *v.* United States, 3 Fed. (2d) 803; Smith *v.* Hayes, 10 Fed. (2d) 145.

[5] United States *v.* Curran, 16 Fed. (2d) 958.

[6] *Ex parte* Yabucannin, 199 Fed. 365.

[7] United States *v.* Sisson, 220 Fed. 538.

of Labor determines he is a native, an executive officer is without authority to change the warrant of deportation by substituting a different country.[1]

THE DEPORTATION PARTIES AND TRAINS

With the issuance of a warrant of deportation, the procedure is at last complete and the alien deportee is ready to be sent from the country as soon as he obtains a passport. He faces one more delay, for unless he is to be sent merely across a near-by part of the land boundary between the United States and Mexico or Canada, he must await one of the great deportation trains which at stated intervals wind their way through the country picking up some deportees as they go and leaving others to be deported from points en route. Because of the great numbers of persons deported annually from the United States it is not possible to convey each deportee separately to the port of deportation. So "in order to handle aliens ready for deportation in the most economical and efficient manner," parties are formed under the supervision of the deportation division of the bureau of immigration, going from coast to coast and from interior points to the coasts or borders.

The number and frequency of such parties are determined by the bureau. At the present time they leave approximately every six weeks, but the number is growing with the increase in deportations. During 1925 forty-eight large groups of parties were authorized sent to ports of deportation [2] but by 1929-30 the number had increased to 174.[3] The routes followed by the parties are as follows:

[1] *Ex parte* Matthews, 277 Fed. 857.

[2] *Annual Report of the Commissioner General for 1925*, pp. 9-10.

[3] *Idem* for 1930, p. 22.

> *West Bound Parties*—New York to San Francisco. This party has two separate starting points, i. e. Chicago and New York, which necessitates the handling of same in two sections as far as El Paso. One section leaves New York and proceeds by water to New Orleans, and thence to El Paso, by way of the Southern Pacific Lines. The other section leaves Chicago and proceeds to El Paso by way of the Rock Island Railroad, joining the New York section at that point, whence the party proceeds to San Franciso.
>
> *East Bound Parties*—San Francisco to New York. This party leaves San Francisco and proceeds to New Orleans and thence by water to New York, all travel being over the Southern Pacific Lines.
>
> *East Bound Parties*—Seattle to New York. This party leaves Seattle and proceeds to New York by way of the Great Northern Railway, Chicago, Burlington and Quincy Railroad, or Chicago and Northwestern, or Chicago, Milwaukee and St. Paul Railroads; Chicago and St. Louis Railroad; and Lehigh Valley Railroad. Guards and attendants are furnished by these railroads free of charge and meals furnished at the rate of 50 cents each.[1]

The deportation division makes arrangements for the parties and advises officers in charge of the districts of the time of arrival, route followed, etc. of the parties. The notice is sent in time to permit all aliens ready and under orders of deportation in the district to join the parties. No deportee may be joined to a party without permission of the bureau in Washington, by letter if there is time and by telegraph in code if there is not.

Two inspectors are designated by the bureau as deportation party officers to accompany the parties. Their exclusive work consists in accompanying and caring for the details of management of such parties. They take turns on the differ-

[1] Bureau of immigration, General Order No. 152: *Transportation and Deportation of Aliens.*

ent routes,[1] each one serving in charge of one party. The inspector in charge of the party is responsible for the delivery of the deportees at the port from which they are to be sent. There is no limit to the number allotted to his care,[2] but he has aid from the doctor,[3] matrons and guards [4] who accompany them.

All types and conditions of deportation cases are brought together, without segregation. All who are scheduled and ready to leave are taken to the nearest railroad station on the

[1] The law permits the acceptance and use of free transportation on railroads in the United States by immigration officials who are engaged in official duty and are District Directors, or Assistant District Directors, Assistant Commissioners, Inspectors in Charge, Immigrant Inspectors and Patrol Inspectors. Officers bearing the title of Commissioner but who are not appointed by executive order are included, but not other Commissioners, clerks, matrons, guards, etc. To save expense, officers entitled to such free transportation are detailed as far as possible to accompany deportation parties.—Bureau of immigration, General Order No. 75.

[2] The largest deportation train in the history of the bureau of immigration reached Jersey City to transfer to Ellis Island on January 11, 1931, carrying 317 aliens, "including more than a hundred women and twelve lunatics."—*The Evening Sun*, New York, January 12, 1931, vol. xcviii, no. 111.

[3] A doctor always accompanies the party, except during such parts of the trip as may be made by water, when the ship's doctor attends the deportees if necessary. (The doctor who accompanies the party is apt to be a young private physician who wishes the trip.) He is allowed actual subsistence expenses not to exceed $5 a day while traveling on official business.—Bureau of immigration, General Order No. 77: *Subsistance in Deportation Cases.*

[4] The number of matrons depends on the number, physical and mental condition of the women in the party. The matrons are usually stenographers or other employees of the bureau of immigration who wish the trip.

Two guards for each car are furnished by the railroad companies. Any attendant of whatever kind to accompany deportation parties or individual aliens is appointed only under authority of the Department of Labor.—*Bureau of immigration*, General Order No. 152.

line over which deportation parties travel [1] and are there added to the varied assembly. Each alien is supposed to have his luggage labeled and sent with him,[2] but often his physical or mental condition is such that he is not responsible for his own belongings and despite the efforts of immigration officials, the luggage is lost or rifled en route. Another common occurrence is to have the alien joined to a deportation train with such speed that no notice is given him to pack and secure his possessions before deportation and he leaves the country minus both bags and money. Notification of the date of his joining the deportation train is sent to the district from which he is to be deported before he is joined to the party. Thus the officer in charge of the district containing the port of embarkation may fix "upon the time when and the vessel upon which deportation will occur." [3] In some circumstances a deportation train may come through the place where an alien is detained before he is completely ready for deportation. If he is almost ready, he is sent by the train, and arrangements are then continued at the port.

Eastbound trains gather up deportees and drop others off as they go. For instance, if a person deported from Seattle is to be sent from the port of Montreal, he would probably be taken from the train at Buffalo and sent in custody of an immigration official from there to Montreal, while the rest of the party continued to New York, for deportation from Ellis Island.

[1] Should it be found expedient to join aliens at other than the nearest station, permission is first secured from the bureau. If the district director considers it advisable for any reason to convey aliens to seaports or elsewhere separate from regular parties, he must also request authority therefor, by wire, letter, or telephone, giving reasons for the request.—*Ibid.*

[2] *Immigration Laws, op. cit.*, Rule 19, Subdivision Q.

[3] Third supplement to General Order No. 70.

When the train reaches the port terminal of the railroad at Jersey City, the deportees are transferred to a government tug or barge for the last short lap of their journey in the United States. Once they reach the island criminals are separated from non-criminals, women and children are separated from men.[1] The length of detention there varies according to whether the deportation formalities were complete before reaching the island. An attempt is made to ship all deportees within a few days or at most within two weeks from their arrival at the port, but even the latter is not always possible. There is room for detention at Ellis Island, for the days of intolerable crowding no longer exist, and restrictive immigration prevents the island from being filled nearly to capacity.

Ellis Island is not the only place where deportation cases are held in the last stage of their sojourn in the United States. Perhaps chief of the other stations used for detention is that at Gloucester City, near Philadelphia, where there is room for about 450 aliens. Angel Island at San Francisco, the Boston immigration station at East Boston, and the immigration station at Seattle are other important centres for deportation. Galveston, Texas, began to be used about 1925 as a detention and deportation station for those aliens whose cases originated principally in the southwestern states.[2]

[1] These classifications are maintained as long as the deportees are on Ellis Island, except that families are allowed certain visiting hours together.

[2] In 1925 alone, 329 aliens were deported through Galveston, resulting in a saving of approximately $20,868 in transportation costs to the government, by deporting the aliens from there instead of Ellis Island.—*Annual Report of the Commissioner General*, etc., *for 1925*, pp. 9-10.

THE VOYAGE

At length the alien is ready to be deported from the country. When he boards the ship he is usually given the money, valuables, etc. kept from him during detention.

If the deportee is sent within five years of his landing here and his steamship trip to this country can be verified, he is sent at the expense of the steamship company which brought him here. The statute provides:

If deportation proceedings are instituted at any time within five years after the entry of the alien, such deportation, including one-half of the entire cost of removal to the port of deportation shall be at the expense of the contractor, procurer, or other person by whom the alien was unlawfully induced to enter the United States, or, if that can not be done, then the cost of removal to the port of deportation shall be at the expense of the appropriation for the enforcement of this act, and the deportation from such port shall be at the expense of the owner or owner of such vessels or transportation lines by which such aliens respectively came, or, if that is not practicable, at the expense of the appropriation for the enforcement of this act. If deportation proceedings are instituted later than five years after the entry of the aliens, or, if the deportation is made by reason of causes arising subsequent to entry the cost thereof shall be payable from the appropriation for the enforcement of this act.[1]

If the alien's trip to the United States cannot be verified, no matter when he entered, or if he has been here more than five years before deportation takes place, the government pays the deportation expense.[2]

[1] Immigration act of 1917, sec. 20. *Vide* also *Immigration Rules*, etc., *of January 1, 1930*, Rule 19, Subdivision M. par. 2.

[2] *Entry* here obviously means entry by sea, for it would be difficult for the government to make a steamship company assume deportation expense for an alien it had brought to this country 30 years previous and who had crossed the Niagara river to Canada and returned within a few minutes and had then become deportable within five years after entry.

If after deportation has been ordered, the alien requests and obtains an extension of time that seems unusual or unreasonable he must deposit in advance a sum sufficient to cover such expenses as may be incurred by the government during the additional time here.[1]

Similar arrangements are made for European aliens who enter the United States through Canada. By the Transatlantic Passenger Conference Agreement [2] between the United States government and steamship lines carrying passengers to Canada, companies transporting passengers to Canada agree to assume the same liability as imposed by American law on bringing passengers to the United States. In other words, if a man lands in Canada and then enters the United States within five years and becomes deportable from the United States within that period, the steamship company which took him to Canada is responsible for his transportation expenses back to Europe. The United States government, however, pays the land journey to the port in Canada through which the steamship is going to deport him. As steamers run irregularly in winter from certain Canadian ports, some lines with service to both Canada and the United States arrange to deport such aliens on their ships running from New York instead of waiting until Canadian ports are open. Difficulties of transportation and expense are thus lessened.

Statutory authority for such agreements was finally given by the immigration act of 1924, where it is provided:

> The Commissioner General, with the approval of the Secretary of Labor, shall have power to enter into contracts with transportation lines for the entry and inspection of aliens coming into the United States from or through foreign contiguous

[1] *Ibid.*, par. 3.

[2] November 24, 1919.

territory. In prescribing rules and regulations and making contracts for the entry and inspection of aliens applying for admission from or through foreign contiguous territory due care shall be exercised to avoid any discriminatory action in favor of transportation companies transporting to such territory aliens destined to the United States, and all such transportation companies shall be required as a condition precedent to the inspection and examination under rules and contracts at the ports of such contiguous territory of aliens brought thereto by them, to submit to and comply with all the requirements of this act which would apply were they bringing such aliens directly to ports of the United States.[1]

There is no such agreement between the United States government and steamship lines running to Mexico. Unless an alien entering this country from Mexico had gone there by a steamship complying with the United States immigration regulations, he would have to live there two years before applying for legal entrance into the United States.[2]

The deportee is supposed to be provided with a ticket to the point where his ticket of embarkation to the United States was bought, if it is possible to find out where such purchase was made. Otherwise he is supposed to be given a railroad ticket or further steamship ticket to the city or town from which he came. If he is physically and mentally well and of adult age, no attempt is made to follow him up and see that he uses his ticket beyond his landing overseas. In practice it becomes the responsibility of the country where he debarks to see that he goes further. So an Italian entering the United States illegally would supposedly be provided with a ticket to the town in Italy whence he came, but if the boat on which he was deported from the United States landed at LeHavre, he would not have to proceed further, unless the

[1] Sec. 17.

[2] *Ibid.*

French government insisted on his continuing the journey. France, incidentally, has received so many deportees with no ticket, passport, or money, that she is beginning to insist that they be routed through the country.

The immigration act of 1924 requires special care and attendance during the trip in cases of any kind of serious illness:

When in the opinion of the Secretary of Labor the mental or physical condition of such alien is such as to require personal care and attendance, the said Secretary shall when necessary employ a suitable person for that purpose, who shall accompany such alien to his or her final destination, and the expense incident to such service shall be defrayed in the same manner as the expense of deporting the accompanied alien is defrayed.[1]

It is furthermore provided that:

a failure or refusal on the part of the masters, agents, owners or consignees of vessels to comply with the order of the Secretary of Labor to take on board, guard safely, and transport to the destination specified any alien ordered to be deported under the provisions of this act shall be punished.[2]

There are various special regulations in order to carry out these provisions. In the first place, notice is sent to the steamship company of *any* deportation, whether at government or steamship company expense, together with a brief description of the alien "and other appropriate data," including cause of deportation, physical and mental condition, and destination, so that attendants may be provided where necessary. The attendants for care of insane and diseased aliens are supplied by arrangement with the steamship company[3] "to provide such care and attention as his (the

[1] Sec. 20.

[2] *Ibid.* The fine is $300 for each violation.—Sec. 18.

[3] Under the Transportation Agreement.

alien's) condition requires, not only during the ocean voyage but also . . . during the foreign inland journey."[1] The practice is as follows: The deportee who is insane or seriously ill is delivered to the master or first or second officer of the steamship. The master is then given a report form in three parts,[2] each of which is to be filled out and returned to the United States immigration service at the proper time. Thus the first sheet is a receipt for the alien and his luggage, money, valuables, etc., and is signed and returned immediately to the immigration officer who delivered the alien[3] on board the boat. The other two sheets are kept on the vessel until the end of the voyage. Then the second sheet is mailed back to the United States immigration service, describing the condition of the deportee during the trip, the care and attention given him en route, and the place in the ship where he was carried.

Last of all, the steamship company at its expense[4] forwards the alien from the foreign port of disembarkation to his destination

in charge of a proper attendant except only in cases where foreign public officials decline to allow such attendants to proceed and themselves take charge of the alien, which fact must be shown by signing the form provided in the lower half of sheet C. If the foreign public officials do not take charge at the port of disembarkation, but at an interior frontier, both forms on

[1] *Immigration Laws,* etc., *of January 1, 1930,* Rule 20, Subdivision A, par. 1.

[2] Form 597, Sheets A, B and C.

[3] *Immigration Laws,* etc., *of January 1, 1930,* Rule 20, Subdivision A, par. 2.

[4] The Transatlantic Passenger Conference Agreement provides that steamship companies parties to it agree to transport mentally or physically defective deportees at $150 (plus regular fare for each individual) for special care and attention, for parties of five or less.

sheet C must be filled out, the former in relation to the inland journey as far as such frontier.[1]

Usually, the report returned to this country contains the signature of the relative, friend, or official to whom the deportee was finally delivered. In some countries such as Italy, public authorities take the alien into custody as soon as he arrives in his own country and do not allow the custodian of the steamship company to continue. Thus an insane Italian girl landing in Naples and destined to Florence, would not be accompanied to Florence by the steamship representative, but would be delivered in Naples to the custody of an Italian official, who would sign the receipt for her.

In case the steamship company fails to comply with the rules or does not return the forms properly executed within 90 days after the departure of the alien," the Secretary of Labor shall thereafter and without notice employ suitable persons, at the expense of such company, to accompanying aliens requiring personal care and attendance when deported on any vessel of such company." [2] There is nothing in the law or regulations requiring the employment of women attendants for women patients, but the practice is usually to send women in such cases.[3]

THE PERMANENT BAR AGAINST RETURN

The rest is silence. What happens to deportees on their return to Europe from the United States is not known save in a few isolated cases. If they are mentally or physically

[1] *Immigration Laws*, etc., *of January 1, 1930*, Rule 20, Subdivision A, par. 3.

[2] *Ibid.*, par. 4.

[3] The custodians, whether appointed by the steamship company or otherwise, are paid actual expenses of not more than $5.00 a day, plus $1.00 nominal fee for the trip. Often the custodians are friends of inspectors, or are ex-officials of the immigration service.

ill, nobody knows whether they are merely dropped at their destination or cared for; if they are in economic straits, it is not known whether or not financial readjustment is possible; if they are criminals whether or not they continue their criminal careers is unknown. As far as the United States is concerned the deportee and his social problems drop into the void.

One thing is certain. A person once deported from the United States may not ever legally return to this country. Formerly only such "undesirables" as prostitutes, criminals, and anarchists, were permanently debarred from reentry into the United States. Others might return at any time after the expiration of a year from the date of their deportation, and if special permission were granted even within the year. All that has been changed, for an act of March 4, 1929,[1] "in some respects the most drastic immigration law ever enacted,"[2] provides that anyone now arrested and deported from the United States, no matter for what cause, may never again enter the country. Should he attempt to enter or succeed in so doing, he is guilty of a felony and upon conviction is punishable by imprisonment for not more than two years or by fine of not more than $1,000 or both.[3]

The act as originally adopted prohibited return to the United States of anyone *ever* arrested and deported in pursuance of law. That is, the prohibition against returning applied to those deported prior as well as subsequent to the passage of the law. The serious effects of such arrangement became so apparent that on June 18, 1929 the Senate passed a bill which eliminated the retroactive aspect of the law by vesting in the Secretary of Labor power to readmit aliens deported prior to March 4, 1929, provided of course

[1] Public No. 1018, 70th Congress, 2nd Session.

[2] *Annual Report of the Secretary of Labor for,* etc., *1930,* p. 62.

[3] Unless a different penalty is otherwise expressly provided by law.

they were not otherwise excludable. The bill was amended in the House and passed in this form, that only where prior to March 4, 1929, the Secretary of Labor gave permission to reapply is it possible for a deported alien to return to the United States. Otherwise he may never come back. There are doubtless many cases where the Secretary would have given such permission had there been any reason for doing so.[1] His permission often would have been only a gesture, for the demand for visas was so great that many deported aliens could not possibly hope to obtain a place in the quota for years ahead. Furthermore, a deported alien was free to return to the United States at the end of a year from the date of his deportation, unless he fell among the group of those mandatorily excludable. The amendment alleviated the difficulties of those who had received permission to reapply for admission to the United States and who had suddenly by legislative enactment been forbidden to use such permission.

For those who did not receive permission before March 4, 1929, deportation is permanent banishment. Deportation may occur for a mere technical violation of law, possibly unwitting on the part of the alien, yet even in such case he may not legally return. Even if his home, family and business connections are in this country, he still is ineligible to return. Many of the officials of the Department of Labor, charged with administration of the law, feel that the rigors of the act are far too great and need modification on humanitarian grounds. Both the Secretary of Labor[2] and the Commissioner General of Immigration[3] have recommended that the Secretary of Labor be author-

[1] *Vide Foreign Language Information Service Interpreter Release*, vol. vi, no. 20, June 26, 1929.

[2] *Annual Report, etc., for 1929*, pp. 46-7.

[3] *Annual Report*, etc., *for 1929*, p. 32, and *for 1930*, p. 48.

ized to permit aliens deported before March 4, 1929 to apply, in meritorious cases, for readmission, while the Commissioner General extends his recommendation to those aliens *hereafter* deported. An Assistant to the Secretary has also voiced his opinion of the matter, for on June 10, 1930 he stated:

I do not think there is anyone who has to do with the enforcement of the immigration law who does not agree that the Congress ought to modify the drastic provisions of the Act of March 4, 1929 which forbids the readmission of an alien who has been expelled at any time in the past, or who has been ordered expelled. So many hardships and injustices arise under this statute that one finds difficulty in excusing the failure of Congress thus far to amend this harsh enactment.

My classic illustration is that of two adventurous youths who entered the United States last summer by way of the freight tunnel under the Detroit River. They entered surreptitiously, evading inspection, and by so doing clearly violated the law. They rode on to the Middle West, beating their way on freight trains. They were en route to the harvest fields of Kansas and Nebraska. They were put off the train in a small Missouri town. The immigration officers were notified, and after they had been in jail a few weeks they were ordered deported. The Washington representative of a Canadian newspaper came to me about the matter, he having heard of it through some anxiety of kinsfolk in his home city. He wanted to secure authorization for the voluntary departure of these young men, so that they would not be in the status of deportees. Unfortunately there was nothing that could be done. They had been ordered deported—expelled—quite properly, as the law by its mandatory terms provides. . . . The very making of an order of deportation would forever prevent the readmission of these two lads.

I submit that the statute which justifies, or attempts to justify, this sort of a situation is unnecessarily harsh. God only knows what is in the future for these two boys. One of them may become an honored citizen of the Dominion within the next decade or two. But even if he should attain distinction, or acquire wealth, he could not at any time be readmitted to the United States because of this deportation record, resulting from an adventurous undertaking of his youth, which had no real criminal aspect, which worked no one any great harm, and which certainly ought to be curable by the passage of time. . . .

It seems to me that once we have accomplished the expulsion of a law violator the question of his readmission, should he desire it, ought to be for the consideration of those who are charged with enforcement of the law . . . there ought to be authority in a particular case for the readmission of an alien whose violation of our law has been of a technical nature, or who has been shown to be lacking in viciousness of intent. . . . I am convinced that the perpetual barrier of the existing statute is too drastic, and that the denial to administrative officers of authority to consider the merits of particular cases is a reflection upon the probity and judgment of such administrative officers and as great an injustice to them as to the aliens whose cases they must consider.[1]

Permanent banishment from the United States has worked such hardships in many cases that administrative officials have developed a practice of withholding an order of deportation, or withdrawing it when issued, if the alien in volved has an American-born wife or children or both; in such cases they allow the alien to depart from the country within a certain period of time. For instance, a German entering illegally in 1924 and since married to an American, and the father of two American-born children, would suffer great hardship if deported in 1930 from the country of his wife and children and never allowed to return. In such a case, he would be allowed to depart, without issuance of a warrant of deportation. This practice is not sanctioned in

[1] Address of the Hon. Peter F. Snyder, Assistant to the Secretary of Labor, before the National Conference of Social Work, Boston, June 10, 1931.

either statute or regulation but has developed with silent assent within the Department of Labor as a administrative measure of relief from a statute which otherwise would oppress not only aliens but American citizens as well.

The issuance of a warrant of deportation and its uncancelled existence is the all-important factor in determining permission for a deported alien to return to the United States. The act of March 4, 1929 further provides:

> any alien ordered deported (whether before or after the enactment of this Act) who has left the United States shall be considered to have been deported in pursuance of law irrespective of the source from which the expenses of his transportation were defrayed or of the place to which he departed.[1]

When the warrant of deportation states that the alien involved may ship foreign as a seaman or otherwise voluntarily depart, it has been held that the alien is merely complying with the deportation warrant and is technically deported.[2] Therefore voluntary departure with no warrant of deportation in existence has a different effect from voluntary departure with such warrant outstanding. In the former case there is no bar to return to the United States, while in the latter, banishment is permanent. It is of note that " there is not now, nor has there ever been, statutory authority even

[1] Sec. 1 (b).

[2] Bureau of immigration, General Order No. 152. This order also provides that where the warrant of deportation provides for shipment foreign without any provision . . . for voluntary departure by other means, such voluntary departure may be permitted, with consent of the sureties, if the alien is at large or under proper safeguards if he is not at large under bond, and such departure will be regarded as a compliance with the terms of the warrant. . . . In every case of such voluntary departure of shipment foreign, the warrant of deportation must be so indorsed as clearly to show either that the alien departed. . . . Such voluntary departure of shipment foreign will be regarded as deportation, so far as the right of the alien to return to the United States is concerned.

for the sort of voluntary departure that, wisely, justly, and for economy's sake, has been permitted by the Labor Department throughout a long period of years."[1] There is not even any order of the Department providing for such departure.

With the administration of the provisions providing permanent exclusion for persons deported from the country, another government department comes into the picture. How is the consul in a foreign country to know that a person applying to him for admission to enter the United States has been deported and so cannot reapply? Word is sent to the Department of State of every deportation since the act of 1929 went into effect, together with information descriptive of the deportee, and the place to which he is deported.[2]

The difficulties of such procedure may be imagined. It is feasible to notify the American consuls *in* the country to which the deportee is sent, but it becomes a well-nigh impossible task when notification must be sent to all the consular posts. A man might be deported to France, and later go to China, there to apply for admission to the United States. If he were otherwise admissible and had changed his name,[3] he could easily slip by, for it would be a difficult task for the local consul at the place in China where the man applied to check up on *all* deportations throughout the world.

Here again it is impossible to make the administration of the law absolutely water-tight. Aliens once deported from the country still continue to re-enter. It is possible that the provision of the act making reentry after deportation a felony has a deterrent effect on some attempts at readmission. It also seems possible that the more law-abiding persons, those who would make the most desirable citizens, are the

[1] Speech of Hon. Peter F. Snyder, *op. cit.*

[2] The Department of Justice is also notified. General Order No. 151.

[3] He would have to have identification papers, etc.

ones deterred from entry, and that criminals and law-breakers generally would feel scant concern over the fact of being a felon on attempted reentry.

So the process may continue indefinitely and deportation be but a temporary solution for the United States. It is certain that from the point of view of the social problems involved deportation offers merely an international passing along and not solution.

The Warrant of Deportation in the Cases Studied

In general the charges in the warrants of deportation were the same as in the warrants of arrest, though after consideration by the board of review, various charges were recommended to be dropped, the most common being " L. P. C." In all cases where this recommendation was made, the Assistant to the Secretary accepted it and issued the warrant accordingly. In nine cases, the board recommended an additional charge, and in each of those instances, the hearings was reopened and the additional charge lodged against the alien; in no case was there objection raised.

As may be seen from the cases in chapter XI, the country to which deportation is to take place is largely determined by what country will take the deportee. In fourteen of the total number of cases, the warrant of deportation was amended to read to a country not the original one named.

Two of the cases contained no warrants of deportation. These may have been held in the local records, although when served they are supposed to be returned to the files of the bureau in Washington for completion of the case.

The Deportation Parties and Trains

The author met two deportation parties on their arrival in New York, one by Southern Pacific boat from New Orleans having started in San Francisco and taken ship in New

Orleans for New York; the other by train from Seattle, detraining at the New Jersey pier terminal of the Lehigh Valley Railroad after six days en route. The party arriving by boat contained twenty-four deportees, all men, with an inspector in charge and seven guards provided by the Southern Pacific, as there were eight insane men among the party. The men all travelled III class,[1] with the insane segregated from the others, and kept two in a room with barred portholes, and guarded outside the door day and night. The "others" included both criminals and illegal entries, all kept in one room at night but allowed on the III class deck during the day.

On reaching the dock in New York, the deportees were tagged. Then they walked, those that were able carrying their own luggage, to the government tug waiting to carry them to Ellis Island. On the tug the insane were kept in the deck-house separate from the others, and closely guarded.

The party arriving from Seattle by train contained 159 persons on arrival, though fifteen had been put off at Buffalo, for deportation from Montreal, and thirteen had been dropped at Bethlehem, Pa., to be sent to the Gloucester City immigration station near Philadelphia for deportation from there. The number reaching the eastern end of the journey had among it about eighteen women, four children ranging in ages from a baby in arms to nine years, about fourteen insane men and women, one tuberculous girl and two men on stretchers (one of these had attempted to escape from a local county jail and had broken his back in so doing). Families were kept together in the train, but in general there was no segregation, and insane and convicts, children, and illegal entries travelled in the same car.

[1] If there had been women in the party, they would in general have been sent second class. Married couples, however, are sent together third class.

The train consisted of eight or nine cars of the "tourist" type[1] or else of out-dated Pullman cars, carrying a porter and two guards in each of the cars, which had barred windows.[2] Warm meals had been brought into the train at various points en route until Chicago, but after that "box lunches" were carried.

The motley assembly was sent by barge to Ellis Island and there taken immediately to a room where identification was made. The insane and ill were first identified and then sent to the hospital on the island for care until deportation. The remainder were gradually separated into categories of criminals and non-criminals and each male class was held in one great room pending deportation. The women deportees were sent to the main quarters of the island, where other aliens, not deportees, were held. An effort was made to separate prostitutes from others.

Just before deportation occurs, any money or other possessions, taken from the alien for safekeeping must be returned to him. In the records read, amounts of money varying from twenty-seven cents to $200 were so returned. In two cases accusation was made by the deportees that the jailers had taken their money and not returned it, but no investigation was reported. In a number of cases, it was stated that the persons deported had money in the bank, or that they had furniture or other possessions. No mention is made in the record of securing such money; it is possible the local record would contain the information. However, the record does state the personal baggage taken with the alien.

[1] A cross between a Pullman and a day coach.

[2] On this particular train, none of the insane were violent, but had they been, they would have been kept in straight-jackets or in the ladies' or men's rooms of the train.

The Voyage in the Cases Studied

Two hundred and one cases of the total were deported at steamship company expense, and the rest at government expense. In three cases the steamship companies felt they should not have to bear the expense of deportation, and so the warrants of deportation were amended to read " at government expense," as shown in the following:

Pasquale Picco (Case 99).

Pasquale Picco was born in 1900, near Milan, Italy. He entered the United States on April 3, 1923, on the S. S. *Conte Rosso* of the Lloyd Sabaudo Line, as a passenger in transit to Canada. He went immediately to Canada and stayed there (place unknown) until May 23, 1925, when he entered the United States in a rowboat across the Detroit river, paying $40 to a smuggler for the trip.

He was apprehended and taken to police headquarters in Detroit where he was detained five days before being released on bond. He was then held under court order as a witness in the prosecution of his smuggler.

Mr. Picco was given a hearing at the Detroit immigration office on June 16, 1925, through an interpreter. He was represented by a lawyer who presented a brief a week later. At the hearing, Mr. Picco stated he had been legally admitted to Canada and so wanted to return there; this the lawyer reiterated in his brief. Furthermore, Mr. Picco insisted that he had not known it was wrong to enter the United States as he did, but thought paying $40 for the trip was a legitimate method of entry.

A warrant was issued for his deportation on October 3, 1925, on the same grounds as in the warrant of arrest, i. e. (1) " L. P. C.", (2) that he entered without inspection, (3) that he was not in possession of an unexpired immigration visa on entry. Deportation was directed to Italy at the expense of the steamship line. However, the Lloyd Sabaudo protested on November 14, stating that as Mr. Picco had left the United States in 1923 immediately on entry, going to Canada, where he had been destined, the steamship line's liability for deportation ended, particularly as Mr. Picco had lived for two years in Canada. On November 20, the board of review directed the warrant to be amended to direct deportation at government expense. Mr. Picco was deported on December 5, 1925, on the S. S. *Giuseppe Verdi,* at government expense.

In those cases where there was serious physical or mental disability, a report was supposed to be sent back as to the condition of the patient during the trip and his delivery at his final destination. In twenty-six of one hundred and thirty six cases where such report might have been made the record did not contain any report beyond deportation. This might be explained by the possibility of delay in returning the forms, or by their loss en route from Europe.

Reports as to the ocean voyage were perfunctory, stating merely that the deportee was transported in the ship's hospital, or elsewhere, and that he was " seasick," " disturbed," " quiet," etc.

The reports of arrival and delivery show European transportation, usually overland, in company with an attendant sent by the steamship lines. So far as could be discovered from the names, all but three of the ill or insane women deportees were accompanied by a woman attendant, but in a number of cases, it was merely stated that the women were sent to their destination, cared for by " an attendant." The sex of the attendants in the cases of children who were deported alone is known in but one case, where a woman was employed.

Those who had received special care were signed for by relatives, police officials, heads of institutions, etc. The signatures in many cases were entirely illegible. Many signatures of relatives were made with a cross, and the name written in below.

Cases not involving illness presented a different situation.

It is not possible to learn from the records with any degree of assurance whether a person who had come to this country first or second class was deported in that class in which he arrived but it is thought not. Save in 4 instances where deportation was made in the second class of the steamer, it is probable that deportation in the cases examined were made in the third class.

It is particularly difficult to find out what happened on arrival to deportees who were not ill or insane and so were not accompanied to their destinations. The records tell us nothing beyond the date and steamer on which deportation took place in all cases where the deportees were in good physical and mental health and were fully grown. The records state nothing in regard to provision with tickets, etc. for further travel.

The Permanent Bar Against Return in the Case Studied

A number of the persons deported had previously been deported from the United States and had then reentered, either legally or illegally. Those of the 1925 group who were not members of the seriously "undesirable" classes could have secured permission legally to return. Seventeen had previously been deported from the country and only two had secured permission to reenter before they came back and were again deported. The other fifteen had not received such permission but had slipped in anyway. They included eight criminals, two prostitutes, one insane public charge, two tuberculosis public charges, and two "L. P. C."

The following are cases of people more than once deported from the United States.

John Clancy (Case 100).

John Clancy was born in 1896 in County Mayo, Ireland. In February, 1925, he entered the United States as a seaman, deserting the steamer in Mobile, Ala. The following year he was admitted to the United States army and served there for two years, receiving an honorable discharge.

On April 27, 1927, Mr. Clancy was sentenced to 1 year, 3 months—2 years, 6 months in Sing Sing for attempted grand larceny, second degree. A warrant of arrest was issued for him on June 7, 1927, and he was given a hearing at prison on August 16, 1927. An application for a passport was made on October 7, 1927, to the Irish Free State legation, and the date of its issuance is not known. A warrant of deportation was issued on September 30, of that year, but deportation did not take place until June 23, 1928. The grounds in the warrant were the same as in the warrant of arrest, i. e. (1) that he entered without inspection, (2) that he entered by water at a place or time other than as designated for entry (seaman); (3) that he had been sentenced subsequent to May 1, 1917 to a year or more for a crime involving moral turpitude committed within five years of entry.

Mr. Clancy next came to the United States as a stowaway on the *Leviathan*, on October 2, 1928, but when taken before a board of special inquiry was rejected, and returned to England on the same boat three days later.

He then went from England to Canada, landing in Montreal as a stowaway on April 19, 1929, and getting ashore unseen. He walked across the border at Nyando, N. Y., by crossing the New York Central bridge, on May 21, 1929. He was soon apprehended as a suspicious person and held in the custody of the sheriff at Malone, N. Y. Mr. Clancy was sentenced on July 12, to serve six months in the Onondaga Penitentiary at Jamesville, N. Y. for violation of the act of March 4, 1929, in entering illegally. He escaped from prison in September but was recaptured the next day, and held in the penintentiary until April 23, 1930. A warrant of deportation was meanwhille issued (date unknown) on the grounds (1) "L. P. C.", (2) that he entered without inspection, (3) that he entered the United States within 1 year of deportation, etc., (4) that he entered by land at a time or place not designated for entry, (5) that he was sentenced to imprisonment for the commission of a crime involving moral turpitude previous to entry, (6) at the time of his entry he was a member of 1 or more of the classes excluded by law, namely, sec. 1 (a) of the action approved March 4, 1929, being an alien who has been arrested and deported in pursuance of law.

Mr. Clancy was deported on May 24, 1930 at government expense.

The following is a case where permission was granted to reapply for admission:

Frank Doonan (Case 101).

Frank Doonan was born in 1901 in County Down, Ireland. He went to Canada as a harvester, landing in Quebec on August 3, 1923, but he decided he would like to go to the United States. He was three times refused admission at the border, and so he remained in Montreal, earning $40 a week as an automobile washer.

On August 1, 1925, Mr. Doonan entered the United States on a train from Montreal, but was taken from the train by an immigrant inspector, and detained in the Caledonia County Jail, St. Johnsbury, Vt. A warrant was issued for his arrest on August 3, and a hearing was given him at the jail two days later. Mr. Doonan had secured a lawyer, who requested deportation to Canada rather than England as he had paid the passage there of Miss Mary Andrews and her 2-year old son, and was expecting them to join him in Canada or the United States. Mr. Doonan was the father of the child, and was planning to marry Miss Andrews on her arrival.

A warrant of deportation was issued on August 23, 1925, with the same charges as in the warrant of arrest, i. e., " L. P. C.", (2) that he entered the United States within one year from the date of exclusion, permission to reapply not having been granted, (3) that he was not in possession of an unexpired immigration visa on entry. Deportation was directed to England. The Canadian immigtation authorities were also notified at the same time to be on the watch for Miss Andrews and her child, so that they might be deported to England from Canada.

Mr. Doonan was deported on September 18, 1925, from Montreal, at the expense of the steamship company. Overland travel was less in deporting him from there than from New York. On November 23, he wrote the bureau of immigration that he had married Miss Andrews and had returned to Canada with her and the child, and would like permission for them to reapply for admission within one year from his deportation. This was granted.

The following case shows deportation of someone formerly excluded:

Bridget O'Toole (Case 102).

Bridget O'Toole was born on July 4, 1898 in County Galway, Ireland, as one of seven children. She attended the parochial school near her home, but it is not known at what age she stopped.

Three older brothers emigrated to the United States and in 1921 Miss O'Toole arrived in New York, landing at Ellis Island on April 27. She was detained there six weeks, as when examined on May 6 by a board of special inquiry, she was found to be pregnant. One of her brothers appealed the case, but the exclusion order was upheld on May 19 of that year, and she was returned home on June 11. On June 6 her child had been born prematurely, at the Ellis Island hospital, and died the same day. Only four days later Miss O'Toole was returned home.

However, as she was afraid to let her parents know what had happened, she persuaded the matron of the steerage passengers on the boat on which she was returned to allow her to go to Liverpool and not go to Ireland. She remained in a convent in Liverpool for two years, then went home and stayed a year.

In May, 1924, she sailed with her younger sister to Quebec and then went to Toronto. Their brother drove across the border from the United States on June 18 and then drove the two girls back into the United States. He took them to St. Paul, Minn. There the older girl, Bridget, got work in a laundry, but had been here less than a month when she was reported to the immigration authorities by a " confidential " source, on July 23.

A warrant was issued for her arrest on July 23[1] and she was released on bond of $500, provided by her brother on August 12. From July 23 to August 12, she had been held in the local jail (?) On August 13, a hearing was given her at the St. Paul immigration station.

On September 26, 1924 a warrant of deportation was issued, on the same grounds as in the warrant of arrest, i. e. " L. P. C.", (2) that she entered without inspection, (3) that she entered in violation of the " passport act." On December 31, 1924, a lawyer retained by the brother wrote the bureau of immigration that Miss O'Toole would be glad to pay her own and her sister's expenses to Canada if they could return there. On February 24, 1925, the bureau wrote direct to Dublin to ascertain if a passport could be granted through the British Consul General, but no passport was available until July 6. Five days later, Miss O'Toole and her sister were sent to Ellis Island, and deported on July 18, at the expense of the steamship company which had brought them. They would normally have been deported from Montreal, but as the line at whose expense they were sent had sailings from either port, they were sent from New York to save overland transportation expense.

None of the cases in the 1930 group, no matter for what reason they were deported, may ever return to the United States, and deportation for them is permanent banishment, unless they enter illegally. Many of the cases already cited will furnish food for thought as to the seriousness of permanent deportation from the United States, for as a 19-year old girl stated in one of the cases " never is such a long time." One further case may serve to show the situation of the person permanently deported from the country:

[1] A warrant was also issued for her sister, but she forms a separate record in the bureau.

Giorgio Amato (Case 103).

Giorgio Amato was born on April 16, 1885 in Zennevetro, Italy. He came to the United States in 1913, and lived in North Haven, Conn. until 1920. He kept the same position all those years, with a brick-making concern. In 1919 he went to school to learn English and prepare for citizenship.

In November, 1920 Mr. Amato's father wrote him it was time for him to marry, and said he had picked out the girl in Italy. On December 8, his son sailed for Italy to marry. He wanted to return to the United States immediately after his marriage in February, 1921, but when he applied for return, he found he could not secure the entry of his wife. He stayed in Italy until 1928, and then finally secured admission to the United States temporarily as a visitor, thinking he could arrange for permanent entry after landing here. He landed July 22, 1928.

Mr. Amato returned immediately to North Haven, where he secured his old job at the brickyard, earning from $3.50-$4.90 a day. It is not known how his whereabouts became known to the immigration service. A warrant was issued for his arrest on September 6, 1929 and has served on him at work in the brickyard. He was taken to the jail at Hartford, Conn., and held overnight when he was released on $500 bond. A hearing was given him at home on September 15. There he stated that he had $1027 in the savings bank, $500 in the Bank of America and $500 in Italian government bonds, as well as eight acres of land in North Haven. It is not known whether he had bought the land before 1920 or since his return, as the record does not make it clear. He also had his first papers.

A warrant of deportation was issued on November 20, 1929, on the ground that Mr. Amato had stayed longer than the time allotted for a visit. He urgently requested that he be allowed to pay his own way, to save the stigma of deportation, and this was granted. However the warrant of deportation was still outstanding, and his voluntary departure on January 2(?), 1930 constituted deportation. He had a valid passport of his own, and departed without being identified, so the bureau of immigration recommended that a certificate be required from the

American consul in Genoa as evidence of Mr. Amato's departure from the United States. He appeared before the consul on March 21. He can never return to the United States.

CONCLUSIONS

As already indicated, what happens to deportees on their return to the country of origin is not known save in a few isolated cases. In many cases the records are incomplete. There is need of careful study abroad of repatriation procedure, care taken of deportees, adjustments made, attempts at reemigration to the United States or elsewhere, before the entire procedure can be evaluated from either the domestic or international points of view.

One thing, however, seems certain. From the cases included in this study one may discover that in many instances deported persons are not themselves necessarily "undesirable" and might prove desirable in the United States if allowed to reenter on a legal basis. It would seem eminently humane and desirable from every point of view that the Secretary of Labor be given the discretion for which he asks in certain cases to readmit deported aliens to the United States. That a technical violator of law should be permanently banished from a country in which he may have his every association is beyond measure in the severity of punishment inflicted.

CHAPTER XIII

Conclusion

ADDISON tells in his day of a mountebank who traveled from one country fair to another selling pills good for the earthquake. Unfortunately here there is no one pill which will prevent eruptions or effect a cure, for the factors are too many and too varied. Even if such a remedy were available, this would not be the place in which to prescribe it, as the field of the study at hand is necessarily limited and its aim is primarily descriptive. There is need for further investigation of facts concerning many other aspects of deportation before conclusions may be reached with any degree of finality.

Even the facts collected here point the way to several possible conclusions in regard to law and administration as well as the international and social aspects of the problem. Congress has enacted piecemeal laws to meet particular immigration problems as they have arisen, with the result that there are many fragmentary and often conflicting and discriminatory enactments.[1] There is need not only for simplification and clarification of the mass of acts relating to deportation but for their codification into one comprehensive and clear statute which in so far as possible does not protect the strong at the expense of the weak.

Several possibilities for change arise on the statutory side. First of all, "moral turpitude" seems to have outlived its usefulness and is, in some jurisdictions, at least, of no protection to the alien in preventing his deportation for trifling offenses or for acts which do not necessarily indicate that

[1] *Annual Report of the Secretary of Labor for*, etc., *1930*, pp. 16 and 18.

he will become a disturbance to our body politic. Secondly, the law seems to bear with particular severity on those aliens whose deportation from the country can be accomplished without time limit after their entry. A number of cases cited in this study indicate that even in regard to persons of the most undesirable sort there is unfairness in lack of any statute of limitations for certain categories. Aliens entering the United States as babies or small children, and later in life becoming prostitutes, criminals, narcotic traffickers or anarchists, have become such, due in no small measure to social conditions in the United States. Countries from which such persons came many years ago feel it unjust to hold them responsible for what happens so long after the arrival in the United States of one of their citizens. The removal of all time limit for deportation of especially " undesirable " aliens and the particular interpretation given to the word " entry " by the United States Supreme Court often cause deportation to countries from which a person has long been absent. It would seem that a five-year statute of limitations for deportation from the United States is a fair limitation from the points of view of both the United States and foreign countries. It may be said that aliens long in this country should have been naturalized, but ignorance of the implications of the law, verification of landing, and many other reasons may have prevented.

Another desirable statutory change would be one forbidding deportation of children alone and unaccompanied. The First General Child Welfare Congress in 1925 called attention to indiscriminate dumping of alien children from one country into another and suggested that it should never be resorted to if it is likely to be harmful to the interests of the child. The three cases studied of children deported without relatives or friends to other countries indicate that the United States has not yet abandoned the practice.

A particularly desirable statutory change would be one amending the provisions of the 1929 immigration law which forever forbid reentry to aliens once deported from the United States. The Department of Labor officials most intimately associated with the administration of the law have clearly stated their feeling of the necessity of alleviating the hardships of permanent banishment from the country in cases where particular difficulties are involved. The cases cited in this study indicate the manifest desirability of such change.

How is it to be decided what cases involve particular difficulty and hardship? At present, the extra-legal decision which may prevent technical deportation is reached on the basis of whether or not the deported alien has an American-born wife or husband or children. If he has, the warrant of deportation is not issued, or is cancelled, and he is allowed voluntarily to leave the country, to prevent hardship to the American members of his family. Such a practice is but one indication of the necessity of giving the Secretary of Labor discretion to grant readmission to the United States after deportation if he deems such readmission necessary to mitigate hardship.

It would seem wise, in fact, for the Secretary to have somewhat larger discretionary powers than he now possesses in regard to deportation in general. If a person under the existing law falls definitely within one or more of the categories or deportable aliens, he is deportable and the Secretary has no authority to prevent it. This is particularly true in such cases as anarchists, prostitutes, criminals involved in moral turpitude, insane persons, etc., where because of the manifest undesirability of such persons in the community, deportation is mandatory. There is need for study of such cases as already exist where deportation has not been carried out, and of the reasons therefor, which might range from political considerations to lack of passports. If the Secretary of Labor were given statutory discretion to prevent deportation in cases where particular hardship is involved, or to grant re-admission to those deported who otherwise qualify, abuse of discretion could be prevented by a requirement that he must specify in writing over his official signature and upon the official record in each case the reason for his favorable exercise of special discretion, and that each year he must report to Congress all the cases in which he has during the year exercised this authority, together with a statement of his reasons.[1] The danger of political influence would seem to be no greater if the Secretary were given the discretion he desires than it is at present where it would be possible to make the finding in some instances that the aliens held in deportation proceedings did not come under the given deportable categories. Of course the standard of discretion laid down in statute must be a definite one, else it will be void for want of constitutionality.[2]

No one can deny that there has been a varying range of court decisions on the subject of deportation. It seems probable from the court cases read that the courts have tended to lay a restraining hand on administrative interpretation, but the courts too have often given strange interpretations. Once an interpretation, like that of "entry," has been established by the Supreme Court there is little that can be done but call attention to the problems entailed by such meaning and await the possibility that some day the

[1] This suggestion was made by the late Louis F. Post, in an unpublished MS. that he lent to the author.

[2] In People *v.* Klinck Packing Co., 214 N. Y. 121, the power given the New York commissioner of labor by the 1913 labor law to exempt such persons in continuous industries as he saw fit from the 1-day-rest-in-7 requirement of the labor law was declared unconstitutional. The reason stated by the court was that no definite standard was laid down for the commissioner.

court may reverse itself or that Congress may change the act. It is all too common for scathing criticism to be made of administrative officials with complete forgetfulness of the fact that the path of the courts, although doubtless less devious of the two, has itself not been entirely straight.

Let us turn for a moment to the criticisms of the administrative procedure. Deportation procedure, we are told,[1] reminds us of the verse in *Alice in Wonderland:*

> " I'll be judge. I'll be jury,"
> Said cunning old Fury;
> " I'll try the whole cause
> And condemn you to death."

In other words, an administrative official hears the case, makes recommendations and then a higher official of the administrative staff of the Department of Labor makes final decision without intervention of court authority. The only appeal from decisions of immigrant inspectors of the bureau of immigration of the Department of Labor is to the Secretary of Labor, who is thus made final judge of his own cause. In actual practice, even he is not final judge, for decisions are made by an Assistant Secretary or an Assistant to the Secretary, and the Secretary himself neither sees nor hears of the general run of cases. Executive justice, it is argued, is no justice at all but is the modern version of Star Chamber proceedings.

It must be conceded that the present procedure affords opportunity for deprivation of rights considered fundamental to Anglo-Saxon law where personal liberty is involved. Deportation may technically not involve punishment but practically a procedure where anonymous reports are received, where complete information against a person may

[1] Z. Chafee, *Freedom of Speech, op. cit.*, p. 232.

be obtained from him and others before his right to counsel is made known to him, where the hearing is held in secret and where appeal to the courts is so rigidly restricted as in deportation cases, savors in actual practice of lack of due process of law. In time of stress, as in the deportation raids of 1920, and again in the economic depression of 1930 with its renewed deportation raids and activity, anti-alien sentiment so manifests itself that fundamental rights guaranteed by the Constitution may be completely disregarded in a procedure which at best is obligated to regard them only in small degree.

A method of guaranteeing those safeguards more completely than by an entirely executive process has often been advocated,—namely, that of jury trial for the person held in deportation proceedings. On the other hand, in a day when jury trial is no longer regarded as the panacea it used to be, the possibility arises of developing increased safeguards on the administrative side.

Personnel is the all-important problem on the administrative side of the law. It is important that inspectors in deportation cases regard themselves as seekers after justice rather than as prosecuting officials. In periods of anti-alien feeling such as developed in the days following the World War and again in the economic depression ten years later it is difficult to maintain the judicial attitude of mind necessary in the work. At such times, immigrant inspectors in seeking to pile up the list of deportations which public opinion seems to demand may disregard fundamental human rights in the exercise of their large administrative powers. In this connection, it may be well to note the rules which the Court of Criminal Appeal in England laid down for the prosecuting officer of the Crown: "Counsel for the prosecution ought not to struggle for a conviction, but should regard themselves as ministers of justice, assisting in its administration rather than advocates."[1] To press for a conviction in England is not merely to violate the tradition of the bar, but is also a violation of the declared principles of the court. As deportation is not a punishment for crime, it seems even more important that inspectors in charge of deportation cases should regard their task primarily as that of establishing facts. It is not too much to hope that eventually they will be trained in methods of social investigation.

On the side of actual administration, several changes may be suggested. In the first place, there is need for better correlation in reporting cases of possible deportation to the immigration service, that it may no longer be the unfortunate alien whom the arm of the law happens to strike. There is further need for increase in inspectors and patrol officers if the deportation laws are to be adequately enforced, but such men should be appointed with regard to their judicial turn of mind rather than their detective and prosecuting powers, and they should never resort to the method of raid.

It seems obvious that it is necessary to have some available review of immigration decisions, but the important fact for the alien seems not so much that review be granted by the regular judicial system, as that review be freely granted by a higher body, whether it be administrative or judicial. In fact, the overcrowding of federal courts makes apparent the necessity for review to be found elsewhere than in the regular judicial system. A statutory authorization and powers of review might be granted to the board of review in the Department of Labor, instead of the merely advisory functions it possesses today, but the final power of decision would still rest in the hands of the Secretary of Labor. On the other hand, an entirely separate administrative board

[1] *Journal of Criminal Law and Criminology*, 1926, p. 567, note.

could be set up by Presidential appointment, similar in organization to the Interstate Commerce Commission, the Federal Trade Commission and the Board of Tax Appeals. The latter suggestion seems the better one, designed to secure a procedure for review unbiased by the exigencies of administration. A full hearing by a kind of administrative court would then be granted to determine the rights of an alien before he is sent from the country. Such a tribunal should be composed of men with legal and, if possible, social training, and they should take into account social as well as legal factors in the cases before them. Social agencies may well consider the possibility of providing counsel or other representation before such tribunal, and indeed at all stages of the proceedings. It seems obvious that many aliens, without sufficient funds, and entirely without understanding of the nature of the proceedings against them, need more adequate representation than is often given them today.

Such a tribunal would in time establish its own procedure and safeguards. But always on general questions of *law,* appeal to a court of law should be available, as under present circumstances.

The findings of this board, and indeed the whole record, should be public rather than as the proceedings are at present. In order to have such public proceedings, the record should be very complete and contain social as well as legal data. Records should never contain re-phrasing or omissions by the inspector but testimony of the alien at all stages of the procedure should be inserted in the record *in toto* so that there may be no opportunity of misinterpretation.

Last of all comes the necessity for realization that the problems involved in deportation are more than the legal questions of one country alone. It is true that the United States has rid itself of many "undesirable" foreigners by deporting them from its shores, and it is doubtless true that American deportation laws have prevented many others from entering. However, it seems increasingly clear that from the point of view of the social and international problems involved, deportation is "passing the buck" and in itself offers no real solution. Passing problems on does little to solve them, for they are of deeper import than saving a particular country in some measure from undesirable citizens or from spending public money on aliens. Many individuals with points of view stretching beyond the confines of one country realize the challenge of such problems from the international standpoint. But as nations we are still in a day of international "law of settlement" when the socially inadequate are passed from country to country as they formerly were from town to town. The day may arrive when the individual will be regarded internationally and will be thought of as the product of more than the country where he happens to have his legal citizenship and nationality. But then, it seems, the millennium may have come.

Meanwhile the important problem is one of public opinion in regard to those of foreign birth in the United States. An unscientific but too prevalent tendency seems to be to regard them as malefactors merely because of the accident of their birth. The main remedy for that, as indeed for the other evils of public opinion, is,—in the words of Mr. Justice Holmes,—"for us to grow more civilized."

APPENDIX

I

CASE OF MARY TAMSON

The following case is an exact replica of a case in the files of the bureau of immigration of the Department of Labor, save that file numbers, addresses, and all names except those of such administrative officials as commissioners of immigration and an Assistant Secretary of Labor have been changed to prevent identification.

Buffalo, New York
September 14, 1926

Sworn statement of Mary Tamson made before Inspector Mark A. Herron at the Juvenile Detention Home, this date.

Alien sworn.

Q. What is your correct name? A. Mary Tamson.
Q. How old are you? A. 15.
Q. What date were you born? A. November 16.
Q. Will you be 16 on your next birthday? A. Yes.
Q. Where were you born? A. Liverpool, England.
Q. You are single? A. Yes.
Q. Have you been going to school? A. Yes.
Q. Have you been doing any work at all? A. I helped in my brother's store sometimes.
Q. Can you read and write? A. Yes.
Q. Of what race are you? A. Scotch.
Q. Where was your father born? A. I don't know.
Q. Did your father ever live in the United States? A. I know nothing about him.
Q. When and where did you enter the United States the last time?
A. May, 1925 I came to Buffalo.
Q. Who came with you at that time? A. Mr. and Mrs. William Downs.
Q. Did you go to the Immigration Office when you came to the United States?
A. Yes.

Q. Did you pay a head tax? A. Yes.

(Records at this office show the admission of this alien on April 25, 1925.)

Q. With whom have you been staying since you came to the U. S.?

A. Mr. and Mrs. David Tamson, 411 West Street, Niagara, New York.

Q. When did you come from England? A. I don't know.

Q. Have you had any trouble at your home lately? A. Yes, with Andrew Tamson.

Q. Did you have immoral relations with him? A. Just twice.

Q. Did you have immoral relations with any other boys? A. One in Scotland.

Q. When were you in Scotland last? A. In 1924.

Q. When did you come back from Scotland? A. August or September, 1924. I came to Montreal on the Donaldson Anchor Line. We got on at Glasgow.

Q. How long were you in Scotland that time? A. About three years.

Q. Who came with you that time? A. David Tamson, Sr.

Q. Who is this David Tamson? A. He is my foster father.

Q. Did you stay in Canada from 1924 to 1925? A. Yes.

Q. Have you any relations in Canada? A. A foster sister.

Q. Have you any relatives in Scotland? A. No.

Q. Did you have any trouble before? A. No.

Q. Where did you live last? A. 411 West Street, Niagara.

(Signed) MARK A. HERRON,
Immigrant Inspector.

Buffalo, New York
September 28, 1926

Sworn statement of David Tamson made before Inspector Mark A. Herron at the Immigration Office, this date.

Witness sworn.

Q. What is your correct name? A. David Tamson.

Q. What is your address? A. 219 John Street, Niagara, New York.

Q. Where were you born? A. Scotland.

Q. How long have you been in the United Etates. A. Since December, 1924.

Q. Were you registered when you entered the United States? A. Yes.

(Registration verified.)

Q. When did you land in Canada the last time? A. August 26, 1924, at Montreal, S.S. Minerva.

Q. Are you related to the girl known at Mary Tamson?

A. Yes, we took her when she was about 1½ year old.

Q. Where did you take her? A. Glasgow, Scotland.

Q. Did you ever legally adopt her? A. No, I registered her as our own at the Registrars Office in Glasgow, Scotland.

Q. Did you get any papers showing the registration? A. No.

Q. What are the names of this girl's parents? A. She is an illigitimate child. Her mother's name is Maggie Brewer. I do not know anything about the father.

Q. Where is the mother now? A. In Canada somewhere as far as I know.

Q. Where was this girl born? A. In Liverpool, England.

Q. How do you know she was born in Liverpool, England? A. Through relatives.

Q. How old is she? A. She will be 16 in November.

Q. When did she come to Canada the last time? A. She came with me in August, 1924.

Q. Did you have a passport? A. We did not need to have a passport to come to Canada.

Q. Under what name did you bring her to Canada? A. Mary Tamson.

Q. When Mary came to the United States, did you come down to this office and appear before the Board of Special Inquiry in her behalf? A. Yes.

Q. Did you tell the Officers at the Immigration Office that she was your daughter?

A. Yes, because we adopted her.

Q. Have you had any trouble with this girl? A. There was trouble with boys and my son turned her over to the authorities.

Q. Is she in the Juvenile Detention Home now? A. Yes.

Note: Mary Tamson or Brewer was admitted at this port as the daughter of David Tamson.

(Signed) MARK A. HERRON,
Immigrant Inspector.

Form 541
U. S. Dept. of Labor
Immigration Service

Port of Buffalo, New York
Date September 25, 1926

Name Mary Tamson Age 15 Sex Fem.
Native of England Race Scotch Date Arrival 4-25-25
S.S. train Class ______ Manifest No. ___

THIS IS TO CERTIFY THAT the above-described person has this day been examined and is found to be afflicted with CONSTITUTIONAL PSYCHOPATHIC INFERIORITY, Class A, at the time of entry.

(Signed) Howard B. Lashin, A.A. Surgeon

U. S. DEPARTMENT OF LABOR
IMMIGRATION SERVICE

No. 1900/620 Place Buffalo, New York
Through District Director, Buffalo September 30, 1926

The Undersigned respectfully recommends that the Secretary of Labor issue his warrant for the arrest of MARY BREWER alias MARY TAMSON: Age 15: female: single student: literate: native and citizen of England: landed at the port of Montreal, Canada, August 26, 1924, S.S. Minerva: last entered the United States at the port of certificate, upon the following facts which the undersigned has carefully investigated, and which, to the best of his knowledge and belief, are true:

1. (Here state fully facts which show alien to be unlawfully in the United States. Give sources of information, and, where possible, secure from informants and forward with this application duly verified affidavits setting forth the facts within the knowledge of the informants. Application for a warrant based on conviction for a crime committed in the United States should be accompanied by a copy of the alien's commitment obtained from the warden of the institution wherein he is confined, or a certificate of conviction obtained from the clerk of the court wherein sentence was pronounced.)

From the attached sworn statements and medical certificate, it would appear that this alien is in the United States in violation of the Quota Act (Act of May 19, 1921, as amended May 11, 1922), the quota for the country of which she is a national having been exhausted at the time of her entry; that she entered by false and misleading statements thereby entering without inspection; that she was of constitutional psychopathic inferiority at the time of entry; that she was under 16 years of age at the time of entry, unacompanied by and not coming to one or both parents; that she was a person likely to become a public charge at the time of entry Issue W/A Defectible Liken Unapt Exquota

(Case reported by Juvenile Detention Home.)

2. The present location and occupation of above-named alien are as follows:

Juvenile Detention Home, Buffalo, New York

Pursuant to Rule 18 of the Immigration Regulations there is attached hereto and made a part thereof the certificate prescribed in subdivision B of said rule, as to the landing or entry of said alien, duly signed by the immigration officer in charge at the port through which said alien entered the United States.

File No. 3722/ 239

Approved and forwarded:

(Signature) Mark A. Herron

District Director (Official Title) Inspector in Charge

District No. 10

Bureau of Immigration
Form 8 C

Warrant—Arrest of Alien

UNITED STATES OF AMERICA

DEPARTMENT OF LABOR

WASHINGTON

No. 66568/1042

TO DISTRICT DIRECTOR OF IMMIGRATION, BUFFALO, NEW YORK.

Or to any Immigrant Inspector in the service of the United States.

WHEREAS, from evidence submitted to me, it appears that the alien

MARY TAMSON or MARY BREWER

who landed at the port of Montreal, Canada, ex SS " Minerva " on the 26th day of August, 1924, subject to be taken into custody and returned to the country whence she came under section 19 of the immigration act of February 5, 1917, being subject to deportation under the provisions of a law of the United States, to wit: The Act of May 19, 1921 as amended by Public Resolution 55, approved May 11, 1922, in that the quota for the year ended June 30, 1925 allotted to the country of which she is a native, is exhausted.

and, WHEREAS, from the evidence submitted to me, it appears that the said alien has been found in the United States in violation of the immigration act of February 5, 1917, for the following among other reasons:

That she was a person likely to become a public charge at the time of her entry, at Buffalo, New York, on or about April 25, 1925; that she was a person of constitutional psychopathic inferiority at the time of her entry; and that she was under 16 years of age at the time of her entry, and unaccompanied by or not coming to one or both of her parents.

I, W. W. Husband, Second Assistant, Secretary of Labor, by virtue of the power and authority vested in me by the laws of the United States, do hereby command you to take into custody the said alien and grant her a hearing to enable her to show cause why she should not be deported in conformity with law.

Pending further proceedings the alien should be permitted to remain in her present location without expense to the Government.

Verification of landing in Canada should be submitted with record of hearing.

For so doing, this shall be your sufficient warrant.

Witness my hand and seal this 14th day of October, 1926

W. W. Husband
Second Assistant Secretary of Labor.

Form 617 PASSPORT DATA FOR ALIEN DEPORTEES

U. S. DEPARTMENT OF LABOR

Immigration Service

District Headquarters at

District file No.......4-1900/620 ......Buffalo, New York......

Bureau file No.......66568/1042 ......October 21, 1926 ....

(Date)

Name of alien (in full)........ ... Mary Brewer or Mary Tamson ....

Where detained......Buffalo, New York......Juvenile Detention Home..

(Town or city) (Institution)

Age...15 Date of birth...November 16, 1910 Nationality...England..

Race .....Scotch...... Subject of......England...... Occupation..... None

(Country)

Place of birth.........Liverpool, England ....

(Give P. O., village, town, or city; county, parish, or province, and country)

Nearest large city............... ....

(City) (Distance and direction from place of birth)

Last address in native country............Liverpool, England..................

Date left native country........... About 14 years ago.... ....

Last address in country of citizenship............Liverpool, England........

Last foreign address.......Glasgow, Scotland and Montreal, Canada......

Date left last foreign address...... ......April, 1925.................................

Date of arrival in U. S.............April 25, 1925 ....

Port of arrival.........Buffalo, New York Name of vessel .....Train......

Married or single............Single................ ....

Name and address of wife or husband ....

Father's name and place of birth..... Do not know (Illegitimate child)

Father's present address.................. " " " " "

Mother's maiden name and place of birth......Maggie Brewer....... ......

Mother's present address ....Unknown ....

Names and addresses of near relatives in U. S.............None................

Names and addresses of relatives abroad.........Uncle, William Brewer, c/o Municipal Tramway Co., Glasgow, Scotland ....

Names and locations of foreign schools attended ....Towser School, Arch Street, Glasgow ....

Names and locations of foreign churches attended ....

Where baptized?............Don't know ....

Name and address of last employer in country of citizenship......None..

.... Has alien passport?. .....No...........

Other documentary evidence? ....No..... ....

Charges against alien in W/D ....Excess quota; L. P. C.; Constitutional psychopathic inferiority; under 16......................................

Personal description: Height....5′ 2″.... Weight....110 Eyes....Blue Hair...Brown Face...Round Nose...Straight Mouth...Normal Distinctive marks............Small scar above left eye...........................

Ordered deported at expense of............Steamship Company.................

Government Printing Office

DEPARTMENT OF LABOR
IMMIGRATION SERVICE

Your file No. 1900/620

District Headquarters
U. S. Commissioner of Immigration
Montreal, Canada

In replying refer to
No. 736/ 589

September, 26, 1926

Immigrant Inspector in Charge
Buffalo, New York

The following is a correct record and statement of facts as taken from the Canadian Manifesto relative to the arrival and presumed landing in Canada of the alien named below:

NAME OF STEAMSHIP Minerva LINE Anchor CLASS 3rd.
SHEET NUMBER LINE NUMBER FORM 40-B 226
PORT OF LANDING Montreal DATE OF LANDING 8/26/24
NAME OF ALIEN Mary Tamson
AGE 14
SEX female
MARITAL STATUS single
OCCUPATION school
RACE Scotch
DESTINATION Sister, Mrs. Lippincott, 1011 Cedar Street, Montreal
REMARKS With David Tamson, 48

(Signed) H. S. Landis
Commissioner

Buffalo, New York
October 11, 1931

To whom it may concern,

This is to certify that the alien Mary Brewer or Mary Tamson is able to travel without danger to her life. She will not require an attendant for the trip.

Howard B. Lashin
Acting Assistant Surgeon
U. S. Public Health Service

Form 561

Warrant—Arrest of Alien

UNITED STATES OF AMERICA
U. S. DEPT. OF LABOR
WASHINGTON

No. 66568x1042

To DISTRICT DIRECTOR OF IMMIGRATION, BUFFALO, NEW YORK OR to any Immigrant Inspector in the service of the United States.

Whereas, from evidence submitted to me, it appears that the alien

Mary Tamson or Mary Brewer

who landed at the port of Montreal, ex S.S. " Minerva "

on —— the 25th day of Aug., 1924, is subject to be taken into custody and returned to the country whence she came under section 19 of the immigration act of Feb. 5, 1917 being subject to deportation under the provisions of a law of the United States to wit; The Act of May 19, 1921, as amended by Public Resolution 55, approved May 11, 1922 in that the quota for the year ending June 30, 1925, allotted to the country of which she is a native, is exhausted.

and, WHEREAS from the evidence submitted to me, it appears that the said alien has been found in the United States in violation of the immigration act of Feb. 5, 1917, for the following among other reasons. That she was a person likely to become a public charge at the time of her entry, at Buffalo, N. Y., on or about April 25, 1925; that she was a person of constitutional psychopathic inferiority at the time of entry; and that she was under 16 years of age at time of entry and unaccompanied by or not coming to one or both of her parents.

I, W. W. Husband Second Assistant Secretary of Labor, by virtue of the power and authority vested in me by the laws of the United States, do hereby command you to take into custody the said alien and grant her a hearing —————— to enable her to show cause why she should not be deported in conformity with law.

Pending further proceedings the alien should be permitted to remain in her present location without expense to the Government. Verification of landing should be submitted with record of hearing.

For so doing, this shall be your sufficient warrant.

Witness my hand and seal this 4th day of October, 1926

(Signed) W. W. Husband
Second Assistant Secretary of Labor

Form 607

U. S. DEPARTMENT OF LABOR

IMMIGRATION SERVICE

File No. 1900/620

REPORT OF HEARING in the case of MARY BREWER OR MARY TAMSON	Under Department warrant No. 66568/1042 Dated October 4, 1926 Hearing conducted by Insp. Mark A. Herron At Buffalo, N. Y. Date, 10-11-26

Alien taken into custody at Juvenile Detention Home, Buffalo, N. Y., October 11, 1926, 2:00 P.M., by Inspector Mark A. Herron and detained at the Juvenile Detention Home, Buffalo, N. Y.

(State if released on own recognizance or bail; or if detained, where.)

Testimony taken and transcribed by Inspector Mark A. Herron

Said Mary Brewer or Mary Tamson, being able to speak and understand the English language satisfactorily, no interpreter, named , competent in the language, was employed

(If other than regular Government employee, state as to being first duly sworn.)

Said Mary Brewer or Mary Tamson was informed that the purpose of said hearing was to afford her an opportunity to show cause why she should not be deported to the country whence she came, said warrant of arrest being read and each and every allegation therein contained carefully explained to her Said alien was offered an opportunity to inspect the warrant of arrest and the evidence upon which it was issued, which privilege was accepted. The alien being first duly sworn , the following evidence was presented:

(If not sworn state reason.)

Q. What is your correct name? A. Mary Tamson is the only name I know.
Evidence shows her legal name to be Brewer.
Q. Have you ever been known by another name? A. No.
Q. You are advised that under these proceedings you have the right to be represented by counsel. Do you desire to obtain the services of a lawyer? A. No.
Q. Do you waive your right to counsel and are you ready to proceed with this hearing? A. Yes.
(David Tamson was notified to appear at the hearing and he did not show up.)
Q. How old are you? A. 15, I will be sixteen on November 16th.
Q. Where were you born? A. Liverpool, England.
Q. Did you make a statement before me on Sept. 14, '26? A. Yes.
(Statement read to alien.)
Q. Is this statement correct? A. Yes.
Q. Is everything you said in this statement true? A. Yes.

I will introduce this statement as evidence in your case, same exhibit " B ".

Q. Where was your mother born? A. I don't know.
Q. Did you ever hear your father's name? A. No.
Q. Where did you live last in Scotland? A. Glasgow.
Q. How long did you live there? A. About three years. Lived in Canada before that.
Q. Did you live in Scotland before you came to Canada the first time? A. I do not know.
Q. Do you remember living in England? A. No.
Q. Who did you live with in Scotland? A. With David Tamson.
Q. Did you tell the Immigration Officers at Buffalo when you came from Canada in April, 1925, that you were coming to your father, David Tamson? A. Yes, I always thought he was my father.
Q. Records at this office show that you were admitted to the United States on April 25, 1925, is that correct?
A. It was about that time.
Q. Certificate of landing issued by the Commissioner of Immigra-

tion at Montreal shows that you arrived at the port of Montreal on Aug. 25, 1924, on the S.S. Minerva, is that correct?

A. Yes.

I have here sworn statement of David Tamson made before me on Sept. 28, 1926, which I will introduce as evidence in your case, same marked exhibit " C ". (Statement read to alien.)

Q. Is this statement correct as far as you know? A. Yes.

I have here medical certificate signed by Dr. Howard B. Lashin, A.A. Surgeon, U.S. Public Health Service, which I will introduce as evidence in your case, same marked exhibit " D ". (Certificate read to alien.)

Q. Have you anything to say in regards to this certificate? A. No.

Q. Have you any relatives in the United States? A. No.

Q. Did you know of any relatives in England or Scotland? A. No.

Q. Have you any papers of any kind showing where you were born?

A. No.

Q. Is there anything further you wish to say to show cause why you should not be deported? A. I would not have anybody to go to if I am sent back. The only people that know me are Mr. Tamson's people and I do not know where they live.

Miss Buelah Stone questioned as follows:

Q. What is your name? A. Buelah Stone.

Q. What is your position in this institution? A. Deputy Chief Probation Officer, Juvenile Court, Girls Dept.

Q. How was the alien known as Mary Tamson brought to your attention? A. She was brought in as a delinquent.

Q. Is she a ward of the Juvenile Court at this time? A. No, not yet. The Court could not act in the case on account of her not being a legal resident. The Court found that she was of low grade mentality. The case is being held up pending what disposition your Department will make of the case.

Q. Is there any possibility of this girl being turned back to the home of the Tamsons?

A. No, we could not turn her back to the people in whose home she became a delinquent. Some other relatives of the Tamsons asked to have her turned over to them but we have not seen fit to do so.

Q. With whom did she live before she was brought to this institution? A. With Mr. and Mrs. David Tamson, Jr.

Q. Have you found that this girl was legally adopted by Mr. Tamson?

A. No, she was not.

Hearing Closed.

FOREIGN DESTINATION IN CASE OF DEPORTATION

Final destination not determined. Alien has uncle, William Brewer, residing in Glasgow, Scotland, address unknown, but is employed by the tramway company of the city as conductor.

EXHIBITS

" A " Warrant of arrest.
" B " Alien's statement of September 14, 1926.
" C " David Tamson's statement of September 28, 1926.
" D " Medical certificate signed by Dr. Howard B. Lashin.

DISPOSITION OF ALIEN

Alien was left at the Juvenile Detention Home, Buffalo, N. Y.

PERSONAL DESCRIPTION

Height, 5-2; fair complexion; blue eyes, brown hair; small scar over left eye.

DOCUMENTARY EVIDENCE

Old British passport issued to Mrs. David Tamson in 1920 to return to Scotland from Canada and on which alien appears as a daughter, on file at this office.

BAGGAGE

Clothing with David Tamson, 219 John St., Niagara, N. Y.

SUMMARY

From the foregoing evidence and exhibits, I, Mark A. Herron, duly authorized examining officer in this case do find the following facts:

That Mary Tamson or Mary Brewer, is an alien namely a native of England, British Subject.

That she last entered the United States at the port of Buffalo,

N. Y., on April 25, 1925, at which time she was admitted as the daughter of one David Tamson. She landed at the port of Montreal, Canada, on Aug. 25, 1924, ex S.S. Minerva.

This alien is an illegitimate child, was taken into the family of Mr. and Mrs. David Tamson, Sr., citizens of Scotland, in Glasgow, as a daughter when she was about two years old but was never legally adopted. Since coming to the United States alien has been living with Mr. & Mrs. David Tamson, Jr. (Mrs. David Tamson, Sr., died in Scotland), became a delinquent in their home and was turned over to the Juvenile Court. Alien is now held in the Juvenile Detention Home, Buffalo, no disposition in her case having been made by the Court up to this time.

Alien is certified by the Medical examiner as being of Constitutional Psychopathic Inferiority at time of entry.

All charges in the warrant of arrest are fully sustained.

Immigrant Inspector

IMMIGRATION SERVICE

DISTRICT NO. 11

No. 1900/620

Detroit, Mich.
October 21, 1926

Commissioner-General of Immigration,
Washington, D. C.

Through District Director, Buffalo.

NAME OF ALIEN:	Mary Brewer or Tamson
NATIONALITY:	England, Scotch
COUNTRY TO WHICH DEPORTABLE:	England or Scotland
ADDITIONAL CHARGES:	None
WHETHER DETAINED AT GOVERNMENT EXPENSE:	No
PASSPORT STATUS:	No passport. Form 617 executed.
COMMENT:	Deportation respectfully recommended.

s.s. Mark A. Herron
Inspector in charge

Oct. 23, 1926 File No. 3722/39
Approved and forwarded:
s.s.
District Director
District No. 10

66568/1042—Buffalo October 29, 1926

In re: Mary Tamson or Brewer, 15.

This case comes before the Board of Review on warrant proceedings.

No interested parties.

This record relates to a native of England, of the Scotch race, presumably a citizen of Scotland, where she has lived the greater part of her life, 15, single, who landed at Montreal on Aug. 25, 1924, ex S.S. "Minerva" and was admitted at Buffalo in May, 1925, as the daughter of David Tamson. It appears that David Tamson was in fact her foster father.

She admits immoral conduct in Scotland and also since arrival in the U. S. and is certified for constitutional psychopathic inferiority. She was under 16 years, unaccompanied and not destined to her parents at the time of entry and the quota for her country for the year ending June 30, 1925 is exhausted.

Hearing was held at Buffalo, N. Y., by Inspector Mark A. Herron and alien has been released to the local authorities, who are holding her as a delinquent.

Deportation may be at the expense of the line.

It is recommended that the alien be deported to Scotland, at the expense of the line, on the grounds:

That the quota for the year ended June 30, 1925 allotted to the country of which she is a native, under the Act of May 19, 1921, as amended by Public Resolution approved May 11, 1922 is exhausted;

That she is in the U. S. in violation of the Act of Feb. 5, 1917, in that she was a person likely to become a public charge at the time of her entry;

That she was a person of constitutional psychopathic inferiority at the time of her entry;

And that she was under 16 years of age at the time of her entry, unaccompanied by and not coming to one or both parents.

So ordered

s.s.
Chairman. Secy & Comr.
Genl's Board of Review.

W. W. Husband
Second Assistant Secretary

U. S. DEPARTMENT OF LABOR
BUREAU OF IMMIGRATION
WASHINGTON

No. 66568/1042

Official copies of Warrant of Deportation in the case of
Mary Tamson, or Brewer
are furnished the District Director of Immigration, Montreal, Canada, for his information. The alien will be conveyed to his port in connection with a party.

1362 Acting Commissioner General.

Form 45

U. S. DEPARTMENT OF LABOR
BUREAU OF IMMIGRATION
WASHINGTON

In answering refer to
No. 66568/1042 Nov. 5, 1926

District Director of Immigration,
Buffalo, New York

Sir:

The Bureau acknowledges the receipt of your letter of October 21, 1926, 1900/620 transmitting record of hearing accorded the alien

Mary Tamson, or Mary Brewer

who landed at the port of Montreal, Canada ex S. S. " Minerva " on Aug. 25, 1924

After a careful examination of the evidence submitted in this case, the Department is of opinion that the alien is in the United States in violation of law. You are therefore directed to cause her to be taken into custody and conveyed to such point in Can. as the U.S. Commissioner of Immigration, Montreal, Canada, may designate for deportation, the expenses incident to such conveyance, including the employment of an attendant to assist in delivery, if necessary, at a nominal compensation of $1.00 and expenses both ways, being authorized, payable from the appropriation " Expenses of Regulating Immigration, 19 26."

Conveyance of the alien to Canadian seaport should be effected in connection with a party.

(Signed) W. W. Husband Respectfully,

Approved:

Acting Commissioner General.

Second. Assist. Secretary.

Inclose W. D. No.

Bureau of Immigration
Form 8 D

Warrant—Deportation of Alien

UNITED STATES OF AMERICA
DEPARTMENT OF LABOR
WASHINGTON

No. 66568/1042

To DISTRICT DIRECTOR OF IMMIGRATION, BUFFALO, NEW YORK

Or to any Officer or Employee of the United States Immigration Service.

WHEREAS, from proofs submitted to me, after due hearing before
Inspector Mark A. Herron held at Buffalo, New York
I have become satisfied that the alien
Mary Tamson or Mary Brewer
who landed at the port of Montreal, Canada, ex S.S. " Minerva " on the 25th day of August, 1924, is subject to be returned to the country whence she came under section 19 of the immigration act of February 5, 1917, being subject to deportation under the provisions of a law of the United States, to wit, The

Act of May 19, 1921, as amended by Public Resolution 55, approved May 11, 1922 in that the quota for the year ending June 30, 1925, allotted to the country of which she is a native, is exhausted.

and WHEREAS, from proofs submitted to me, after due hearing before Inspector Mark A. Herron, held at Buffalo, New York I have become satisfied that the said alien has been found in the United States in violation of the immigration act of February 5, 1917, in that:

She was a person liable to become a public charge at the time of her entry into the United States, at Buffalo, New York, on April 25, 1925; that she was a person of constitutional psychopathic inferiority at the time of her entry; and that she was under 16 yrs. of age and unaccompanied by or not coming to one or both parents.

I W. W. Husband Second Assistant Secretary of Labor, by virtue of the power and authority vested in me by the laws of the United States, do hereby command you to return the said alien to Scotland the country whence she came, at the expense of the steamship company bringing her to Canada.

For so doing this shall be your sufficient warrant.

Witness my hand and seal this 15 day of November, 1926

W. W. Husband
Second Assistant Secretary of Labor.

U. S. DEPARTMENT OF LABOR
IMMIGRATION SERVICE
DISTRICT NO. 11

Telephone: CADILLAC 6485

In answering refer to
No. 3624

Office of District Direction
Buffalo, New York

November 15, 1926

Commissioner General of Immigration,
Washington, D. C.

With reference to my letter of November 12, requesting authorization for Montreal party scheduled to leave Detroit the 21st instant, via Canadian Pacific train #22, 4:30 P.M. in addition to the aliens listed in letter November 12, authorization is requested to join the following aliens to Montreal party of the 21st instant:

Bureau F.	Alien	District F.
66568/1042	Mary Tamson, or Brewer	3611/128
66568/839	Jules Henrigues	3611/73

District Director, P. L. Prentis

WESTERN UNION RUSH

66315/108 November 19, 1926

Immigration Service,
Buffalo, New York.

Answering your letter fifteenth (Stop) Attach special Detroit Montreal party twenty first Jules Henrigues and Mary Tamson if provided with valid passports.

Tolman

Attest:

Assistant Commissioner General,
G. E. Tolman

File
Nov. 20 '26

U. S. DEPARTMENT OF LABOR
IMMIGRATION SERVICE
DISTRICT NO. 1

In replying refer to
No. 736/589

District Headquarters
U. S. Commissioner of Immigration
Montreal, Canada

Nov. 23, 1926

Commissioner General of Immigration
Washington, D. C.

Herewith returned the Department's warrant dated November 5, 1926, 66568/1042, directing deportation to Scotland of the alien Mary Tamson or Mary Brewer.

This alien was delivered at Montreal with other deportees on the morning of November 22nd, by Inspector John Gonzales of the Buffalo staff, and was placed aboard S.S. " Minerva " for deportation, steamer sailing at 10:00 A. M. yesterday.

Commissioner, H. R. Landis

SN
Encl.—67798

U. S. DEPARTMENT OF LABOR
IMMIGRATION SERVICE
DISTRICT NO. 11

In answering refer to
No. 1900/859

Office of Inspector in Charge
Buffalo, New York

November 28, 1926

Commissioner-General of Immigration,
Washington, D. C.

Through District Director, Buffalo.

Referring to Bureau file No. 66567/1042, in case of the alien Mary Tamson or Brewer, there is returned herewith warrant of arrest for cancellation. This alien was conveyed to Montreal for deportation on the 12st instant by Inspector George P. Wells. The expenses incurred will be covered in the voucher of the deporting officer.

Nov. 29 '26
Approved and forwarded:

Mark A. Herron
Inspector in Charge

s.s.
District Director,
District No. 10

U. S. DEPARTMENT OF LABOR
IMMIGRATION SERVICE
DISTRICT NO. 1

In replying refer to
No. 736/620

District Headquarters
U. S. Commissioner of Immigration
Montreal, Canada

Suboffice

December 17, 1926

Commissioner General of Immigration
Washington, D. C.

For the completion of the Bureau's file No. 66568/1042, there is forwarded herewith Sheets A, B and C Form 597 showing the condition en route and delivery at final destination of the alien Mary Tamson, or Brewer, deported on S.S. "Minerva", November 22, 1926.

H. R. Landis
Commissioner

Enc.—96195

Form 597 — Particulars concerning alien requiring special care & attention — Sheet A original

---

No.

U. S. Department of Labor
IMMIGRATION SERVICE

Port of Montreal, 1926

To the Master of SS. " Minerva "
Sailing November 26, 1926

The below described alien is to be returned by you to the final destination hereinafter stated, and requires special care and attention en route. You will retain this sheet marked " A ", causing to be filled out and mailed to me as soon as practicable sheets " B " and " C ".

Particulars

Name Mary Brewer or Tamson
Age 15 sex F Occupation None
Married or single S Nationality Scotch
Cause of deportation Excess quota; LPC; Constitutional Psychopathic Inferiorty; under 16
Physical and mental condition
Last residence in U. S. (exact address) 219 John St., Niagara, New York
Names of relatives or friends (if any) by whom accompanied None
Baggage, money, or valuable 1 bag

H. S. Landis
Commissioner of Immigration

Form 597 Receipt for alien and baggage

No.... Port of .... 19....

Received of Commissioner of Immigration (or Immigrant Inspector in Charge)and alien (more fully described in Sheet " A " forming part of this record), and the baggage, money and valuables named in said sheet.

viz: ....

....

Master (First or Second Officer)

s.s. ....

Form 597 Record of Ocean Voyage Sheet B

Det. F. 2611/128

Bur. F. 66568/1042

Mont. 736/589

U. S. DEPARTMENT OF LABOR

IMMIGRATION SERVICE

No. Place and Date Glasgow, 30 Nov., 1926

To The Commissioner of Immigration,

PORT of Montreal, Canada,

We, the undersigned, Master and chief Surgeon of S. S. " Minerva " certify that the alien Mary Brewer or Tamson more fully described in Sheet " A ", forming part of this record, received during the ocean voyage *all* necessary care and attention as called for by her condition

We further certify as follows:

Portion of ship in which alien was carried 3rd Class Accomodation

Whether attended by surgeon, nurse, or hospital steward Yes surgeon

Daily condition:

1st day	good
2d day	do
3d day	do
4th day	do
5th day	do
6th day	do
7th day	do

8th day do
9th day do
10th day do

Master
ss Minerva Chief Surgeon

Note.—The above report must be accurate and complete. Any special incidents be set forth in a special report on a separate sheet of paper.

Record of Land Trip and Delivery at Final Destination

form 597 Sheet C
Det. F. 2611/128
Bur. 66568/1042
Mont. 736/589

U. S. DEPARTMENT OF LABOR

IMMIGRATION SERVICE

(For use where custodian selected by steamship company proceeds with alien to final destination.)

No. ________

Place and Date ________ , ________ 19

To the Commissioner of Immigration,
Port of Montreal, Canada,

We certify that the alien Mary Brewer or Tamson (more fully described in Sheet " A " forming part of this record) was, on 19 , conveyed by from , the seaport of debarkation, via and to , the place of final destination, where he was left with the person whose signature is attached to the receipt at the bottom hereof, who is

(here state such person's relationship to alien, or his official position).

Special remarks:

____
Agents S. S. " Minerva "

Received this day of 19 , the above-named alien.

____

(For use where foreign public authorities decline
to allow custodian to proceed.)

Place and Date Glasgow, Oct. 30, 1926

TO THE COMMISSIONER OF IMMIGRATION,
Port of Montreal, Canada,

We certify concerning the alien Mary Tamson or Brewer (more fully described in Sheet " A ", forming part of this record), that at Glasgow the public authorities (namely, The Glasgow Southern Parish) took her into their custody and declined to allow her to be accompanied by any custodian of our selection, although we declared that we stood ready to furnish one. We thereupon delivered to them a copy of the particulars found on Sheet " A " hereof and informed them in writing that she required special care and attention. Said authorities stated that she would be sent to the final destination mentioned on Sheet " A ".

For Canadian Pacific Railway
Agents S. S. " Minerva "

Note.—The custodian must be some proper attendant selected by the steamship company *unless* the authorities at the port of foreign debarkation, notwithstanding request that such custodian be allowed to proceed, decline to consent thereto and insist on taking charge of the alien.

In that event the public officials so taking charge must be requested to receipt for the alien in the space above provided. They will be informed that the receipt is desired by the United States Government. If, notwithstanding such request, they decline to sign the receipt, then this fact should be stated in the space provided for such receipt.

SELECTED BIBLIOGRAPHY

Abbott, E., "Federal Immigration Policies," *University Journal of Business*, vol. ii, nos. 2, 3, 4, March, June, September, 1924.

——, *Historical Aspects of the Immigration Problem* (Chicago, 1926).

——, *Immigration: Select Documents and Case Records* (University of Chicago, 1924).

Abbott G., *The Immigrant and the Community* (New York, 1917).

Alexander, N., *Rights of Aliens* (Montpelier, Vt., 1931).

Annals of Congress, vol. ii, *in re* Alien Act of 1798.

Bevis, H., "Deportation of Aliens," *University of Pennsylvania Law Review*, vol. xlviii.

Beveridge, A. J., *Law and Order*, Report to a Sub-Committee of the Republcan National Committee (1920).

——, *Life of John Marshall*, vol. ii.

Borchard, E., *Diplomatic Protection of Citizens Abroad*, esp. §§ 11 and 319.

Bouvé, C., *A Treatise on the Laws Governing the Exclusion and Expulsion of Aliens in the United States* (Washington, D. C., 1912).

Chafee, Z., *Freedom of Speech* (New York, 1920), ch. v.

Claghorn, K. H., *The Immigrant's Day in Court* (New York, 1923), chs. ix and x.

Coolidge, M. R., *Chinese Immigration* (New York, 1908).

Cook, A. and Hagerty, J., *Immigration Laws of the United States Compiled and Explained* (Chicago, 1929).

Corpus Juris, vol. ii, p. 1043.

Donnell, C. C., "Settlement Law and Interstate Relationship," *Social Service Review*, vol. iv, no. 3, September, 1930.

Fairchild, H. P., *Immigration*, Revised Edition (New York, 1925).

Flournoy, R. W. and Hudson, M. O., *A Collection of Nationality Laws of Various Countries* (New York, 1929).

Foreign Language Information Service Interpreter Releases.

Foreign Relations, 1892, pp. 106-158, *in re* deportation of Chinese.

Freund, E., "Deportation Legislation in the Sixty-ninth Congress," *Social Service Review*, vol. i, no. 1, March, 1927.

Garis, R., *Immigration Restriction* (MacMillan, 1927).

Kansas, S., *United States Immigration, Exclusion and Deportation* (Washington, D. C., 1927).

Kelso, R. W., *Poor Relief in Massachusetts* (Boston, 1922).

Leonard, *Early History of English Poor Relief* (Cambridge, 1900).

McKenzie, R. D., *Oriental Exclusion* (Chicago, 1928).

Mears, E. G., *Resident Orientals on the American Pacific Coast* (Chicago, 1928).

Migration Laws and Treaties, vols. i-iii (Geneva, International Labor Office, 1922-1929).

Miller, D. H., " Nationality and Other Problems Discussed at the Hague," *Foreign Affairs*, vol. viii, no. 4, July, 1930.

Moore, J. B., *Digest of International Law*, vol. lv, sec. 550.

O'Brian, J. L., " The Menace of Administrative Law," *Proceedings*, 25th Annual Meeting, Maryland State Bar Association, 1920, p. 153 *et seq.*

Oppenheimer, R., *The Enforcement of the Deportation Laws of the United States* (1931).

Panunzio, C. M., *The Deportation Cases of 1919-1920* (Federal Council of Churches, 1921).

Post, L. F., " Administrative Decisions in connection with Immigration," *Political Science Review*, vol. x, 1916.

——, *The Deportations Delirium of 1920* (Chicago, 1923).

Stevenson, G. M., *History of American Immigration* (New York, 1926).

Van Vleck, W. C., *Administrative Control of Aliens* (About to be published).

Webb, S. and B., *English Poor Law History* (London and New York, 1927).

Wheaton's *International Law Digest*, sec. 206, *in re* the right of a State to deport.

Works of John Adams, vol. ix, *in re* Alien Act of 1798.

INDEX

Bei Fragen zur Produktsicherheit wenden Sie sich bitte an:
If you have any questions regarding product safety,
please contact:

Walter de Gruyter GmbH
Genthiner Straße 13
10785 Berlin
productsafety@degruyterbrill.com